IN LAND WE TRUST

ACTS Environmental Policy Series No. 7

A Change in the Weather: African Perspectives on Climate Change edited by S.H. Ominde and Calestous Juma

Gaining Ground: Institutional Innovations in Land-use Management in Kenya (revised edition) edited by Amos Kiriro and Calestous Juma

Weathering the Storm: Climate Change and Investment in Kenya by Wilbur K. Ottichilo, Joseph H. Kinuthia, Phares O. Ratego and Godfrey W. Nasubo

Biodiplomacy: Genetic Resources and International Relations edited by Vicente Sánchez and Calestous Juma

A Climate for Development: Climate Change Policy Options for Africa edited by H.W.O. Okoth-Ogendo and J.B. Ojwang

Towards Common Ground: Gender and Natural Resource Management in Africa edited by Asenath Sigot, Lori Ann Thrupp and Jennifer Green

Other relevant ACTS publications

Juma, Calestous, and Jackton B. Ojwang, eds. 1989. *Innovation and Sovereignty: The Patent Debate in African Development*. Nairobi: ACTS Press.

Juma, Calestous, John Mugabe and Patricia Kameri-Mbote, eds. 1994. *Coming to Life: Biotechnology in African Economic Recovery*. Nairobi and London: ACTS Press and Zed Books.

Juma, Calestous. 1989. *Biological Diversity and Innovation: Conserving and Utilizing Genetic Resources in Kenya*. Nairobi: ACTS Press.

Juma, Calestous. 1989. *The Gene Hunters: Biotechnology and the Scramble for Seeds*. London and Princeton, NJ: Zed Books and Princeton University Press.

Kituyi, Mukhisa. 1990. *Becoming Kenyans: Socio-economic Transformation of the Pastoral Maasai*. Nairobi: ACTS Press.

Odera Oruka, H., ed. 1994. *Philosophy, Humanity and Ecology*. Nairobi: ACTS Press and African Academy of Sciences.

Okidi, C.O. 1994. *Environmental Stress and Conflicts in Africa: Case Studies of Drainage Basins*. Ecopolicy Series 6. Nairobi: ACTS Press.

Okoth-Ogendo, H.W.O. 1991. *Tenants of the Crown: Evolution of Agrarian Law and Institutions in Kenya*. Nairobi: ACTS Press.

Sánchez, Vicente, and Calestous Juma, eds. 1994. *Biodiplomacy: Genetic Resources and International Relations*. Nairobi: ACTS Press.

Sigot, Asenath, Lori Ann Thrupp and Jennifer Green. 1995. *Towards Common Ground: Gender and Natural Resource Management in Africa*. Nairobi and Washington, DC: ACTS Press and World Resources Institute.

Tiffen, Mary, Michael Mortimore and Francis Gichuki. 1994. *More People, Less Erosion: Environmental Recovery in Kenya*. Nairobi and London: ACTS Press and John Wiley.

IN LAND WE TRUST

Environment, Private Property and Constitutional Change

Editors

Calestous Juma
J.B. Ojwang

With Foreword
by Goran Hyden

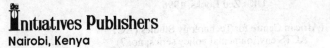

Initiatives Publishers
Nairobi, Kenya

Zed Books
London

1996

© African Centre for Technology Studies (ACTS)
and the Contributors, 1996

Published by

Initiatives Publishers
A division of Initiatives Limited
P.O. Box 69313, Nairobi, Kenya

and

Zed Books
7 Cynthia Street
London N1 9JF, UK

Printed by English Press Limited, P.O. Box 30127, Nairobi

Cataloguing-in-Publication Data

In land we trust: environment, private property and constitutional change/Calestous Juma
and J.B. Ojwang (eds.) — Nairobi, Kenya : Initiatives Publishers : London
UK : Zed Books, 1996.

(African Centre for Technology Studies (ACTS)
ACTS environmental policy series; no. 7)

Bibliography: p.
Includes index

ISBN 9966-42-042-8   UK ISBN 1 85649 417 9 Hb;   UK ISBN 1 85649 418 7 Pb

Contents

Part III: Customary rights and sustainable land use

Part IV: Private property, environment and constitutional change

List of tables

List of figures

Foreword

This important book marks the dawn of a new era in African scholarship. Never before have African scholars applied their minds so creatively to solving Africa's socio-economic problems by addressing the complex relationships between environment and governance. *In Land We Trust* deals with the intricate linkages between land tenure and natural resource management in Kenya. These two themes were previously studied separately but have now been brought together with a high degree of intellectual creativity. The results are policy options that are not only relevant for Kenya, but for many other countries, including industrialized ones. The book is not only an excellent piece of interdisciplinary research, but it brings to the national level issues that have been discussed largely in international forums on the one hand, and tried out at the local level on the other. It reveals a deep understanding of theoretical issues and their applicability to the African situation. It brings much-needed knowledge to issues that are marred with political controversy in many parts of the world.

It is appropriately titled *In Land We Trust* because of the primary role of land in an agricultural country such as Kenya. But as the contributors show in various ways, their chapters do not deal with the technical and economic dimensions of land tenure and natural resource management, but something more fundamental: the legal and constitutional aspects of these two issues. In this respect, this book deals with the ground rules, in a more generic sense, of the country's development.

For a long time, legal and constitutional issues were not seen as related to development, but this has shifted in recent years. When analysts speak of the need for an enabling environment, they do not typically refer just to the macro-economic context, but also to the legal and constitutional environment. If the laws are too constraining or not adhered to, the environment is hardly hospitable for national development. Investors and others wish to know what the rules of the game are; what they can expect if they engage in a certain activity. Most students of development today accept that without predictable and reliable rules, people will not make the contributions to building their nation that government expects. How the latter treats the law of the land, therefore, is of crucial significance.

In the literature on development, this aspect has more recently been identified as "governance". It refers to how government, in collaboration with civil society, manages the rules that make up the regime, in other words, the normative order. These rules are both formal and informal, written and unwritten. Some would appear in the official constitution of the country, others in various statutes that have been passed by parliament. In addition, however, there are rules that may be best described as customary. People follow them and are in that sense aware of their significance. For instance, in Kenya as in many other countries around the world, land tenure is regulated both by formal law and by customary rules applied by distinct ethnic groups.

When we are talking of environmental governance, we refer specifically to the rules that apply to the task of managing a country's natural resources. The ultimate responsibility for it lies with the government, but it is unrealistic to expect the latter to do it on its own. Individuals and groups belonging to civil society, i.e., the sphere that we do not call the state, have an important role in this exercise too. In short, environmental governance is likely to be successful only if the responsibility for managing the rules of natural resource management is shared between government and non-governmental actors. We know that women's groups, community associations and parent-teachers associations in collaboration with school authorities in Kenya already make an important contribution to environmental governance. Their involvement is likely to grow in importance in the future. This task will involve a combination of monitoring and evaluation of existing forms of coping with environmental conservation and development and, as a result of the feedback from such activities, the appropriate reformulation of the relevant rules. Environmental governance, as identified here, is likely to become increasingly complex and involve a growing number of actors in Kenya. This book is an important contribution to the application of knowledge to public policy problems. It is a courageous effort to bring clarity to complex policy issues and to offer innovative solutions.

Goran Hyden
Professor of Political Science
University of Florida, Gainesville
January 1996

Acknowledgements

This book is the culmination of seven years of research at the African Centre for Technology Studies (ACTS) that has involved many organizations and individuals in Kenya and in other countries. The idea of carrying out this study came to us in 1988 while working on issues related to industrial property protection. Our first study on property rights, *Innovation and Sovereignty: The Patent Debate in African Development*, became a background document for the preparation of the 1989 Industrial Property Act. It set out for the first time in Kenya's legal history the basis for integrating environmental considerations into property rights.

This was followed by two books, *Tenants of the Crown: Agrarian Law and Institutions in Kenya* and *Constitutional Development in Kenya*, which mapped the constitutional terrain on which property rights systems are rooted. More specific studies such as *Becoming Kenyans, Gaining Ground* and *Life in the Balance* helped to sharpen our understanding of natural resource management systems. This book thus builds on the ACTS tradition of bringing detailed research to inform complex public policy issues.

We are grateful for the initial grant for this work provided to ACTS in 1989 by the Ford Foundation to review the relationships between property rights and natural resource management in Kenya. Additional financial support came from the Swedish Society for Nature Conservation (SSNC), the World Resources Institute (WRI) and the International Institute for Environment and Development (IIED). We have more recently been able to further the research with assistance from the Pew Scholars Program in Natural Resources and Environment based at the University of Michigan (USA), the Swedish Agency for Research Cooperation with Developing Countries (SAREC), the Mennonite Central Committee (MCC), the Government of Norway and the Biodiversity Support Programme (BSP) supported by the United States Agency for International Development (USAID). Much of the material has also been assembled or updated during research assignments for various institutions including the Swedish International Development Cooperation Authority (SIDA) and USAID. We would like to thank the Finnish International Development Agency (FINNIDA) and the Regional Soil Conservation Unit (RSCU) for their support for the book's publication.

We want to acknowledge the intellectual contributions and support we have received from Prof. H.W.O. Okoth-Ogendo (University of Nairobi), Prof. Goran Hyden (University of Florida, USA), Prof. John Bruce (Land Tenure Center, University of Wisconsin, USA), Dr. Dianne Rocheleau (Clark University, USA), Dr. Eric Rusten (Ford Foundation, Nairobi), Dr. Eric Loken (USAID, Nairobi), Dr. Kate Newman (BSP, Washington, DC), Dr. Charles Lane (IIED, London), Prof. Anders Hjort-af-Ornäs (Department of Water and Environmental Studies, Linköping University, Sweden), Dr. Mukhisa Kituyi (Member of Parliament, Kenya), Dr. Michael Ståhl (SIDA, Addis Ababa), Mr. Mikko Pyhälä (Embassy of Finland, Pakistan), Dr. Hartmut Krugmann (International Development Research Centre, Nairobi), Mr. Stephen Mwenesi (K.S. Osmond Advocates, Nairobi), Mr. Arman Aardal (Ministry of Foreign Affairs, Oslo), Mr. Harold Miller (All Africa Conference of Churches, Nairobi) and Mr. D. Dean Bibles (Policy on Land Tenure, US Department of the Interior, Washington, DC). They have directly and indirectly inspired much of the effort that has gone into this book. They have readily assisted us to clarify many of the technical issues and we owe much to them for their work and dedication to intellectual enquiry.

We also want to thank the researchers who worked on the various ACTS projects that contributed to this work and whose ideas and inputs have shaped the current study. Those who have contributed in various ways to the research include Prof. Arthur Eshiwani, Prof. Kivutha Kibwana, Dr. Albert Mumma, Mr. Smokin Wanjala, Mr. Arthur Okoth-Owiro, Ms. Janet Kabeberi-Macharia, Ms. Patricia Kameri-Mbote, Prof. Makau Kiamba, Dr. Casper Odegi-Awuondo and Dr. Peter Ondiege (University of Nairobi), Mr. Caroli Omondi (the Attorney-General's Chambers), Mr. David Mukii, Mr. Philip Wandera, Mr. Wilbur Ottichilo and Mr. J.M. Ndung'u (Kenya Wildlife Service), Dr. Mark Stanley-Price, Mr. Edmund Barrow and Mr. Njoroge Ngure (African Wildlife Foundation), Mr. Nehemiah Rotich, Mr. Mwamba Shete and Mr. Amani Komora (East African Wildlife Society), Prof. Stephen Njuguna (IUCN-The World Conservation Union), Mr. Francis Mbote (Ministry of Agriculture), Dr. Owen Lynch and Dr. Kirk Talbott (World Resources Institute), Dr. Bondi D. Ogolla and Prof. Charles O. Okidi (United Nations Environment Programme), Dr. George Krhoda

(Netherlands Embassy, Nairobi), Mrs. Margaret Mwangola (KWAHO), Mr. Hadley H. Jenner (MCC, Nairobi) and Ms. Alison Field-Juma (ACTS). Part of the research for this work was carried out when one of us was on sabbatical leave at the WRI. Over this period we benefited greatly from research support and direction provided by Dr. Walter Reid (WRI), Prof. Mark Sagoff and Ms. Cheryl Cort at the University of Maryland, College Park. Others who have contributed in various ways to our efforts include Dr. Jan Olof Lundberg (SAREC), Dr. Peter Western (SSNC), Dr. Anders Tivell (Forests, Trees and People Programme at the University of Uppsala, Sweden) and Dr. Norman Clark (University of Sussex, UK).

Within the southern Africa region, we appreciate having had the opportunity to discuss some of these ideas with colleagues at the University of Zimbabwe, especially Prof. Sam Moyo (Institute of Development Studies), Prof. Victor Nkiwane (Faculty of Law), and Dr. Jeremy Jackson (Centre for Applied Social Sciences), as well as Mr. Simon Anstey (IUCN-ROSA). We would also like to thank Ms. Aninka Claassens and Mr. Andrew Murphy (Centre for Applied Legal Studies, University of the Witwatersrand), Mr. Brendan Pearce (National Land Committee), Dr. Catherine Cross (Centre for Social and Development Studies, University of Natal), Dr. David Fig (Group for Environmental Monitoring), Dr. Essy Letsoalo (Ministry of Land Affairs), Mr. Saliem Fakir and Ms. Helen Meintjes (Land and Agriculture Policy Centre), and Mr. Jack Blaker (Environment and Development Agency Trust) for the useful materials and insights they provided on governance processes within the new South Africa.

Over the years we have relied heavily on the library of the United Nations Environment Programme whose staff (Ms. Mary Rigby, Ms. Ruth Okuthe, Mr. Samwel Theuri Mwaniki, Ms. Ruth Kamau and Ms. Elizabeth Amolo) have always been prepared to assist us. Ms. Meryl Federl (Documentation Centre of the Centre for Applied Legal Studies, University of the Witwatersrand, South Africa) provided invaluable materials on short notice for which we are most grateful. We want to finally thank Ms. Elizabeth Larson, Mr. Andrew Akhonya, Ms. Mary Muthoni, Mr. Franklin Mwango and Mr. Justus Maganga (Initiatives Publishers) for their assistance in a variety of technical matters essential to the publication of the book.

The contributors to this volume have done so in their personal capacity and do not in any way represent the views of their institutions.

Introduction

CALESTOUS JUMA

Access to and ownership of land is a central aspect of African development in general and political change in particular. Most of the development strategies adopted by African countries are related to the use of the land. But these strategies and the legal arrangements that come with them have not taken into account ecological principles and the importance of long-term natural resource conservation. While traditional development plans have placed emphasis on maximizing economic returns from the available land, new approaches to development are calling for the use of a conservation ethic to guide growth strategies. The way land use is governed is not simply an economic question, but also a critical aspect of the management of political affairs. It may be argued that the governance of land use is the most important political issue in most African countries. Land issues, therefore, should be a central aspect of the constitution as the overall scheme of national governance.

This book examines the relationship between land ownership and the sustainable use of natural resources in the context of constitutional change in Africa. The relationship between land tenure and natural resources has often been examined from the point of view of agricultural development, a subject of much research and debate over the last four decades. Until recently, it had been taken for granted that private ownership and the related legal as well as administrative instruments such as land titling, were a prerequisite for increasing agricultural productivity in the developing world. This argument had become so entrenched that it was an act of development heresy to question it. Much research and academic persuasion went into sustaining the view. Dissenting views were dismissed with little consideration. This position, which has its roots in older individualistic models of development borrowed from the western world, remains a central pillar in the economic strategies of developing countries.

But after decades of development practice evidence is starting to reveal a number of weaknesses in this position. A recent study of a number of African countries has concluded that "title does not equal security of tenure; the extent to which it does depends on the quality of the title surveyed and the broader context of respect for law. Unsuccessful attempts to substitute state titles for customary entitlements may reduce security by creating normative confusion, of which the powerful may take advantage."[1] The study stresses that security of tenure does not by itself lead to greater investment or productivity. "Its effect may be entirely insignificant if farmers are overwhelmed by other risks and disincentives, such as frequent drought, or if the economic environment is otherwise stagnant."[2]

The study concludes that the way forward for Africa is to adopt "more incremental approaches to change in indigenous tenure systems."[3] It recommends an "adaptation paradigm" which builds on customary tenure systems and stress that such a "paradigm requires a supportive legal and administrative environment for evolutionary change in indigenous law. Such a supportive environment implies a clear recognition of the legal applicability and enforceability of indigenous land tenure rules."[4] While the study focusses on agricultural productivity, it provides a basis upon which to extend the analysis to deal with broader issues of environment and development. This broader context is the theme of this book.

The main argument of this book is that current constitutional arrangements in many countries, especially in Africa, put excessive emphasis on the protection of private property rights without requiring the corresponding duty of ecological stewardship. In the absence of such a duty on the part of private property owners, the expectations that humanity places in land to guarantee its survival cannot be met. Meeting such long-term expectations, which is one of the primary goals of sustainable development, cannot be achieved unless a balance is struck between private ownership of land (and the related natural resources) and public interest. A similar balance between conservation and growth is still lacking despite the popular claims about the adoption of sustainable development strategies.

The enforcement of private property rights in land without the corresponding duty of ecological stewardship has resulted in the failure of government policies and development practices to fully integrate environmental considerations into growth strategies. Redressing this, the book notes, requires that environmental rights are recognized in national constitutions and that transactions regarding private property and environmental management are carried out with regard to the due process of the law. Using Kenya as an example, the book shows that the legal system provides extensive and simplified procedures for converting public land to private ownership with little regard for ecological, social or developmental impacts. The same system provides constitutional safeguards against the taking of private property in the public interest without adequate compensation. The system is heavily biased against public interest in general and environmental considerations in particular. The ecological ignorance that prevailed at the time when the legal system was designed cannot be used to deny the call to bring the constitutional order in line with the requirements for sustainable development.

The incorporation of environmental provisions into national and state constitutions is emerging as an important aspect of the governance of public affairs in many countries.[5] This process has evolved from the statements on freedom from pollution and the right to a clean environment towards the adoption of sustainable development principles. This transition is an indication of the growing recognition that environmental protection is central to the goals of achieving sustainable development. Many of the early environmental provisions were influenced largely by concerns over environmental pollution in general and the awareness generated in connection with the 1972 United Nations Conference on the Human Environment held in Stockholm. Many of the constitutions which extend rights to citizens also impose duties on them to protect the environment. Sustainable development is an express objective of a number of them.

This book builds its analysis on the experiences of many countries worldwide. It sets out its argument through chapters clustered into four parts. The first part presents the conceptual foundations upon which the rest of book is built. It presents the linkages between governance and natural resource management and stresses that the sound management of natural resources—which are the natural capital for economic growth—is a critical aspect of national governance. The rules for a governance scheme that takes into account environmental management should therefore be a central part of the constitutional order. This part looks more specifically at the constitutional aspects of environmental management with particular emphasis on the provisions of the Constitution of Kenya dealing with private property. These provisions are further elaborated in the context of land tenure systems in Kenya.

The second part of the book analyses in detail the relationships between the management of specific natural resources and land tenure, with particular emphasis on soils, water, forests and wildlife. It explores the strengths and weakness of current tenure systems and gives indications of alternative approaches that could be adopted in a revised constitutional order. This part presents evidence in support of a flexible land tenure regime under which the state acts as a genuine public trustee.

Part three of the book presents evidence to show that traditional or customary land use practices already embody ecological principles which should be recognized by the law and reflected in constitutions. This part provides evidence from pastoral lands, tenure over trees and medicinal plants to argue the case for recognizing of customary land rights as basis for enriching common law. It demonstrates that the provisions of the Constitution of Kenya are inimical to the use of customary rights as a basis for the development of environmentally-sound property rights systems. This argument is based on the view that customary land rights reflect many of the principles of sustainable development. The very principle of community and its fundamental principles of governance such as reciprocity, citizen oversight and government responsiveness are consistent with ecological laws.

The final part is devoted to presenting options for constitutional reform. It sets out the relationships between ecology and jurisprudence and compares the implications of different constitutional arrangements for environmental management. Of particular interest is the comparison between unitary and federalist constitutions and how such arrangements facilitate or hinder environmental management. This part ends with an outline of options for constitutional reform dealing mainly with the use of doctrines of public trust, customary use and the rights of nature to balance between private property rights and public interest. It suggests measures for effecting the enforcement of the proposed constitutional provisions.

This part notes that the failure to include environmental provisions in national constitutions is likely to lead to activism on the part of the judiciary. This is mainly because the citizenry and the judiciary are rapidly recognizing that environmental change is directly linked to the right to life, which is the most fundamental of all human rights. In countries undergoing democratic change, it has not taken much for the judiciary to given most of the fundamental rights environmental interpretations. Such judicial activism, and the growing recognition of the links between democratic change and environmental management, will create new avenues for furthering the call for political reform. The material basis for such interpretation has been provided by examples such as the destruction of forests upon which local communities depend, onset of health problems associated with industrial and vehicular pollution, loss of life from industrial accidents, destruction of community livelihoods due to the privatization of public lands and the disruption of local populations by large-scale development projects.

This book has been written for a broad audience covering the general public, stakeholders in natural resources, political leaders, policy analysts, policy-makers, researchers, development practitioners, writers and students of social and political change. It seeks to balance between the need for gen-

IN LAND WE TRUST

eral constructive discussions while at the same time serving as a guide for those interested in carrying out further research on the subject. This book does not seek to further any partisan political views, but to present a range of policy options that can be considered by those interested in the relationship between property rights and natural resource management.

Notes

1. Bruce and Migot-Adholla, 1994, p. 260.
2. Bruce and Migot-Adholla, p. 260.
3. Bruce and Migot-Adholla, 1994, p. 261.
4. Bruce and Migot-Adholla, p. 261–262.
5. Brandl and Bungert, (1992) have provided the most comprehensive review of the entrenchment of environmental provisions into conventions.

5

PART I

GOVERNANCE, PRIVATE PROPERTY AND ENVIRONMENT

Governance and sustainable development

1

ALISON FIELD-JUMA

Introduction

The systems of governance currently prevailing throughout the world were largely developed and codified during eras when short-term economic gain guided the concept of development. In many countries, governance systems were modified by social requirements when the negative result of purely economics-driven approaches became visible. Since the United Nations Conference on the Human Environment held in Stockholm in 1972 it has become increasingly clear that the management of national affairs must recognize the limitations of the biosphere and that economic development must take place within the Earth's finite natural resource endowment. Further, the understanding that future generations could only benefit from advances in consumption made by the current generation has started to give way to the reality that unsustainable utilization of natural resources could in fact undermine the very existence of ourselves and our offspring.

This chapter argues that the fundamental reorientation taking place under the banner of sustainable development requires that those norms and rules which guided the affairs of nations be revisited. The first section introduces the relationships between ecology and social change. The second section presents the conceptual basis of this argument and states what we mean by "governance". The interaction between governance and natural resource use from the pre-colonial period to the present is reviewed in the third section.

This section shows how the link between the natural resource base and governance systems was broken during the colonial period and that independence failed to repair the link. The fourth section argues for a new approach to governance in the context of sustainable development. An indication of areas which require a new conceptual approach as argued in the foregoing chapters is provided in the last section.

Ecology and social change

Laws and policies around the globe have been based on the logic that increased consumption is the primary stimulus to economic growth and hence human development. Limitations on consumption, such as anti-pollution regulations, are generally only accepted in as much as they do not violate the primacy of the individual's right to utilize that portion of the natural environment to which he or she has access. This same logic has been applied at the international level, where countries are loath to relinquish their access to common natural resources, such as the oceans or the atmosphere, where it may impinge on their economic development.

Rules for natural resource utilization under this scheme have been guided by the logic of economic and political power. "The intriguing ease with which Neoclassical economists left natural resources out of their own representation of the economic process may not be unrelated to Marx's dogma that everything nature offers us is gratis. . . . Perhaps the absence of any difficulty of securing raw materials by those countries where modern economics grew and flourished was yet another reason for economists to remain blind to this crucial economic factor."[1] However, it became clear that this approach could not be sustained. Over the past few decades appreciation for the complexity of systems has challenged the previously accepted mechanistic economic models. This theoretical revolution in the life sciences has spilled over into other sciences, including economics. It is increasingly being recognized that "real world economic phenomena have had much more in common with biological organisms than with the mechanistic world . . ."[2]

The study of ecology has had a major impact on this realization, providing a model of dynamic systems with interconnected flows of energy and information. Application of ecological principles to social systems has engendered a greater appreciation for the dynamism and complexity of social structures. The emerging field of environmental economics is attempting to develop new tools for factoring environmental externalities and the value of environmental amenities and functions into decision-making. Complex systems approaches have also been found relevant in political science and the study of institutions. It is argued that the reason it has taken so long for governance to take centre stage in the development debate is "due partly to the traditional dominance of quantitative economics."[3] Complicating factors such as ethnicity, corruption and environmental impacts have driven home the point that holistic and dynamic approaches are needed to understand development issues.

Re-examination of indigenous natural resource management systems has shown that far from being static, they have embodied the responsiveness, resilience and complexity of the ecology upon which they are based. This is in stark contrast to the majority of the current systems of governance based on the nation-state and on a model which evolved in the course of industrialization. In most cases these norms and rules were entrenched in developing countries during the colonial era and re-affirmed at independence. National systems tend to be characterized by centralized structures which separate the resource users from the decision-makers and hence circumscribe the flow of information.

The suitability of current systems of governance can, therefore, be questioned on two grounds. First, whether the governance systems recognize the ecological limitations imposed on human activity. In rethinking environmental law, Hunter notes: "The absolute finiteness of the environment, when coupled with human dependency on the environment, leads to the unquestionable result that human activities will at some point be constrained. . . . In short, the environment imposes constraints on our freedom; these constraints are not the product of value choices but of scientific imperatives of the environment's limitations."[4] Secondly, we must ask whether our systems of governance respond to, and effectively utilize, the complexity of the ecological and social context in which they exist to solve development problems. If we accept that we must live within ecological constraints, there is still considerable latitude as to how to do this. Whether it is successfully done will depend on the choices made by individuals, their communities, the nations in which they are located and the international community as reflected in the routines, norms and rules of their governance systems.

Since the natural environment creates the very basis of social and economic development and specifies the limits of the resources available for such development, it is a reasonable starting place for defining the basic limits of our actions. While public attitudes towards the environment have clearly come to recognize the twin threats of pollution and natural resource depletion over the past three decades, changes in behavioural norms and their codification in law and institutions have lagged behind. This chapter argues that if we intend to achieve sustainable development it is time to revisit our systems of governance so that they refer to the ecological basis of

11

our societies, at the local, national and international levels. This review cannot be limited to legislation or policies, but should reach from the capacity of communities to manage their natural resources to the rights embodied in the supreme law of the land—the constitution.

Concepts of governance

Governance and government

The meaning of the term "governance" can be confusing due to its diverse uses. Two approaches currently dominate development discourse: one focussing on government, and the other on civil society as a whole. While we will present both approaches, it is the latter which will inform our analysis. First, let us examine the case of the former. In its 1989 report on development in sub-Saharan Africa, The World Bank defined governance as the "exercise of political power to manage a nation's affairs".[5] In a 1994 document the Bank emphasized "the practical exercise of power and authority by governments in the management of their affairs in general and of economic development in particular".[6] Hence The World Bank has focused on management of public economic resources, establishment of policy and legal frameworks, regulation of markets, national planning, and accountability in decision-making, all relating ultimately to maintaining credit-worthiness. This approach has its roots in the study of public administration and the requirements of industrial society.

In discussing the issue of governance and development Boeninger expands this notion slightly, stating that governance is the "good government of society". He notes that the quality and effectiveness of government enhances the capacity of the state in strategic areas which are vital to development, including: the just exercise of authority, a capacity for problem-solving and conflict resolution and efficient performance of functions. Hence Boeninger retains the government focus, but qualifies it by suggesting that governance is not a neutral act, manner, fact, or function of governing, but represents the achievement of excellence in governing, including the existence of a "societal coalition for development" (referring to a business-labour coalition) and a "committed political consensus".[7] The question of how such coalitions and consensus are built remains unanswered.

Practical action has already been taken along the above lines to improve the efficiency and effectiveness of government by reducing its role in provision of social services and production, using market mechanisms to manage economic affairs and increasing private sector involvement. This has also been applied to the use of market-based instruments for environmental management rather than the "command and control" regulatory approach.

Governance and civil society

Let us now turn to the second approach to governance which encompasses civil society. A number of efforts focussing on governance have been linked with "democratization", with a focus on the exercise of political power. Civic education, strengthening of electoral procedures, political pluralism and a free press have been encouraged to improve the capacity and inclination of elected governments to represent and respond to their citizens. Literature on the governance of institutions in industrialized countries has dealt with topics such as the internal management of schools and hospitals, particularly regarding the decision-making roles of teachers and parents, and doctors and patients, respectively.

In his study of governance in Africa, Hyden defines governance as "the conscious management of regime structures with a view to enhancing the legitimacy of the public realm".[8] Four properties are particularly important to achieving this end: authority, reciprocity, trust and accountability. The more regime management is characterized by these properties "the more it generates legitimacy for the political system and the more, therefore, people will participate in the public realm with enthusiasm."[9] In order to allow practical application of this approach Hyden suggests three main empirical dimensions of governance—citizen influence and oversight; responsive and responsible leadership; and social reciprocities among citizens. The legal framework, policies and institutions are then the mechanisms through which governance finds expression, from the local to the global level.

It is our premise that the mechanisms of governance must derive from the specific circumstances and needs of each individual country. They will reflect the state of the knowledge base and of institutional development in each country. Hence, this approach does not prejudge the locus or character of knowledge and problem-solving, and the roles of formal and informal institutions are left open to explore. This approach can be used to look at activities at all levels of society—and interactions between levels—rather than being limited to the plane of the state.

This inclusive method can enable us to look at how society communicates with itself, how it solves problems, generates ideas and organizes action in order to utilize and conserve natural resources. Countries throughout Africa as well as in many other parts of the world, are currently engaged in revising, and in some cases overhauling, their systems of governance. In order to understand the depth of this process and the potential that it has for supporting sustainable natural resource management, it is useful to examine Hyden's definition of governance further and then illustrate how environmental imperatives may be brought to bear on its functioning.

Mechanisms and dynamics of governance[10]

The mechanisms of governance comprise the legal framework, policies, and formal and informal institutions of a society. These mechanisms are used by the State and by the public in maintaining reciprocal relations within society. The legal framework of governance comprises binding international agreements, the national and sub-national constitutions, legislation, regulations and rules. As such it includes both statutory and traditional systems, as in the case of traditional rules of access to common property. Policy instruments comprise non-binding international agreements (such as Agenda 21) and national policy statements, plans such as national development plans and environmental action plans, and approaches such as decentralization strategies.

Institutions are the most broad-based element of governance, existing at the formal level yet including the norms and behaviour at the local level. Institutions may implement government strategies and plans, but may also originate from the daily activities of communities (such as revolving credit associations, traditional decision-making systems, women's groups, etc.). Community groups, professional associations and traditional resource management norms are localized mechanisms of governance which are to varying degrees outside of the formal governmental system.

The existence of the mechanisms outlined above by no means ensures the existence or quality of governance. Human agency is required to give life to these structures, and their creation and evolution is by necessity the result of citizens' capacity to express their interests.[11] The degree to which such agency exists can be assessed through Hyden's three principal empirical dimensions of governance—citizen influence and oversight; responsive and responsible leadership; and social reciprocities among citizens (Figure 1). We will now examine each of these in the context of natural resource management, what we will call "environmental governance".

There is ample evidence that citizens of African countries are active managers of their environment at the local level, in most cases directly as small-scale farmers and pastoralists. The first question relating to citizen influence and oversight is whether and how their interests and knowledge as direct users and managers of the environment become reflected in instruments of governance (such as government laws, policies and procedures) and in institutions. Formal structures, such as the District Focus for Rural Development Strategy in Kenya or the mobisquads in Ghana have the potential of providing two-way avenues for the flow of knowledge.[12] However, if citizens do not believe that they will be able to affect government sufficiently they may choose to not invest their energies in the formal process. Citizens may abandon the public realm and turn to traditional or informal means of ensuring their welfare. For example, informal personal contact with intermediaries who have access to decision-makers and elected representatives may be used.

Figure 1 The three principal empirical dimensions of governance

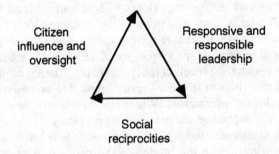

Citizen influence and oversight

Responsive and responsible leadership

Social reciprocities

Source: Hyden and Bratton, 1992, p. 15.

This makes it more difficult for the state to receive the correct signals or be able to implement policies which are for the public good rather than the good of a lesser number of individuals. The same applies to non-governmental organizations (NGOs) or religious organizations involved in development. Unless the information upon which policies, technologies, interventions or institutions are developed is drawn from local experience, these investments are unlikely to reflect the needs of local resource users. When this happens, the citizens are likely to cease investing in the land (e.g., in soil conservation, tree planing, genetic resource conservation) and instead mine what is there and then abandon it. It must also be recognized that communities are not homogeneous and may not have well-defined boundaries. There are also important differences between the way women and men value and utilize natural resources.[13] This may result from differences in land ownership, land management and household duties by gender. Some of these differences are quite pronounced while others cannot be discerned without in-depth knowledge of the community. There may be other differences according to income level, age, religion or other factors.

The second question is, do citizens have the standing, ability and motivation to oversee the implementation of development activities. This is largely

15

a matter of communication and access. Stakeholders must be able to assess whether the solutions provided have the desired effect, and have some recourse if they do not. Are there official mechanisms for this, or does it happen informally? Do citizens have the information they need to make intelligent claims and decisions in natural resource use? Do citizens have the "right to know" about decisions which will affect them? It is not the *existence* of formal structures which matters. What is important is the *performance* of the system—does it work, do citizens have confidence in it, and do they have the ability to maintain its functions?

The question of responsiveness and responsibility of leadership can be approached at various levels—clan elders, village leaders, local and central government. The main interest is to solve the problems identified by citizens, analysts and academics before the problems become so intractable that the solutions will undermine the system itself. The loci of problem-solving could be at the community level, in independent think-tanks, in universities, in government ministries or in other organizations. The common need is for accurate and relevant information. Where the information originates from and is utilized will depend on the nature of the problem.

Government decisions affecting the environment will often need to integrate local knowledge with information about national or regional trends plus scientific information generated by national or international research. Government policies and plans are needed to give coherence and predictability to government actions but will only do so if they are communicated to the citizens and are well understood. Ultimately the government has the responsibility to facilitate capacity-building at all levels of society to ensure that the institutional and knowledge infrastructure are developed where they are needed.

In terms of social reciprocity, reference to ecology teaches us one fundamental point: everything is connected to everything else—both in time and in space. Simply stated: "The basic insight of ecology is that all living things exist in interrelated systems; nothing exists in isolation."[14] The environment includes a mix of "common property" resources (water, air, fisheries, etc.) as well as privately-owned land and fixtures. In many African countries large areas of land are under some form of common property regime, particularly in the arid and semi-arid areas.[15] In addition, the impacts of land use tend to spread across property boundaries and national borders. Efforts to solve environmental problems based purely on self interest and private property have not met with success. In the case of soil and water management, the approach is shifting to watershed and catchment-based efforts, such the establishment of river and lake basin development authorities in Kenya and the "catchment approach" to soil conservation used in eastern Africa. Atmospheric pollution has such global effects that only global approaches to mitigation seem appropriate.

However, all these approaches to problem-solving require collective action based on consensus—between men and women, between villages and between nations. This may be achieved through customary consensual decision-making processes, conflict resolution methods, consultative processes required by policies and laws, or other means. These approaches to development will benefit from conscious government facilitation of collective thinking. Reciprocity can be the result of mutual dread of an impending disaster such as global warming, where governments commit themselves to actions which they would not otherwise take. Reciprocity can also be encouraged through policies or laws such as water pricing or fuel alternatives, where individuals, firms or communities may agree to change their consumption patterns due to a new array of choices.

It has become clear that people, or nations, can only make and successfully implement these choices if they are provided with adequate information and if the options provided have been developed based on accurate knowledge. This may be relatively easy at the local level, where citizens have strong cultural ties, often expressed through social reciprocity. But we should not be mislead by the evidence of strong local associations if they cannot transcend their locality and accommodate similar associations from a different locales and ethnic groups.

Natural resources and governance

Traditional resource management and governance

Environmental governance was the main preoccupation of traditional resource management systems in Africa. Indigenous resource management systems reflected the way communities organized their lives within the constraints of the environment in which they lived. Decision-making institutions focused on utilizing and managing environmental resources based on the knowledge of the community. This was done within the framework of their world view, in other words in accordance with their ethics, norms and beliefs.

Despite the diversity of traditional resource management systems on the continent, it can be said that traditional institutions were part of the community, and the resource users and the decision-makers were in very close proximity, if not one and the same. Decision-making was knowledge-intensive in that the decisions were made based on knowledge accumulated over time, in addition to the immediate experiences of the resource users as well

17

as of scouts and travellers. Indigenous knowledge of the environment allowed classification of soil and vegetation types, prediction of resource availability and planning of use strategies. This knowledge enabled communities to avoid over-utilizing an area through monitoring its status and adjusting their resource use patterns.

Resource use systems relied upon building reciprocal relations among families and communities, for example through livestock sharing, and with other groups and communities through trade, marriage and advisers. These relations redistributed risk and strengthened social obligations to be utilized during times of drought, pestilence or war. The land was generally held by the community with fairly clearly defined spatial and temporal use rights allocated to its members. The same applied to other natural resources, such as in the case of customary tree tenure among the pastoral Turkana.[16] Intergenerational transfer of family rights proceeded under the control of the community through its decision-making body according to prevailing rules of succession. Accordingly, indigenous tenure systems often provided high levels of tenure security.

Indigenous natural resource tenure systems were rarely static, and showed a notable degree of change over time in response to social and economic changes, new technologies, natural calamities, migration and population changes, subordination and war. It has been observed that over time customary tenure systems in Africa have spontaneously evolved "from more diffuse and collective to more specific and exclusionary individual rights" in response to population pressure and commercialization of agriculture.[17]

Colonial political and economic imperatives

As nation-states came into existence the distance between the resource users and the overall decision-makers increased by virtue of their having different world views (particularly with the advent of colonial states), being physically located farther from each other, and having more indirect forms of representation (where there was representation at all), all of which hindered the sharing of information and norms. The specific functions of government came to operate at different levels isolated from the resource managers. Environmental problem-solving was done in the ministries of agriculture or livestock and other agencies. Research came to be conducted in special-focus institutes rather than in the course of resource management activities. These institutions drew their models and concept of science from Western traditions and generally disregarded indigenous knowledge. Hence the flow of knowledge was seriously disrupted; research results were disseminated to resource managers through one-way extension activities with few mechanisms for feedback.

During the colonial period, development was driven by political and economic imperatives. The natural environment was seen as a free good and the preoccupation of colonial governments was how to control as much as possible of it for their own economic benefit. While the legal justification differed slightly between protectorates and colonies of the different colonial powers, the process was essentially the same. Administrative power was used penetrate the local production systems and either co-opt or remove indigenous populations. In the case of Kenya, between 1890 and independence in 1963, the colonial government progressively alienated land from the indigenous population for European settlement, and then entrenched European private property rights as a buffer against the impending African rule.[18] As independence approached, the property rights of some Africans were also entrenched in order to ensure the development of an African landed middle-class which would share the same economic and political interests as the settlers.

It is argued that the African sector of the colonial economy was systematically exploited and underdeveloped in order to support the settler sector.[19] In Kenya, attempts at European "self-rule" were halted, unlike in Rhodesia. However, the European settlers sought security "in an arrangement that had been in operation in South Africa for many years, namely, the creation of native lands or reserves segregated both juridically and territorially not only from the settler enclave, but internally among the Africans themselves as well."[20] This *de jure* dual economic and social system resulted in continual crises in land management and environmental degradation throughout the African areas. Major colonial government efforts to intensify land use through application of technology in the high and medium-potential areas were used to diffuse demands for extensification and hence land redistribution in these areas. In the African reserves, land "betterment" was done by administrative directive using coerced labour, forced destocking and other uses of the police power.

A similar dualism was created in Rhodesia between the high-potential areas settled by Europeans and the less fertile Tribal Trust lands. In those regions where large-scale expropriation for European settlement was not undertaken, colonial administrators often forged alliances with local rural elites as a strategy of control, as with the Buganda, Toro and Bunyoro kingdoms in Uganda. "Chiefs" and tribal boundaries were also created in order to provide a locally-based administrative unit with which colonial authorities could deal. This had the effect of reducing the reciprocity possible between ethnic groups—such as trade, multiple resource use and marriage—by heightening ethnic identity and competition for increasingly scarce natural resources. It also froze the ecologically-sound migratory processes

19

through which communities had responded to land shortage and patchiness and temporal variability in the natural environment.

In pastoral areas of Kenya administrative control was also used to restrict seasonal movement of livestock by delineating grazing blocks, fixing grazing borders between communities and establishing livestock quarantines with heavy penalties. While pasture and water resources may have been adequate within the fixed areas during years with adequate rainfall, during low rainfall years they were not, exposing the local economies to high levels of stress. In his study of northern Kenya, Oba notes that: "The policy ignored the obligatory relationships between neighbouring pastoral communities, instead it aimed at controlling stock movements within the delimited borders. . . . The artificial partitioning of tribal grazing lands gave rise to ecological, political, administrative and economic problems."[21]

Post-colonial continuity

Immediately prior to independence, the colonial government in Kenya ensured that settlers' agricultural leases were converted into freehold tenure, private property was made sacrosanct, and expropriation was outlawed except on payment of prompt and full compensation. The legal arrangements which had been codified in the run-up to independence were preserved in the Independence constitution under the sanctity of private property in high potential areas, and the control by the state of the arid and semi-arid areas through the continuation of a trust mechanism. Okoth-Ogendo concludes that ". . . the colonial status quo weathered the independence storm in its entirety, both in terms of production relations and the legal and institutional norms and structures that were complementary to it . . . . In this sense the continuity of agrarian law was simply an aspect of the wider process of the continuity of the political economy of colonialism as a whole." He further suggests that the validity of the colonial legal system was assumed in the Independence constitution, hence becoming part of the "foundation upon which the legitimacy of the independent state rested".[22]

In Zimbabwe, the independence period has been "characterized by tensions between the goal of preserving the productive potential of a broadly capitalist economy geared to meeting the needs of a small high-income minority, and the goal of redirecting state and economy to meet the basic needs of a rapidly growing population."[23] The less fertile Tribal Trust lands were renamed "Communal Areas" after independence and continued to experience environmental degradation and resource scarcity due to the high population density and lack of services. The ability of the independence government to address this continuation of the colonial duality was constrained by a clause in the constitution protecting settler lands which prohibited seizure without full compensation for ten years. Legislation to permit acquisition of land for resettlement without full compensation was quickly passed after 1991.

The situation in other African countries differed only in degree. Some countries revised the legal instruments which they had inherited, but the governance systems overall tended to bear the imprint of the centrality of state power, particularly through the executive branch of government. In countries which followed a socialist path, such as Tanzania, Angola, Mozambique and Ethiopia, all land was vested in the state. In most countries key natural resources were part put under the control of the government, including water, minerals, forests, wildlife and land. Control of finance was an important element of central government authority, making the operations of *de jure* local authorities difficult if not impossible.

Throughout the drylands of eastern and southern Africa policies to bring certain services to rural populations were implemented without consideration of the environmental impact, such as sedentarization of pastoral peoples. The prevailing belief among government planners in southern Somalia during the socialist period 1969–76, which was typical for the region, was that "common ownership was environmentally degrading, nomadic pastoralism was unproductive, and traditional institutions were ineffective and outmoded. The reforms were thus intended to vest land management in the hands of the state, to draw the population into settled farming, and to substitute modern institutions of production and marketing for traditional forms."[24] Provision of water points, and in some areas problems of insecurity, drew pastoralists into forming settled communities, disrupting the ecologically-sound movements of livestock and concentrating demand on woodlands for fuelwood and construction and fencing materials. Sedentarization and other programmes such as villagization in Tanzania, disregarded those community governance structures which had survived colonization and the natural resource management systems and knowledge which they embodied.

Private property, productivity and conservation

The colonial emphasis on exclusive private property rights in land, and its continuity into the independence era had a number of impacts. Only Kenya continued with a generalized privatization campaign, while other countries opted for an overall state-ownership approach. The emphasis on privatization received a boost throughout the region in the mid-1980 when a number of major bilateral and multilateral donors called for large-scale privatization and title registration programmes to provide tenure security in order to increase investment in agriculture.

Where it occurred, privatization undermined many traditional common property resource management systems, particularly in the agro-pastoral areas, creating a confusing mix of "modern" and traditional authority rules and norms. Private property entrenched ownership in a landed elite which monopolized the most productive agricultural resources and denied access to other agriculturalists and pastoralists leading to environmental stress in the remaining areas. For the small-holder, private property also failed to deliver the benefits which were widely touted both before and after independence: security of tenure, improved access to credit, reduced land conflicts, economic size of land-holding, an effective land market, and hence incentives for investment and sound resource management.

Recent studies have shown that registered titles do not ensure security of tenure.[25] Furthermore, security of tenure does not by itself result in greater investment or productivity since factors such as drought or poor producer prices may provide overwhelming risks and disincentives.[26] Nor does private title eliminate the social responsibility of the land owner to provide for the extended family. Individual title-holding, in most cases by an elder male family-member, has also undermined the rights in land of the women and children in the family, and of the community as a whole. In addition, cultural norms have hindered the development of land markets to the extent that sources of credit are hesitant to accept title in rural land as collateral. Hence land purchases are more likely to be made by urban middle or high-income individuals rather than farmers interested in expanding their holdings. A growth in landlessness has been reported in countries where land markets have not developed.[27]

As noted above, the institution of private property allowed for *exclusive* ownership of the most productive land for agricultural production. It also facilitated continued encroachment of agricultural land use into drylands which were more susceptible to ecological degradation. Pastoralists were denied access to what had been their dry season grazing and water points which were a critical part of their environment-based socio-economy. Loss of access undermined both the economic and ecological viability of pastoral systems.

Pastoralists were also affected by attempts to integrate them into the private property system in Kenya through granting of individual title to ranches starting in 1954 and then through granting private group title under the Land (Group Representatives) Act of 1968. Having group title to a limited area gave that group some security of tenure but it also further circumscribed their ability to maintain reciprocal relations among their own communities and with others and reduced their access to critical grazing and water resources outside the group ranch boundaries.

Excision of game reserves and national parks from the remaining pastoral areas starting in the 1950s further limited pastoralists' access to water and dry season grazing resources. In pastoral areas "[t]his process represents an ongoing spread down the ecological gradient of the adjustments of land rights and use involving the replacement of livestock by crops as the basis of production, and ownership of cattle by land as the objective of accumulation."[28]

The concept of "exclusive" use bears examination. Land is generally taken to mean the soil and the natural resources which exist above and below that soil, such as water, plants and wild animals. Private property law has generally taken rights to the use and consumption of all of those resources throughout time as a right of ownership (although regulated to some degree by other laws). This creates a rigidity which cannot respond to changing environmental conditions, such as drought, seasonal events, such as wildlife or livestock migrations, or reciprocal relations between people, such as shared water or fuelwood resources.

It is evident that a single landowner may not use all of these resources all the time yet other people may have some use for them. Traditional land use systems were based on use rights to certain resources bounded by time and the needs of other community members. Not only does the shift to exclusive use of the whole quantum of rights severely disrupt traditional land-use systems, it has the effect of limiting the natural resource utilization strategies of society as a whole. This is very relevant today as many countries in the region face severe shortages of natural resources, particularly water and arable land. Tenure systems which allow for multiple use of resources and simultaneous production (e.g., of wildlife, livestock, tree crops, fuelwood, medicinal plants, etc.) are as likely to be relevant today as they were 100 years ago. Hence governance structures suited to multiple use should be considered especially in the context of community-based natural resource management, discussed later in this chapter.

The administrative approach

Many governments in eastern and southern Africa have opted to declare public (government) ownership of land and other natural resources and, to varying degrees, have attempted to eliminate community rights and resource management systems. Such attempts have included instituting collectivized agriculture to reorganize relations of production and villagization schemes in Tanzania, Mozambique and Ethiopia. These systems have not provided the economic or productivity benefits envisaged. National parks and reserves are also under exclusive government ownership.

Government ownership of natural resources provides for resource access either through lease arrangemen's or delegation of trusteeship to lower levels of authority. The primary control is retained in the relevant government ministry and administered through its machinery such as, in the case of Kenya, administrative chiefs and local authorities. The sector-based authority of those line ministries which are responsible for land management and policy (e.g., forestry, agriculture) does not allow for the highly interdependent nature of the various resources on these lands or the varied needs of the resource users. The political nature of organs such as administrative chiefs and local authorities opens up opportunities for inconsistency in access and insecurity in tenure with limited channels of redress.

Recent studies have shown that title vested in the state may "reduce security by creating normative confusion, of which the powerful may take advantage."[29] On the one hand, such administrative organs are located in reasonably close proximity to the people and have the power to demand and enforce actions which could enhance the sustainability of land utilization. While on the other hand, there are few checks and balances which would control the abuse of such power. The Chiefs' Act in particular provides broad police powers to the chief, a government appointee.

The degree and breadth of action taken on environmental issues by the executive branch of government in Kenya indicates both the importance attributed to environmental concerns and the power of that office in matters regarding natural resources. A case in point is the Permanent Presidential Commission on Soil Conservation and Afforestation which has far-reaching powers; the Commission can break through the bureaucratic limitations of the Ministry of Agriculture and take direct action on particularly urgent matters on both public and private land.[30]

The effectiveness of the centralized approach to resource management has come under increasing scrutiny. Recent evidence of re-assessment of the centrality of the state in natural resource management comes from Tanzania. In his analysis of the constitutionality of the 1992 Regulation of Land Tenure (Establishment of Villages) Act which extinguished customary tenure and re-asserted state title in Tanzania, Shivji notes the ". . . unviability of piling up *ad hoc* legislation on the substratum of the Land Ordinance, which puts enormous power over land in the hands of the executive by vesting the radical title in the President (State). He concludes:

> The authoritarian state-controlled and centralized model which guided the colonial and post-independence land tenure system has become bogged down. . . . the way out of the impasse is thoroughly to democratize and legitimize the land tenure system by devolving power to the Village

Assemblies and an independent National Lands Commission, on the one hand, and rooting land tenure in the custom and culture (albeit modified by democratic and accountable institutions and procedures) of the people, on the other. People are crying out for nothing less that a democratic constitutional dispensation on land to resolve their problems.[31]

Governance for sustainable development

The sustainable development paradigm

Traditional African ethos towards the land has taken many forms and been enunciated in various ways, but to select only one, Kenyatta in 1936 wrote: "Since the land is held in trust for the unborn, as well as for the living, and since it represents [the owner's] partnership in the common life of generations, he will not lightly take it upon himself to dispose of it."[32] Unfortunately, Kenyatta was voicing an indigenous ethos of land stewardship which was being consistently stamped out by colonial enterprise around the globe. In 1966 Aldo Leopold, the oft-quoted American environmentalist lamented the dominant attitude of his time: "There is as yet no ethic dealing with man's relation to land and to the animals and plants which grow upon it . . . . The land-relation is still strictly economic, entailing privileges but not obligations."[33]

The 1972 Stockholm Conference on the Human Environment is a convenient landmark for the emergence of popular consciousness of the limits of the natural environment which challenged the logic of the economic imperative. Whether it was the fear of pesticides so vividly described by Rachel Carson in the late 1960s, the oil crisis of the 1970s or the waves of famines and droughts across Africa that brought the message home, the importance of "environment" to economic and social development was on the road to acceptance. Although the conference declaration was non-binding, it described a new international agenda in which the role of the environment in human development could no longer be ignored. While there are still quarters where environmental concerns are seen to be alarmist, the reality of the connection is nowhere as vivid as in developing countries where the buffer between human welfare and environmental conditions is thin or non-existent. Notable lack of success of projects which aimed to bring technical solutions to the problems of poverty in the Third World also suggested that a more systematic approach was needed.

The work of the World Commission on Environment and Development published in 1987 as *Our Common Future* showed how the two seemingly contradictory goals of environment and development were in fact interdependent. These events led up to the adoption of Agenda 21, the non-binding consensus document of the United Nations Conference on Environment and Development (UNCED) in Rio de Janeiro in 1992, which provided the operational framework for efforts to attain sustainable development. The signing and ratification of two binding environmental conventions, on biological diversity and climate change, and subsequently the convention to combat desertification proposed by African governments, put environmental governance on the international negotiating table together with trade and political agreements.

However, perhaps the most difficult question raised by Agenda 21 and all three environmental conventions remains to be answered: how to implement their provisions at the national and local levels within the context of national development goals. Agenda 21 emphasizes the important roles to be played by local authorities, NGOs and indigenous people and their communities.

Within independent Africa the development imperative—encompassing economic growth, social transformation and political control—had ruled the evolution of governance mechanisms and dynamics. However the intractability of the problems of environmental degradation started to become apparent and influence the political dialogue in the 1970s. Growing recognition of the importance of the proximate resource users—small-scale farmers, pastoralists, fisherfolk—to sound resource management decision-making suggested that governance systems should strengthen local-level mechanisms and institutions. Several approaches to natural resource management emerged as a result of this convergence of international and domestic awareness which challenged the centralized administrative methods which had prevailed since the turn of the century.

Decentralization of government

In response to failures in state-controlled resource management and appeals to have a more bottom-up approach, governments in eastern and southern Africa have experimented with various forms of decentralization. Decentralization can take a number of forms, with varying degrees of reform of existing power structures.[34] It is useful to distinguish between these forms since their effect may be quite different. UNDP describes three types of decentralization: deconcentration, delegation and devolution. The most common form is deconcentration, where the functions of central government ministries are assigned to sub-offices. "In effect, deconcentration extends central government tentacles to the periphery through the creation of sub-units of government . . . . which does not encourage the development of autonomous local governments, and makes little allowance for horizontal integration at the local level."[35] With delegation, responsibility for specific functions is transferred to an entity outside of, or indirectly controlled by, government, such as special authorities or parastatals. This is often seen as a means of improving the delivery of key services. Lastly, devolution "results in the establishment or strengthening of sub-national units of government which are largely independent of central government control, and which have broad authority for operating across a number of sectors."[36] Full devolution is not common in developing countries.

Decentralization of national development planning has been attempted in both Zimbabwe and Kenya through the establishment of development committees which operate from the village level to the provincial or district level, respectively. Concerns have been raised as to the effectiveness of this deconcentration approach in Kenya, in particular its bureaucratic nature and the tendency of interests to flow from the top-down rather than from the bottom-up. Uganda's Resistance Council system has arguably provided an innovative democratic mechanism of governance, strengthening citizen oversight, and responsiveness and accountability of leadership and reciprocity within the public realm.[37] The impact of this system on natural resource management will be an important area of study.

In the search for viable land reform Botswana has opted to develop a new local land administration institution which administers land under indigenous tenure rules but operates subject to certain statutory provisions. This system attempts to balance the need to recognize indigenous tenure rules with state interests, without taking over the administration of all land. Under this system, "the land is vested in several Tribal Land Boards, who hold it for the tribe. These are elected, and considerable resources have been devoted to training and equipping them. They are responsible for both customary land allocations for farming and homes, and leases for commercial ranching, residential plots in town, and commercial sites."[38] This attempt to devolve authority was implemented nation-wide and involves appeal and supervision systems tying the new local institutions to national ministries. However, the limitations of the system have emerged as the boards have been less effective in gaining control over use of communal grazing land or allocation of arable land than in allocation of large ranches. "In both cases, much land allocation is still carried out by traditional authorities, subject to appeals to the new institutions."[39]

The centrality of the state in natural resource management may also be challenged simply by its inability to provide the financial resources and infrastructure to assert control. During the 1980s and 1990s there has been a progressive weakening of state interventions in community development. The lack of economic growth coupled with reductions in donor support has considerably reduced the ability of governments in sub-Saharan Africa to provide the planned level of social services and infrastructure to their citizens. This has been coupled with the pressure to reduce state involvement in marketing and production, reduce the size of the civil service and increase private sector participation under structural adjustment programmes. Agricultural extension, health, education, veterinary services, water supply development and other state programmes relating to natural resource management have been cut back.

There has been no systematic replacement of these services at the local level, however, and in many cases communities have had to fall back on their own capacity to cope. There has been an upsurge in non-state institutions and organizations, both non-governmental and private sector, which have emerged to fill the gap to some degree. But decentralization cannot be a panacea: "There will be circumstances, where development of the people will be better served by centralized control, or by some degree of decentralization in some form other than by complete self-determination. In countries characterized by wide inter-regional economic disparities, central control and authority might be necessary to remove these disparities."[40]

Social innovation and environmental governance

Whether the form of governance is a traditional system or a national government, the existence of some degree of the three dynamics of governance—citizen influence and oversight; responsive and responsible leadership; and social reciprocities—is critical to sustaining the use of natural resources in light of their increasing scarcity. A recent study on environmental change and violent conflict concluded that:

Scarcities of renewable resources are already contributing to violent conflicts in many parts of the world. These conflicts may foreshadow a surge of similar violence in coming decades, particularly in poor countries where shortages of water, forests and, especially, fertile land, coupled with rapidly expanding populations, already cause great hardship.[41]

The authors suggest that we need to know more about "the variables that affect the supply of human ingenuity in response to environmental change". This includes social ingenuity "for the creation of institutions that buffer people from the effects of degradation and provide the right incentives for technological innovation".[42] This knowledge is important for policymakers, researchers and development workers to have in order to plan their local strategies and suggest policy and legislative reforms which will strengthen institutions, rules and behaviour which can help society solve emerging resource management problems.

Where do we look for this ingenuity? It is becoming increasingly accepted that traditional means of local decision-making and governance hold important lessons regarding sustainable resource use and options for reform of statutory institutions. Chapter 26 of Agenda 21 says: "Indigenous people and their communities have an historical relationship with their lands and . . . have developed over many generations a holistic traditional scientific knowledge of their lands, natural resources and environment. . . . national and international efforts to implement environmentally sound and sustainable development should recognize, accommodate, promote and strengthen the role of indigenous people and their communities." The importance of understanding local and traditional governance systems has been particularly well documented in terms of management of common property resources.[43]

As argued in this chapter, and supported by evidence from around the world, neither state ownership and regulation nor the market have had much success in enabling individuals to sustain long-term, productive use of natural resource systems. However, "communities of individuals have relied on institutions resembling neither the state nor the market to govern some resource systems with reasonable degrees of success over long periods of time."[44] Such systems may be called "common property resource management systems" which imply that the resources are co-owned by a group which manages those resources and is able to exclude others from outside the group from to access them. For the purposes of our discussion, the relevant resources may be fisheries, forests, water, wildlife or pasture.[45]

The effective functioning of common property resource management systems depends on the existence of appropriate institutions; these are often local and informal, community-based rather than government-sponsored, flexible yet durable. Such institutions play a crucial role in economic development. Berkes and Farvar note that:

> Institutions seen as necessary for development planning cannot be created anew. . . . the local people cannot be divorced from the social structures of which they are a part. The logical approach for development planners is to deal intelligently with existing community structures, including those for handling production and resource-management issues. . . . Having developed within specific historical, cultural and ecological contexts, their strength is in their suitability for specific areas and resource types.[46]

When investigating local resource management systems, the influence of traditional means of local decision-making and governance must be considered. Traditional systems in themselves are not the answer. Rather, they illustrate systems which worked to some degree in the past, but usually under different social and ecological conditions than today.

As traditional systems, technologies and institutions evolve over time they incorporate elements from the environment and thus are generally specific to the culture and natural surroundings of the people practising them. Unfortunately, they are often seen as static remnants of a primitive past which have been (or should be) supplanted by statutory or other "modern" systems. Efforts to facilitate their continued evolution, recombining them with new information from today's society in a way that leads towards sustainable resource management is often what is needed. In other cases, conditions have changed so much that completely new technologies and institutions are required. Community development workers in Kenya confirm this point: in Taita, strengthening village-level leaders who are legitimate in their community's eyes and evolving new institutional structures by merging traditional and statutory systems has enabled villagers to make long-term decisions about their water resources.[47]

Resource depletion on state-controlled lands has largely been caused by the lack of effective management systems—rules, sanctions and management decision-making—resulting in an open access situation, the true "tragedy of the commons". The re-establishment of governance with a strong local presence and legitimacy in such areas is likely to be the best option for sustainable management.

Many forms of non-state institutions have emerged over the past few decades, from small resource-user groups and interest groups to registered NGOs. Private sector organizations, such as consultancy and law firms, have also engaged in environmental assessment, planning, advocacy and policy advice. This growth of the institutional capacity of civil society has great potential to contribute to sustainable development from different vantage points.

Assistance to developing countries provided by and through non-governmental organizations has increased rapidly and by 1993 amounted to almost one-fifth of net bilateral flows.[48] This enthusiasm results from a number of perceptions by development assistance organizations: First, NGOs are seen to have a role in increasing pluralism and strengthening civil society. Second, they are seen to be in closer contact with the population and hence be able to be more responsive to local development needs than the state. Third, it is believed that NGOs are more accountable and less corrupt than the state, and less bureaucratic. This should increase the cost-effectiveness of development assistance channeled through them.

While not necessarily agreeing with all of the foregoing, governments of developing countries hope that NGOs may share some of the burden of development in ways that the state is no longer able to do. Their flexibility and issue- and problem-specific mandates enable NGOs to mobilize funds comparatively quickly. This also places them in a position of conflict with developing country governments. "[NGOs] have the money, personnel, and rapid-response capacity for programs and projects, while national governments claim sovereignty and gate keeping authority."[49]

The rapid increase in the number of NGOs is remarkable, particularly in countries such as Tanzania where non-state and non-party organizations of any description were suppressed from 1964 until the mid-1980s.[50] Tanzania provides a vivid example of the recent ascendance of NGOs and their potential contributions. By the late 1980s, social sector development aid in Tanzania was starting to be directed through local non-state channels which were emerging to fill the gap left by declining state resources. Grass-roots, member-run, self-reliant bodies were springing up and challenging the local power bases of the state and ruling party; local formally-organized community development activities (counterparts of foreign NGOs or donor governments) and international NGOs without local counterparts also increased in number. A large number of NGOs, either government-organized or elite-organized became particularly evident in areas where there was "widely-publicized donor interest to support local-level activity", especially in environment and women-in-development activities. These heterogeneous organizational forms arose out of varied interests and showed varying degrees of patronage, durability, accountability, capability and legitimacy.

In his study of ten urban and rural districts in Tanzania, Kiondo was surprised to find "genuinely locally-rooted organizations . . . providing or attempting to provide a comprehensive set of social services across a number of sectors." These so-called Development Trust Funds appeared to have nearly replaced the local state organs and had as their central features "the integration of local state-based and private elites in leadership roles, and the marriage of state (taxation) and private (donation) forms of revenue-raising."[51] Their effectiveness and accountability remain to be studied, but the social ingenuity involved is evident. The impact of such local-level institutions on natural resource management may only be answered in time.

In Kenya, Zimbabwe and other countries in the region NGOs have been seen to have a positive role to play in research and extension activities relating to the environment. A survey in 1991 identified over nineteen NGOs actively engaged in agricultural and environmental technology development in Zimbabwe.[52] These were mostly working in collaboration with the government research system to disseminate technical packages such as improved seed, but some also worked on community mobilization and empowerment. Some NGOs engaged in their own research, particularly focussing on areas that they felt were neglected by mainstream research institutions.

31

Kenya has a similar number of NGOs with some 17 per cent of NGOs involved in environmental protection by 1990.[53] During the colonial period traditional self-help groups were co-opted into compulsory environmental rehabilitation work through the "betterment" schemes on the reserves. Since independence, a large self-help movement encouraged by the heads of state and institutionalized as a national development mode, *harambee*, has made substantial contributions to national development. This long history of community organization in Kenya, based on the traditional modes of organization in many areas, has provided some social memory of institutional organization, accountability and purpose. While it is unlikely that this provides a sufficient basis for large-scale natural resource management systems, it does provide a foundation for community-based conservation and development as described below.

The participation of people and communities in the decisions which govern their well-being has been identified as a key to sustainable natural resource management. In the context of international and domestic calls for democratization and liberalization, and spurred on by withdrawal of the state from a number of social and economic activities, grassroots, participatory and community-based conservation and development activities have gained a large following. Many methods have been tried to secure the participation of community members, or the participation of the larger group of stakeholders in the natural resource in question. However such interventions have generally fallen short of achieving enduring natural resource management systems.

Despite some degree of international consensus on the unity of environment and development, tensions have grown between developed and developing nations, and between conservationists and those concerned with social and economic development. "At the root of these tensions are two opposing rights: the rights of communities to assume control over their land and resources, and the right of outsiders to deny the use of species and resources."[54] This tension can be seen as poorer nations struggle to assert their sovereignty in the face of demands from industrialized countries, and as communities within the former demand control over their own resources from the state.

Drawing from the Zimbabwe experience Murphree suggests that the reason participatory conservation efforts have generally fallen short is that "participation usually is undertaken in ways that segregate responsibility from authority."[55] Efforts to include community participation assume that communities have the institutional capability for decision-making and management and the authority to implement resource management responsibilities. However, this is rarely the case, due in part to the colonial legacy of centralized authority and underdevelopment of the African sector. To have true community-based natural resource management requires proprietorship of the resources: "sanctioned use rights, rights of access and inclusion, and the right to benefit fully from use and management."[56] Such group proprietorship would allow communities to negotiate resource management arrangements which take advantage of multiple-use opportunities. For example, where proprietorship over wildlife is devolved to some communities, as in the case of Zimbabwe, there are clear economic incentives for sustainable utilization by the local people. The same lessons obtain in Kenya; where communities have had proprietorship over wildlife reserves they have had strong incentives to protect wildlife from poaching.

This approach requires that the state, donors and other interested parties devolve a substantial portion of authority and responsibility. It is also critical that the requisite institutional capacity is built at the community level. The evolution of this capacity is a protracted and dynamic process which reflects the peculiar characteristics of time and place. There are few shortcuts in building a sound institutional foundation for such schemes of governance, despite the urgency of the problems which they seek to solve.

The ecological imperative

The preceding sections have shown that natural resources have been codified in the instruments of governance as the property of individuals and the government with a primarily economic value. This property regime was based on the colonial and post-colonial views of development driven by economic rationale and stoked by the fuel of unlimited natural resources. The question at hand was limited to who would have access, essentially a political matter. Today we know that the world in which we live not only has finite resources, but these resources are connected in a web where disruption of one strand can destabilize the whole system on which human livelihoods depend.

Science has also shown us that ecology is dynamic and is constantly changing, but that change need not lead to instability. The environment has a robustness derived from its diversity at all levels, from the genetic makeup of individual organisms to continent-wide ecosystems. Diversity also extends to social systems. The diversity of governance systems present over time allows us to reach back to traditional common property management systems and across from pastoral to agricultural systems to devise what we need today and for the future.

This chapter has provided a rough sketch of the evolution of governance systems relating to natural resources in the eastern and southern Africa region. Environmental management can be improved by redefining the inherited roles of some of the key players, namely the citizens, their government and their institutions. This section examines areas in this regard: intergenerational public trust; generation and utilization of knowledge; and local institutional development.

Intergenerational public trust

The approach to governance taken in this chapter seeks to close the gap between the demands of the recognized ecological interdependence among people and nations and the specific needs and path of each. This requires reciprocity between parties on the same level, and between those on different levels—as well as between generations. The material presented leads to an unavoidable conclusion. We can no longer rest assured that our development efforts today will necessarily provide for the health and livelihoods of future generations. This can only be done if the norms by which we live reflect ecological principles.

There is much evidence that these norms are starting to recognize environmental limitations, such as general acceptance of environmental policies and regulations by the public. However, there is as yet no overarching framework to guide the development and use of governance mechanisms—laws, policies and institutions—which reflects this ecological imperative. Piecemeal reform of laws and institutional capacity-building can only be frustrated by the provisions of most national constitutions in the region which are still based on the logic of consumption of natural resources for the economic gain of the present generation. What should be considered now is a system of governance which provides a robust—diverse, dynamic and interconnected—framework for intergenerational responsibility for natural resource management.

In many countries in the region large tracts of land and certain resources are held by the state "in trust" for the citizens. In the case of Kenya trust lands are not just referred to in the constitution; a large section of the document is devoted to defining the boundaries and provisions pertaining to the use and authority over such lands. The question then may be posed: is trusteeship a suitable means of governing natural resources for current and future generations? If so, are there some forms which may work better than others, under certain conditions. Trusteeship may be an appropriate legal mechanism for holding land outside of a private individual tenure scheme. If so, who should be the trustee, in trust for whom, and with what structure of decision-making, may be investigated as well as the appropriate level and type of codification of such provisions.

Knowledge-intensive resource management

Resource management based on an ecological imperative requires a sound knowledge-base which can be used at all levels of society. Traditional resource management systems drew from a broad base of knowledge. Some current resource use systems, such as agriculture, have well developed research infrastructure. However, the weakness lies in the links between the research institutions and the knowledge of the resource users (e.g., the farmers), and with those who could commercialize the technologies which are developed (e.g., the private sector). In other sectors, such as construction and mining, research has been limited and focused on extraction of materials rather than on the ecological consequences of such extraction, or on substitute processes or materials. There are many activities in our societies which have ecological consequences of which the vast majority of the population, including policy-makers, are unaware.

Hence a more knowledge-intensive society is required in order to make sound resource use decisions and plan for future needs. This requires strengthening both the institutions which generate knowledge and the links between them and the resource users and policy-makers. In this regard it is important that these activities happen at all levels of society with proprietorship over knowledge and resources devolved as appropriate, and respected. This requires a degree of reciprocity between, for example, the herbalist and the research institution, the informal sector artisan and the industrialist, where the rights of the weaker party are strengthened through legal and institutional mechanisms and access to knowledge.

In order to understand how the flow and utilization of information can be enhanced for these purposes it would be instructive to analyze a number of systems where relevant knowledge is generated or required. This would include traditional and indigenous governance mechanisms to provide alternative models and principles which complement or contrast with those from industrialized countries. The utilization and generation of knowledge by community-based organizations which mange their natural resources or have influenced the management, such as through participating in policy reform or enforcement of legal provisions, would be another such system.

A comparative analysis of the flow and utilization of information looking at centralized *versus* decentralized systems may also prove instructive. This is particularly important as governments consider decentralizing some quantum of authority to local-level institutions. Increasing the effectiveness of public or parastatal research institutions continues to be an important area for improving environmental management. It may be asked, to what degree they facilitate a two-way flow of information between themselves and resource users, entrepreneurs and policy-makers.

Institutional development

One of the most challenging areas with respect to sustainable natural resource utilization is how to balance the diverse interests of local communities with those of the state in the long-term common interest. Communities cannot act in isolation from each other or from other stakeholders. They are part of a larger ecological, economic and political system. Murphree notes that ". . . communities need allies, including the state, if they are to realize proprietary claims. They also need assistance with collective arrangements to overcome internal division and reach external actors. Communities themselves seek integration with and need the assistance of actors in the outside world."[57] This requires strengthened institutions of local governance which can mobilize knowledge, organize support, and communicate and negotiate with parties outside themselves. It also requires that those "actors" in the outside world, such as research institutions, NGOs and governments have the capacity and the institutional space to contribute to local, national and international-level problem solving in natural resource management.

How institutional capacity can best be developed and supported in the region is a hotly debated question. One may ask how much of the effort and finance invested in development projects, supports local institutional development, rather than undermining it. This is a key question if governance systems are to have the diversity, resilience and responsiveness which we argue they require.

Conclusions

This chapter has attempted to give operational meaning to the term environmental governance in the context of eastern and southern Africa. It has taken an evolutionary approach to understanding the current governance structures and mechanisms in the region. The emphasis on centralized authority and control over natural resources has undermined environmental management, due in part to the inhibition of the generation and flow of knowledge both laterally and vertically. This lack of information, combined with the lack of what Murphree calls "proprietorship" of natural resources at the local level, result in a system which is unable to respond to the complex and constantly changing social demands and environmental conditions present in the region. It is now generally recognized that governance systems in the region need to be revised if they are to be responsive to local needs and conditions, as well as be able to hold their own in the global political and economic fray.

This requires a fundamental reorientation away from the blinders of economic rationale and towards the logic of the ecological systems upon which human economic life is based. This logic is based upon a highly interconnected flow of information, a diversity of approaches, dynamic processes and complexity. Governance systems which recognize this—in their constitutions, laws, policies and institutions—are more likely to exhibit higher levels of reciprocity, citizen participation in the public realm and responsive and responsible leadership. This will in turn reinforce suitable governance mechanisms and structures.

Such governance systems allow for a stable yet dynamic society which has the resources to solve problems at whichever level they may emerge before they undermine the society itself. The evolution of governance systems, both traditional or indigenous and contemporary, needs to be better understood in order to identify where reform may be effective. There are ample examples of experimentation over the past century to assist in this task, and to indicate options which may be used in the current reform process.

Notes

1. Georgescu-Roegen, 1971, p. 2.
2. Hodgson, 1993, p. 22.
3. UNDP, 1994, p. 25.
4. Hunter, 1988.
5. World Bank, 1989.
6. World Bank, 1994.
7. Boeninger, 1992.
8. Hyden, 1992, p. 7.
9. Hyden, 1992, p. 12
10. This section draws from the author's contribution to Field-Juma, *et al.*, 1995.
11. For example, the development of the landmark US National Environmental Policy Act of 1970 was the result of years of consensus building about trade-offs between different public, government and private sector interests (Yost, 1982).
12. Dorm-Adzobu *et al.*, 1991.
13. Sigot, *et al.*, 1995; Cleaver and Elson, 1995; Rocheleau and Edmunds, 1995.
14. Science for Action Coalition, quoted in Hunter, 1988.
15. In many cases the ownership of these areas has a statutory definition, such as "trust land", putting them under state control. However, traditional resource management systems often remain active in decision-making over resource use and access. See Berkes (1989) and Ostrom (1990) for discussions of common property resource management.
16. Barrow, 1992. See Chapter 10 in this book for a discussion of tree tenure.
17. Migot-Adholla and Bruce, "Introduction", in Bruce and Migot-Adholla, 1994, p. 4.
18. Okoth-Ogendo, 1991.
19. Okoth-Ogendo, 1991.
20. Okoth-Ogendo, 1991, p. 170.

21. Oba, 1994, p. 7.
22. Okoth-Ogendo, 1991, p. 164.
23. Copestake, 1993b, p. 15.
24. Roth *et al.*, 1994, p. 201.
25. Bruce and Migot-Adholla, 1994.
26. Barrows and Roth, 1989.
27. Bruce, Hoben and Rahmato, 1994.
28. Campbell, 1993, p. 265.
29. Bruce, Migot-Adholla and Atherton, 1994, p. 260.
30. The mandate of the commission includes, *inter alia*, making the necessary consultations to advise on which areas should be declared protected catchments, and continually evaluate the performance of the various government agencies with the responsibility of implementation in respect to soil conservation, afforestation and flood control.
31. Shivji, 1994.
32. Kenyatta, 1938, p. 27, quoted in Kiriro and Juma, 1991, p. 21.
33. Quoted in Hunter, 1988.
34. As Chapter 28 of Agenda 21 says: "Because so many of the problems and solutions being addressed by Agenda 21 have their roots in local activities, the participation and cooperation of local authorities will be a determining factor in fulfilling its objectives. As the level of governance closest to the people, they play a vital role in educating, mobilizing and responding to the public to promote sustainable development."
35. UNDP, 1994, p. 65.
36. UNDP, 1994, p. 65.
37. Hansen and Twaddle, 1991; Tideman, 1994.
38. Bruce, Hoben and Rahmato, 1994, p. 74.
39. Bruce, Hoben and Rahmato, 1994, p. 74.
40. UNDP, 1994, p. 66.
41. Homer-Dixon *et al.*, 1993, pp. 38–45.
42. Homer-Dixon *et al.*, 1993, pp. 38–45.
43. See: Ostrom, 1990; Verhelst, 1990.
44. Ostrom, 1990, p. 1.
45. The atmosphere, radio wavelengths, the deep seabed and Antarctica are examples of global common property resources.
46. Berkes and Farvar, 1989, pp. 13–14.
47. World Neighbors, Kenya, 1994, pers. comm.
48. J. Farrington, "Preface", in Wellard and Copestake, 1993.
49. Murphree, 1994, p. 416.
50. Kiondo, "The New Politics of Local Development in Tanzania", in Kanyinga, Kiondo and Tidemand, 1994.
51. Kiondo, 1994, p. 76.
52. Copestake, 1993b.
53. Copestake, 1993a.
54. Western and Wright, 1994, p. 7.
55. Murphree, 1994, p. 405.
56. Murphree, 1994, p. 405.
57. Murphree, 1994, p. 418.

The constitutional basis for environmental management

2

J.B. OJWANG

Introduction

The ultimate concerns of environmental law are two-fold: to provide a regulatory framework for those human activities which may undermine the vital natural assets that support normal economic and social life; and, to provide appropriate legal theory to explain and guide the path of the law in environmental management.

Human beings today live with major economic and social crises which, in summary, originate from atmospheric pollution, depletion or destruction of biological resources, contamination of water and soil and noise pollution. As a result of these crises, current generations are damaging the natural basis that supports their own welfare and begrudging future generations the benefit of the natural capital from which to make a good life for themselves. This warning is poignantly expressed in Queen Beatrix's Christmas message to the Dutch people: "The earth is slowly dying, and the inconceivable—the end of life itself—is actually becoming conceivable. We human beings have become a threat to our own planet."[1]

The gravity of the environmental crisis at once brings the question into the domain of political arrangements, and of the constitutional order which exists to validate and regulate those arrangements. Conventional wisdom in the interplay between politics and the constitution easily leads to contradictions with the essential concerns and principles of the environment. This relationship is well stated by Goodland et al.:

Two realisms conflict. On the one hand, political realism rules out income redistribution and population stability as politically difficult, if not impossible . . . . On the other hand, ecological realism accepts that the world economy has already exceeded the sustainable limits of the global ecosystem and that a five-to-tenfold expansion of anything remotely resembling the present economy would simply speed us from today's long-run unsustainability to imminent collapse.[2]

The authors propose that "in conflicts between biophysical realities and political realities, the latter must eventually give ground."[3] Such a case is emphatically made in the *Global Biodiversity Strategy* which ascribes the inability to provide an effective framework for the conservation of biodiversity to legal and institutional constraints. In other words:

Largely because of . . . legal and institutional constraints, biodiversity conservation has typically been piecemeal and concentrated on traditional wildlife protection techniques—a protected area here, a regime for managing an endangered or threatened species there. Even multiplied many times, such efforts seldom fulfil species' habitat requirements, particularly those of migratory animals, since land-use practices outside protected areas can alter water supplies, introduce pollutants, and change micro-climates. And such efforts do nothing to ensure *that policies for sustainable resource use are integrated* . . .[4]

The strategy calls for an integrated legal arrangement and policy framework, as the best approach to the sustainable use of resources. It is obvious that the environmental crisis has to be accorded priority in the political and legal arrangements of any well-managed state. This chapter is thus logically concerned with the primary legal arrangements—the constitutional order.

A constitution has two main aspects—substantive and formal. The first consists of the norms which establish the state entity and its various components—norms which determine the mode of exercise of the sovereignty of the state, and norms which relate to rights and duties, as between the state and the individual.[5] Within a constitution, as Hauriou and Gicquel observe, such fundamental norms are generally found in the preamble, or in a section devoted to major state commitments (i.e., directive principles). The second aspect rests on the fact that the constitution generally falls in that portion of the state's laws which, on account of its pre-eminence, is made following special legislative procedures, and can only be amended in the same manner.[6] The constitution thus represents the primary obligations of the state and the public institutions, and constitutes the basic organizational norm of the public domain. Other legal norms are of a secondary nature, and their burden on the state's organs of decision-making and policy implementation is therefore subsidiary. This further accounts for the concern with the constitution.

These other norms remain highly important, and material to the full discharge of the original constitutional mandate.

Outside the framework of constitutional initiatives, the norms affecting the environment would largely fall to international conventions—whose enforceability entails special limitations associated with international law in general.[7] Insofar as such international norms may be seen as the external facet of the domestic constitutional undertaking, and in the measure in which they have a bearing on environmental issues, they may be a significant device of environmental protection.[8] Indeed, the territorially unlimited character of environmental degradation, as well as the distinctly common interest of humankind in a healthy planet, points to the international legal framework as the model of environmental protection. But currently the reality of national sovereignty, and the international power structure, place the most crucial environmental functions in the hands of the individual states. The constitutional arrangements of these states, accordingly, play a decisive role in the reality of environmental protection. The domestic constitutional framework, where it lends itself to the tasks of environmental management, may also be an important basis for statutory, policy and administrative functions designed to achieve a well-ordered state of environmental protection.[9]

The environment and the public interest

The environmental concern with nature's role in human economic and social development, readily makes an agenda for political business. But more specifically, problems related to the environment have turned out to be inextricably linked to immediate concerns of government, such as: types, varieties and levels of national resources; operative modes of resource use and development; and productive capacity that determines the level of national development (e.g., irrigated agriculture, soil fertility, forest and genetic resources, wildlife resources, fisheries, water resources, hydro-electric power capacity).

In the early 1970s, especially in the run-up to the 1972 United Nations Conference on the Human Environment, it was acknowledged that, whereas the outstanding environmental issues in the developed countries were mainly pollution and deterioration of settlements, the developing countries were primarily concerned with the environment as a medium for, and a factor in, sustainable development. Their main concern was *poverty*—how to lift themselves from this scourge through more intensive use of resources which did not destroy nature's support systems for such undertakings.[10] This broader notion of the environment is reflected by Okidi, who defines it to "include land/soil, water, forests and vegetation cover, livestock, fish and other wildlife; the minerals under the land and the air which envelops the earth's surface; and human beings. Then the artificial infrastructures include the intrusion [into] that natural setting in the form of human constructions for human settlement."[11]

Development, which is at the very core of the environmental concern in the new nations, has been thus defined:

Firstly, development is the process by which a country provides for its entire population all the basic needs of life, such as good health and nutrition, education, and shelter, and provides every one of its population with opportunities to contribute to that very process, through employment as well as scientific and technological construction. Secondly, it is the process by which the national government authorities construct and maintain productive mechanisms and infrastructure which diversify and perpetuate the productive base of the country, such as agriculture and industries, so as to ensure that the society can overcome the pressures and necessities of the national and related economic system for the present and for all future times.[12]

The attributes of "development", as thus defined, clearly form the most basic issues for policy choice, legislation, adjudication or mediation, *within the constitutional framework*. The development agenda, which is a political and ultimately a constitutional and juridical question, is intimately intertwined with the environment.

There is little doubt that the broad government mandate, which is first and foremost a "development mandate", should anticipate environmental protection as a central element in public policy-making, and as an aspect of appropriate law-making—and of good administration under the law. It is an open-ended mandate, at the level of basic choices of approach, which falls to the constitutional machinery of the political set-up. Its due discharge is destined to inure *to the public*—as a matter of vital interest, and in certain cases, as a matter of constitutional and legal rights. The mode of exercizing such policy, law-making and administrative options must become the basis upon which the rights of the constitution may be exercised. Questions of human rights, as understood in international law, are intimately related to this scenario.

There is thus a dynamic relationship between environmental goals and the operations of governmental machinery (which constitutes the main public interest apparatus). The public interest in the environment arises, too, by dint of the natural interplay of the environment, and the conditions of human survival. Such conditions require constant adaptation and transformation to the economy, so as to provide for changing levels of human needs. The effectiveness of such adaptation will depend on the predictability of the ecosystem, and will necessarily dictate initiatives for the maintenance of ecological integrity. Dangers to the environment which must be of great concern to the governmental set-up, have been thus summarized by Ogolla:

> First, irrational land use practices may result in soil erosion with adverse impact on soil fertility and water quality; secondly, the use of fertilizers and pesticides for improved agricultural production pose the danger of water pollution through chemical residue with possible debilitating impact on human health and plant and animal life; thirdly, the process of industrialization leads to the generation of deleterious byproducts whose capacity for environmental media degradation is immense—the production of effluents without proper treatment and disposal mechanisms and the uncontrolled emission of fumes and particulates by factories undermine human, plant and animal life and upset delicate ecosystems.[13]

The primary duty of regulation and policing, in respect of such activities, must lie with the state's authorities as defined in the public law, and must be conducted on the basis of detailed laws and regulations founded on a constitutional mandate.

Law and environmental management

The complexity of environmental problems dictates, for any given country, that a well-designed scheme of environmental management, with clear policy, law, implementation and policing machinery, should be in place. Environmental management, as understood here, has been thus defined:

> [The] control or management of the environment essentially means measures taken to balance the natural resources. The measures may be of two kinds: one aspect may be to ensure . . . balanced utilization so as to prevent over-exploitation, or to restore those that have been utilized to strenuous levels. The other aspect may be measures taken to prevent [the] introduction . . . of any substances or energy which might immediately or in the long run, cause deleterious consequences to the natural resources. This second aspect is known as pollution control.[14]

In the above definition, the second facet of environmental management may be broadened to include more than just pollution, and encompass all the deleterious by-products of human intervention in the ecosystem—such as soil leaching owing to imperfect agricultural practices; plant and animal poisoning through toxic substances, etc.[15]

At any rate, the central referent in environmental management is *natural resources*, in both quantitative and qualitative strength, and the dependability of the medium in which they are used. Natural resources constitute the most basic raw material for the fabrication of commodities essential to human beings. But these resources are no less essential to other members of the biotic community—either as habitat, nourishment, or both. Irrational appro-

43

priation of these resources, moreover, may not only lead to permanent wasting and damage to the biotic co-users, but their exploitation and processing will generate excess energies into the biosphere which will undermine the ecological integrity, causing injury to the ecosystem.[16]

The removal of plant and animal habitats, for instance, through the destruction of forests, also destroys the natural carbon reservoirs and sinks, with the effect that deleterious gases are discharged into the biosphere. These are likely to lead to climate change and other grave consequences for human economic and social activities.[17] Such factors affect the symbiotic relationship between the natural resources and the biotic entities—a relationship which lies at the core of the concern for environmental protection.

The delicate interests built around the advantages of the environment, have for a long time been protected, in some form or other, under state law.[18] But the comprehensiveness of such protection has not been the same throughout modern history. Indeed, the quest for a detailed scheme of protection, even today, remains largely unfulfilled, with significant differences in the accomplishments made in different countries. It is becoming clear that even the national achievements so far made bear little relation to the growing burden of scientific evidence which underlines the planetary and common character of the main problems of environmental protection.

In the case of Kenya, hardly any policy or law designed for environmental management in broad terms, existed in the early colonial period.[19] In that period one would have had to resort to contracts and torts as the main branches of law which involved some measure of environmental concern. At that time, and to the limited scope of its efficacy, environmental law was essentially a *private law* concern—as it was not known to the main branches of public law, namely constitutional law, administrative law and criminal law.

Contracts, at English common law (which forms part of the law of Kenya),[20] operate on the principle of *pacta sunt servanda* (agreements must be honoured),[21] and so they could only provide for environmental considerations in those situations in which an occupant of property was placed under contractual duty, or covenant, with regard to the environmental impact of use-options. The obligations created were, moreover, confined to the parties to the contract. Members of the public who were not party to the contract, would have no legal interest in the environmental rights or duties that might be provided for; and the courts could not give redress for any environmental injury they suffered as a consequence of breaches of contractual obligations.

The law of tort (also part of the received common law) offered a slightly wider scope for environmental claims. Tort law generally steers clear of conflict with the long-established rights of property law,[22] and in particular, the principle that the owners of landed property have unrestricted rights of use and abuse over their land.[23] However, the common law rights of property are qualified by the maxim *sic utere tuo ut alienum non laedas* (so use your property in a manner that does not interfere with your neighbour).[24] The owners or occupiers of land may not emit from their land noises, vibrations, smoke or dirt which may cause injury to their neighbours. The injured party may seek redress in the form of damages and injunctions.[25] Tort law's protection takes the form of the law of nuisance and of "strict liability" (as in *Rylands* v. *Fletcher*). In the latter case, the law provides that the occupiers who bring any potentially dangerous thing upon their land, must ensure it does not escape and cause injury to their neighbour.[26] The law of nuisance, in addition, has a broader aspect, which links up with the machinery and principles of public law, and on this account gives slightly more scope for environmental protection. The public law aspect, unlike in private nuisance which depends on the fortuitous factor of litigation, allows the state to prosecute persons who create a nuisance on such a great scale that a large number of persons are inconvenienced.[27] Whereas such prosecution takes care of the general public interest in a safe environment, any particular person or persons who, on account of the nuisance, suffers special injury, may file a suit for damages.[28]

In Kenya, the concept of public nuisance has been incorporated into the Penal Code, and the relevant provision states: "Any person who does an act not authorized by law or omits to discharge a legal duty and thereby causes any common injury, or danger or annoyance, or obstructs or causes inconvenience to the public in the exercise of common rights, the misdemeanour is termed a common nuisance, and is liable to imprisonment for one year."[29] This provision is broad enough to apply to incidents of plain environmental damage, with direct injury to the public. It cannot however, cover large-scale degradation resulting from ecological changes caused by economic activities.

Perhaps not much more environmental protection could have been expected from the common law, since this tradition of law evolved on the foundation of property rights, which gave it its standards of measurement, and compromised it to the restitutive goals of ownership of property.[30] Ownership, rather than rational use of natural resources, was the first consideration. The position is clear from colonial and post-colonial Kenya, when it was found necessary to enact a plurality of sectoral laws, dealing with, *inter alia*, specific conservation issues. Notable in this respect are: the Agriculture Act; the Food, Drugs and Chemical Substances Act; the Cattle Cleansing Act; the Fertilizers and Animal Foodstuffs Act; the Forests Act; the Plant Protection Act; the Grass Fires Act; the Public Health Act; the Water Act; the Merchant Shipping Act and the Factories Act.

While such laws have diverse objectives,[31] their concern (to varying degrees) with the environment cannot be doubted. The Forests Act, for instance, which was originally passed in the mid-colonial period (1942), is "[a]n Act of Parliament to provide for the establishment, control and regulation of Central Forests, forests and forest areas in the Nairobi area and on unalienated Government land." Its environmental purpose is plain from a number of the provisions. Section 6(2) is illustrative: "[i]n a nature reserve, no cutting, grazing, removal of forest produce or disturbance of the flora shall be allowed except with the permission of the chief conservator, and permission shall only be given with the object of conserving the natural flora and amenities of the reserve." Section 8 prohibits certain activities in forest areas, without the authority of the chief conservator. Such activities include: felling or burning of trees, erecting buildings or cattle enclosures, setting fire to grass or undergrowth, introducing smoke or fire, allowing cattle to gain access, cultivation, capturing or killing animals, making roads or paths. Breaches of these prohibitions are punishable by fine, imprisonment, or both.

The Plant Protection Act gives a similar example. Originally passed in 1957, this is "[a]n Act of Parliament to make better provision for the prevention of the introduction and spread of disease destructive to plants." It empowers the minister to, *inter alia*, make rules in respect of "the methods of planting, cleaning, cultivating and harvesting to be adopted, and the precautions and measures to be taken by any person for the purpose of preventing or controlling attacks by, or the spread of, any pest disease."[32] This legislation gives effect to the spirit of the International Plant Protection Convention of 1951, to which independent Kenya became a party in 1974. The broad concern of the Convention is the conservation of biological diversity in the case of plants. Such laws impart the state's direct sanction, within the framework of public law, and their effect is to bring the relevant environmental issues within the public domain—no longer just a restitutive claim confined to the litigants. The outlook becomes broader, the basis of implementation ceases to be private *locus standi*, and the whole question no longer rests on the random occurrence of litigation.

Apart from private law and public law at the domestic level, international law, too, contains important norms that create environmental obligations. Currently there are over 200 multilateral treaties and agreements which have been adopted on environmental issues.[33] Kenya is a party to some 10 per cent of these. The obligations created commit Kenya, through the legal instruments as well as the policies and administrative procedures that manifest her sovereignty, to provide for and perform the relevant environmental undertakings. Insofar as such international agreements have a bearing on the provisions of the municipal law, and on important aspects of domestic administration, they form part of the framework of environmental law in place. One sees that law, firstly private law, secondly public law, and thirdly international law, comes to play an important role in efforts to protect the environment. While at the present level, in private and public law, no systematic notion of environmental management exists, the sectoral concern with environmental issues is evident; and it seems to be accepted that the state's most effective device of control is the law. The central position of the law in environmental protection, is thus acknowledged.

Law, in general, must be seen in that light, for the plain reason that it gives the most solemn expression of the state's commitment; it is the state's normative launching pad for imperative courses of public action. Law is the culmination of the state's integrity, and of international recognition of its sovereign character.[34] The quest for legitimacy is still more important in the sphere of environmental protection, where common sensations of human comfort would readily sacrifice sustainable projects, for the sake of present material advantages.

The nature of environmental law

The ascendancy of environmental issues virtually everywhere, to a position of priority in the public policy agenda, has led to a recognition among scholars, of the discipline of environmental law. Okidi has defined the concern of this area of law as follows: "Environmental law is the ensemble of norms . . . statutes, treaties and administrative regulations to ensure or to facilitate the rational management of natural resources and human intervention in the management of such resources for sustainable development."[35] He underlines the two basic elements in that definition—the capacity to "ensure", and to "facilitate": Laws which "ensure" are those that are rule-oriented, requiring the role occupants or citizens to perform certain actions failing which they face penalties. On the other hand, law may be management-oriented, requiring measures that facilitate the prevention of the deleterious effect on the environment.

While the concept of "laws that ensure" would appear to be plain in meaning, that of "laws that facilitate" lends itself to at least two meanings. A "law that facilitates" could in the first place be law that establishes certain patterns of legality, such as might be done by tax relief laws, or monetary benefits made payable under some law, provided as a device for encouraging private initiatives in environmental protection. Such laws are not imperative in the normal sense; but they give rights only to those who come to satisfy the basic conditions prescribed. In this manner, they facilitate the goals sought. But laws that establish agencies to perform management and discretion-oriented duties, for instance, in the cause of environmental protection, may also be said to be facilitative, albeit in a different sense. By establishing management machinery, such laws will facilitate the task of environmental protection. It is, of course, to be expected that such machinery would derive part of its authority from legal sanctions. Hence there is an important overlap between this kind of "facilitative law" and the "ensuring law".

Although it is not clear if Okidi intended both aspects of "facilitative law", it is nonetheless apparent from his discussion that environmental law will remain a mixed bag for some time, without the relatively sharp boundaries such as those associated with property law, contract or tort. For environmental law has both the sanction-based element, and the "positive", facilitative angle which will not, in all cases, have yet crystallized into any enforceable rights or duties. This latter aspect becomes wider still when it incorporates "management support" functions, or when it provides for incentives of varying categories, for a rational management of the environment. This somewhat amorphous character is further enhanced by the essential characteristics of international legal obligations, which, where they relate to the environment, are not as readily enforceable as would be the case with ordinary municipal legal obligations.[36]

Environment and public law

Public law has been defined as: "[t]he totality of rules that set up the state and its component parts, and which regulates the interplay between the public authorities and the individual units."[37] Now, to what extent can environmental law be regarded as an aspect of public law? In the earlier part of its development, environmental law, as already noted, was an uneven amalgam of public law and private law principles and rules. It no doubt lacked the character of a uniform juristic discipline and was largely a pragmatic category for the lawyer's paraphernalia.

However, the increased use, especially from the middle decades of this century, of sectoral legislation to serve (if mainly incidentally) environmental ends had the effect of linking environmental issues to recognized public law concepts. An example is the concept of "police power", which originates from American constitutional law and means "the governmental power to regulate matters of safety, health, welfare, and morals for the general public good.'[38] In recent practice this power "has been extended beyond safety, health and morals to the conservation of natural resources . . ."[39] The concept, thus applied, provides a logical explanation for the sectoral environmental legislation already referred to. Insofar as the police power enhances the standing of public authorities, and has certain implications for the rights and duties of the governed, it clearly falls in the domain of public law. Hence, those environmental issues that depend on this power for their implementation become public law issues.

Even as the sectorial, natural resource-based "environmental" laws remain in force, new management strategies are being adopted which must enhance the standing of environmental law in the public law domain. The most striking development in this respect is the gradual acceptance of environmental impact assessment as a device of environmental conservation. The persistent concern with obvious indices of economic development, that has attended the preoccupation with natural resource exploitation, tended to obscure to many African countries the broader picture of environmental degradation. This condition was exacerbated by the lack of effective methods for assessing environmental impact. Environmental impact assessment, which is a relatively new device holding promise as a tool of sustainable development, has been defined as "an activity designed to identify and predict the impact on the biogeophysical environment and on man's health and well-being, of legislative proposals, policies, programmes, projects and operational procedures, and to interpret and communicate information about impacts."[40]

Environmental impact assessment requires certain steps to be taken, in the course of preparation for a development project. These include: a full description and analysis of the project proposal; a complete inventory of the environment affected; an identification of the expected consequences of the proposed actions; a description of the environmental risks involved in the proposed action; and an assessment of alternatives to the proposed action.[41]

But it is hardly possible to secure compliance with such steps unless a legal framework, which creates appropriate executing and monitoring institutions, is provided. These would be institutions of public law, by their mode of operations, their scheme of accountability, and by virtue of the fact that their authority would have to be secured by legislation which imposes sanctions. While, in the case of Kenya, environmental impact assessment is recognized as a practical approach to the prevention of environmental degradation, and while a capacity exists in a number of institutions for conducting environmental impact studies, no binding legislative commitment has yet been made. The state's undertaking remains only at the level of policy and administration.

Legislation of this kind, with a back-up of sanctions and which not only deals with a major public policy issue but vests in government special powers to superintend the course of economic activities squarely belongs to the sphere of public law. Such legislation at the same time establishes and describes new public bodies, reposing in them a competence to affect the domain of private rights and interests. Insofar as the scheme of environmental protection dictates the creation of new policy-making institutions, and the promulgation of new laws of sanction, the whole question must come under public law. To this extent, environmental law for all practical purposes must be regarded as a public law subject. The various manifestations of police power, as conferred by environmental law, have a central place in both constitutional and administrative law, and a partial role in criminal law. The main issues of rights and duties, which flow from the interaction between the state and the subject, are matters of constitutional law; while the technical questions of the application of statutory procedures in the implementation of environmental law, belong to the discipline of administrative law. The application of any penal sanctions stipulated in legislation, is by-and-large the subject of criminal law. Such bodies of domestic law, of course, have no monopoly over the disciplinary pedigree of environmental law. For an important part of this body of law could well be treated squarely under the discipline of international law.

The specific ingredients of environmental law will inevitably vary from one economic region to another, and even from one country to another. The more economically advanced countries, as they have a more sophisticated framework for environmental protection, would be expected to have a more coherent body of environmental law than the developing countries.[42] Besides, whereas common natural resource-subjects, such as soil, water, forests and the atmosphere will attract similar regimes of conservation, the more complex resources such as nuclear energy are likely to be the basis of developments in environmental law that are unique to the wealthier countries.[43] Indeed, the pattern of adherence to international agreements already shows clearly that many developing countries have little in common with the industrialized countries, in respect of the more technologically complex energy sources. It may thus be affirmed that the exact state of environmental law at any given time must vary from one region to another—given the current distribution of developmental advantages. Such variations should ultimately diminish, given the rising level of international concern with "the global commons" such as the ozone layer, the high seas, the atmosphere.[44]

From the foregoing discussion, it emerges that environmental law is a discipline-in-formation. On the whole it still lacks independent characteristics, as it is largely derived from bodies of law the disciplinary boundaries of which are well settled. It may be expected that in the longer term, and with greater environmental awareness and international co-operation in the protection of the environment, a gradual fusion of the relevant disciplinary spheres should lead to a more coherent and a conceptually neater discipline of environmental law. In any event, this body of law will have to rely significantly on techniques of public law, even as it incorporates a substantial set of facilitative and management-oriented procedures which must lie at the core of any viable scheme of environmental protection.

The constitutional basis for conservation

That developing countries must act to contain the current run-away levels of environmental degradation, is an imperative public duty. But, in the very nature of environmental conservation initiatives, policies, laws and public institutions must be brought into effect and put in place which have a significant impact on, and cut across, the recognized rights, interests and claims of ordinary people. That is to say, the operation of such environmental initiatives is bound to have *constitutional implications*. What then, is the constitutional basis of such initiatives?

The constitutional basis for environmental conservation, in the Kenyan experience, comprises several factors: the state's mandate to provide for the people's welfare; the crystallization of specific rights, out of the state's public-welfare initiatives; individual rights-claims *vis-a-vis* public development programmes; and the emergence of new public institutions, and their constitutional characteristics.

The state's mandate in public welfare

The very legitimacy of government rests on its capacity to provide for the people's welfare in economic, social and political terms. This is a basic mandate which lies at the root of the political system. The first task of the constitutional order is to avail machinery for the discharge of this mandate. Thus the constitution vests in the executive the responsibility for policy-making and public administration. This facilitates the making of public-welfare policies, their conversion through the legislature into binding laws, and their efficient administration.

The constitution views the environment, a basic capital input for economic and social development, as a prime sphere of executive policy-making. Insofar as conservation of the environment supports good health, and ensures the sustained production of products and resources essential to life, it is a matter of constant concern to the governmental process. In this sense, environmental protection has a pre-eminent place in the due execution of the main constitutional tasks.

Rights-creation and the environment

The state's role in rights-creation is an incident of its mandate to provide for the people's welfare. The precise nature of this mandate emerges from several international legal documents which relate to recognized roles of state

51

authorities. The Universal Declaration of Human rights (1948) states that "[e]veryone, as a member of society, has the right to social security, and is entitled to realization, through national effort . . . and in accordance with the organization and resources of each state, of the economic, social and cultural rights indispensable for his dignity . . ."[45] Such rights include the rights of women, who are central to the process of natural resource management. A positive public duty is here being placed on the state, to manage policy and programmes in economic, social and cultural matters, in such a way as to confer upon the individual certain interests and entitlements. It is acknowledged that the organization and management of such programmes will rest upon the country's resources.

This brings us back to the question of "sustainable development" which relates to the management of natural resource management in order to maintain the integrity of ecosystems. The state will not be able to discharge the obligation in question—which has a basis both in international and constitutional law—in the absence of proper environmental management. Thus, failing an effective approach to environmental protection, the state is in danger of breaching important obligations.

Article 23(1) of the Universal Declaration of Human Rights states that: "[e]veryone has a right to work, to free choice of employment, to just and favourable conditions of work and to protection against unemployment." The availability of work, in sufficient variety, depends on the strength of the economy, whose sustainability in turn depends on effective environmental management. The state's policy, in quest of this requirement, is therefore limited by the extent to which it ensures environmental protection. Article 25 of the Declaration stipulates: "Everyone has the right to a standard of living adequate for the health and well-being of himself and his family, including food, clothing, housing and medical care and necessary social services . . ." The standard of living contemplated must incorporate a healthful environment; and the clauses relating to food, clothing and housing must contemplate environmental conditions that will facilitate sustainable sources of supply.

Although the Universal Declaration of Human Rights is essentially a moral code for the conduct of states in their domestic affairs,[46] its terms are substantially reproduced in international instruments of a binding nature (for parties to the instruments). Examples include the International Covenant on Economic, Social and Cultural Rights (1966),[47] the International Covenant on Civil and Political Rights (1966), and the African Charter on Human and Peoples' Rights (1981).[48]

Such obligations of the state rest on both public international law, and domestic constitutional law. The international laws impose on states a duty to observe constitutionalism in domestic practices. Constitutionalism, in this sense, imposes upon the state both negative and positive duties. The negative duty is that of restraint in the exercise of public power. The positive duty is the creative one of facilitating national development by enhancing the economic and social spheres of life. This phenomenon has elsewhere been analyzed as follows:

> Constitutional practice indicates that any initiative to attain good government, as the notion of constitutionalism imports, must rest on . . . political arrangements that accord with the primary social, economic and cultural conditions holding sway . . . . Such conditions, as regards Africa, are still in the ferment of socio-economic dynamics which must be regulated and processed in development efforts. Such developments must be pursued, as they alone will enhance the material base for the enjoyment of social and personal liberties . . . . The African context is . . . a context of . . . construction, of larger rights and liberties, *through orderly and well-conceived management of national resources* . . . [49]

The emphasis in the above passage points directly to the environmental questions, and underlines the sustainability of development as the key to the discharge of the state's foremost constitutional duties, and to the enhancement of the civil liberties that are so highly cherished as the ideal condition in a well-managed society. This is clear evidence of the constitutional basis for environmental protection. Apart from the foregoing more general scheme of rights-creation, some countries have attempted to replace the top-down orientation in environmental protection, by a bottom-up approach, which specifically empowers private individuals and interest groups to employ the state's legal machinery in the control of actions that are likely to lead to environmental degradation. The National Environmental Policy Act (1970) of the United States, for instance, provides:

> [It] is the continuous policy of the Federal Government, in co-operation with . . . concerned public and private organizations, to use all practical means or measures . . . to create and maintain conditions under which man and nature can exist in productive harmony, and fulfil the social, economic and other requirements of present and future generations of Americans.[50]

A constitutional right is thus created for the ordinary citizen to act in pursuit of a healthful environment which is conducive to sustainable development, alongside the various public initiatives in place. Such a commendable approach to legislation ought to be adopted in other countries as well, even though its effectiveness is unlikely to be as great in the developing countries as it would be in the developed countries, since litigation is an expensive means of redress which is only available to a limited degree in the poorer countries.

The individual and development activities

The rights of the *self* are an abstraction from a secure social condition which, in its turn, rests upon a fully productive economy. The relationship between economic stability and the environment, makes the latter a vital factor in the ideal social condition that would facilitate the full enjoyment of the rights of the *self*. Moreover, maintaining ecological integrity remains vital to the rights of the individual, even when the economic objective has already been satisfied. A clean and healthy environment is an essential component in the totality of social welfare. So important is it to personal well-being, that it may be equated to the various civil rights that often make headlines. Addressing himself to this issue, MacCormick says: "This requires an admission that environmental goods may be brought into the balance against the good of freedom of action . . ."[51] He, however, cautions that such an admission entails certain dangers for constitutional rights, as the position easily lends itself to abuse. This caveat further underlines the clear constitutional complexion of environmental issues.

It follows that many rights-claims that come up for redress within the constitutional machinery, whether through courts, administrative tribunals, or ombudsmen,[52] ultimately rest upon constitutional actions that have a clear bearing on the environment and its protection.

Constitutional bodies and environmental issues

As already noted, established constitutional organs such as the executive and the legislature are intimately involved with environmental issues. So far, the African public—and this is true of Kenya—have barely been litigious in environmental matters. The courts therefore have not been much involved in environmental rights-claims. But examples from other countries depict this as a potential area of constitutional activity.[53] In India, where environmental litigation has been more common, public authorities have appeared as defendants in court for allowing pollution to take place in urban areas.[54] In one such case, the High Court stated the principle that the statutory duty imposed upon a public body (including environmental duties) was enforceable by a writ of the court.[55]

In Kenya, new institutions concerned with environmental issues have recently come into existence. Insofar as the issues are of constitutional character, they must be seen as a further basis for the practice of environmental conservation. With the growing awareness of the environmental factor in matters of national development, Kenya is, at the policy level, committing itself to a centralized approach to management in this sphere. This orientation which has appeared in policy declarations right from 1965,[56] and especially in the five-year development plans, took its most concrete form with the establishment of the National Environment Secretariat in 1974 under the Office of the President and subsequently under the Ministry of Environment and Natural Resources. More recently, it has seemed as if the government finds the existing bureaucratic framework of management too limiting. Thus a body with executive authority—the Permanent Presidential Commission on Soil Conservation and Afforestation—was set up in 1981 under the Office of the President. Its objectives are to effect co-ordination of environmental initiatives and take action to rectify present or impending injuries to the environment, when such is apparent.[57]

The establishment of such public agencies with a mandate which seeks to enhance the public welfare but the work procedures of which could also lead to conflicts with private claims, gives rise to a new forum of constitutional issues. The potential conflict is all the more real, as the private claims of aggrieved persons would be resting on settled law (common law or parliamentary enactment), whereas the new agencies, in spite of their public-welfare goals, would have no recognized body of law as the foundation of their activity.[58] This is an undesirable situation, and a clear scheme of coordinated environmental management, supported by appropriate legislation and institutional arrangements, would be preferable

Current constitutional developments

In the background of the traditional cornerstones of the constitutional order of many developing countries (the executive, the legislature and the judiciary) there has often been, in the post-independence period, a monopolist political party, the machinery and development programmes of which are coincidental with those of the state.[59] In those conditions, and with there being a clear commitment to environmental protection, there was little difficulty in managing programmes of environmental conservation, despite the lack of a supporting framework of legislation. In Kenya, the unity of politics and power machinery had the tendency to limit the scope for constitutional conflicts in the matter—even though the endeavour would then have been short on impelling pressure for uncompromised action in the protection of the environment. Since 1991, a multi-party system has come into being. With the resulting enlargement of constitutional space, it is only to be expected that conflicting rights and interest-claims over environmental issues will now come into the open. If such a development would work in favour of greater environmental consciousness and more determined environmental conservation, then it would also enhance the basis of economic and social welfare, and consequently, the scope of constitutional rights for individuals.

In any event, given the fundamental nature of environmental issues today in the context of public affairs, it is to be hoped that the current political developments will lead to a re-thinking of the place of the environment in the constitutional framework. For a more assured basis of commitment to environmental protection, it is desirable that future constitutional change should formally incorporate a declaration of this commitment in the constitution—either as the subject of a special section, or as part of a set of directive principles of state policy. If such a commitment should take the form of a detailed provision, then it will be important to formally recognize environmental impact assessment as the central tool of environmental management. It will be just as important to provide for a clear environmental monitoring procedure, involving a duly empowered constitutional agency.

One of the key features of future constitutional developments in Kenya will be the demand for popular and democratic participation in forging new schemes of governance as well as implementing sustainable development programmes. The effective implementation of environmental programmes, because of their very decentralized nature, will require the effective participation of people at different levels. Such involvement will not only draw on the constitutional provisions, but will also generate new ideas that will influence the constitution as well as specific laws.

The rise in the demand for democracy in Kenya is not necessarily associated with the rise in environmental awareness. Despite the major efforts made to promote sustainable development in general and environmental management in particular, political activists have not had a chance to link the growing environmental awareness to democratic reform. Environmental issues tend to be used in the early stages of advocating for political change but the issue is not taken seriously when formulating the agenda for political change. Unlike in eastern Europe, where rapid industrialization has left behind a sad heritage of ecological destruction, Kenya's major ecological problems cannot be directly linked to unsatisfactory economic management. Other factors such as drought tend to mask the impacts of environmental degradation on agricultural productivity.

There are opportunities to integrate environmental concerns into expected constitutional and legal reforms. However, there is a danger that this opportunity may be lost, partly because of the lack of awareness, and partly because political discourse is still to come to terms with the emerging global concerns. The discourse is largely governed by the basic demands for accountability, transparency and good governance. The details of such demands, for example the relationship between corruption and ineffective environmental performance in enterprises, have yet to be articulated in political terms. Furthermore, the vital alliances between researchers, the media and political activists necessary to effect public accountability in environmental matters, have yet to take shape. In Kenya, for example, political reforms are taking place at a rapid pace, leaving hardly any time to take stock of global changes and to reflect on the future.

The first major step in this direction is to improve the rights of the public to have access to information. Most of the "right-to-know" provisions are still restrictive. This is compounded by the fact that the technical nature of environmental information concentrates authority in the hands of scientists and civil servants. The restricted nature of such information is often used to limit public access to information. The transition towards a more democratic system will require more open provisions that allow for the "right-to-know-more". Democracy can be significantly expanded through guarantees of public access to information. Environmental awareness and rights can be considerably enhanced through such guarantees. It is notable that the current demand for greater democracy in the developing countries is based more on the principles of accountability and transparency. The assumption here is that governments will necessarily make efforts to conduct their business in a manner that ensures that all the relevant information is in the public domain. This expectation, however, can only be realized if effective mechanisms are instituted that will guarantee the right of the public to know and know more.

Communities affected by development projects are often the last to know about planned activities. Legislation or administrative measures that guarantee the community the right-to-know would go a long way in enlarging the participation of the people in environmental management. But such legislation would need to be accompanied by measures that ensure that information on key environmental issues is regularly made available. It is only through such institutional measures which not only guarantee access to information, but also actively provide it, that the public can genuinely participate in activities designed to lead to sustainable development.

But the right to know, by itself, is not enough unless it is accompanied by reforms that allow for the right-to-participate in decision-making processes. Information is not an end in itself, but a means to enable the public to improve their capacity for participation in decision-making. The transition towards more open political systems enhances the scope for realizing the right to participate. On the whole, the road to sustainable development is indeed a political challenge that can only be resolved in an open and participatory system.

Conclusion

At what point in the conduct of public affairs does such a momentous reality as the environment become an element in the state's vital legal machinery? This is the essential question at the centre of this inquiry. It emerges that the

J.B. OJWANG

relationship between the environment and the productive processes—which lie at the root of the entire scheme of social welfare—constitutes a crucial issue of public policy. It is thus a major item on the constitutional agenda of the state. Beyond this threshold, the task of environmental protection leads to complex interactions with known areas of constitutional rights—further triggering questions of ideal constitutional balances and touching on the basic principle of constitutionalism.[60]

The complex relationship between economy and environment leads to a sensitive balancing act, to be performed by the state, as between the creative process which will crystallize new areas of rights, and rights-claims that are based on established principles of law. There is no perfect answer to the puzzles posed by the resulting organizational, moral and juristic dilemmas. And the constitutional lawyer's task, ordinarily, would be to merely illuminate the likely crisis areas—sounding cautions and suggesting approaches that would be likely to accommodate the ideal of constitutionalism.

However, bearing in mind the gravity of the present environmental crisis, and the fact that it is likely to seriously undermine the material supports to human survival and comfort, it may be suggested that the scales should be gradually tilted against those rights and interests that rest mainly on property values and in favour of more planned social life and use of natural resources. Specific constitutional amendments are therefore necessary to provide for natural resource management in line with the imperatives of sustainable development.

Notes

1. Ekins, 1991, p. 47.
2. Goodland *et al.*, 1991, pp. 10–11.
3. Goodland *et al.*, 1991, p. 11.
4. World Resources Institute *et al.*, 1992, p. 13 (emphasis added).
5. Hauriou and Gicquel, 1980, p. 324.
6. Hauriou and Gicquel, 1980, p. 324.
7. Waldock, 1980, pp. 1–2; Brownlie, 1973, pp. 179–189.
8. There are already numerous treaties on the environment, their main authority resting on their moral direction rather than on binding legal force. See Kiss, 1983.
9. Caldwell, 1984; Ojwang, 1992a.
10. Okidi, 1988, p. 28. Okoth-Obbo, 1985, notes that while the developed countries were plagued with problems which arose from a high and irrational level of development, the developing countries had problems arising from their status as developing countries. He relies on the pre-Stockholm, Founex Report (1972), which rightly remarked that the environmental problems of developing countries were "predominantly problems that reflect poverty and the very lack of development of their societies. . . Not merely the 'quality of life' but life itself was endangered by poor water, housing, sanitation and nutrition, by sickness and disease and by natural disasters."

11. Okidi, 1988;
12. Okidi, 1984, p. 93.
13. B.D. Ogolla, 1988, p. 118.
14. Okidi, 1984, p. 7.
15. Ogolla, 1988, pp. 118–119.
16. Caldwell, 1984, Goodland *et al.*, 1991, Kondratyev *et al.*, 1992.
17. Ominde and Juma, 1991; Ottichilo *et al.*, 1991; Baraclough and Ghimire, 1990.
18. See Brownlie, 1973.
19. It should be noted that a number of treaties were made in the colonial period, whereby colonial powers assumed environmental responsibilities affecting African countries. Examples include the London Convention Relative to the Preservation of Fauna and Flora in their Natural State (1933); the Paris Convention for the Protection of Birds (1950); and the Rome Plant Protection Convention (1951).
20. Judicature Act (Cap. 8), Section 3(1)c.
21. Treitel, 1970, pp. 1–8.
22. Wieacker, 1990, pp. 1–29; Neumann, 1953, pp. 901–935; Veblen, 1978, p. 121.
23. *Bradford Corporation* v. *Pickles* [1895] A.C. 587.
24. Brownlie, 1973.
25. Street, 1972, pp. 212–241.
26. *Rylands* v. *Fletcher* [1866], L.R. 1 Ex. 265; Street, 1972, pp. 242–257.
27. Street, 1972, pp. 238–241.
28. Street, 1972.
29. Penal Code (Cap. 63), s. 175(1).
30. Ackerman, 1977; Dietze, 1971.
31. The commercial aspect emerges clearly, for instance, from the Legislative Council debates of 1948 and 1949, on the Forest (Amendment) Bill. In those debates the general attitude prevailing among the ruling elite was thus expressed:"...I think it should be said that the timber industry of this Colony is in a very bad way at the present moment, due to the system of tenure given out by the Forest department. The tenure is given out at the maximum for ten years, with the right of cancellation annually. This means that no sawmilling company operating in the forests can raise any capital for machinery suitable for the milling of timber. ...[This] timber industry will eventually be by far the biggest asset in the whole colony. It will enable us to develop and improve the standard of living of all people and the general prosperity of this territory. ..." Legislative Council Debates, *Official Report*, vol. 30 (19 January, 1949), cols. 1093–1094 (Hon. L.R. Maconochie-Welwood).
    This attitude is also apparent from the 1945 debates on the National Parks Bill, a major concern in that case being for incomes to be derived from the tourist industry: Legislative Council Debates—Official Report, vol. 20(3 January 1945), cols. 437–445.
32. Cap. 514, s. 3(g).
33. Kiss, 1983; UNEP, 1991.
34. Lutz, 1976, pp. 506–520; Seidman, 1986, pp. 15–25; Ogolla, 1988, pp. 118–120.

35. Okidi, 1988, p. 130.
36. Waldock, 1980; Brownlie, 1973.
37. Guillien and Vincent, 1978, p. 151. To the same effect see Duverger, 1977, p. 6.
38. Walker, 1980, p. 965.
39. Walker, 1980, p. 965.
40. Munn, 1977, p. 1, quoted in Okoth-Obbo, 1985, p. 4.
41. Okoth-Obbo, 1985, pp. 5–6.
42. Schramm and Watford, 1989; Sarokin and Schulkin, 1991, pp. 175–189.
43. Evidence of this can be seen in the fact that many developing countries have not become parties to international conventions dealing with nuclear resources; for example, the Convention on Third Party Liability in the Field of Nuclear Energy (1960); the Vienna Convention on Civil Liability for Nuclear Damage (1963); the Treaty banning Nuclear Weapon Tests in the Atmosphere, in Outer Space and Under Water (1963); the Convention Relating to Civil Liability in the Field of Maritime Carriage of Nuclear Material (1971).
44. Goodland *et al*, 1991; Weiss, 1989; WCED, 1987.
45. Art. 22.
46. Starke, 1978, pp. 113–131.
47. Arts. 6, 7, 11, 12.
48. Arts. 15–17.
49. Ojwang, 1990b, pp. 219 (emphasis added).
50. Quoted in Lutz, 1976, p. 478.
51. MacCormick, 1982, p. 152.
52. See Ojwang, 1990b (pp. 187–194) for a discussion of the role of environmental ombudsmen.
53. Bakshi, 1987, pp. 260–261.
54. *Citizens Action Committee* v. *Civil Surgeon, Mayo (General) Hospital, Nagpur*, A.I.R. 1986, BOM. 136.
55. *Municipal Council Ratlam* v. *Uarthichand, A.I.R.* 1980 S.C. 1622.
56 Republic of Kenya, 1965.
57. See Ojwang, 1990b, pp. 180–184.
58. See Ojwang, 1992a, pp. 12–17.
59. J.B. Ojwang, 1992a. In the case of Kenya this has been the Kenya African National Union.
60. It has been argued elsewhere that an objective view of this principle ought to accommodate the fundamental economic and social reality obtaining in different parts of the world (Ojwang, 1990a, pp. 57–74).

Property rights, public interest and environment

3

R.S. BHALLA

Introduction

This chapter aims to show how Western constitutional theories regarding property affect environmental management in general and the management of natural resources in Kenya in particular. The chapter, more specifically, explores the various concepts of property and property relations, as they are modified and controlled under the Constitution of Kenya, to serve the state and society. It also discusses how far, under the stress of the modern urge for technological development, socio-economic forces have influenced property relations. At the end, some reflection will be made on the implications of property doctrines for environmental goals.

Property in context

Property is in every sense a legal concept. Its significance changes in consonance with the changes in the legal system. From the times of primitive societies, through the feudal systems until modern industrial and commercial societies, each phase of human society has given its own content to the notion of property. One thing, however, is not in doubt. At each stage of society, the institution of property has remained vital to human existence. It is also another way of saying that acquisitiveness is a primal human instinct. To deprive a person of property is to deprive him or her of life. The presence of the institution of property in human society is necessary for order and stability. It is this simple and primitive fact that Bentham expresses in his oft-quoted dictum: "Property and law are born together and die together. Before laws were made there was no property; take away laws, and property ceases."[1] Bentham stresses the importance of the regulation of property in society. The centrality of the institution of property in Kenya is affirmed in the constitution which establishes the right to property and alludes to its social functions.[2]

In every society, whatever its level of development, property relations and other elements of social order such as political groups and economic policies are closely linked. Even where property relations are not regarded as the basis upon which the whole social order rests, it is undeniable that the concept of property and the relations it entails have wide implications on the life of the community.

Legal institutions set the rules for the relationship between differing economic activities. To judge and design legal institutions, one must know what economic game one wants to play—though the test for determining it is very difficult.[3] This chain of cause and effect is very long, but when traced it is found in a man-made legal order. Thus the relationship of the legal order to the economic order can be seen from the consistency in the relation between the two.[4] This relationship between the legal order and the economic order is not a development of modern times. It has always been a characteristic of human society.

In modern times, economic efficiency is secured through legislation. The Constitution of Kenya, which is not an evolutionary constitution like that of Great Britain or the United States, controls property relations via certain principles, to achieve certain economic goals. Property relations under the constitution are important both as a source of national power and as a restriction on state power. It is, therefore, necessary to assess the concept of property and property relations regulated under the Constitution, and to explore the wider values regarding the social relations on which the Constitution is based. It is only then that one can state whether these values are consistent with the provisions regarding property relations and provide a guide to the law-enforcement agencies. Such an exploration is made not only by examining the provisions of the Constitution as simple propositions of law (or positive law), but by a careful study of them as they operate in practice, and affect economic relations.

A functional approach is important, since it brings out the discrepancies between law and social reality. It maintains a constant dialogue between law and action. It enables the state to avoid unpalatable consequences before it is too late. The judicial wisdom also favours functional, rather than logically consistent choices. While making such a study one must realize that law is not an abstract thing, just a printed page, a volume of statutes or a statement by a judge. So far as it is of any consequence to the observer, law, to take a real form, must govern actions, must determine positive relations between people, must prescribe processes and juxtapositions. A statute may lie fallow on the book for ages unless under its provisions, a determined arrangement of human relations, is brought out or maintained. Separated from economic life and the social fabric, by which it is conditioned, and which it in turn helps to condition, law has no reality. This chapter analyzes the patterns emerging from the right of property guaranteed under the Constitution of Kenya. In discovering emerging patterns, the writer has analyzed decided cases as examples of how property law governs human relations.

With the emergence of new property patterns, customary property relations are under constant strain. Under customary law, as Kenyatta states it with reference to the Gikuyu,[5] the elders enjoy a broad discretion in relation to land disputes and land transactions. However, in modern times, the elders' power in relation to land has been limited. It is not only in a technical sense that their powers have been restricted, but in spirit they have lost their old grandeur. Under the Magistrates' Courts Act the elders, that is, persons who because of age, experience or other cause are recognized by custom to be responsible persons having knowledge on the subject, are vested with power to decide matters relating to land disputes. But where no elders are found, or the parties to the disputes do not agree on the choice of elders, the District Commissioner has the power to appoint such elders as he thinks fit. Such a technical arrangement runs against the spirit of customary law because it challenges the integrity of the elders. But it is quite consistent with the modern developments in the application of natural justice. Again, the powers of the elders are limited to making only a consultative judgement. It is the court that shall enter the binding judgement and make a decree. The court has also power to reject the recommendation of the elders, if it finds any legal flaws in the recommendation. The power of the elders to deal with land disputes, however, is in respect of both land registered under the Registered Land Act and unregistered land. This provision thus covers cases where customary land rights are still held by the parties. This provides a link between customary land rights and the new rights of ownership. This is important from a social point of view.

The reliance on the system of elders has other problems as well. It depends largely on the traditional norms prevailing in society and may be blind to emerging social realities. For example, most traditional systems discriminate against women when it comes to the ownership of property. The same is true of the "modern" system. In reality, unless the rights of women are clearly articulated by law, the two systems tend to reinforce gender inequalities. This point is particularly important because women play an important role in the management of natural resources and other public goods and their interests need to be given force in the Constitution.

When a constitution is consciously formulated, it lays down the principles on which property is to be held and acquired. These principles are laid down in Section 75 of the Constitution of Kenya. This section does not reveal any ideological picture of the scheme of property relations. There are at least two contending ideologies with regard to the right of property—the theory of property based on natural law (free market economy) and the socialist theory of property. Out of these two theories, one can easily see which one is enshrined in the Constitution. According to John Locke, who represents the naturalist theory of property, property is an inalienable human right.[6] Therefore, all acquisitions and dispositions of property depend on the will of the holder. Whatever the defects of the natural law theory, the right of property is recognized because of its inalienable nature.[7] It is a primal human instinct. Its existence is necessary to maintain social order. The socialist theory of property places all property in the means of production in the hands of the state, which administers it as a "trust" for the society.

Both the free market and socialist systems look upon property relations as a means of power for the state, as well as a means of social control. The distinction between the two theories lies in the modes of enjoyment of property. It is the ambit rather than the nature of property that is different. Locke's theory under which property in all its forms is a natural human right, is recognized in the Kenyan Constitution; the natural law theory has provided the philosophical basis of Section 75. The natural law idea has become the highest positive law through its incorporation in the Constitution. The economic significance of such a philosophy is revealed in measures to attract foreign investment to meet economic needs, such as the guaranteeing of the right of property to all persons. Undoubtedly, the Constitution is built upon the recognition of the right of property. This reveals the ideological picture of the scheme of property relations as reflected in Section 75.

Conceptual foundations

Property defined

The term property is not defined in the Kenya Constitution but it is used in a comprehensive sense. Section 75(1) states: "No property of any description shall be compulsorily taken possession of, and no interest or right over property of any description shall be compulsorily acquired." These words include all categories of property, movable or immovable, corporeal or incorporeal, that can be appropriated and enjoyed. It is concerned with property in a legal sense, as a bundle of rights. It refers to all the different degrees of ownership, since all interests that have an insignia of property are protected under the Constitution. In *Haridas Chhagan Lal* v. *Kericho Urban District Council*,[8] the plaintiff was granted a lease over a piece of land in 1928. The lease was granted on the condition that the land was to be used only for residential and business purposes. In 1960, the plaintiff wanted to erect a petrol pump on the land. The land board in charge of the area refused permission on the grounds that to operate a petrol pump would be contrary to recently enacted by-laws passed under the Local Government Ordinance of 1960. The court, however, held that the provision of the by-laws that takes away the property interest without compensation is in conflict with Section 75 of the Constitution. A person cannot be deprived of his or her property without compensation even if there is a clearly expressed intention in an enactment.

Viewed from this perspective, the court simply reinstated the principle of "rule of law" in regard to property; any interference with the property interest is sufficient to attract the application of Section 75. Deprivation, thus, need not be total. Any deprivation is an impairment of the right of property. Section 75 is broad enough to cover all cases of deprivation—whatever the extent. It breaks up the unitary concept of ownership[9] into its component units of enjoyment and control, a position more favourable to property owners.

Section 75(1) covers all those rights that have an insignia of proprietary right. It is the marketability and exchangeability of the right which is considered property under Section 75(1). Anything that has an economic value is regarded as property. For example, the right of a shareholder to vote at the meeting of the company, as distinct from the shares he or she holds, is not a property right. The property right in the Constitution is stated in the negative, so as to include any other form of property that may come into existence in the future. Positive assertions would exclude future forms of property—a fact which would necessitate changes to the Constitution each time it was necessary to provide for a new property right.

Again Section 75(1) guarantees liberty of the person to acquire and dispose of a thing that has acquired an insignia of property. However, the right to acquire and dispose of, refers to any lawful manner, or by lawful pursuit. Thus the section provides both protection for the right of property (not just the right to possess and enjoy), and the guarantee of liberty in acquiring and disposing of property.

Public interest and private property

The inviolability of the right of property is recognized not only in the municipal law of the great majority of states but also by international law, both in times of peace and war. Private property is not affected by conquest, annexation or cession of territories. In the peace treaties after World War I the principle of inviolability of private property was recognized. Article 17 of the United Nations Declaration of Human Rights states that everyone has the right to own property, alone, as well as in association with others, and that no one shall be arbitrarily deprived of his or her property.

All these lofty notions about private property do not make it an absolute right. In fact, property as an absolute right never existed, nor can it exist. It is in this qualified sense that the notion of property is enshrined in the Kenyan Constitution—that the material resources of the community must be used to serve the best interests of the community. The very fact that property is a legal institution, logically makes it subject to the law-making process. And its content will change with the law. Law as a major instrument of social change, has to labour under socially beneficial options. It has to maintain its stability and at the same time look to the socially progressive and beneficial interests. In the wider interests of the community, it may be justifiable to restrict the ambit of the property right.

It is the social control of property that brings into context the power of compulsory acquisition. Social control of property is exercised by putting restrictions on the use of property,[10] and by compulsory acquisition.[11] However, one can also argue that the reconciliation of private interests in property with the public interest raises no major dilemmas, since property is a social concept. It is often assumed that society's demands on property are not explicit because of the general view that the proprietor's own interest requires him or her to use the property in such a way that it advances both individual and social interests.

It is possible that the restrictions imposed on the right of property vary in different societies. Such a variation will be due to differences in needs and values. For example, pre-industrial societies in Western countries imposed fewer restrictions on property during their period of industrialization than the restrictions that the developing countries are imposing on property rights during their period of industrialization. This is due not only to the differences in the nature of societies, but also to the socio-economic and technological pressures on present-day developing societies that are suddenly exposed to the machine age.

Having in view the need to protect private property, and society's demands on private property, the constitution-makers have given power to the state to acquire private property for public purposes. Under the Constitution, property can be compulsorily acquired "in the interest of defence, public safety, public order, public morality, public health, town and country planning or the development or utilization of any property in such manner as to promote the public benefit."[12] Compulsory acquisition is a form of social control quite different from putting restrictions on the use and enjoyment of property. Given these forms of social control, it is evident that the controlling agent of economic activity is no longer the individual but the entire community. This method of specific adjustment of private property to social needs can also be looked at from the point of view of deliberate rational and equitable control and distribution of property, through the agency of the state. It is against this background that the idea of acquisition of property, as enshrined in the Constitution, should be understood. Under the Constitution, encroachments on the right of property are made in the public interest.

Since any encroachment or interference is to be made only in the public interest, it can be regarded as a fulfilment of the social function of property. It is an imposition of obligations on the owners, on the basis that their possessions are for social needs. Such a principle is expected to put an end to all known and imagined abuse of property, that might be perpetrated to the disadvantage of society. The same law which creates property also assigns it a social function. It is within the sphere of law that the various aspects of property are regulated. Under the Constitution, the only condition to the state's control is that the law must be a valid law. Property, therefore, is a creation of law. It is a system of legal rights and duties relating to external objects which have economic value.

Private property can be compulsorily acquired only if "the necessity therefor is such as to afford reasonable justification for the causing of any hardship that may result to any person having an interest in or right over the property."[13] "Necessity" does not require the statement of a specific purpose. It refers not only to the present demands of the public but also to the future demands as may fairly be anticipated. In *Destro* v. *The Attorney-General* it was pointed out that "the government of a developing country such as Kenya must have a land bank available for development when required in order to take advantage of aid offered by developed countries and such institutions as the World Bank."[14] Thus no restrictions as to the time of acquisition would apply as the benefits from the acquisition were anticipatory.

The Constitution imposes two types of restrictions under Section 75(1) (a) and (b), to ensure the acquisition is in the public interest. These are the conditions subject to which interference can be reasonably justified. These two provisions, read together, stress Blackstone's idea of the "despotic dominion", which is, however, subject to control and diminution in the public interest. The idea is based on the superior claims of the community over those of the individual. All restrictions on property rights, whether amounting to total deprivation or falling short of it, can only be imposed in the general interest of the society. Therefore, no property interest or right can be interfered with without a consideration of the public interest or it would amount to confiscation. The Constitution does not allow confiscation. Were Section 75(1) (a) to be deleted, it would exclude the public-purpose requirement, and allow the state to take private property at will. In such a situation the purpose of the acquisition, or taking of possession of property would not be subject to question in a court of law.

The liberal complexion of Section 75 is restricted by the state's policy of controlling or reserving to itself certain areas of development. It is recognized that in a developing country it would be inappropriate to leave certain matters of development in private hands. The state has to assume leadership in such matters, because of the exceptional burdens of social and industrial development. The magnitude and complexity of such development call for centralized co-ordination. In this development process, the state sometimes needs to acquire private property for the wider interests of the community. But a simple assertion by the government that the necessity exists to carry on an operation in the public interest, would not satisfy the court. There must be evidence to prove it. Public interest is a condition precedent if property rights are to be interfered with. It is immaterial whether the deprivation is total or only partial.

Acquisition or taking of possession of property is possible only if such an action is authorized by law. Whenever law is referred to in the Constitution, it means a valid law, that is, a law that is not inconsistent with the Constitution. Authority of law is necessary for any government action that deprives a person of any right or interest in his or her property. In fact, this is no more than an assertion of the rule of law in regard to property, and an assertion of the principle of English Law, that the executive cannot take private property without the authority of law. It should be noted that even before the Constitution came into existence in 1963, there were laws regulating the compulsory acquisition of private property, and they were based on the concept of public interest.[15]

In *B.P. Bhatt and Another* v. *Habib Versi Rajani*[16] the term "purpose in the public interest" came up for interpretation. The court defined it with reference to aims and objectives which showed the general interest of the community, as opposed to the particular interests of individuals, to be directly and vitally concerned. Public purpose does not include propping up the financial position of one person at the cost of another by the state. The idea is not to take from the rich and give to the poor, so as to establish economic equality. The phrase is not limited to business necessities and ordinary conveniences. It extends to public matters such as the settling of squatters and highway improvements. It includes not only present demands but also fairly anticipated demands of the future.

The problem of reconciling the idea of private property with social well-being is engaging attention all over the world. The task of adjusting the old institution of property to a harmonious relationship with new social forces, and new goals such as environmental management, is a vexing question. It is the adjustment of an old concept to changing circumstances. Such an adjustment, in the Constitution of Kenya, is attempted by two methods: by imposing restrictions on the circumstances for promoting the public interest, and by widening these restrictions to deal with a special social *mélange* in the preservation of social order. But under no circumstances can a proper equilibrium be achieved between individual rights and social interests.

Efforts in the quest for some equilibrium are to be found under Section 75 of the Constitution.[17] *Prima facie* the government, though not the absolute judge, is the judge of the existence of the public interest. The question is a judicial one because, according to Section 75(2)(a) of the Constitution, "every person having an interest or right in or over property which is compulsorily taken possession of or whose interest in or right over any property is compulsorily acquired shall have a right of direct access to the High Court for . . . the determination of . . . the legality of the taking of possession or acquisition of the property, interest or right."

What constitutes public interest is largely a question for the legislature although democratic practices create greater space for public involvement in defining public interest issues. The courts will not interfere except to enquire whether the legislature could reasonably have considered the use to be a public one. It is in this respect that the question becomes a judicial one. The courts, in deciding whether an acquisition is for public use, take into account the diverse local conditions, but otherwise accord great respect to the legislative declaration as to public purposes. The courts are not concerned with the prudence, or even the necessity of the use for which the property is acquired. These are legislative matters. Nevertheless, the courts will pose a subtle question as to the balance between an individual's interest and the interest of the community.

No hard and fast definition of public interest or purpose can be given. It is a question of fact whether under certain conditions public interest exists or not. In India, in *State of Bihar* v. *Kemeshwar Singh,* the Supreme Court stated in 1952:

> With the onward march of civilization our notions as to the scope of the general interest of the community are fast changing and widening, with the result that *our old and narrow notions as to the sanctity of the private interest of the individual can no longer stem the forward flowing tide of time and must necessarily give way to the broader notions of the general interest of the community.*[18]

R.S. BHALLA

The US Supreme Court has given a very liberal construction to the term "public purpose". In *Clark* v. *Nash*,[19] it stated that a purpose which is for the benefit of an individual may still be a public purpose, provided that such an individual benefits not as an individual but in furtherance of a scheme of public utility. This is true. A purpose will still be public even if it benefits an individual not as an individual, but as a member of the community. For example, where the state acquires a house to rehabilitate flood victims and it turns out that there is only one person who qualifies for the state's assistance, it is still a public purpose. Apart from such cases, any liberal interpretation of public purpose in terms of public utility, public advantage or public benefit will hardly leave any case that will not be covered under public purpose. Not all powers given to, and duties imposed on the executive by the legislation are directly concerned with public purpose. Unless the powers given and duties imposed are directly concerned with public interest, their exercise should not be cast exclusively within the ambit of public interest.

Public purpose does not cover all cases where there is government approval or which are directly or indirectly related to objects mentioned in the statute. Such a relationship can also prove very tenuous. For example, in *Barkya Thakur* v. *State of Bombay*,[20] property was acquired to house a private industrialist, and acquisition was made under public purpose. The court upheld the acquisition. In *R.L. Arora* v. *State of Utar Pradesh* the acquisition was made for the purpose of setting up a textile plant.[21] The court held that it was not in the public interest. In *Somaranti* v. *State of Punjab*,[22] the manufacture of fridges was regarded as a public purpose. These uncertainties created by the courts do not augur well for the establishment of the confidence which the public needs, and which flows from the sanctity of property. Moreover, these cases do not leave anything outside the category of "public purpose".

There is a public purpose if the thing is useful to the public, or entails the participation of the public. The complexities of modern developments, and of human interdependence, have made it necessary to limit individual activities. The term public interest is to be construed in the light of the particular legislation, taking into account the circumstances of its enactment. Its definitions may provide a legal solution, but the public need to be aware of its existence. For court decisions represent no more than a fictional victory.

Any use of compulsorily acquired property that is not public in nature not only conflicts with the law, but erodes public confidence in the authority doing this. It is an abuse of power. It is a case of bad faith and bad motives. If such cases occur frequently, the public will doubt that all cases of acquisition of private property are in good faith. Such a distrust will be neither in the best interests of the government, nor conducive to national development.

PROPERTY RIGHTS AND PUBLIC INTEREST

If, for example, such a provision were to authorize the government to compulsorily acquire private property for public purpose and then sell it later, where the necessity for acquisition has passed, this would not fit well with the constitutional scheme of Section 75.[23] The necessity of causing hardship to the owner should lie in public benefit, not government or state benefit. One can argue that such any such sale or transfer of compulsorily acquired property would be necessitated by some ulterior motive. Moreover, if the authority acquiring private property cannot visualize its present or future programme of publicly beneficial works, the policies of that authority are not conducive to social progress and cannot create confidence in the public.

"Taking possession of" and "acquisition"

The term "taking possession of" referred to in Section 75(1) of the Kenyan Constitution suggests the taking of physical possession, as generally understood in traditional agricultural economies. Immovable property such as land and houses can only be held by taking actual physical possession or control. The term "acquisition" refers to well-developed, modern economic interests and rights, such as patents and shares, which can only be acquired since there is no physical possession involved. Thus the use of "compulsory taking of possession" and "compulsory acquisition" takes care of both types of property—corporeal and incorporeal, movable and immovable. It covers property both in the traditional sense, with reference to agricultural societies, and in the newer sense in which the term is used in modern societies, to cover such property as intellectual property. It is in the light of the complexity of tradition and modernity, that the concept of property is understood and entrenched in the Constitution. The incorporation of such modern developments in the basic law is essential and beneficial to economic development. This concept has been extended to the intellectual property regime through the enactment of the Industrial Property Act.

One of the issues that Kenya will need to deal with in future is the possible expansion of the concept of "taking" to include reductions in value associated with regulatory measures. The concern here is that government regulation which reduces the value of land and renders it unusable (either in part or in whole) should be considered a taking and should be subject to compensation. So far the question of "regulatory takings" of property has not been an issue but it is bound to emerge as land becomes more scarce and the conflict between private and public interests is heightened. The takings jurisprudence as developed in the US judicial system may be a source of ideas on how to solve this complex issue. What is critical, however, is that the takings issue needs to be considered in a framework that accommodates other legal doctrines such as public trust and customary use.[24]

R.S. BHALLA

Interpretation of constitutional provisions

Sanctity of private property

The sanctity of private property, and the right to property, are given paramount importance in the Kenyan Constitution. This is clear from Section 83(1) which states:

> Nothing contained in or done under the authority of an Act of Parliament shall be held to be inconsistent with or in contravention of section 72, 76, 79, 80, 81 or section 82 [of the Constitution] when Kenya is at war, and nothing contained in or done under the authority of any provision of Part III of the Preservation of Public Security Act shall be held to be inconsistent with or in contravention of those sections of this Constitution when and in so far as the provision is in operation by virtue of an order under Section 85.

This section curtails fundamental rights contained in Chapter V (Protection of Fundamental Rights and Freedoms of the Individual) in times of war and under the Preservation of Public Security Act *except the right to property* guaranteed under Section 75. Clearly the institution of property is one of the bases of the Constitution. In spite of variations and qualifications, the sanctity of the right of property is preserved. There are two possible reasons for this deliberate approach. Firstly, the right of property, like all other fundamental rights guaranteed under Chapter V of the Constitution, is subject to restrictions under normal circumstances in the general public interest. Secondly, while a person can be deprived of his or her property in the public interest and paid compensation even under exceptional circumstances, a further derogation of the right of property under any circumstances is untenable. As far as other fundamental rights are concerned, however, there can be a near-complete derogation.

The placing of property in the category of fundamental rights is in itself of great significance. Prior to the enactment of the Constitution, there was no restriction on the enactment of laws affecting the right to property. Property relations were regulated by the ordinary law of the land. Kenya attained independence from Britain in 1963 and became a sovereign republic in 1964. With the background of foreign domination and exploitation, the founding fathers secured the right of property against ordinary-law encroachments, by instituting the right of property in the Constitution as a fundamental right. The ordinary law's protection of private property is very wide. Indeed, the governmental system sustains a corresponding system of property relations through varied legal arrangements. It is not only the property laws that create and protect property relations. Property relations are protected through

PROPERTY RIGHTS AND PUBLIC INTEREST

many devices. For example, the law of torts deals with economic torts; the law of contract secures property relations; and likewise criminal law is concerned largely with the protection of property. In modern societies administrative law has developed a theory that an individual's right of subsistence is to be protected from the executive's arbitrary interference.

Adhering to the human rights principles set out in the UN Charter, the Universal Declaration of Human Rights (1948) and the International Covenant of Economic, Social and Cultural Rights (1966), the Constitution provides protection to all persons subject, of course, to domestic laws, and the prevailing social and political considerations. The right of property is granted to all persons. Hence, any person can buy property in Kenya subject to permission under the Land Control Act. Once people have acquired property, they are not at the mercy of the state and are free to exercise their property rights like any citizens. All protections and safeguards provided under Section 75 apply to them.

Compensation

There is nothing anti-social or anti-property in the compulsory acquisition of private property in the public interest. The question of compulsory acquisition of private property is a constitutional principle relating to the exercise of a sovereign power expressed in the doctrines of eminent domain and police power—offsprings of political necessity.[25] Sovereign government has the power to acquire the private property of people under its protection, for public use, irrespective of the wishes of the owners. This power presupposes the existence of property, and nullifies its absolute character. However, public use is a pre-condition to the exercize of this power. Under the US Constitution, three powers have been recognized, in relation to control on private property. These are: *eminent domain, police power* and *taxation*, which are distinct categories of sovereign powers, with different connotations, and serving different needs.

They include all of the forms of social control recognized in law but have different applications. Police power is the legal capacity of the sovereign or any of its state agents to delimit the personal liberty of individuals by means which affect the end to be achieved for the protection of social interests. Taxation is the legal capacity of the sovereign to impose a charge on persons or their property for governmental purposes and for the payment of any other public purpose which it may legally carry out. Eminent domain is the legal capacity of the sovereign or any state agents to take private property for public use provided that just compensation is paid.

One can see that public purpose or public interest runs through all the three powers inherent in sovereignty, and furnishes justification for their exercise. There is a very thin line between police power, where there is no obligation to pay compensation, and eminent domain, where there is an obligation to pay compensation. In *Pennsylvania Coal Co.* v. *Mahon*,[26] Chief Justice Holmes took a pragmatic approach in which he endeavoured to distinguish between police power and eminent domain. He stated that up to a certain extent the government has a right to regulate private property, but a stage may come when the regulation amounts to taking. He said: "Government could hardly go on if to some extent values incident to property could not be diminished without paying for every such change in the general law. As long recognized, some values are enjoyed under an implied limitation and must yield to the police power . . . . The general rule at least is, that while property may be regulated to a certain extent, if regulation goes too far it will be recognized as a taking."[27]

The governmental intervention then, instead of being confined as a valid exercize of police power, becomes an exercize of the power of eminent domain, and an obligation to pay compensation then arises. Each case of taking possession is to be seen in the light of how far the government can go without interfering with the enjoyment of private property. Publicly justifiable criteria, and reasonableness are to be applied in each case. Section 75(1) of the Constitution refers to both police power and eminent domain. It refers to both payment of compensation in cases of compulsory acquisition of private property, and the imposition of restrictions in the public interest. Though the right of compensation does not directly follow from the theory of eminent domain, it is always considered that the payment of compensation is an essential element in the valid exercise of such a power.[28] Section 75(1)(c) imposes an obligation on the state to pay full compensation when an individual is deprived of his or her property.[29]

What is the "police power" of the state? It is the power of the state to impose restrictions for the purposes, *inter alia*, of health, safety and public morality. These restrictions on the private property which clearly bring out the idea of police power are found in section 75(6)(a)(v):

> Nothing contained in or done under the authority of any law shall be held to be inconsistent with or in contravention of subsection (1) or subsection (2) [of this section] (a) to the extent that the law in question makes provision for the taking of possession or acquisition of any property . . . (v) in circumstances where it is reasonably necessary so to do because the property is in a dangerous state or injurious to the health of human beings, animals or plants.

Therefore, deprivation of property falls into two categories: deprivation of property by taking possession, or acquisition on payment of compensation; and deprivation of property *simpliciter*. Deprivation of property that takes place as a punishment, or in the cause of administration under certain conditions, is a case of deprivation under police power. Private property can also be acquired to secure public safety as where animals are destroyed to prevent spreading of disease.

Reading Section 75(1) and Section 75(6) together, one can see that the Constitution incorporates the American doctrines of eminent domain and police power. These two doctrines are judicially developed principles to deal with cases involving the fundamental right to property, and government's authority to put restrictions on and to extinguish the right—by appropriation or otherwise. Therefore, these two principles, whether or not expressly incorporated in the Constitution, are bound to correspond with Section 75 which deals with the right of property. Section 75, when interpreted in the constitutional text itself, involves these two doctrines.

The two doctrines are an incident of sovereignty in all civilized states. The powers they give are essential to the independent existence and perpetuity of government. It is absolutely necessary that government has the means to perform its functions and perpetuate its existence and should not be liable to control or defeat by want of consent on the part of private parties or any other authority. The compulsory acquisition of property is founded on the superior claims of the whole community over the claims of the individual citizen. It is applicable only in those cases where private property is required for public use. The right of eminent domain does not imply a right in the sovereign power to take the property of one citizen and transfer it to another, even for full compensation, where public interest will in no way be promoted by such transfer.

The takings debate has recently been advanced in the 1992 case of *Lucas* v. *South Carolina Coastal Council*, in which the US Supreme Court ruled that "[w]here the State seeks to sustain regulation that deprives land of all economically beneficial use . . . it may resist compensation only if the logically antecedent inquiry into the nature of the owner's estate shows that the proscribed use interests were not part of his title to being with."[30] In this case, South Carolina argues that the Beachfront Management Act that prohibited David Lucas from developing his beachfront property was aimed at abating a public nuisance (the destruction of a public beach). Indeed, the nuisance doctrine has been a key pillar of the takings jurisprudence. But the most important factor in the *Lucas* case is that it puts economic value above other land uses.

Adequacy of compensation

Whether or not compensation is adequate is an important matter in the social and economic wellbeing of an individual, since acquisition, in whatever form, is always considered an intrusion upon private property. No matter how substantial the compensation paid, the satisfaction found in one's own belongings can never be assessed in monetary terms. In fact, compensation can never cover the owner's esteem and reverence for his or her property nor the personal identity associated with property. Nevertheless, the life of the community, its welfare, its needs, its development and progress demand a sacrifice of the individual's interests. The community, however, endeavours to compensate this sacrifice in monetary terms.

When the state takes possession of or acquires the property of an individual for a public purpose, it is under an obligation to pay "full compensation" as provided in Section 75(1)(c) of the Kenyan Constitution. The provision regarding full compensation, which dates back to the colonial constitution in its later years, came up for interpretation in *Puran Chand Manay* v. *The Collector*.[31] Under the 1894 Indian Land Acquisition Act, the term was interpreted as a market value, and compensation was "the price which a willing vendor might be expected to obtain from a willing purchaser;" a "willing purchaser" is one who, although being a speculator, is not a wild or unreasonable speculator. Therefore, the compensation should be according to the market value.[32] This interpretation is later followed in a number of cases. The time of acquisition is of the essence in fixing the compensation. The value must not be entirely conjectural, and future potential use of the property should not be considered. It must be estimated by prudent business calculations, and not by mere speculations and impractical imagination. However, the amount of compensation can be questioned in the High Court. Though valuation is not an exact science, arbitrary or artificial compensation cannot be regarded as compensation within the meaning of Section 75(1)(c).[33] This also represents the American approach on the authority of judicial review or due process, in relation to private property.

The level of compensation cannot be less than the market value, otherwise it will be arbitrary. For fixing the amount of compensation, rules have been laid down in the schedule to the Land Acquisition Act.[34] These rules are quite liberal, and take into consideration the inconvenience, disturbance or damage caused by the interference, or by the acquisition of property—but they are still inadequate.[35]

Property and the subsistence question

Private property is a legal regime in which property is vested in a determinate individual who enjoys perfect freedom in its disposition. It gives him or her an area of choice. It is argued that such a regime places confidence, security, management ability and stability in the property holder. However, such a regime bears hardly any reference to the economic needs of the individual. Thus, private property as a legal concept, cannot be justified in terms of such socio-legal consequences. Public property on the other hand is a regime of property whose legal character resides in a corporate body, as opposed to a determinate person. Unlike in private property, legal character in public property is not visible. It is common property, or a trust, created in the government for the use of the whole society. Its advantages, functions and utility to the public in general depend on the policies of the government in power, which determines its distribution.

The Kenyan Constitution deals with both types of property. Section 75 deals with private property. It gives ample powers to the state over private property, even to the extent of acquisition for public use (with compensation). The Constitution also lays down a framework for trusts, or public property. These trust lands vest either in the central government or in the county councils. Overall supervision to regulate, distribute and manage these trust lands rests with the government. In respect of these lands, customary rights, privileges, grants, occupancy rights and interests (including those related to environmental management) are null and void, to the extent of their inconsistency with written law either already in existence or enacted in future. Customary law in respect of land, is giving way to modern law, owing to the modernization ethos underlying the objectives of the Kenyan state. In fact, customary land rights are made readily subject to qualification, and a person can be deprived of these rights by payment of compensation. The old grandeur of community life has given way to individualized and impersonal needs dissociated from the right of subsistence under customary land. Agriculture has become an industry rather than a profession. This is a departure from the community living of the past.

The institution of property arose in answer to the society's economic needs. This in turn gave the individual control over economic goods. Besides the economic justification of the institution of property, it is also socially and morally justified because, without control over the means of livelihood, human survival is impossible. Different theories developed to justify the institution of property are only explanatory and do not address the right of subsistence on which the institution of property is based. With these points in mind it is futile to discuss the advantages of private property to the general public. The question of public and private property, in fact, is a question relating to the legal regime of ownership, not the economic needs of the individuals. Therefore, the important question is not as regards the regime of public or private property, but rather, the regime of property that meets the economic needs of individuals on a sustainable basis. The question is not who owns the land, but who owns the produce. The classification of property into public and private property is to be judged only from the point of view of the system of property that sufficiently satisfies a society's minimal economic needs. No such question is raised in the Constitution, nor is there a reference to it in any other legislation dealing with the institution of property; yet it is one of the most fundamental concerns of the majority of the people.

The means of production can be said to have been distributed if the ownership of the produce vests in the producer, even if he is not the owner of the land. Therefore, the ownership of land can vest in the community, but it must be parcelled out to its members who should own the produce. It is only then that the means of production can be said to have been allocated so as to meet the economic needs of the individuals. In this way, the regime of property can be said to answer the economic needs of the individuals and the related natural resource concerns.

Legal doctrine and environmental goals

Property can be viewed as a slice of natural resources, or a fabrication therefrom, which has been appropriated by a particular person. To the lawyer, property is only a juridical symbol, which represents a person's ownership and control of something. The law's guarantees of property rights allow only the most limited room (in the form of police power, eminent domain, and taxation) for varying such rights with public interest. This is bound to present a major obstacle for environmental goals.

The main areas of concern, in relation to environmental goals, are: air pollution; depletion or destruction of biological resources; poisoning and loss of soil and water. All these problem-areas are unbounded by territorial limits; and they thus transcend the redress-capability of the positive laws of individual countries. The various regimes of municipal law do treat property rights as fundamental rights, that are safeguarded by the judicial process under the Constitution. The national constitutions have built walls of protection around property rights, thus raising serious practical difficulties for those governments which may be genuinely committed to international co-operation, by virtue of treaty law, for the reduction of greenhouse gas emissions, the conservation of biological diversity, the prevention of desertification, etc. Where such global measures tend to come into conflict with private property rights, they run the risk of being nullified by the courts. Narrow exceptions such as that afforded by the concept of eminent domain, whereby private property may be acquired in the public interest, are likely to operate as exceptional situations only, and will not give a wide-enough opening for large-scale environmental-protection initiatives by the state.

As already noted, the institution of property arose in answer to society's economic needs. Such a development took place when the pressures on the environment were still relatively low, and at a time when the fundamental links between economics and environment, under the notion of sustainable development, had not yet been sufficiently clarified. The constrictive burdens of legal doctrine have, unfortunately, been carried over into the modern constitution, which now sanctifies individualist principles that are in sharp conflict with collectivist goals of environmental conservation. Although the Constitution does provide for the acquisition of private property, under the concept of eminent domain, this opening is narrow, and the legal system as a whole remains essentially restrictive, in relation to broad-based environmental goals. One way forward is to define public interest to include environmental conservation.

Conclusion

This chapter has explained the general direction of property relations under the Constitution of Kenya. It indicates that the Constitution and its legal system, constitute a bedrock of norms that are built around certain settled doctrines; and that these doctrines, with their individual-centred characteristics, will be found to constitute a major obstacle in the way of environmental initiatives. However, it may be taken that the restrictive doctrines of property, as currently enshrined in the Constitution and other laws, will continue to be exposed to certain pressures, especially those wrought by international environmental initiatives. Already, in the *Destro* case, it appears that the needs of the public are growing, and the state is gaining a grip over development, rather than letting it fall completely in private hands. This will lessen the cost of development related to public consumption, and will save the public from private developers who are more concerned with profit than with public service. Indeed, in *Destro*, the main reason why the government moved to seek compulsory acquisition of the land was to avoid imminent speculative purchase of the land by a prominent businessman.

The acquisition of land by government, however, will not necessarily eliminate private property. Indeed, the land that was acquired was subsequently allocated to private interests. But public acquisition is likely to adjust the relations between the public sector and private enterprise. Major public developments will be removed from the ambit of private developers, who will remain largely confined to the consumer market. The effect will be to lessen the conflict between private and public capital. Development in this case can go with those needs recognized by the state, in an order of priority. This will enable the country to rely on comprehensive socio-economic planning, rather than on the mechanisms of market forces. Although such a policy is not revealed in Section 75 of the Constitution, the court decisions, and the reasoning proffered on acquiring private property, point to such a conclusion.

Lastly, it should be observed that the Constitution should in principle be subjected to appropriate reforms, aimed in particular at tempering the more antiquated property doctrines, and establishing a clear juridical capacity for the public management of natural resources, in consonance with the dictates of environmental conservation. Another aspect of the Constitution that should be reviewed is the potential abuse of the provisions for compulsory acquisition of land by the state which in turn is transferred to private individuals under circumstances that would not qualify as being related to the public benefit.

Notes

1. Bentham, 1967, p. 113.
2. The Constitution of Kenya, Section 75. All sections referred to herein are sections of the Constitution of Kenya.
3. The Constitution of India was designed to suit the socialist economic pattern. Since its inception in 1950, it has served different economic patterns: socialist, mixed, and capitalist.
4. For example, anti-trust laws in the US are being used not only to establish and maintain perfect competition but to discipline large corporations.
5. Kenyatta, 1938, Chapter 2.
6. Locke, 1946, pp. 15–26.
7. Bhalla, 1984, pp. 15–26.
8. [1965] E.A. 370.
9. Bhalla, 1984, pp. 15–26.
10. *Haridas Chhagan Lal* v. *Kericho Urban District Council.* [1965] EA 370.
11. *Destro* v. *The Attorney-General*, 1980, KLR 80.
12. Section 75 (1) (a).
13. Section 75(1) (b).
14. [1980] KLR 80, p. 84. This case involved a decision to acquire land compulsorily for purposes of industrial development. The government resorted to compulsory acquisition when it was learnt that negotiations to purchase the land were likely to be frustrated by the interest of a prominent businessman to buy the land, possibly for speculation. Laterm Destro and others filed a case in which they sought to regain the land on the basis that the compulsory acquisition was *ultra vires*. Part of the claim was based on the knowledge that parcels of the land had been transfered to private individuals who in turn had sold them at considerable profit. The idea of questioning the validity of the compulsory acquisition "only occurred to them seven years later when they heard of the enormous profits made by two speculators" (p. 82).
15. See Indian Land Acquisition Act, 1894 (applicable in Kenya).
16. [1958] E.A. 536.
17. In fact, such an approach is found in all fundamental rights guaranteed under Chapter 5 of the Constitution.

18. AIR, [1952] SC 275 (emphasis added).
19. [1905] 190 US 361.
20. AIR [1960] SC 1203.
21. AIR [1962] SC 764.
22. AIR [1963] SC 151.
23. As in Section 144 of the Local Government Act.
24. See, for example, Babcock, (1995) for an innovative approach to the takings issue.
25. Police power is an American public law concept, concisely explained in Walker (1980, p. 965) as follows: "[It is the] title given in American constitutional law to the governmental power to regulate matters of safety, health, welfare, and morals for the public good. The Supreme Court held, in the *Charles River Bridge* case (1837) . . . that, though Congress had the power to regulate interstate commerce, a state's police power entitled it to make reasonable laws for regulatory purposes even though such might not be expressly authorized by the Constitution. After the passage of the Fourteenth Amendment the Supreme Court frequently, under the 'due process' clause, struck down legislation creating regulatory functions, but latterly the Court has taken a much more liberal view of such regulation. Moreover more recently the police power has been extended beyond safety, health and morals to *the conservation of natural resources* . . . and other purposes not so narrowly limited as in earlier interpretation" (emphasis added).
26. [1922] 260 US 393.
27. [1922] 260 US 393, pp. 393–415.
28. See Lord Atkinson's judgement in *Central Control Board* v. *Cannon Brewery Co. Ltd.*, [1991] AC. 757.
29. But so far as the question of compensation is concerned, the Constitution has brought no marked change. The 1894 Land Acquisition Act provided for compulsory acquisition of property on payment of compensation. So this aspect of the law was well known before Kenya became a sovereign republic.
30. [1992] 112 S. Ct., 22 ELR.
31. [1957] EA 125.
32. Compensation based on market value is, therefore, cited to achieve the objective of satisfying the owner whose property is compulsorily acquired by the state. However, such a basis of compensation breaks down when the property compulsorily acquired commands no market value but is nevertheless of substantial value to the owner, for example, a private place of worship designed to the owner's convenience, in a manner that does not command any market value. In all cases of compulsorily acquisition of property the compensation should be not the market value, but should be based on the need to compensate the owners to the nearest use of the property to their full satisfaction.
33. *Haridas Chhagan Lal and Others* v. *Kericho Urban District Council*, 1972, EA 370.
34. *New Munyu Sisal Estate Ltd.* v. *The Attorney-General*, 1972, EA 77; *Institute of the Blessed Virgin Mary* v. *The Commissioner of Lands*, 1980, KLRS 5.
35. Land Acquisition Act, schedule, section 1–4.

PART II

LAND TENURE AND NATURAL RESOURCE MANAGEMENT

Land tenure systems and natural resource management

4

BONDI D. OGOLLA

WITH JOHN MUGABE

Introduction

Concern about land tenure and its impact on land-use and the management of environmental resources is not a recent phenomenon in Africa. Radical changes that have been deliberately initiated in tenure arrangements prior to and after independence in African countries have been justified on the basis of the expected improvements in productivity, land-use planning and decision-making which they would generate. However, until recently debate on the interface between land tenure and land-use has been restricted to how to enhance agricultural production. Yet land tenure, since it determines access to land and the environmental resources linked to it, is a critical variable in the management and conservation of the environment.

This chapter starts with a summary of the natural resource endowment of Kenya which provides the country's economic foundation. It points to some of the current threats to the resource base which may undermine the nation's economic growth and stability. It then provides an overview of the land tenure systems in Kenya and the role of the state in land-use regulation. It concludes with some proposals for alternative land tenure and land-use policies which define property rights in a way that incorporates the conservation ethic.

Figure 2 Land classification in Kenya

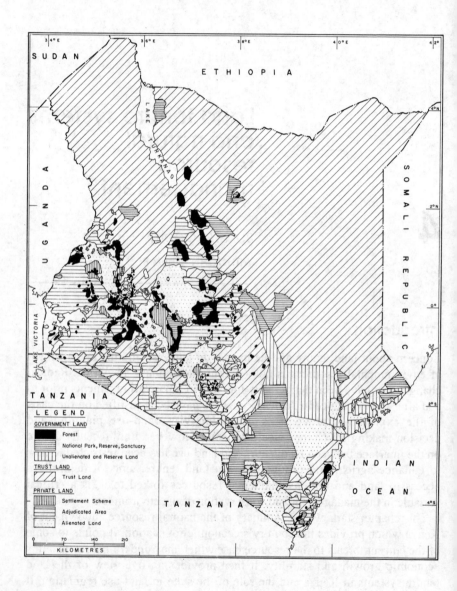

Figure 3 Vegetation of Kenya

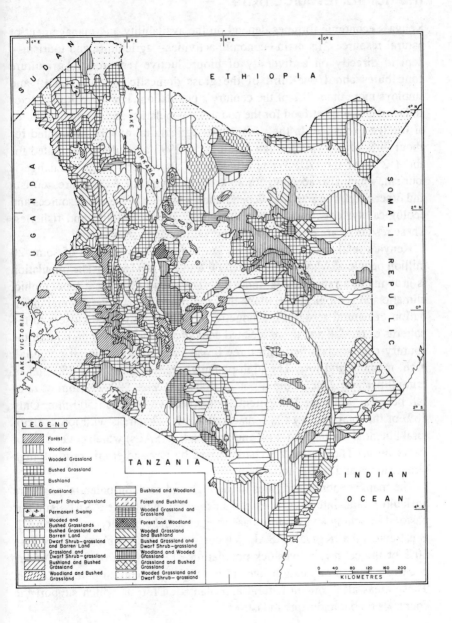

The natural resource base

Kenya's economic fortunes depend on the availability and management of natural resources. Its main economic activities—agriculture and tourism—depend directly on a diversity of bioproductive resources. Agriculture contributes about one-third of the gross domestic product (GDP) and employs more than 70% of the country's population. The agricultural sector is the main source of food for the country's population and is a major source of foreign exchange. In the early 1990s agricultural exports accounted for about 70% of Kenya's foreign earnings. In 1993 agriculture accounted for about 25% of the GDP.[1] The other major source of foreign exchange is tourism, which also accounts for 10% of employment.[2] Agriculture, tourism and other economic activities depend upon a number of natural resources and ecological systems, including soils, water, forests, wildlife and fisheries. These resources are mediated by the prevailing land use systems.

Kenya's total area of 582,646 sq km supports a population of some 26 million people of whom an estimated 80% live in rural areas. The population is growing at a rate of 3.5% annually.[3] The country has great topographic, climatic and ecological variations that contribute to the diversity and distribution of natural resources. Productive activities are related closely to the patterns of rainfall and the associated ecological zones. Based on rainfall the country can be classified into three broad zones of agricultural potential: high, medium and low. The high-potential areas receive over 750 mm of rainfall per year. The medium-potential areas receive 500–750 mm of rainfall per year while the low-potential ones receive less than 500 mm. Only 18% of the total land area is considered arable. The areas with low agricultural potential are the semi-arid and arid lands (ASALs) which cover 82% of the country.[4] These areas are characterized by low and erratic rainfall, high temperatures and fragile ecosystems.

The main economic activities in the high and medium-potential areas are agriculture and intensive livestock husbandry, while the ASALs support pastoral, ranching and wildlife-based systems and some dryland farming. It is estimated that Kenya's ASALs support six million people and more than 50% of the country's livestock population.[5] In contrast, over 75% of the country's human population lives in the high and medium-potential areas. These areas also contain natural and plantation forests which support the country's timber and paper industries.

Figure 4 Agro-climatic zones of Kenya

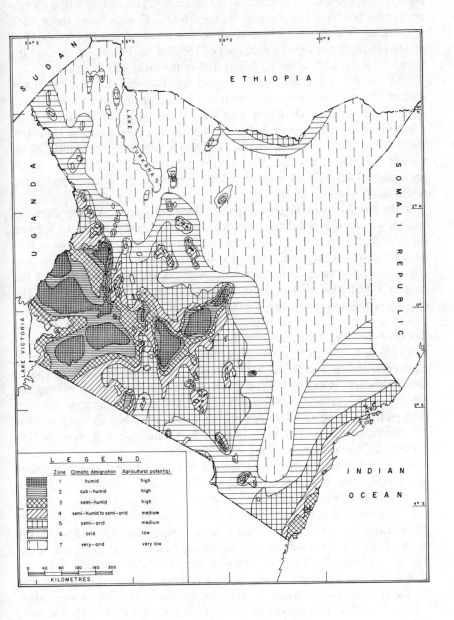

Kenya contains significant biological diversity. It is estimated that there are 8,000–9,000 species of plants in the country. Of this about 2,000 species are shrubs and trees found mainly in the ASALs. Forests cover about 2.5% of the total land area, of which about 85% are indigenous forests. In 1993 plantation forests covered a total area of 159,600 ha. Forest reserves are the habitat of about 25% of the birds and 40% of the mammals in Kenya.[6]

The country has considerable animal wildlife resources. It has many species of large herbivores and carnivores including unique and endangered species, as well as abundant bird life. Some wildlife is managed in government-controlled protected areas, such as parks and reserves. However, about 70% of the country's wildlife, much of which is highly mobile, exists outside the protected areas. Migration corridors and dispersal areas which are essential for the survival of wildlife are often outside the parks and reserves.

In the last 20 years the area of public lands designated as protected areas has grown. At independence there were four national parks and six game reserves in Kenya. By 1992 this had increased to 26 national parks and 29 national reserves. Terrestrial national parks, reserves and sanctuaries now cover a total area of some 4.4 million hectares, eight per cent of the country's land area. Most of the protected areas are found in the ASALs. The country also has an estimated 114,000 ha of marine parks and reserves.[7]

The tourist industry competes with agriculture for generating the most foreign exchange. It depends heavily on wildlife resources in national parks and reserves, particularly the large "charismatic" wild animals such as elephants, rhinos and lions. Many tourists also come to Kenya's Indian Ocean beaches. Between 1977 and 1987 the number of tourists visiting the country increased by 318,000 and the country's foreign exchange earnings through tourism increased by 244 million Kenya pounds.[8] The total number of tourists visiting the country's national parks and reserves grew by 42% between 1976 and 1986, reaching 730,000 in 1989.[9]

Water resources are a critical natural resource system which supports agriculture, tourism and domestic needs. The country has about 12,000 sq km of inland waters and an extensive coastline. Some of the most important water bodies and catchment areas are the Tana River Basin, Athi River Basin, Lake Victoria basin and lakes Nakuru, Naivasha and Turkana. Many of the country's rivers are seasonal which makes it difficult to harness water for development. Furthermore, the distribution of water bodies is uneven with Rift Valley Province having the most rivers and lakes. The lakes, rivers, coastal ecosystems and wetlands have plant, wildlife and fisheries resources essential for domestic consumption, tourism and agriculture. By the early 1990s the country was using about 600 million cu m of water per year. Of this 13% went to industrial uses, 18% to domestic use and 69% to agriculture. It is estimated that the country will be using at least 2,500 million cu m of water by the year 2000.[10] The ability to realize the potential for agricultural and industrial development in large sections of Kenya is limited by access to water. Since the water supply is inadequate to meet demand and is unevenly distributed, conflicts over the resource are emerging in many parts of the country.

Forests and woodlands are another important economic and ecological resource for Kenya. They provide about 70% of the energy consumed annually; 95% of rural energy demand is met from fuelwood.[11] The national annual demand for fuelwood and charcoal of 31 million cu m is met from forests and woodlands.[12] Forests also provide the raw materials for the timber and paper industries. In 1990 some 389,000 tonnes of wood materials from forests were used by pulp and paper industries to manufacture paper, cardboard, bags and other related products. The domestic production of wood and paper is estimated at US$100 million per year and over 100,000 people are employed in wood-based enterprises.[13]

Forests are also an important ecological resource. Despite their relatively small size (two per cent of the land area), they support much of the country's biological diversity. It is estimated that 40% of Kenya's animal species, 30% of bird and 35% of butterfly species are found in forests. Some 70% of plant species are found in forest areas.[14] Forest ecosystems are also critical for the survival of endangered species. For example, the coastal forests, which account for less than 0.1% of the remaining closed-canopy forest area, support 50% of the threatened plant species. They also support 60% and 65% of the threatened bird and mammal species, respectively. These forests are also the home of 25 endemic plant, four endemic bird and five endemic mammal species and sub-species.[15] Forests perform an important function by allowing groundwater recharge, regulating stream flow and controlling floods. They also contribute to the regulation of climatic variations and rainfall that are crucial for agricultural production. Forest biodiversity is a source of raw materials for human and veterinary medicine, forage for live-stock and cultural and handicraft materials. The 1994–1996 national development plan recognizes that "[f]orests produce many economic benefits as well as generation of jobs in the rural areas."[16]

Another important natural resources sector in Kenya is freshwater and marine fisheries. This sector contributes to national employment and provides inexpensive protein to rural households. The fisheries sector has experienced considerable growth over the past two decades. Total fish output has risen by about 125,600 tonnes in the past twenty years and per capita fish consumption has increased from 2.23 kg in 1964 to 5.3 kg in 1989. In 1992 total revenue generated by fisheries was over US$2 million and the total fish exports were 11,763 metric tonnes. Total revenue generated by the sector has increased sharply due to a rapid rise in fish prices attributed to a recent reduction in supply.[17] It is estimated that the country's fish farming potential is 50,000 metric tonnes per year.

Given the importance of natural resources in the country's economic life as summarized above, it is imperative that the management of these resources be an issue of national concern. In the past, natural resource management was seen to be only a scientific issue; it is clear today that it also has a political and economic character. For a country whose economy is vulnerable to global political and economic changes, it is crucial that measures aimed at improving economic performance take into consideration the need to manage the natural resource base sustainably.

Kenya's economy has experienced considerable stress during the past five years or so. From the late 1980s the economy has performed poorly in terms of growth. Since 1989, the GDP growth rate has continued to fall. The decline in economic growth could be explained in terms of the decline in agriculture in real output and poor performance of the tourist industry in early 1990s. The economic slowdown is partially a result of political instability in the country during the early 1990s.

The Kenya government has instituted a wide range of measures to deal with the macroeconomic problems related to this slowdown. These include mobilizing revenue by improving the taxation system, privatizing public enterprises, reducing government expenditure, and devaluing the currency. These measures have been instituted within the framework of the stabilization and structural adjustment policies advocated by the International Monetary Fund and the World Bank. Some of these measures have had, at least in the short-term, considerable impact on the social and economic life of the population. For example, the devaluation of the Kenya shilling against major currencies resulted in a large increase in the prices of agricultural inputs and consumer goods. The purchasing power of most households was severely cut. Some of these measures increase income disparities, reduce investment by rural households and hence contribute to the depletion of natural resources.

In order to meet the challenges facing the country, there is a need to ensure economic growth and stability by increasing the range of economic activities. This will require approaches that deliberately integrate the management of natural resources into economic planning and management. It should be noted that diversification of Kenya's economy and creation of employment will, at least initially, be possible through the creation of more natural resource-based enterprises. But this will undermine long-term economic growth and security if the resource base is not managed sustainably.

Kenya is currently experiencing a number of environmental problems which are largely associated with natural resource degradation. Strategic natural resources, such as wildlife, soils and forests, are being lost at rapid rates. The loss of these resources is associated with the rapidly growing population and changes in the social modes of production with limited growth in the corresponding technological knowledge and skills to manage the ecological base. The growing human population is putting more pressure on the environment in all regions. This is particularly so in the drylands where human migration has dramatically changed the land-use systems. This has occurred without sufficient adaptation of production technologies to the ASAL ecology. It has also coincided with the disruption of customary common property management regimes. As a result, land degradation, devegetation and diminished water resources are increasingly becoming common features in these areas.[18]

The country is also losing some of its unique and economically vital biotic resources. By 1989 it was estimated that five per cent of trees and shrub species, and eight per cent of herbaceous plant species in ASALs were endangered.[19] By 1986 the country had lost about 48% of its wildlife habitat. The 56.95 million ha of wildlife habitat in the 1940s and 1950s had fallen to only 29.6 million ha in 1985.[20] This trend has continued up to the present. The population of elephants decreased from 165,000 in 1973 to 18,000 in 1988; and that of black rhinos decreased from about 20,000 in 1970 to 350 in 1986.[21] Furthermore, it is estimated that 15% of the species of birds in the country are endangered. For example, the population of crowned cranes declined to about 19,000 in 1987 from 35,000 in 1978.[22] It is also reported that the populations of unique wildlife resources such as the Tana River mangabey and the Tana River red colobus have been declining over the past ten years due to extensive forest fragmentation.[23] While it may be possible to protect certain species from threats such as poaching, decreasing wildlife habitat portends a more intractable crisis.

The irreversible degradation of natural resources undermines prospects for economic development. Thus issues of management of and access to natural resources are of relevance to the short-term and long-term development of the country. These are not only economic issues, nor issues for resource management specialists alone. The sustainable management of natural resources depends in large part on the governance systems which define the relations between people, and between people and the resources, as discussed in the preceding chapters. In order to be able to address the question of how to increase the productivity and economic benefits of the country's natural resources, we must understand how access and rights to those resources are determined.

The concept of land tenure

The term land tenure is derived from the Latin word *tenere* which means "to hold". Generally, tenure is a right, term or mode of holding. Tenure defines the social relations between people in respect of the object of the tenure, in this case land. "Those with tenurial rights have a certain social status *vis-à-vis* natural resources in comparison to those without tenurial rights to those resources."[24] Land tenure defines the methods by which individuals or groups acquire, hold, transfer or transmit property rights in land. Property rights may include a variety of different rights (e.g., to use, to transfer, to build on, to mine, etc.) commonly referred to as a "bundle of rights". The rights may be transferred or transmitted either together or individually ("unpackaged") at the discretion of the holder with or without limitations, depending on the tenure system. Formal rules of tenure, therefore, define the nature and content of property rights and determine how society will allow individuals or groups to hold property rights in land or other resources and the conditions under which those rights are to be held and enjoyed.

Land tenure is both culture-specific and dynamic. It is culture-specific because it is determined by the history, social organization and land-use patterns of a given community which reflect, among other things, the ecological characteristics of the region. Pre-feudal African societies, characterized by diffuse political systems, kinship bonds, shifting cultivation and pastoralism, thus developed tenure systems whose main focus was to guarantee rights of access to individuals or families and to invest relevant political entities with rights of control over allocation and land-use. In the post-Norman Conquest feudal England, all land was vested in the king, who granted interests therein to his subjects. The subjects held land of the king.

Land tenure is a dynamic system which responds to social change. In Africa, there are many instances where the system of guaranteed rights of access and overlordship by political entities has slowly broken-down as a response to the emergence of modernizing centralized states, population pressure on limited arable land, and the development of new land-use patterns. The private property rights system of industrialized Western societies, developed under *laissez-faire* capitalism, has had to increasingly accommodate an ever-expanding concept of *police power* in response to the changing public health and welfare imperatives of those societies.[25] It is this dynamism that provides a basis for integrating environmental considerations into land tenure systems.

Land tenure and environment

Land is not just another form of property that can be appropriated and used at the absolute discretion of individuals or groups without regard to wider social and ecological interests. Land is essential for our food production and security. Sustainable agricultural development is critically linked to questions of access to, utilization and husbandry of land resources. In addition, land embodies, nurtures, or supports important biological resources and processes. In this respect, it forms part of intricate natural systems that guarantee essential ecological processes. These attributes transcend the property rights of individuals or groups over particular parcels of land both in terms of space and time.

The rules governing access to land resources and the manner of their current use will affect not only the welfare needs of present and future generations but also the ecological status of the natural systems of which land is part. In effect, the nature and quantum of property rights society invests in individuals or groups and the manner in which those rights are exercised, have important implications for the sustainable use of land, the conservation of natural resources, and the maintenance of essential ecological processes.

It follows, therefore, that, in relation to the wider social and ecological interests, any definition of property rights should incorporate a sustainability or conservation ethic. Society must therefore retain overriding powers to *qualify* the property rights of individuals or groups in cases where this ethic is not respected. For, in the final analysis, land resources are vested in society as organized in the state for the welfare of present and future generations, and for the survival of humankind and other species.

Theoretical debates on the interface between land tenure and land-use and the conservation of environmental resources have centred, until fairly recently, on the virtues of private (individual) property rights and the inherent vices of "communal ownership". The perceived superiority of private property rights as a tool for the rational management of land and other natural resources arose out of and was buttressed by the economic efficiency paradigm.[26] The reasoning was that investing individuals with private property rights in land would contribute to and enhance proper resource management because individual actions are informed by enlightened self-interest. Adam Smith thus asserted: "A small proprietor . . . who knows every part of his little territory, who views it with the affection which property especially small property inspires and who upon that account takes pleasure not only in cultivating but in adorning it, is generally of all improvers, the most industrious, the most intelligent and the most successful."[27]

Individual ownership of land and other natural resources is thus seen as the most rational, efficient and productive way for managing those resources. Denman, a modern exponent of this theory, has thus forcefully affirmed that "[p]roperty rights [in the narrow sense meaning private rights] or rights analogous to them are in the last analysis the only power by which man can execute positive plans for the use of land and natural resources."[28]

B.D. Ogolla with J. Mugabe

What is ignored in this land-use theory is the fact that enlightened self-interest emphasizes short-term economic interests at the expense of wider and long-term social interests. In seeking to maximize economic gains, an individual invested with private property rights may not pay appropriate attention to the long-term sustainability of the resource nor to the impact of its use on the natural systems to which it is linked. In effect, private property rights in land may, in the short-term, exploit efficiently the productive potential of the resource but may be inimical to the imperatives of sustainable resource utilization and conservation.

In academic debates on how land tenure systems affect resource management, private property rights have often been juxtaposed to the so-called "communal tenure" or systems based on overlapping rather than exclusive property rights. Hardin writing in 1968, and basing his analysis on communal grazing, characterized resource use in such situations as the "tragedy of the commons".[29] Since the full environmental costs arising from resource over-use are shared, rather than borne by a single herder, he argued that rational herders will be tempted to increase their herds beyond the carrying capacity of the commons. The ultimate consequence is ecological collapse.

Hardin's thesis has now been largely discredited. In the first instance, as Ciriacy-Wantrup and Bishop have argued, Hardin confused situations of "open access" with "common property regimes".[30] The former is a common use situation characterized by an absence of defined property rights governing access and use, the latter is "a distribution of property rights in resources in which a number of owners are co-equal in their rights *to use* the resource."[31] In terms of the distinction, Hardin's hypothetical pasture is not an example of common property but of open access. Open access is characterized by an absence of regulatory mechanisms regarding resource use. In the context of scarcity and competition, resource degradation is indeed likely to result.

In the second instance, the common property regimes generic in Africa before colonial intervention, possessed in-built mechanisms of control with important implications for sustainable resource use and conservation. The use-rights of individuals and families were circumscribed so as to avoid over-use of common resources. There are many instances where, due to land-use patterns and ecological factors, common property regimes are the most economically and ecologically appropriate land tenure arrangement for the management of land and other natural resources.

The nature and structure of land tenure

Land tenure systems in Kenya can be classified as customary tenure, "modern" tenure, and public land tenure.[32] These systems have a direct effect either individually or in articulation, for land-use and the management and conservation of environmental resources.

Customary land tenure

The thrust of official policy since the middle 1950s has been to systematically replace customary or traditional systems with a "modern" tenure system through the processes of adjudication of individual or group rights under customary law and their registration. Nevertheless, though official policy is one of replacement, the process of adjudication and registration has been so slow (and costly). Notwithstanding nearly 40 years of implementation of the modernization programme, customary land tenure remains the most widespread and dominant tenure system in the country. Moreover, there does exist a remarkable persistence of customary norms, values and practices in areas where registration has been completed.[33]

Kenya is a diverse country in terms of its ethnic composition. One needs therefore to talk of multiple customary tenure systems rather than of a single customary tenure system. In addition, apart from the variations in norms and practices of each community, customary land tenure systems have also evolved due to demographic changes, the intensification and diversification of agricultural production, and climate and ecological changes. It is, however, possible to isolate certain dominant legal concepts that characterize most customary tenure systems.

First, individuals or groups, by virtue of their membership in some social unit of production or political community, have *guaranteed rights of access* to land or other natural resources.[34] Such access is an incident of membership, specific to a resource management or production function, and linked and perpetuated through continued participation in the process of production. Individuals or families thus claim property rights from political entities (chiefs, clan-heads, family-heads) by virtue of their affiliation to the group. The content of these rights are determined by status within the group and the performance of multifarious reciprocal obligations.

Secondly, *rights of control* are vested in the political authority of the unit or community. This control is derived from sovereignty over the area in which the relevant resources are located. Control is for the purpose of guaranteeing access to the resources and is redistributive both spatially and inter-generationally. Its administrative component entails the power to allocate land and other resources within the group, regulate their use, and defend them against outsiders. Historically, the locus of control was dependent on the land-use type and the social organization of the community.

Among the Luo, for example, land was held and used as a collective asset by the *jokakwaro* (lineage members). The common grandfather of this group was usually recognized as the land controlling authority. He allocated cultivation rights and controlled types and scope of use. With regard to land-use types which required more expansive access rights, for example grazing, rights were allocated and controlled by a council of common grandfathers (*jodong gweng*). Among the Nandi and Kipsigis, the *kokwet* elders (a council similar to *jodong gweng*) controlled all pastoral and agricultural land rights. Among the Kikuyu, allocation of land rights and the regulation of use was effected by the *mbari* (sub-clan level) or assigned to a *muramati* (the head of the family in charge of the land). In predominantly pastoral communities such as the Maasai and the Samburu, because of ecological constraints and the need for wider access rights, control was located in a larger social unit.[35] The social category may be a clan as among the Samburu or a sub-tribe as among the Maasai. Below this group there may be smaller units controlling what may be termed local resources.

Thirdly, rights analogous to *private property rights* accrue to individuals out of their investment of labour in harnessing, utilizing and maintaining the resource. Thus, there are no people with greater rights to parcels of land than their present cultivator. Their rights transcend mere usufruct and encompass transmission and, in certain communities, transfer.[36]

Lastly, resources that did not require extensive investment of labour or which by their nature, had to be shared, for example, *common pasturage*, were controlled and managed by the relevant political entity. These may be termed public lands or resources and every individual member of the political community has guaranteed and equal rights of access thereto.

The regulatory mechanisms imposed by the political units such as exclusion of outsiders, seasonal variations in land-use, and social pressure ensured sustainable resource utilization. The breakdown in traditional authority engendered by the systematic imposition of the institutions of the modern state has undermined the capacity of the political units that regulated land-use to effectively fulfil their regulatory functions. In addition, population pressure and tenure insecurity introduced into land relations by the process of land tenure reform have encouraged competition for access to land and other natural resources. These processes have, in many instances, transformed the common property regimes into situations of open access with concomitant adverse impacts on land-use and the conservation of natural resources. In our view, environmental degradation manifest in regions under customary land tenure is due largely to interference in rural resource management by a "modernizing" nation-state rather than the "inherent vices" of customary property relations.

The decline of the regulatory capacity of customary land-tenure systems implies that policy initiatives aimed at sustainable resource utilization at the local level must perforce focus on identifying, reviving and strengthening the traditional norms and institutions that propped-up the common property regimes.[37] It implies rethinking the role of the state in land-tenure and land-use issues at the local level; empowering local institutions to determine questions of access to and use of land and other natural resources; enabling women to own property and have access to land; and encouraging collaboration between state agencies and local-level institutions in the management of natural resources.

"Modern" land tenure

Exclusive property rights over parcels of land have been conferred on individuals and corporate entities through a process of land tenure reform. This was initiated by the colonial government in 1956 in the native reserves. Areas under settler occupation had been registered as freeholds or leaseholds from the early 1900s.

Colonial legislation and superseding post-colonial legislation outlines three distinct stages in the process of tenure reform.[38] The first stage involves ascertaining individual or group rights under customary tenure approximating to ownership, that is, the process of adjudication. Such rights are to be determined according to "native law and custom" and with the assistance of adjudication committees constituted from the inhabitants of the adjudication section. The second stage involves the aggregation of all pieces of land over which each individual or group has rights and the allocation to the individual or group of a single consolidated piece approximately equivalent to the several units, that is, the process of consolidation. The last stage involves the entry of rights shown in the Record of Existing Rights or Adjudication Register into a state-maintained Land Register and the issuance of a certificate of ownership, that is, the process of registration.

Land registration in the Native Trust Land Areas (now known as Trust Land and vested in the respective county council before registration) started in 1956 in Central Province. To date most of the agricultural regions with high potential, such as Central and Western Provinces (except for Busia District) and Kericho, Uasin Gishu, Embu, Meru and Kisii districts, have been completely adjudicated and registered.

With regard to the areas with lower agricultural potential, mostly arid and semi-arid parts of the country where the dominant land-use is pastoralism, a different registration system was instituted in 1968. This is the regime of the Land (Group Representatives) Act. Here, the registration of group ranches was viewed as a compromise between individual ownership and the need for access to wider resources in drylands. Under this system "communal lands" are divided into smaller units (ranches) which are then registered in the names of group representatives (three to 10 members) elected by the members of the group. Every member of the group has rights in the ownership of the group land in undivided shares. The members are entitled to reside therein free of charge with their family and dependants. The important point to note is that the members are supposed to make exclusive use of the group ranch resources.

However, the group representatives are empowered to mortgage or lease the property or part thereof for the benefit of the members. There is considerable movement across ranch boundaries as a response to dry conditions. Most ordinary Maasai do not observe land boundaries, whether of group ranches or individual holdings. Indeed many Maasai have been known to settle permanently with their herds in ranches in which they have no membership.

This system is now in transition. In the better-watered areas of Maasailand, individual ownership is becoming the norm. Besides, many areas which initially accepted group ranches are now pressing for subdivision into individual holdings. This pressure is coming mainly from the educated and wealthy Maasai. It has forced the government to alter its policy with respect to group ranches, at least in Maasailand. From 1990, the operative government policy has been to sub-divide existing ranches into individual holdings, issue titles thereto to individuals and stop further adjudication and registration of group ranches. In Narok District, two group ranches have been completely sub-divided and eight group ranches in the Kilgoris Division have been surveyed and demarcated for sub-division.

The current moves to sub-divide group ranches may portend an economic, ecological and a cultural disaster for the Maasai. This is mainly for two reasons. In the first instance, practical experience has demonstrated that faced with adverse climatic and ecological conditions the Maasai are unlikely to benefit from or respect the sanctity of private land holdings. The likelihood of constant herd intrusions into private lands in times of ecological crisis is therefore a real one. In the second instance, given the level of existing land-use technology, the nature of ecological factors in the area and the cultural context, land-use in the region will for some time demand wider access rights to land and other natural resources. Restricting access rights through the sub-division of group ranches and the creation of private property rights will not only imperil the existing pastoral economy but also adversely affect the cultural practices and traditions of the Maasai. The case of group ranches is discussed in more detail in Chapter 9.

Tenure reform has a number of important implications for the smallholder farmer. The Registered Land Act lays down the legal framework that governs registered land. It provides that the registration of a person as the proprietor of land vests in that person the absolute ownership of that land together with all rights and privileges relating thereto. Such rights cannot be defeated save as provided for in the Act and are to be held free from all other claims and interests. They are, however, subject to such leases, charges, conditions and restrictions shown on the Register and to the over-riding interests specified in Section 30. Those over-riding interests include rights of compulsory acquisition by the state and the rights of a person in possession or actual occupation of land. It is however stated that nothing contained in these provisions shall be taken as relieving a proprietor from any obligations or duty to which he is subject as trustee. But it is not mandatory that a person be described in the Register as holding land as a trustee.[39]

It is clear from the history of tenure reform and the relevant statutory provisions that the interest in land granted on registration is in the nature of a freehold estate. Registration was therefore calculated to transform the legal status of registered land from one susceptible to multiple customary rights and interests to individual absolute ownership. The process also converted land into a commodity which can be sold, leased, charged or mortgaged at the absolute discretion of the proprietor. Part of the rationale for the programme was that it would enable peasant farmers to have access to credit facilities on the security of registered title. The English institutions of mortgage and charge therefore became important aspects of the new property regime. However, financial institutions were granted wide powers of sale of charged property in cases of default in repayments. This has caused considerable difficulties to peasant families who often found themselves landless due to the imprudence of certain members, drought or other causes of default. The Government was forced to intervene and administratively restrict powers of sale of financial institutions.

Despite the modernization programme, customary property rights have continued to exist in the adjudicated areas. The provisions of the Registered Land Act have caused considerable difficulties of interpretation particularly with respect to the effect of registration on customary property rights and interests. Indeed, two interpretations have emerged in the High Court as to the precise impact of registration on these rights and interests; interpretations which the Court of Appeal has done very little to reconcile.

The dominant view is that registration of a person as an absolute proprietor destroys all rights and interests not noted in the Register.[40] The only exceptions are over-riding interests and beneficial interests under a trust. Customary rights and interests if not noted in the Register are consequently extinguished since they are not over-riding interests within the meaning of the Act. A section of the Court of Appeal has advanced this view further by asserting that once land is registered, not only are such rights extinguished but customary property law is also, by the fact of registration, ousted by the common law and statute.[41]

Apart from a few reservations on the ouster of customary law, given the history and objectives of tenure reform and the wording of the relevant statutory provisions, this is the correct interpretation of the effect of registration on customary rights. The intention of the reformers was definitely to radically change the traditional land tenure system and to redefine the content of property rights. The reform was calculated to introduce fundamental changes with respect to customary norms, values and practices. In this scheme the survival of customary rights after registration could not therefore have been envisaged.

However, a minority opinion in the High Court, which has also found support in the Court of Appeal, asserts that in settling disputes arising out of land registration, the vital consideration is to determine the capacity in which the "absolute proprietor" was registered.[42] If in the capacity of a trustee then he or she must be called upon to perform the obligations inherent in that status. Further, that there is nothing in the relevant legislation which prevents the courts from declaring and giving effect to a trust in relation to registered land. This is a mere restatement of, first, the protection of beneficial interests under a trust by the Act and, secondly, the inherent power of the courts to create a trust in order to prevent the perpetuation of a fraud or the unjust enrichment of the registered proprietor. The judges supporting this view have, however, invariably read a trust in all cases where the disputed land is former family or clan land and have subsequently ordered the rectification of the register to accommodate the interests of the plaintiff. This state of affairs has led Okoth-Ogendo to conclude that judicial attitudes now tend to regard the tenure reform programme merely as an "exercise in the regionalization of *land administration* rather than in the *privatization* of rights."[43] This attitude is understandable given the sort of iniquities which "absolute proprietorship" may occasion to a peasant society wholly dependent on land. However, its basic postulate that the programme was not designed to expropriate family or clan title but merely to guarantee it, is clearly misconceived.

The point to note is that the process of tenure reform and its aftermath have caused considerable confusion and insecurity of tenure in rural Kenya. In that milieu, land is still largely regarded as a collective asset. The predominant belief is that registration did not oust family or clan title. In areas of severe land shortage such as Central Province, and Kisii and Kakamega districts, there is a marked increase of disputes and litigation related to registered land. Registered title has been challenged on the ground that land is former family or clan land. Rights to cultivate and occupy land registered in the name of a family member have been asserted simply because the land is "former" lineage land. In most cases, such cultivation and occupation subsist without any legal disputes.

Another factor is the prevalence of land-use practices which are based on customary norms in areas where land has been registered. In some cases, land-use practices are driven by the diversity of soil types and the related crop diversity. Under such conditions, communities have continued to use customary rules of access to multiple sites instead of relying solely on their registered parcels.

It has been argued that the modernization programme has had a number of positive impacts on resource management. In general, there has been a marked improvement in land-use and environmental management in many areas after registration. A notable example in both Central and Western provinces is the development of agroforestry both for commercial and domestic purposes. Field officers emphasize the upsurge of tree-planting activities after land registration. This may, however, be partly explained by the fact that land registration eliminates communal sources of wood and therefore forces landholders to develop individual sources.

Land registration has also facilitated access to credit on the basis of registered title, at least for the medium- to large-scale agricultural producers in parts of Kenya. Remarkable improvements in agricultural output were recorded in the country in the 1960s and the 1970s. It has, however, been asserted that several factors (e.g., improved agricultural infrastructure, more purposive extension services) rather than tenure reform *per se*, have been responsible for improvements in land-use in the high-potential areas of the country.

At least two adverse impacts with regard to resource management have resulted from the creation of private property rights in land. First, there have been important and increasing instances of absentee landlords. Large tracts of land remain idle notwithstanding recurrent food shortages and landlessness in the country. Private property rights thus encourage accumulation and speculation thereby withdrawing land resources from productive use. Secondly, the dualism in tenure arrangements and the concomitant conflicts that arise from their articulation have had important implications for land-use and land-use decision-making. In areas not yet registered, tree-planting has largely been regarded as an attempt to assert title. In registered areas, the insecurity of tenure that arises from the articulation between the modern and the traditional compromises long-term land-use planning by title holders. In both instances, improvement in land-use is largely undermined.

One of the issues that is often ignored when dealing with land reform is its impact on women. In many societies women are the ones responsible for the management of natural resources.[44] They are often more involved in agricultural production and energy provision than men. Changes in land ownership often affects the ability of women to have access to land that was previously under customary tenure. There is ample evidence that land reform measures often reduce women's access to basic resources such as fuelwood.[45]

Public land tenure

Public land tenure refers to the phenomenon of the government as a private landowner. It originated from the Crown Lands Ordinance of 1902 which declared all "waste and unoccupied land" in the protectorate "Crown land". The concept of Crown land was redefined by the 1915 Crown Lands Ordinance to include land in actual occupation by the "natives". In 1938, the Crown Lands (Amendment) Ordinance of that year excised native reserves from crown lands. These were subsequently vested in an independent Native Lands Trust Board by the Native Lands Trust Ordinance of 1938. At independence, land in native reserves became Trust Land and was vested in the respective county councils which hold the land for the benefit of the residents. Upon adjudication and registration such land ceases to be Trust Land.

At independence, the 1915 Crown Lands Ordinance, as subsequently amended, became the Government Lands Act. By virtue of this instrument, government lands are vested in the President who, *inter alia,* has powers to make grants or dispositions of any estates, interests or rights in or over unalienated government land. Some of these powers have been delegated to and are exercised by the Commissioner of Lands. Interestingly, the framework of the Government Lands Act does not contain any notion of trusteeship as is the case with the Trust Land Act. Yet the public has an interest in the manner in which land resources vested in the government are utilized or disposed of. The government thus has some sort of *carte blanche* in dealing with such land.

The total area of government land is some 116,088 sq km. There are several categories of government land: forest reserves; other government reserves; townships and other urban centres; alienated government land; unalienated government land; national parks; and open water bodies. Some of the government land has been alienated for settlement purposes. By early 1990, there were about 302 settlement schemes in the country with some 2,182,360 acres. As population pressure on land outside the government estate has increased, there has been a tendency to alienate more and more government land for settlement. For example, between 1963 and 1971, a total of 48,000 ha. of government forest land was converted to agricultural settlement through official excisions under the Forests Act.

The regime of government land has constituted an important framework for the conservation of the country's biodiversity. The system of biodiversity conservation established both by the Forests Act and the Wildlife (Conservation and Management) Act follows the classical model of wrapping nature in protected areas that exclude other forms of land-use. In effect, the two instruments have vested designated zones under public control for the propagation, protection and preservation of wild fauna and flora. Forest reserves, national parks and national reserves are the product of declarations made under the two instruments regarding the use of un-alienated government land. The effect of these declarations is to exclude other forms of land-use and to vest monopoly rights of management and conservation in the government.[46]

The vesting of monopoly rights in the state has been justified on a number of grounds. First, biological resources such as forests and wild animals serve important functions and possess values that transcend the scope of immediate individual pre-occupations: the protection of water catchments, the propagation of species, the maintenance of genetic diversity on earth, and the conservation of representative ecosystems. A system of public control is therefore deemed imperative to assert the overriding public interest. Secondly, the management and conservation of biological resources entail the outlay of human, financial and technical resources far beyond the capabilities of the individual. Lastly, that state control is critical since it will ensure an effective and sustainable framework for long-term planning and implementation.

It is not in doubt that there are important public interest considerations in the sustainable management and utilization of biological resources. It is, however, questionable whether the public interest can only be served through exclusive state control over those resources. Exclusive control and legal prohibition of other forms of land-use may not be viable and sustainable methods of management and conservation. The current practice, except with game reserves under the county councils and national reserves under the central government, is to exclude other forms of land-use from protected areas. In the long-term, however, this exclusion implies that as population pressure on land outside the protected area system increases, there will be mounting political pressure to convert portions of protected areas into human settlements and agriculture.

Already large chunks of forest areas have been officially excised and converted to agriculture and settlement to satisfy the demands of adjacent populations. There have also been increasing incidents of illegal conversions by populations bordering forest areas. As regards game and national reserves, adjacent communities have opened-up more and more areas for agriculture and pastoralism thereby gradually pushing wildlife to smaller and drier areas.[47] The process has also severely circumscribed the space available for migratory species. Moreover, local communities around protected areas increasingly view wildlife conservation as a threat to their livelihood, with no tangible benefits at the local-level. There is an increasing need for new typologies of land-tenure and institutional arrangements that will harmonize the imperatives of conservation and the resource needs of local communities.

In the first instance, legal and institutional mechanisms whose net effect would be to divest the state of monopoly rights and empower appropriate local institutions to collaborate with state agencies in the management of local resources could be devised. The present arrangement where game reserves are vested in and managed by county councils under the overall guidance of the Kenya Wildlife Service could be generalized to other protected areas. The strengthening and use of existing institutions such as county councils would guard against unnecessary proliferation of institutions. The county councils would be required to manage the resources in trust and for the benefit of local communities. Appropriate controls could be imposed regarding the use of revenues derived from the exploitation of biological resources.

In the second instance, the present antagonistic relationship between local communities and protected area systems could be further attenuated by designing management typologies and tenure arrangements that will accommodate both interests. First, a graduated system for each protected area could be developed comprising an inner strictly protected core, surrounded by a limited-use area which is in turn surrounded by a multiple-use area. Secondly, the use of the protected area for agricultural and pastoral activities could be based on a tenure system that incorporates a conservation ethic. As regards agricultural activities, a leasehold interest, granted and monitored by the local authority, and conditional on the conservation of certain plant species, proper management of vegetation cover, and non-killing of wild animals could be an appropriate policy alternative. These arrangements will permit local communities to engage in productive human activities, maintain their traditional way of life, and participate in and derive benefits from the conservation of biodiversity.

The regulatory power of the state

In legal theory, the state has two types of residual powers concerning property rights.[48] These are *police power* and *eminent domain*. Under *laissez-faire* capitalism, the role of state and law with regard to property rights in land was seen as limited to defining formal rules of tenure. The actual planning and implementation of land-use were deemed the province of individual initiative, conceived of as the critical element in positive land-use decision-making. State and law assisted this initiative by conferring exclusive rights over particular parcels of land and defining the rules governing the transfer and transmission of those rights, that is, providing a framework for the operation of a land market.

The argument that land-use decision-making and implementation was the exclusive domain of landowners began to be eroded towards the end of the last century for two basic reasons. First, the realization that a particular mode of land-use may affect not only other property users but also the public interest led to the recognition of the concept of *public rights* in private property. State and law intervened by prohibiting or regulating certain forms of land-use to protect public health and safety (for example through public health laws, housing and town planning legislation and public nuisance laws). Contemporary concern and interest in environmental quality and the sustainable use of natural resources has over the years increased the domain of public regulation.

Secondly, the practical imperatives imposed by demographic changes, crises in food production, and the need for rapid economic development, particularly in the Third World, have demanded greater public and government concern and participation in land-use decision-making and implementation. The objective has been to maximize output from the resource base while guaranteeing sustainability over time. However, state intervention has not been limited to regulating land-use. It has included "regulatory takings", that is, the transfer of some private property rights to the public domain, hence diminishing the value of the remaining rights.

Eminent domain

This concept is derived from the Roman *dominium eminens* (sovereignty over territory). It is the right of the state or its assigns (in Kenya, county councils with respect to Trust Land) to take private property for public purposes, i.e., the power of the sovereign to compulsorily acquire land for public purposes. In neo-feudal theory, this right flows from the fact that the state has the *radical title* over all land in the territory and therefore as ultimate owner it can compulsorily acquire any parcel. In compulsory acquisition, the state merely resumes its original grant. The better view, however, is that the concept is an extension of that right of the state to interfere with private property manifest in police power. Eminent domain is therefore an incident of political sovereignty.

The public purpose doctrine has however meant that the state could only acquire land for "public" activities. Traditionally, these were limited to defence, highways, hospitals and education. In modern times, and especially in the Third World, the imperatives of economic development and the necessity of active state participation in the process has raised serious questions about such strictures. It was also accepted from the very beginning that the state must make good the loss occasioned to individual citizens. Modern constitutions therefore incorporate the obligation to pay compensation.

In Kenya, the power to compulsorily acquire land in the public interest is embodied in sections 75, 117 and 118 of the Constitution. Those sections, however, contain three important qualifications. First, the taking must be in the public interest in the sense that it must be shown that it will "promote the public benefit." Secondly, that benefit must be weighed against the hardship that may be caused to the owner. Lastly, the taking must be accompanied by prompt payment of compensation. Section 75 deals with compulsory acquisition generally and the machinery for the compulsory acquisition is embodied in the Land Acquisition Act. Sections 117 and 118 of the Constitution deal with the "setting-apart" of Trust Land at the initiative either of the relevant county council or the Commissioner of Lands.[49] The rules governing the "setting-apart" and the payment of compensation to affected residents are contained in the Trust Land Act.

Compulsory acquisition and "setting-apart" destroy any individual or group (family, clan, tribe) rights and interests in the affected land. However, the public purpose doctrine may be an important obstacle to the state's ability to acquire land for development and resource management purposes. It assumes that the legitimate domain of state activity is restricted to the provision of developmental infrastructure. It is therefore arguable whether the central government or the county councils can acquire or "set-apart" land for the purpose of the conservation of environmental resources. In our context, an extension of the *public purpose or benefit doctrine* to include environmental management is necessary.

In any case, it is neither practical nor fair to the entire social community to condition the fulfilment of an important social imperative such as the sustainable management of environmental resources on systematic state expropriation of private property rights and the payment of compensation to rightholders. What is needed is a reconceptualization of private property rights as incorporating a conservation ethic and a residual power of the state to qualify such rights where tenurial right-holders are in default.

Police power

The power of the state to regulate land-use in the public interest is known as *police power*. Its earliest manifestation was the accepted right of the state to interfere with private property through the taxation of its citizens. It found extension in the so-called "taking" of property for necessities of war, and the regulation of use or even the destruction of property in times of pestilence. In modern times, it has been invoked to secure proper resource utilization and management, such as regulation of filling of wetlands.

This power is an attribute of the sovereignty of the state; it is an incident of political jurisdiction over territory. Its exercise, however, does not extinguish property rights in land, it merely regulates their use in vindication of public rights. For this reason, though its exercise may affect the use and enjoyment of property, compensation for such interference is never provided for by law. In Kenya a number of statutes consecrate this inherent regulatory power of the state, such as the Public Health Act, the Agriculture Act, the Chiefs' Authority Act, the Local Government Act, the Land Planning Act and the Water Act.

The exercise of property rights in Kenya is regulated predominantly, but not exclusively, through land-use legislation.[50] Land-use legislation settles the uses to which land is to be put, seeks to accommodate competing legitimate demands on the resource, and ensures that stated resource management and conservation objectives are adhered to by holders of tenurial rights. In Kenya the relevant statutes include the Land Planning Act, the Agriculture Act, the Local Government Act, the Chief's Authority Act and the Water Act.

In legal theory, it can be argued that the quantum of property rights in land is ultimately a function of the scope of police power. The definition of the nature and content of property rights in the land registration statutes rarely takes this fact into consideration. Yet the scope of police power will determine the rights, powers, privileges, and immunities of the right-holder. There is, therefore, no such thing as an *absolute proprietorship*. Police power always circumscribes the freedom of action available to tenurial right-holders. The larger its scope, the more limited the nature of individual property rights in land and the wider the latitude the state has for implementing sustainable resource management and conservation policies.

A textual analysis of the Kenyan land-use legislation reveals an attempt by the legislature to invest state agencies with power to take measures that will secure sustainable resource management objectives. This is supposed to be achieved through land-use zoning and licensing procedures and the power to issue directives and orders to tenurial right-holders concerning land utilization and conservation. In practice, however, ineffective implementation of these requirements and the limited nature of sanctions attached to non-compliance have given the impression that tenurial right-holders have unlimited rights of use and abuse. The idea of *public rights* in private property is largely down-played and some kind of *laissez-faire* attitude pervades the Kenyan land-use management and conservation scene.

The Land Planning Act regulates land use through the application of the police power. Rational planning of the uses to which land is put is important for two basic reasons. First, productive land resources are becoming increasingly scarce, particularly in developing countries, due to urbanization, land degradation and pollution.[51] Land-use planning is imperative for sustainable development in the context of a limited resource. Secondly, land-use often entails the generation of environmentally adverse side-effects. Land-use controls are therefore necessary to anticipate and pre-empt such negative impacts.

Land-use planning and zoning have thus become important tools in contemporary national policies regarding environmental management and conservation. The basic components of these processes consist of the evaluation of land, the alternative patterns of land-use and other physical, social and economic parameters, and the selection and adoption of land-use types compatible with sustainable resource utilization and environmental conservation objectives. The zoning process facilitates the allocation of land to competing legitimate demands according to ecological and economic parameters. Thus, the whole country or a region may be divided by a land-use plan into broad land-use categories such as residential, industrial, agricultural, forestry or nature conservation areas. In effect, only uses compatible with stated environmental or developmental objectives will be allowed in designated zones.

Kenya's policy documents do recognize the centrality of land-use planning in the country's overall development strategy. One of the major constraints has been the absence of a natural resources inventory to facilitate the process of evaluation and allocation. The government has therefore proposed the establishment not only of a land capability survey but also of a land-use committee to advise it on the most appropriate use where there is an apparent conflict between alternative uses. Currently an inventory of natural resources is being built by the Department of Resource Surveys and Remote Sensing in the Office of the Vice-President and Ministry of Planning and National Development. However, no land-use committee has so far been set up by the government.

Although relevant legislation such as the Land Planning Act and the Town Planning Act exist for the purpose of land-use planning, they are primarily concerned with planning of urban centres and the development of such physical facilities as roads, buildings and factory location. Yet the powers vested in relevant agencies are wide enough to cover land-use planning and zoning for the whole country. In effect, local authorities and the Physical Planning Department have power not only to prepare town plans but also area plans. The former are supposed to ensure co-ordinated economic land-use for development projects within a satisfactory urban environment. The latter ought to offer, in the context of country planning, a broad framework for accommodating competing land-use demands and hence guidance on resource allocation to those uses. But objectives have not been fully realized in practice.

First, no area plans have been formulated of the various ecological regions of the country. Land-use and development are therefore haphazard and land-use decision-making largely *ad hoc*. Secondly, notwithstanding the emphasis in practice on town planning the government does admit that land-use inside the urban centres has sometimes been at variance with the approved plans or is unauthorized and unorganized. The result has been a proliferation of slums in Kenya's major towns, thereby impinging on the available physical facilities (sewage systems, water supplies, etc.) and posing a serious danger to public health.

The techniques of the law in the pursuit of rational land-use are markedly traditional: the use of prohibitions and restrictions to control undesirable uses or unauthorized change in use. Thus, relevant planning regulations prohibit the initiation of development without the prior consent of the relevant authorities. The permit system is supposed to ensure that land development is in accordance with the relevant plans. Failure to observe the conditions attached to the permits may lead to the withdrawal of consent and the demolition of unauthorized developments. Whereas the legislation is capable of accommodating the current world-wide trend of "positive" planning (or growth management) which encourages and promotes economic land uses that are compatible with rational environmental management, the practice of planning in Kenya is still restricted to urban settlements.

In contrast, the post-Stockholm land-use legislation in some developing countries, for example, the 1974 Colombian Environment Code and the 1983 Algerian Loi Relative a la Protection de l'Environnement, increasingly rely on land-use management plans to secure the objectives of sustainable resource management and utilization. These laws establish special management areas and define the specific authorized uses for each area rather than impose prohibitions concerning land-use activities. Under the Colombian Code such areas include integrated management districts, water management areas, soil conservation districts, and various categories of national parks. The Algerian Law provides for the establishment of nature reserves and national parks for the conservation not only of fauna and flora, as is the case in Kenya, but also of the soil, water and the natural environment in general. In addition, whereas the establishment of such protected areas may be accompanied by certain prohibitions regarding land-use activities, provision is made for the declaration of buffer zones around the protected area systems, where measures for social, economic and cultural development are to be implemented for local communities by the relevant state agencies.

The Agriculture Act is another example of the use of the police power. The stated objectives of the Act are to promote and sustain agricultural production, provide for the conservation of the soil and its fertility, and stimulate the development of agricultural land in accordance with the accepted practices of good land management and good husbandry. Wide discretionary powers are, consequently, vested in the minister responsible for agriculture, concerning the preservation, utilization and development of agricultural land. Regulations made under these enabling provisions proceed by way of prohibitions regarding land usage and practices inconsistent with the objective of good husbandry. Authorized officers are empowered to prohibit the clearing of vegetation and the depasturing of livestock and to require, under pain of criminal proceedings, the planting of trees to protect the soil from erosion. The director of agriculture is authorized to issue *land preservation orders* to landowners requiring the undertaking of conservation measures or prohibiting activities incompatible with good land management. A whole range of environmental conservation measures can be implemented under this provision. Thus, the director may prohibit the clearing of vegetation or the grazing of livestock in vulnerable ecosystems, require the afforestation of land to reclaim areas threatened with degradation or demand the use of farming techniques compatible with conservation requirements.

The framework of the Agriculture Act has not been very effective mainly for two reasons. First, the scarcity of good agricultural land and demographic pressure on available land has made legal prohibition an ineffective tool in regulating improper land-use practices. Secondly, the law neither offers incentives for proper land-use practices nor encourages free public participation in their implementation. The population is thus neither sufficiently sensitized to the benefits of good land management nor voluntarily associated in the pursuit of that objective. The command and control posture of the law is thus its greatest liability.

The Water Act provides for far-reaching application of the police power in the water resources sector. It lays out the legal framework for the conservation, control, apportionment and use of the water resources in Kenya. The Act vests every body of water under or upon any land in the government. In effect, property rights in any land are subject to the overriding rights of the state with regard to surface or ground water. Indeed, the legislation vests in the minister responsible for water affairs powers for both compulsory acquisition of land (extinction of property rights) and regulation of property rights in land where these measures are considered essential for the conservation and proper management of water resources.

The minister can compulsorily acquire land where he or she deems it necessary for the conservation, improvement or use of water. Such acquisition is to be construed as compulsory acquisition under the Land Acquisition Act. The provisions of the Act concerning "public benefit" and compensation would, therefore apply automatically.

The regulatory powers of the minister include the power to declare "protected water catchment areas" for the implementation of special measures for the protection of water resources in a given area; the power to construct and maintain in any land works for the protection of the sources or course of any body of water; and the power to issue "conservation area orders" for the protection and conservation of groundwater supplies. On the basis of a declaration of a protected water catchment area, the minister can by order require, regulate or prohibit specific activities in an area. Thus, programmes for enhancing and protecting water catchment areas can be implemented under this provision.

A system of permits for the construction of wells is established for areas in which the minister has issued a conservation order for the protection and conservation of groundwater supplies. It should be noted that where the minister decides to construct and maintain—in the public interest—works for the protection of the source or course of any body of water, it is required that compensation be paid to the land owner affected.

The Local Government Act and the Chiefs' Authority Act are the two final areas where the police power can be extensively exercised. County councils have broad enabling powers under the Local Government Act to regulate land-use in trust land areas under their jurisdiction. These powers comprise the declaration and management of forest reserves and land management in areas actually occupied by the residents. County council by-laws made under Section 201 may empower the councils to prohibit or require the performance of specified activities. Several county councils have consequently declared certain areas within their jurisdictions forest reserves and enacted by-laws for their management. The by-laws employ the same regulatory techniques of the Forests Act. Nevertheless, some by-laws do recognize residual rights of the local communities. For example, the by-laws promulgated by the Narok County Council allow "indigenous residents" to graze their cattle in specified forest reserves.

Section 147 of the Act empowers local authorities to control the cutting of timber and the destruction of trees and shrubs; to prohibit the wasteful destruction of the vegetation cover; and to require afforestation activities within their jurisdiction. Indeed, in certain districts, for example Kericho and Nakuru, local authorities have taken the initiative to ban the production of charcoal under these provisions.

The Chiefs' Authority Act is basically a law and order instrument which defines the powers and functions of administration officials. It is a legacy of the colonial administration and is therefore essentially authoritarian in character. Compulsion and repression are its primary legal techniques. In relation to land-use and the conservation of environmental resources, two sets of provisions are of particular interest. In the first instance, chiefs are empowered to issue orders regulating or prohibiting the cutting of timber and the destruction of the vegetation cover; controlling grass fires; and restricting or prohibiting grazing. In the second instance, the minister may authorize chiefs to issue orders requiring communal work for the conservation of natural resources within their jurisdiction. These provisions are being used by locational, divisional and district environmental committees constituted under the provincial administration to enforce environmental conservation measures. Administration officials have regularly employed them to ban charcoal production and to implement soil conservation measures within their jurisdictions.

The authoritarian character of the statute and its colonial past are major constraints to the implementation of long-term resource management and conservation policies. Its framework does not accommodate *free* public participation in resource conservation activities. It may therefore engender a negative attitude towards such measures. In the long-term, a participatory and incentive-based legal framework may contribute more to sensitizing the population to the imperatives of sustainable development than such command-and-control legislative machinery.

Conclusion

Land tenure systems have important implications for the sustainable use of natural resources for economic development and the maintenance of the ecological processes essential for the survival of humankind and other species. In Kenya, existing land tenure arrangements have contributed in no small measure to environmental degradation and the unsustainable use of land and other natural resources. This has arisen mainly from: the dominant postulate that unrestricted private property rights are imperative for rational land-use decision-making and management; the decline in the regulatory attributes of common property regimes; and the misconception concerning public rights in private property and the attendant ineffectual nature of state regulatory functions and powers.

Alternative land tenure and land-use policies (including legislation delimiting the scope and exercise of police power) should aim at defining property rights in a manner that incorporates the conservation ethic. They should also aim to devolve control over natural resources to local communities and encourage appropriate local-level institutional and normative regimes for sustainable resource management. Empowering society, as organized in the state, to *qualify* property rights in cases where the ethic of sustainable use is breached by tenurial right-holders should also be a goal of such new policies. These proposals may seem radical. However, the imperative of sustainable development requires fundamental changes in our conception of society, its organization, and its production and consumption activities.

Notes

1. Republic of Kenya, 1994a.
2. Nyeki, 1992.
3. Republic of Kenya, 1994b.
4. Republic of Kenya, 1992a, 1994a.
5. Republic of Kenya, 1993a.
6. Mugabe, 1994.
7. Kenya Wildlife Service Databank, 1992.
8. Nyeki, 1992, p. 60, 68–69.
9. Nyeki, 1992; Mugabe, 1994.
10. Republic of Kenya, 1992b.
11. It should be noted that the volume of wood consumed is increasing every year as a result of growing demand. More wood is being processed into charcoal to provide energy for urban households, particularly those with relatively low incomes.
12. Republic of Kenya, 1993a.
13. Republic of Kenya, 1993a.
14. KENGO, 1989.
15. Mugabe, 1994.
16. Republic of Kenya, 1993a
17. Republic of Kenya, 1994a.
18. Darkoh, 1990.
19. KENGO, 1989.
20. IUCN/UNEP, 1986.
21. Nyeki, 1992. Major efforts by KWS during the 1990s have reversed these trends in many cases. However, the decrease in wildlife habitat continues.
22. See KWS News, March 1992 (newsletter of the Kenya Wildlife Service).
23. IUCN, 1990.
24. Lynch and Alcorn, 1994, p. 373.
25. Karp, 1993, p. 735.
26. Karp, 1993, p. 746.
27. Cited in Okoth-Ogendo, 1974, p. 13.
28. Denman, 1969.
29. Hardin, 1968, p. 1243.
30. Ciriacy-Wantrup and Bishop, 1975, p. 713.
31. Ciriacy-Wantrup and Bishop, 1975, p. 714.
32. Lynch and Alcorn (1994) propose an alternative typology of property rights which distinguishes between individual and group rights on the one hand, and public and private ownership on the other. This typology is relevant here due to the overlap of types often observed, and their evolutionary character. Their typology provides "four tenure combinations: private individual, private group, public individual, and public group," where "public" refers to the

government. This is a useful approach because "private ownership is usually deemed synonymous with individual ownership, when, in fact, group ownership can also be private." They also note that the generally accepted typology—private, common, state/public, and open access—"requires that community-based tenurial systems that include both individual and group rights must be disentangled and separated before any of these rights can be recognized by the nation-state concerned." (pp. 375–376).

33. See Okoth-Ogendo, 1979b.
34. Okoth-Ogendo in agreement with V.G. Sheddick argues that a useful scheme for analyzing African land relations is to distinguish between rights of *access* to land and rights of *control*. See Okoth-Ogendo, 1979b; Sheddick, 1954.
35. Grandin, 1987.
36. See Elias, 1956; Gluckman, 1965.
37. On local-level common property management institutions and the viability of such institutional arrangements, see generally Lawry, 1990.
38. The relevant instruments are the Land Adjudication Act, Land Consolidation Act and Land (Group Representatives) Act.
39. *Mwangi Muguthu* v. *Maina Muguthu* H.C.C.C. No. 377/1968.
40. See *Selah Obiero* v. *Orego Opiyo* (1972) EA 227; *Esiroyo* v. *Esiroyo* (1973) EA 388; *Belinda Murai & Drs* v. *Amos Wainaina.* C.A. No. 46/1977.
41. *Belinda Murai & Drs* v. *Amos Wainaina.* C.A. No. 46/1977.
42. *Mwangi Muguthu* v. *Maina Muguthu. Op cit.*; *Samuel Thata Misheck & Drs* v. *Priscilla Wambui & Anor* H.C.C.C. No. 1400/1973; *Edward Limuli* v. *Marko Sabayi* H.C.C.C. No. 22/1978; *Alan Kiama* v. *Ndia Muthunya & Ors* C.A. No. 42/1978.
43. Okoth-Ogendo, 1987, p. 228.
44. Khasiani, 1992; Sigot, Thrupp and Green, 1995.
45. See, for example, Loudiyi and Meares, 1993.
46. It should be noted that total exclusion applies only to forest reserves and national parks. National and game reserves are relatively large conservation areas where various degree of human activities, compatible with conservation imperatives, are allowed.
47. UNEP and KWFT, 1988.
48. See generally, Becker, 1977; Sax, 1971; Sax, 1984; Epstein, 1985. See also Chapter 3 of this book.
49. "Setting-apart" of land under the Trust Land Act has the same legal effect as compulsory acquisition under the Land Acquisition Act.
50. Other important legal frameworks that regulate the exercise of property rights are the Public Health Act and legal provisions relating to public nuisance.
51. See Wilkinson, 1985.

Land tenure and soil conservation

5

PETER ONDIEGE

Introduction

Most developing countries are currently confronted by the urgent need to halt and reverse land degradation and to introduce sustainable agricultural production systems. A number of these countries, especially in sub-Saharan Africa, are not producing adequate food to be self-sufficient although they have the potential to do so. Intensification of agriculture is seen as a means of redressing this problem, but it may have a negative impact on the natural environment. Land tenure types and policies tend to determine the nature of agriculture and also influence the effectiveness of land conservation programmes and policies. In order to achieve sustainable agriculture, countries will need to adopt strategies and tenure policies that promote the conservation of natural resources during the development process.

Developing countries can meet the challenge of sustainable agriculture by addressing critical issues of degradation of cultivated and range lands as a result of soil erosion, salinization and acidification, deforestation and loss of biological diversity. These countries must carefully weigh the social and environmental costs and benefits of various options to improve the productivity of their agricultural systems. Such options include: intensive soil and water management, using improved plant varieties and animal breeds, applying chemical inputs and farm mechanization. Security of access to land, proper soil fertility and pesticide management, conservation and

117

utilization of agrobiodiversity and using agricultural systems and implements that are adapted to local environmental and socio-cultural needs could lead to sustainable agricultural production. Other urgent issues with broader impacts include water contamination resulting from poor management of agricultural chemicals and farms waste products, and waterborne diseases associated with irrigation. Policies for land-use and natural resource conservation with a long-term focus will be necessary to improve the productivity and sustainability of agriculture.

This chapter analyzes the relationship between land tenure, agricultural productivity and soil conservation. It shows that the ability of the state to intervene on private land can result in improvements in land management. It also points out the need to deal with land degradation on a larger scale than that of the individual farm. The experiences of Machakos District in Kenya are used to show how state intervention can promote soil conservation on private land using local and international resources.

The economic role of sustainable agriculture

The World Bank estimates that within the next 40 years, the world population will increase to nine billion and the food requirement will nearly double world-wide. In the developing countries, it will more than double.[1] To meet these increases, world grain production will have to grow at annual rate of 1.6% which is, however, less than the annual rate of 2.0% experienced in the past three decades. This high demand together with demand for other foods, fuel and fibre will exert pressure on all natural resources, especially arable land. This will lead to intensification of current food production areas and expansion into new areas. It will also affect demand for and supply of water, fish and timber.

This high demand for grains and other foods will put considerable environmental strain on developing countries which already face severe financial resource constraints. It will also require adaptation of production technologies. In Africa, for instance, environmental problems are likely to be largely due to livestock and crop pressures on marginal and fragile soils and steep slopes, especially in arid and semi-arid lands (ASALs). These areas are the only remaining agricultural frontier in most countries. Continuing conversion of land to agriculture and increasingly intensive land use systems combined with slow technological change signal serious degradation in the future. In addition, populations are rapidly increasing and household incomes are falling in much of rural Africa.

Figure 5 Crop distribution in Kenya

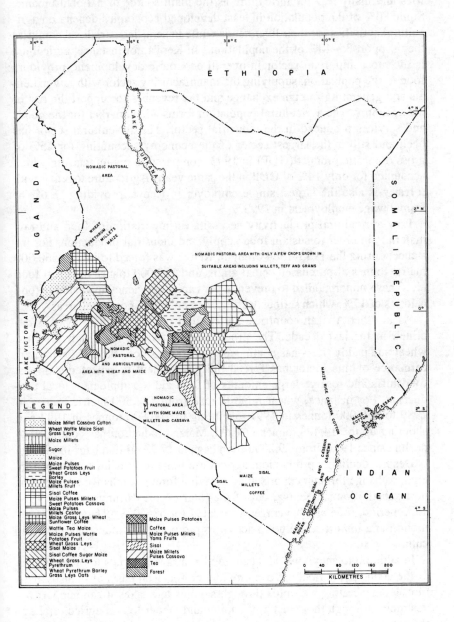

The agricultural sector is the largest employer in most developing countries and many rely on agriculture as the main source of national income. Some 80% of the population in least developed economies depend on agricultural activities for their livelihoods while in semi-industrialized countries they support 35–40% of the population.[2] In Kenya, for instance, agriculture is the most important sector in overall economic development, providing food to the population, supplying the manufacturing sector with raw materials and generating foreign exchange and tax revenues to support the rest of the economy. The agricultural population forms a key market for the goods and services produced in the industrial sector. The agricultural sector has been and still is the largest sector of the economy accounting for 25% of gross domestic product (GDP) in 1993, compared to manufacturing which accounted for only 14% of GDP in the same year.[3] Agriculture together with forestry is also the largest single employer in Kenya, providing 18.6% of formal wage employment in 1993.[4]

Low agricultural productivity necessitates importation of food and raw materials in order to sustain food supply and industrial production. For instance, during the 1983–1984 drought, Kenya was forced to import 560,000 metric tonnes of purchased cereal grains and 122,000 tonnes of cereal food aid. These imports failed to prevent a per capita deficiency in available food calories of 17%, which seriously affected people in remote rural areas.[5]

As in other African countries, agricultural production in Kenya has declined in the last decade. The production of food crops—maize, beans, wheat and paddy rice—has continued to decrease since 1989. The poor performance of this sector has forced the government to repeatedly import foodstuffs and receive large amounts of food aid to supplement local production. For instance, wheat imports rose from 123,500 metric tonnes in 1989 to 450,000 tonnes in 1991, declining to 100,800 tonnes in 1992 and shooting up to 314,400 tonnes in 1993. Maize production has continued to decline since 1989, from 29.23 million bags to 17.73 million bags in 1993.[6]

Despite declining production, agriculture remains a major source of foreign exchange through exports and by saving foreign exchange through import substitution. In Kenya, out of the total export earnings of the 1989–1993 period, food and beverages accounted for 53–60%.[7] Thus export promotion and import substitution activities promote both industrial and agricultural sectors.

In addition to supplying adequate food and raw materials to other sectors of the economy, agriculture can provide the financial basis of industrialization. By generating a surplus through savings and taxes it can support investments through the transfer of capital and labour to non-agricultural activities, especially important during early stages of industrialization. Development of non-agricultural activities plays an important role in reducing the pressure on natural resources by providing alternative productive employment. During early stages of development, the agricultural sector historically dominates, constituting the bulk of the national economy, labour and capital.[8] However, in the long run, non-farm activities must grow at more rapid rate than farm activities in order to allow for a transformation of the economy to that one is no longer dominated by agriculture. This model assumes that the income generated by the agricultural sector is used for investment in the modern industrial sector.[9] For industry to operate and function efficiently, it also requires a strong and a well-developed internal market which a sustainable and developed agricultural sector would provide.

Meier notes that it is possible for the agricultural sector to make large net transfers of resources to other sectors.[10] He argues that if these transferred resources were productively used, the rate of economic development would be accelerated. Hence, the agricultural sector has been seen as a source of sustained growth in the non-agricultural sectors, promoting employment and generating increased real income among the rural poverty target groups of small-scale farmers and landless labourers. .

However, it has been recognized that strategies based on the dual-economy model have failed to generate adequate employment in modern sector industries in most developing countries although a number of these economies have achieved high rates of industrial growth. This has largely been due to the capital-intensive nature of technology that these countries adopted; neglect of agriculture that has led to poor productivity; the unwillingness of the rural rich to be taxed; and rapid population growth rates that have outstripped the surplus generated by small-scale farmers. Most developing economies have increasingly come to rely on imports, foreign aid and borrowing to finance and support the development of their industries.

Current approaches to agricultural development increasingly focus on constraints imposed by land tenure systems and the associated social and political structures of village communities. These new approaches also address technical changes that have arisen from the Green Revolution technologies (especially as applied to grains like rice, wheat and maize) and their environmental suitability. These new approaches recognize the differences in the underlying environmental and technical conditions of different regions. The characteristics of agrarian society and agricultural technology are considered to be most significant determinants of industrial development based on the experiences of Southeast Asian countries, especially Japan, Taiwan, Korea and Thailand.[11]

Land tenure and agricultural productivity

Land is a crucial factor of production in the agricultural sector. In Kenya land uses such as agriculture, tourism, ranching, wildlife management, forestry and water conservation—each of which is a valid and nationally productive use of land—often compete for land and give rise to land-use conflicts.[12] These competing land uses and interests are exacerbated by the demands of the growing number of landless and the burgeoning population. The extent to which these will be resolved will depend very much on the appropriateness of the land tenure system and land-use policies.

The system of land tenure sets the context in which all efforts to raise agricultural output must operate. Land tenure will influence farming systems, social equity and agricultural productivity and hence overall economic development.[13] The tenure regime affects the welfare of the farming family as well as the prevailing degree of political stability. Gillis *et al.* point out that under tenancy type of tenure where an individual family rents land from a landlord, if the rent is too high the tenant family will have very little to feed itself or invest in improvements. Such cases occurred in Korea and China prior to land reform. They further argue that families who own the land which they are farming, as opposed to landless farm labourers and tenants, make efforts to conserve land resources and also tend to have a stake in the existing political order. For example, the landless in China and Mexico were moving forces behind the revolutions in those countries.

Land tenure systems fall into three basic categories: private or "modern", communal or customary, and public or state. A fourth category, open access, may also be observed where property rights have not been assigned or observed. Under the private tenure type property rights are assigned to the individual, while under a communal tenure system these rights are assigned to a group of individuals. The public sector controls the land under state ownership. The open access tenure type often results in lack of incentives or social norms to encourage the efficient use and conservation of land resources.

In Kenya, all of these categories co-exist, and in many cases overlap where conversion from customary tenure has been incomplete. "Modern" tenure systems are primarily absolute private proprietorship, with smallholder freehold tenure comprising about 6% of Kenya's land area in 1990 (Table 1). Public tenure obtains in the former Crown lands, which accounted for about 20% of Kenya's area in 1990 and includes national parks, forest land, unalienated and alienated land. The most extensive tenure type is trust land which is awaiting smallholder registration, comprising some 64% of Kenya's area in 1990. This diversity of tenure regimes has led to various forms of farming, such as large-scale intensive farming or ranching; plantation agriculture; family farms; communal farming; and tenancy. These types affect land use, conservation of land resources and the environment differently.

The Crown Lands Ordinance of 1902 established a dual society when the colonial government set aside 3.1 million hectares in Kenya for 3,600 European farmers.[14] This effectively established the "scheduled" areas (known as the White Highlands) and the "non-scheduled" (or African) areas. The colonial government of Kenya further influenced the current system of land ownership by carrying out land reforms in the non-scheduled areas. The government's Swynnerton Plan of 1954 initiated the change. The objective was to intensify the development of African agriculture in Kenya by concentrating land in the hands of the more efficient producers.[15] The plan also lifted the ban on Africans producing high-value crops such as tea, coffee and dairy products.

Table 1 Land tenure in Kenya, 1980 and 1990 (sq km)

TYPE OF TENURE/	1980	1990	1990 (%)
Government Land	**117,878**	**116,068**	**19.9**
Forest reserves	9,125	9,116	1.6
Other government reserves	1,245	1,970	0.3
Townships	1,911	2,811	0.5
Alienated land	37,013	38,546	6.6
Unalienated land	34,858	28,598	4.9
National parks	22,653	24,067	4.1
Open water	11,073	10,960	1.9
Freehold Land	**7,135**	**8,731**	**1.5**
Smallholder schemes	5,016	6,615	1.1
Other	2,119	2,116	0.4
Trust Land (not for registration)	**34,965**	**59,625**	**10.2**
Forest	7,092	7,084	1.2
Government reserves	443	492	0.1
Townships	1,398	1,812	0.3
Alienated land	13,915	33,397	5.7
Game reserves	9,285	13,691	2.4
National parks	2,832	3,149	0.5
Trust Land (for smallholder registration)	**425,341**	**397,366**	**68.2**
Already registered	27,217	27,279	4.7
Not yet registered	398,124	370,087	63.5
Total Water	**11,230**	**11,230**	**1.9**
TOTAL AREA	**582,646**	**582,646**	**100**[16]

Source: Republic of Kenya, *Statistical Abstracts*, 1983 and 1991.

The Swynnerton Plan was to provide African farmers with sound agricultural development based upon a system of land tenure that availed to them land and a farming system which would support their families. The plan aimed to consolidate fragmented and dispersed pieces of land that African families cultivated within the non-scheduled areas.[17] This approach led to individualization of land holdings in Kenya's arable areas and to an increase in the number of landless families. The process of land adjudication began in Central Province in 1953 and lasted until 1963. From there it was to be continued in the other parts of the country; the process is still being undertaken by the current government. After 1962 most of the resources of the Department of Agriculture were used for establishing settlement schemes which resulted in transferring 1.5 million acres of land owned by 1,325 European farmers to 66,319 African families between 1961 and 1975.[18] This could have contributed to the slowing down of the land consolidation processes in the rest of the country.

Small-holdings dominate the Kenyan landscape; in 1992 the number of small-holdings in Kenya was 2.7 million.[19] The majority of these have no title deeds (see Table 1) though they may have security under a customary tenure system. By the end of 1992, the government had issued 2,127,968 title deeds in the whole country out of which some 90% were issued in the medium and high-potential areas.[20]

Did the consolidation and registration process in fact increase agricultural productivity? During the 1970s and 1980s there has been a growing debate about whether indigenous land tenure systems constrain transformations in the agricultural sector. One school of thought views the traditional tenure as a static limitation on agricultural development as it does not provide adequate tenure security to induce farmers to make investments which would improve productivity. Other scholars argue that the indigenous tenure system are dynamic in nature and evolve in response to changes in factor prices.[21] This latter school of thought argues that there is a spontaneous individualization of land rights over time which allows families to acquire a broader and more powerful set of transfer and exclusion rights over their land as population pressure and agricultural commercialization proceed.

It has been argued that where land is owned communally, everyone has the incentive to use the land to the maximum extent possible but no one has an incentive to maintain and improve that land. For instance, Feder and Feeny observed that in Thailand farmers with land titles had a larger volume of investment, higher likelihood of land improvements, more intensive use of variable inputs, and higher output per unit of land as compared to squatters on state land. They further noted that farmers with title to their land had better access to formal credit and a significantly higher market value for their land when compared to the squatters. Where land is scarce and/or technological changes create new investment opportunities, they conclude that provision of property rights in land may enhance productivity.

However, Migot-Adholla and colleagues argue that empirical evidence from rain-fed farming areas in sub-Saharan Africa (Ghana, Rwanda and Kenya) shows that traditional African tenure systems have been flexible and responsive to changing economic conditions.[22] For instance, where population pressure and commercialization have increased, these systems have evolved from communal rights to systems of individual rights. Tiffen *et al.* confirm this view in their observation that by 1930 in Machakos ". . . customary tenure already recognized private rights, particularly in cultivated land."[23] This is reflected in the customary land nomenclature. *Kisesi* is grazing area to which one family claimed exclusive rights while in actual use, and *ng'undu* is a cleared and cultivated family farm which could be sold, inherited or loaned. Migot-Adholla *et al.* further argue that there is a very weak relationship between individualization of land rights and agricultural yields in the regions they studied in Ghana, Rwanda and Kenya.[24]

Further analysis by Migot-Adholla and others challenges the very foundation of the land titling programmes, concluding that: "[T]he effects of indigenous tenure institutions, through their effects on land rights, do not appear to constrain agricultural productivity. It is likely that farmers feel sufficiently secure in their ability to continuously cultivate their land, regardless of rights category."[25]

Other scholars have questioned the causal relationship between individual tenure and increased agricultural productivity.[26] These researchers argue that the increased agricultural productivity in Kenya seen during the 1950s and 1960s was due to the lifting of the ban prohibiting Africans from growing high-value crops, rather than introduction of individual land tenure systems to Africans. This event was accompanied by substantial investments in communications and transport infrastructure, improvements in extension services and establishment of credit institutions. It should also be noted that the lifting of the ban was accompanied by the implementation of soil conservation programmes which in turn required privatization of land holdings.[27] It is likely that increased productivity resulted from such programmes. For instance, Omoro notes that in Gura Valley in Nyeri District, Kenya, soil conservation measures on small private holdings were being maintained up to the present by the landowners because ". . . with proper care, the land would pay enough to make it unnecessary for some people to seek employment elsewhere."[28]

Agricultural production may also have increased due to the transition, in some cases by force, from pastoralism to intensive agriculture. Thomas-Slayter *et al.*, analyzing the case of Katheka in Machakos District, describe the colonial destocking campaign which pushed the Akamba into intensive agricultural production:

> When [World War II] ended, both the colonial conservation campaign and the villagers' resistance resumed. In Machakos, tensions reached a high point in 1951, when colonial extension officers established a livestock quota for each farm. The losses were sometimes overwhelming; several holdings declined from 500 to 15 head. In Katheka, the massive destocking marked the irreversible change in land use from that of agropastoralism to agriculture.[29]

They further observe that agriculture in this semi-arid area has not been completely successful:

> Farming is risky in Katheka even in the best years. Families plant knowing that drought may destroy their crops every third or fourth year. In such times many families buy most of their food; during the 1984–85 drought, 90% could not grow enough to feed themselves. In good rainfall years, 85% of the 57 households interviewed are self-sufficient in food.[30]

Lele observed that between 1970 and 1985, Kenya experienced an increase in total output and exports of its main agricultural commodities.[31] The share of small-scale farmers' production in exports and food output also increased substantially due to expansion of total cropped area and to a lesser extent, increases in yields. These increases were mainly from the medium and high-potential areas where individualization of land rights and soil conservation programmes have been carried out since colonial days.

The above observations show that individualized land tenure can lead to increased agricultural land productivity if combined with other factors. Evidence from Southeast Asia and Kenya's medium and high-potential areas between 1970 and 1985 indicates a causal relationship between individual tenure and increased agricultural productivity. But it is important to note that land reform in Southeast Asian countries was accompanied by promotion of new agricultural technologies, credit, farm inputs and efficient product markets. Rural infrastructure was provided in both cases.

Clearly there is little consensus among scholars on the impact of individualized land tenure on productivity in Kenya. Conclusions tend to vary depending on the period of analysis. For instance, between 1960 and the early 1970s production rose at a high rate which some scholars have attributed to land reform. In the highlands and high-density settlement schemes, small-scale farmers realized higher yields than those in the low-density, large-scale farms. In the 1980s and early 1990s, production levels have failed to match increases in population due in part to land tenure problems—such as continuous uneconomic land subdivisions—and poor agricultural and land use policies.

Figure 6 Location of case studies in Kenya

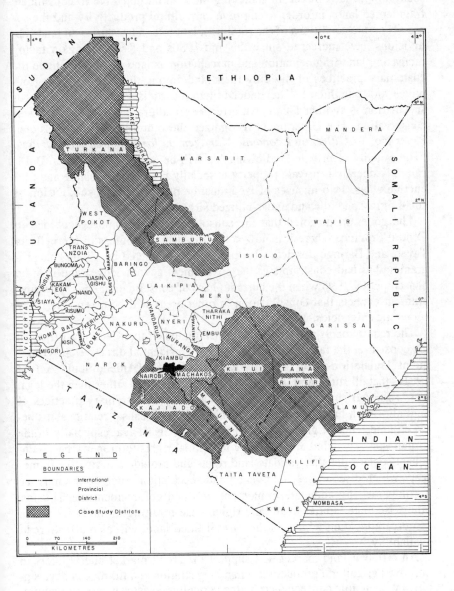

LEGEND

BOUNDARIES

International

Provincial

District

Case Study Districts

0   70   140   210
KILOMETRES

PETER ONDIEGE

Land consolidation and registration programmes which started in 1956 seem now to have failed in achieving their initial objective to consolidate fragmented lands in order to improve agricultural productivity and the socio-economic conditions of the rural population. Landlessness and land subdivisions have increased since the mid-1980s and Kenya is again facing increasing land fragmentation and parcellation as land owners continue the customary practices of dividing their land among their sons (leaving out wives and daughters). The under-utilization of large holdings held for speculation is another factor that affects agricultural productivity and soil conservation. The government recognized these problems in its Sessional Paper No. 1 of 1986 on *Economic Management for Renewed Growth* thus: "The sanctity of private land ownership will be respected in Kenya. But it can only operate if private property is socially used in responsible and productive ways. Two misuses of land must be prevented: The subdivision of small farms; and idle and under-utilized large holdings."[32]

The government noted that the consolidation programme succeeded in Central Province where it is now complete; it is in progress in Meru, Taita Taveta and Baringo districts which are to be completed by 1996. This programme has had constraints as the government acknowledges and is to be phased out by 1996 when the current phase of consolidation ends. The government expects that consolidation in other areas will be taken care of by economic exigencies.[33]

The requirements that individuals wishing to sell their land must first get the consent of the family members, and the Presidential directive and consequent legislation—the Magistrates' Jurisdiction (Amendment) Act of 1981—that all rural land disputes be referred to elders rather than the legal courts for settlement, show that some elements of customary practices of land allocation have been retained. This may mask causal relationships between land tenure rights and land productivity in Kenya, especially in the former non-scheduled areas. Secure individual rights to property need consonant social rules that validate land rights and provide a normative framework which discourages subdivision and speculation. Such norms must be accompanied by adequate implementation and enforcement mechanisms, otherwise uncertainties as to land rights arise resulting in inefficiencies in resource allocation which, in the case of titled land, will also affect credit availability.

An efficient land market will support the credit market and is likely to improve agricultural productivity. Land registration and titling can have significant economic consequences in the agricultural sector where agricultural development is related to the emergence of both formal and informal rural credit.[34] Accessing credit facilities usually requires the availability of explicit or implicit collateral which land may offer. The land's security and its transferability as seen by both the lender and the borrower must be ascertained. A unified land registration system provides a mechanism that can reassure the affected parties as long as there is a functional land market. If security of land tenure and transferability of land are not guaranteed, then productivity of land may not increase by mere individualization of land tenure as observed above. This must be accompanied by land-holdings being of an economic size, security of tenure, credit facilities, infrastructure development, new technologies, soil conservation and promotion of market efficiency.

Land tenure and soil conservation

Land tenure provides the legal and normative framework within which all agricultural activities are conducted. Through land conservation activities (such as soil and water conservation, agroforestry and revegetation) owners of land can preserve the object of their rights by refraining from use that could lead to its degradation and by taking action to improve certain properties of the resource.

Wachter suggests two broad types of land degradation. The first type is *over-exploitation* of land resources through over-grazing, overuse of fertilizers, soil erosion, soil acidification and salinization, overload of soil nutrients, and loss of agricultural land to other uses. The other type is *under-investment* in land which includes the degradation of existing components of land that are not maintained (such as irrigation works, terraces or tree alleys) as well as land improvements that are not made due to lack of investment incentives.[35] Factors that contribute to land degradation include: land tenure insecurity; population pressure; poverty; fragile ecosystems; inadequate price incentives; inadequate knowledge of appropriate technologies; and socio-cultural factors.

Tenure insecurity, whether under customary or statutory tenure regimes, undermines the conservation of land resources, as discussed earlier. Acute population pressure is likely to lead to over-exploitation of the existing productive agricultural land and its degradation, especially when there is inadequate adaptation of farming systems to the new conditions.[36] Soil degradation involves soil erosion, nutrient loss and reduction in organic matter. This in turn leads to reduced moisture-holding capacity and increased vulnerability to drought.

Another problem related to population pressure, soil erosion and productivity is overgrazing due to stocking levels and management systems which are no longer responsive to the rangeland ecology. This may be caused by reduction in rangeland area through encroachment of other land uses, or fragmentation or subdivision of group ranches or common grazing lands.[37] Where pig and poultry farming techniques are intensive, the likely impact on the environment will be water pollution and odour resulting from waste disposal unless increased livestock production is accompanied by strictly enforced environmental protection legislation.

Among the poor in developing countries are landless squatter households, nomadic pastoralists and tenant farmers. The majority of farmers in the developing world are subsistence farmers with low incomes who may not have the resources to sustain environmental conservation programmes. Poverty affects land by affecting the decision-making patterns of people. It reduces the time horizon of land users and discourages long-term planning or investment in land conservation. Socio-cultural factors also affect land degradation by influencing the behaviour of the agricultural decision-makers and their households.

Fragile ecosystems affect the status of land because large parts of the developing world are located in the tropical or arid areas which are more vulnerable to degradation. This factor is closely related to the other factors such as population growth and unequal access to land resources, which drive people into fragile or marginal areas.

Agricultural policies that distort input and output prices also contribute to land degradation. Subsidized inputs and high output prices can lead to over-exploitation of the land through land clearing activities, over application of agricultural chemicals or intensification without adequate investment due to lack of capital.

The land tenure system can provide incentives to use land in a sustainable manner, or invest in resource conservation, if tenure rights are certain. It can thus determine whether the economy will have a solid foundation built on sustainable agriculture. Titling of land will promote resource conservation if it is combined with increased tenure security, increased demand for and supply of credit and functioning land markets. An economic approach argues that "the establishment or strengthening of exclusive property rights to environmental goods will give resource users an incentive to take care of the resources and use them in a socially optimal way."[38] In the case of land resources, the users will have incentives to work and invest in land improvements and conservation and to take advantage of access to credit.

It must be noted, however, that while tenure security and credit may be developed through sound government intervention, land markets may still fail to function adequately in rural areas where traditional norms are strong. In addition, the above argument may not hold for the shared in-between pieces of land or common resources like river beds and valleys in the mountainous areas, as has been observed in Kenya.

Rocheleau argues that the individualization of land holdings through adjudication and registration resulted in the Ukambani region and its communities being more permeable to settlement, exchange and extraction by commercial interests from outside.[39] This led to strengthening of the integrity of individual holdings at the expense of resource management at the community and regional levels of integration. This also allowed the interstitial spaces at the local level to be more vulnerable to extractive use and damage by both local and outside commercial interests.[40] This individualization of smallholdings, she argues, undermined and eventually over-shadowed the legal and moral authority of community groups and cultural norms to govern the use and disposition of shared resources outside of well-defined private and public holdings.

An example of the predicament of conservation of common property within a framework of individualized property rights is sand collection from river beds in rural Machakos by the urban construction industry.[41]

Although Katheka has effectively confronted some of the technical and institutional challenges of ecological sustainability on a local level, villagers have been less successful with externally controlled forces. For example, villagers and mwethya groups are struggling with Nairobi businessmen to gain control of the area's abundant river sand deposits, vital to conserving dry-season water. To accumulate more sand and increase water retention capacity, the mwethya groups construct small rock dams across the river beds and in gullies. At one point in the early 1980s, up to 200 lorry loads were taken from Katheka per day. The water level has dropped in one elder's well from a constant 10 feet to 20 [feet].[42]

Sand harvesting is legal as it is authorized by Machakos County Council and permits do not specify locations. As elsewhere in Kenya, these kinds of activities generate much-needed revenue for local authorities. Yet they contribute to land degradation in the rural areas thereby affecting the agricultural productivity of small-scale farmers.

Brokensha and Njeru observed that in Mbere Division of Embu District, land adjudication changed land rights thereby affecting conservation of trees. Prior to adjudication the people were relatively free to make any reasonable and non-destructive use of anybody's land and the plants on it.[43] Trees were in most cases regarded as communal property. They note that out of 100 households surveyed only 22 said that land adjudication resulted in trees being planted and soil conserved. The Embu County Council was reluctant to reserve certain lands for communal use, resulting in the acceleration of the disappearance of sacred groves that would have remained as a last refuge of biodiversity in the district.

131

PETER ONDIEGE

State intervention

State intervention in soil conservation has primarily been through enacting laws to regulate the rights and powers over land that are conferred upon land owners by the law. The state has also directly promoted soil and water conservation by soliciting donor funds for conservation projects countrywide. Land use legislation in Kenya has focused on land exploitation (Agriculture Act), land control (Land Control Act) and land planning (Land Planning Act).

The Agriculture Act is intended to provide and maintain a stable agricultural system as well as provide for soil conservation through good land husbandry. It empowers the state to intervene in all types of land tenure systems to conserve soil and its fertility. The Land Control Act's concern is with land market regulation while the Land Planning Act is concerned with physical planning. The other related acts include the Water Act, Forests Act and the Wildlife (Conservation and Management) Act due to the relationship between soil, water, forest and wildlife conservation activities. The impact of these laws on soil conservation depends on how they are implemented and enforced and on the responses of the affected communities as well as land tenure and land-holding patterns.

Soil conservation programmes in Kenya can be classified into four phases: the colonial era of compulsory soil conservation (1930–1962); the period of rejection ("the lost years" of soil conservation (1963–1972); the re-introduction of soil conservation on the basis of land users' free-choice and with an on-farm focus (1974–1988); and the current phase (1989–present) which is a modified version of the third phase. The current phase focuses on active involvement of communities and the integrated treatment of catchment areas.[44]

Soil conservation schemes were launched by colonial authorities in Eastern Africa soon after realizing the seriousness of the soil erosion problems during the early 1930s. The authorities forced farmers to undertake conservation activities. As a result, conservation schemes and regulations became associated with the brutality of colonialism and were rejected by most countries upon gaining independence. In Kenya the government had established the Soil Conservation Service within the Agriculture Department by 1938.[45] Land degradation had reached alarming proportions in both the White settler areas and the native reserves. The settlers had applied inappropriate farming methods to the tropical soils. Population pressures in the African reserves was increasing rapidly largely due to alienation of land for settler agriculture and consequent reduction of land available for the African population. This resulted in a reduction of fallow periods in shifting cultivation and concentration of livestock on a limited range. A general sedentarization of population and intensification of farming practices resulted. The colonial government introduced urgent soil conservation measures in those districts with the most serious land degradation problems.

The colonial government had considerable success in constructing soil conservation structures, such as terraces and dams, and on-farm water management. But communities rejected their coercive approach leading to serious and accelerated land degradation during the period prior to independence and thereafter. There were increased environmental problems such as sediment-loaded rivers, siltation of dams, flooding and destruction of coral reefs and beaches. This was as a result of continued clearing of forests during the political emergency periods and for new settlements, and lack of maintenance of terraces together with increasing population pressure and settlement in drier areas. These off-farm environmental impacts of soil erosion had reached such alarming levels during the late 1960s and 1970s that the government became concerned. In 1970, President Kenyatta shared his awareness of the state of the environment while addressing farmers thus:

> There is vital need for farmers everywhere, whether in richly endowed or more marginal areas, to protect their land from soil erosion. This erosion can spring from destroying vegetation from slopes and hillsides, and its consequences, including flooding, can damage the homes and Shambas (farms) of people living far away. After each period of heavy rain, it is possible to see our rivers changing colour, as valuable soil is washed from the land and is swept away. This is an irretrievable loss to the nation, and in the long term could undermine the agricultural development on which the welfare of all our people depends.[46]

As awareness grew during the second phase of soil conservation (1963–1972) research focused on soil erosion processes and modelling. Research priorities included the off-farm impact of soil erosion, such as water pollution, dam siltation, destruction of coral reefs and beaches, and macro effects in the landscape such as landslides and gullies. Soil and water conservation during this period was not a political priority and the advances made during colonial period were neglected or destroyed. During this phase, soil conservation was taken to be synonymous with "stop erosion" and very little effort was made to relate erosion to land productivity.[47]

By the early 1970s land degradation was considered to be the most critical environmental problem in Kenya. Following the 1972 United Nations Conference on the Human Environment, the Kenya government requested help in soil conservation from the Swedish government. The initial project proposal drawn up by the Food and Agriculture Organisation (FAO) of the United Nations, to be funded by the Sweden International Development Authority (SIDA), was rejected by Kenya because the project was based on tractor service and survey by expatriates. Kenya was not interested in a mechanized project since it would not be applicable to small-scale farmers. The Kenya government instead proposed a soil conservation programme that would suit the local conditions. This was agreed upon in 1974.

The rejection of FAO's proposed conventional approach revolutionized the thinking in soil conservation in East Africa and has allowed it to be accepted by the small-scale farmer. In 1974 Kenya became one of the first African countries that had rejected or ignored soil conservation at independence to launch an extensive programme to check land degradation, implemented through the Ministry of Agriculture and Livestock Development.

The third period of soil conservation (1974–1988) started with the SIDA-financed soil conservation programme in four trial areas in Machakos, Murang'a, Nandi and Elgeyo-Marakwet districts.[48] This was extended to cover 39 out of 41 districts in the country by 1985. The objective of this programme was to convince, teach and assist farmers in soil conservation. The early periods of this phase isolated soil and water conservation from other farm activities; conservation officers and engineers were separate from the agricultural extension services. Numerical targets, such as kilometres of terraces, cut-off drains and waterways constructed and number of trees produced and planted, were set. The projects had large central nurseries producing millions of tree seedlings.

This new approach to soil conservation—based on the terrace model developed during the colonial period—became successful not only in Kenya but was also practised internationally. This approach was modified in the late 1980s to include listening to farmers needs; using agricultural extension staff and encouraging methods which did not require mechanization. A significant aspect of this approach was to encourage farmers to do all the work by themselves on their own land.

The current phase of soil conservation (1989–present) emphasizes land husbandry. Soil conservation had been mainly concerned with stopping soil loss on individual farm units, primarily by physical and mechanical means. Land husbandry addresses causes of land degradation and how to improve the sustainability of production. A land husbandry approach recognizes the central role played by land resource users in determining the health and long-term productivity of land resources.[49] The "catchment approach" currently used also recognizes the importance of collective action within a water catchment to deal with common property resources, such as water and common lands. It also encourages common decision-making regarding gullies, streams, paths and other in-between places which were disregarded by earlier private property-focused approaches.[50]

The Machakos case

The National Soil Conservation Programme which started in 1974 mainly focused on areas with high to medium-potential for agricultural production. By the end of the 1970s the ASALs, which account for about 80% of Kenya's total area and about 20% of the population, began drawing the attention of the government. A rapidly growing population had led to substantial migration into the drylands. In the more settled marginal areas the population pressure was resulting in soil erosion and reduced food production combined with drought-induced famine. As a result the government extended soil conservation programmes to the ASALs.

Machakos District is situated in the transition area between the dry southeastern lowlands and the wetter high central region bordering the capital city, Nairobi. It forms part of the lands inhabited by the Akamba, an agropastoral ethnic group, known as Ukambani. The district covers an area of 14,250 sq km, most of which has low–medium agricultural potential.[51] The district is a predominantly semi-arid area with a bimodal rainfall pattern. It experiences inadequate and unpredictable rainfall which on average provides no more than a 60% probability of getting the minimum rainfall required for a maize crop. This together with shallow soils, steep slopes and unstable surface soil structures make soil and water conservation essential for sustainable agriculture.[52]

Since colonial times Machakos has been known as a "problem district" due to perceived problems of over-stocking, soil erosion, over-population and drought. The concentration of population in the 1920s led to decreasing size of land-holdings and by the 1930s there was increasing individual land ownership in the district. Intensified soil erosion by the mid-1930s resulted in poor agricultural production and the need for frequent famine relief.[53] After 1945 the colonial government forced the resettlement of people from the hill areas to Makueni Division within the district, and instituted intensive soil and water conservation programmes. By 1950, the district realized a net surplus in maize production as a result of "successful" soil erosion control measures.[54]

However, this agricultural development was unsustainable as the soil and water conservation programmes failed to integrate the cropping and livestock components of the local farming systems.[55] During the 1940s, households in the district had inadequate food and could no longer generate adequate income through their livestock as they had done in the past. This led to out-migration and many Akamba men joined the army.[56] Migration within the district was primarily in search of land, still available mainly in the drier areas, while out-migration was in search of employment. This process continues up to the present.

Thomas-Slayter *et al.* describe how migration within the district led to over-population and over-stocking of Katheka village, starting in the early 1900s.[57] Due to the development of two large coffee and sisal estates by colonial farmers along the Kalala and Athi rivers some 10 km away by colonial farmers and the growing restrictions on access to prime agricultural lands throughout the country, many Africans were forced to migrate and farm marginal lands. As a result local grazing land in Katheka was reduced by 20–30%. By the early 1900s more migrants from Kangundo and other villages in Machakos began to arrive in Katheka and by the 1920s and 1930s problems of land degradation had become severe.

Meyers observes that by the 1930s all unsettled communal grazing land (*weu*) in the northern parts of the district had disappeared.[58] The remaining traces of the traditional practice of a basic kinship unit of a family (*musyi*) having exclusive grazing rights to an area of land not used for residence or lengthy cultivation (*kisesi*) in the northern and north-central parts of the district also no longer existed. All the available land had become subject to private claim. This eliminated the grazing lands of this agropastoral people, forcing them to accommodate their livestock on small delineated parcels. This both hastened the devegetation and erosion of soil, and undermined the economic and cultural foundation of the Akamba.

The privatization of land holdings in the district had been encouraged since 1938 when the soil conservation programme required the demarcation of land-holdings using sisal hedges. The traditional system where the elders of the community (*utui*) could indirectly veto the sale of land by refusing rights of residence in the *utui* to the buyer began to die. By now there is a fairly active land market in the district based on individual power of disposal.[59]

To meet the growing needs of a rapidly increasing population confronted with a diminishing resource base, the Akamba people have adopted various local-level strategies among which are soil and water conservation and income and employment generation activities.[60] Soil and water conservation works in Ukambani were constructed by communal work groups organized on the basis of the traditional clan-based *mwethya* self-help groups. *Mwethya* groups, predominantly comprising women, are involved in numerous conservation projects, such as, construction of water tanks, developing tree nurseries and controlling gully erosion, as well as building terraces on each others' land.[61]

Due to continued land degradation and poor agricultural productivity in Machakos, the district was designated a pilot area for the 1974 soil and water conservation programme. Machakos was chosen because erosion was a serious problem and the people were concerned with its effects on their crop yields; a suitable soil and water conservation technique (*fanya juu* terracing) was already well established in the district; and strong and active self-help community groups (*mwethya* groups) were ready and willing to work on land resource conservation projects.[62]

The district was also included in the EEC-funded ASAL development programme as the Machakos Integrated Development Programme. MIDP was launched in 1978 and focused on resettling people in the former large settler holdings ("scheduled areas"); promoting crop and animal husbandry; expanding community services; and promoting employment and income generating activities. MIDP also had soil and water conservation and provision of essential infrastructure and water supply components.[63] Rocheleau summarizes the development processes in the district and the rest of Ukambani as follows:

> [T]he region regularly recurs as a classic example of land degradation in accounts dating from the 1930s, and state policies have continuously been devised to address deforestation, overgrazing, soil erosion, fuelwood, and other perceived crises. Those policies, in turn, transformed the landscape and the lives of rural people, and sometimes generated new crises. After a century of colonial, national and international interventions, rural residents report frequent crop failures, livestock numbers are still depressed from the drought and famine of 1984, and food relief has become a permanent feature of rural life. At the same time, researchers note the successful rehabilitation and commercialization of farms in many parts of Machakos and widespread success of grassroots development efforts.[64]

Results of state intervention

State intervention since 1974 has led to vigorous implementation of soil conservation activities in most of the country. It is estimated that between 1974 and 1991, some 1.2 million farms have been conserved, constituting an impressive 45% of the total number of farms requiring soil conservation nationally. It is further estimated that from 1991 an additional 100,00 farms have been conserved annually. The SIDA-supported programme has also trained over 500,000 farmers and about 57,000 other persons including youth, community leaders, government officers and teachers.

In the trial areas, Eriksson concludes that:

> About 80% of the farmers in Machakos District immediately accepted the programme in word and deed when it was launched. After 10 years, almost

100% of farms had good terraces and well-maintained cut-off drains which allows farming on even steeper slope and this increased the area of arable land;

In Murang'a District, about all farmers accepted the programme and it even attracted the farmers from the neighbouring valleys. Within three years, 2,000 farms were terraced and after 10 years few farmers were observed to have neglected the maintenance of terraces. Most farmers said that maize yields had increased by 15%–50%. Some erosion had occurred in natural and artificial waterways without any conservation measures taken.[65]

Other areas in Central Province have also recorded successful soil conservation efforts. Studies of the programme have shown that agricultural productivity increased soon after terracing and that women and self-help groups dominated by women have been at the forefront of conservation programmes in Kenya.

The ASAL areas require different approaches to soil conservation as inadequate water supply compounds the problems of dryland agriculture. Water is considered to be the most crucial element for the success of the ASAL conservation programmes.[66] In the 1982 DANIDA-sponsored Mutomo Soil and Water Conservation Project in Southern Division of Kitui District it was not difficult to get people, especially women, to be involved in the programme. Availing water to residents of Mutomo eased the women's burden of fetching water and thereby gave them time to do soil conservation. By 1986, they had constructed 302 wells, rock catchments and dams in the division, usually using self-help groups of 25 to 30 people. They had also terraced 1,000 km and dug some 1,000 km of cut-off drains along the hills most of which are on private land and only 10% on public sites.[67]

Soil conservation achievements vary from area to area as seen in the preceding examples. For instance, in Elgeyo-Marakwet District which is high potential area, the farmers were less receptive to soil conservation when it was launched in 1974 while other districts were very successful. "In Elgeyo-Marakwet District, erosion . . . was not very obvious and the people were not very interested in terracing. The chief was also not willing to ask the population to participate in the programme so there was very little success here."[68]

In 1984–1985, Central Province accounted for more than 50% of terraced farms in Kenya. It was followed by districts in Eastern and Western Province while Nyanza Province lagged behind.[69] The best soil and water conservation record in Kenya is in Machakos District where over 70% of the arable land has been terraced.[70] Some of the techniques developed to combat land degradation during colonial times were effective. Although these were ignored during the period immediately after independence they were used again by the soil conservation programme from 1974.

Mwethya groups in Machakos District were active in soil conservation during 1976 and with the active support of government, they put up 32,072 m of cut-off drains. Most small-scale farmers began to use a total catchment protection approach from 1989. Participation in soil conservation has mainly been by *mwethya* self-help groups which form the contact groups of farmers; no payment is made to farmers for conservation work done. These activities have clearly resulted in increased productivity. For example, maize yields on terraced farms are higher by 50% when compared to unterraced ones. Where a whole catchment area is conserved, stream flow has improved and water supply increased.[71] The case study of Machakos and examples from other parts of Kenya have shown that active government involvement in soil conservation efforts in Kenya have resulted in increased productivity, and that women have played a crucial role in this through self-help groups and as individuals.

It should be noted that poor farmers, especially female-headed households, have benefited less from soil conservation activities. Because poor women are unable to find time or money to join *mwethya* self-help groups activities their land remains prone to soil erosion and with low productivity. These farmers need to be assisted so that they can also realise the benefits from soil conservation activities.

Conclusion

The SIDA-supported soil and water conservation programme shows that private ownership of land is not a prerequisite for soil conservation. But lack of private ownership may be used as an excuse for not conserving land. Where it exists, the system of communal and public (government) land ownership allows local chiefs to promote soil conservation even when farmers have no title deeds.[72] The Chiefs' Authority Act and the Agriculture Act strengthen their hand further, even in the case of private property. This authority may be used effectively to promote the public good. During this century soil conservation programmes in Kenya have had positive results. However, such authority may also be abused for private gain, as occurred during the colonial period and unfortunately continues to occur. The origin of this authority in the colonial regime and its purposes prejudice its use for the more constructive and focused aims of sustainable agricultural development.

After independence, chiefs and agricultural extension officers have generally had to convince farmers that conservation activities pay. They were assisted in this by major government investment in soil conservation programmes and the personal involvement of the head of state in promoting the idea of conservation for national development. It has been shown that land titling does not necessarily ensure that conservation activities will be undertaken by farmers (as in the case of Elgeyo-Marakwet). But some form of tenure security and a conviction that these activities pay will promote soil conservation.

The case of soil conservation in Kenya shows that, given the mandate, the government can play an active role in promoting environmental conservation on private property. It is also clear that private property as such does not necessarily result in either improved environmental conservation or improved agricultural productivity. For the government to effectively promote environmental conservation on a sustained basis, it needs the relevant constitutional mandate that would allow it to intervene on private land for the public good. In the absence of such a mandate, the private property restriction may create a situation where the possibilities for positive government support for the regeneration of natural capital may be lost. This should be done through legal mechanisms which maximize the public good and minimize the potential abuse of authority.

Notes

1. World Bank, 1992b.
2. Penelope, 1992.
3. Ondiege and Kiamba, 1994. Agriculture's share of GDP has slipped considerably, however. In 1965 it accounted for 35% of GDP while manufacturing accounted for 11%.
4. Republic of Kenya, 1993b.
5. Yeager, 1987.
6. Republic of Kenya, 1994a.
7. Republic of Kenya, 1994a.
8. Lee, 1971.
9. This model is known as the post World War II dual-economy model. Penelope, 1992.
10. Meier, 1984.
11. Feder and Feeny, 1991. See also Chalamwong and Feder, 1988.
12. Kiamba, 1994; Ondiege, 1994.
13. Gillis et al., 1983.
14. Wanjigi, 1972; Eriksson, 1992.
15. Swynnerton, 1955; Migot-Adholla et al., 1991.
16. Deviations in totals due to rounding.
17. The traditional practice of having access to a variety of land parcels provided the farmer with a diversity of soil conditions and crop potential. Farmers strongly resisted consolidation in some areas, particularly in Machakos, due to the damage that it would cause to their farming system. See Wamalwa, 1991.
18. Eriksson, 1992.
19. Eriksson, 1992. Small-holding is defined as those farms of less than 50 acres

but where the majority are not more than one acre.

20. Republic of Kenya, 1993a.
21. Riddel and Dickerman, 1986; Migot-Adholla *et al.*, 1991; Kiamba, 1994.
22. Migot-Adholla *et al.*, 1991; Migot-Adholla *et al.*, 1994.
23. Tiffen *et al.*, 1994, p. 65.
24. Migot-Adholla *et al.*, 1991.
25. Migot-Adholla *et al.*, 1994, p. 137.
26. Heyer *et al.*, 1976; Anthony *et al.*, 1979.
27. Meyers, 1981.
28. Omoro, 1987b, p. 6.
29. Thomas-Slayter *et al.*, 1991, p. 7.
30. Thomas-Slayter *et al.*, 1991, p. 8.
31. Lele, 1989.
32. Republic of Kenya, 1986, p. 89–90.
33. Republic of Kenya, 1993a.
34. Chalamwong and Feder, 1988.
35. Wachter, 1992.
36. Where population growth is accompanied by investment in social and physical infrastructure land conservation may be enhanced. See Tiffen *et al.* (1994) for the case of Machakos, Kenya.
37. Kiamba, 1994.
38. Wachter, 1992.
39. Rocheleau, 1993.
40. Thomas-Slayter *et al.*, 1991; Rocheleau, 1993.
41. Thomas-Slayter, *et al.*, 1991; Ondiege, 1992b; Rocheleau, 1993.
42. Thomas-Slayter *et al.*, 1991, p. 14.
43. Brokensha and Njeru, 1977.
44. See Admassie, 1992.
45. Eriksson, 1992.
46. Republic of Kenya, 1972, p. 26.
47. Lundgren, 1993.
48. Admassie, 1992.
49. Lundgren, 1993.
50. A. Field-Juma, African Centre for Technology Studies, Nairobi, pers. comm.
51. The district is divided into three zones based on agro-ecological potential: low, medium and high. These account for 32.0%, 54.3% and 8.8% of the district's area, respectively.
52. Meyers, 1981; Ondiege, 1992a; Tiffen, 1992.
53. Ondiege, 1992a.
54. Meyers, 1981.
55. Meyers, 1981; Ondiege, 1992a.
56. Tiffen, 1992.
57. Thomas-Slayter *et al.*, 1991.
58. Meyers, 1981.
59. Meyer, 1981; Thomas-Slayter *et al.*, 1991.
60. Ondiege, 1992b.
61. Thomas-Slayter *et al.*, 1991; Ondiege, 1992b.
62. Meyers, 1981; Critchley, 1991; Eriksson, 1992.
63. Ondiege, 1992a.

64. Rocheleau, 1993, p. 2.
65. Eriksson, 1992.
66. Omoro, 1987a.
67. Omoro, 1987a.
68. Eriksson, 1992.
69. Omoro, 1987b.
70. Critchley, 1991.
71. Some farmers also use terracing as a proof of occupancy or a claim of ownership to land.
72. Eriksson, 1992.

Land tenure and water resources

6

CLEOPHAS O. TORORI, ALBERT O. MUMMA AND ALISON FIELD-JUMA

Introduction

This chapter discusses the governance of water resources in Kenya in order to demonstrate that legal, institutional and policy reform is needed to support the development and sustainable management of water resources. It argues that any efforts aimed at improving water resource management must be based on the prevailing land tenure system as this provides the context and defines rights to water. In this regard, the chapter draws from the experiences of the English common law tradition. The chapter first looks at the social and economic importance of water in national development and its unusual character as a scarce public good which is dynamic and linked to many other features of the environment. How these characteristics structured approaches to water rights under English law provides the antecedents for Kenyan water law. The legal and institutional elements of governance of water in Kenya are then assessed demonstrating that water has become the property of the state. The chapter concludes by arguing that the system of water tenure in Kenya needs to be reformed in order to achieve sustainable resource utilization. This will require reassessment of the current ownership of the resource by the state and of the concept of public trust.

The water resource base

The importance of water for socio-economic development cannot be overemphasized. It forms a vital part of social infrastructure, playing a key

143

role in health, industry, agriculture, energy and general consumption for human welfare for which there are no substitutes. Water is essential for all forms of life, yet the total amount of water that is available is limited. It is estimated that 80% of the countries in the world currently suffer from serious water shortages and this is expected to worsen in the coming decades.[1]

Africa, despite its substantial water resources, experiences chronic shortages owing to uneven distribution of water and rainfall, underdevelopment of potential water resources and poor management of existing resources.

Water for socio-economic development

Social and economic development increases water use for domestic, agricultural and industrial purposes and energy production. Water consumption in Kenya is estimated at nearly 600 million cu m per year. Of this, 69% is used in agriculture, 18% in domestic use and 13% in industry. Projections of annual water demand by the year 2000 range from 2,500 to 5,900 million cu m.[2] Although the government has made efforts to make safe water available, only a small proportion of the population has access to such supplies, most of which are concentrated in the urban areas. With the growth of Kenya's population, the pressure on existing supplies and demand for additional water has also grown. The result has been overuse and pollution of the available water resources leading to shortages even where water was previously abundant. To satisfy projected demands, major investment in water development will be needed. This will require that new measures be taken to ensure that the needs of future generations are met while satisfying current demands.

Kenya's freshwater resources comprise water retained at various stages in the hydrological cycle. Surface water includes rivers, lakes, wetlands and reservoirs. A large quantity of water is stored underground at different depths (referred to here as groundwater). The coastal region has important marine resources. The uneven rainfall distribution in the country results in large fluctuations in river flows. In many parts of Kenya, low flows during the dry seasons are insufficient to meet all demands, while wet season flooding causes serious damage and waste of fresh water. Because of the uneven distribution of rainfall and surface water, the water readily available the year round without having to regulate river flows is estimated to be only 1.2% of the gross run-off in the rivers.[3]

Figure 7 Drainage basins in Kenya

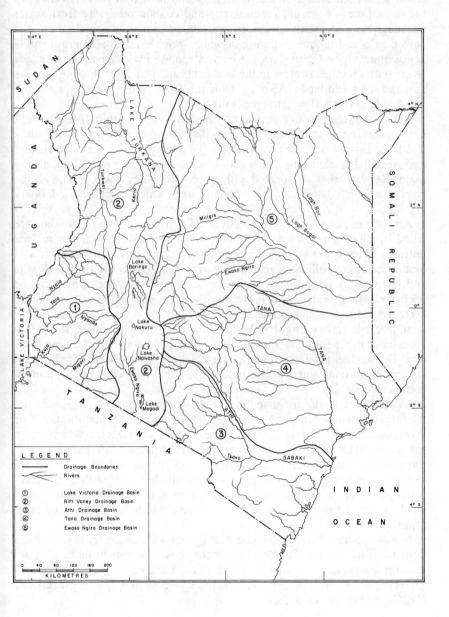

Water resource development has generally emphasized using rivers as sources for domestic, agricultural, energy and industrial uses. Rivers have the advantages of a rapid renewal rate and contain relatively fresh water (although not necessarily clean). In contrast, lakes tend to contain more dissolved salts and require pumping of water which uses more energy, and is hence more expensive to source. Kenya is endowed with a number of major rivers with their headwaters in the highlands and generally flowing into the arid and semi-arid lands (ASALs). Only the Tana, Nzoia, Yala, Nyando and Sondu-Miriu rivers flow throughout the year.

Kenya's surface water resources are distributed within five drainage basins, the Tana, Athi, Ewaso Nyiro (all single river systems), Rift Valley and Lake Basin (multiple rivers). With the exception of Lake Victoria and two small lakes along the Tanzanian border (lakes Jipe and Chala), all the major Kenyan lakes are located within the Rift Valley basin. While all the rivers for which data is available contain fresh water, most are moderately alkaline.

Apart from Lake Victoria, all Kenyan lakes have closed basins—they are filled by direct rainfall and in-flowing rivers but have no known surface outflow. Since water is lost mainly by evaporation, sediment and dissolved matter including pollutants accumulate over time. Lakes Victoria, Naivasha and Baringo are important because they contain fresh water which can be used for agricultural, industrial or domestic use after treatment. All other lakes are either brackish (Lake Turkana) or highly saline and unfit for consumptive use (lakes Bogoria, Nakuru and Magadi). However, the saline lakes have other intrinsic and economic values, however. Lake Magadi is used in soda ash production while lakes Nakuru, Bogoria and Turkana are important tourism and wildlife resources. Lake Turkana also supports a commercial fishery.

Kenya's wetlands are also important water resources. Wetlands are frequently regarded as wastelands suitable only for "rehabilitation" or "reclamation". Wetlands, however, are diverse ecosystems which serve many important functions, including: fish breeding, wildlife habitat, water purification and tertiary treatment for effluents, flood control and groundwater recharge. Wetlands have traditionally provided the only year-round water supply and dry season grazing reserves in many dryland areas, such as the Lorien swamps on Ewaso Nyiro North River and Amboseli swamps.

Many regions of Kenya depend heavily upon groundwater reserves and demand is increasing. The borehole is the most widespread method of accessing groundwater in Kenya. Boreholes are drilled by local and central government as well as by individuals, non-governmental organizations (NGOs) and corporate bodies.

Competing uses and water conflicts

Water resources are basic for sustaining human life and for the production of goods and services. Therefore, it is not surprising that there is competition over access. Water development programmes form a significant part of the national and district development plans. However, the natural limits of water resources constrain their utilization for all development purposes unless priority-setting and vigorous efforts to sustain and develop the resources are taken. Important uses include public water supply, which contributes to public health, and irrigation and provision of water for livestock under the agricultural development programme. Hydropower provides the bulk of Kenya's electricity supply but maintaining river water quality and flow is important for wildlife, fisheries and rural domestic water supply. Flood mitigation is important to the social well-being of people living in flood-prone areas.[4] The utilization of water resources thus involves balancing these competing needs and interests.

A clean and adequate public water supply provides the foundation for the economic and social development of countries, particularly due to its impact on health. The current national Development Plan (1994–96) aims to ensure the availability of potable water within four kilometres of every household by the year 2000. Meeting this goal would require considerable expansion and improvement of municipal water supplies and distribution systems, and a major increase in rural supplies. Many different approaches to rural water supply are currently in use, including river abstraction, capped and piped springs, boreholes, riverbed wells, and rooftop catchment systems mainly put in place by community groups and NGOs.

However, pollution of surface waters is a growing problem with serious health consequences. Women and children also still spend a significant proportion of their time and energy collecting water. Several problems, among them inadequate funds for development and maintenance of water supplies, have reduced the effectiveness of government in addressing domestic water needs. Of particular importance, an inadequate understanding of, and support for, governance systems which would facilitate access to and sustainable use of rural water supplies has hindered community-level development and management of water resources.

Self-sufficiency in food production has been a government objective in developing the agricultural sector, with a focus on rainfed agriculture. However, agriculture is the largest user of water, accounting for nearly three-quarters of the total consumption in the country. There are more than 18 major irrigation schemes in Kenya covering a total area of more than 200,000 ha and creating a very large water demand.[5] Irrigation is even more vital in ASALs if high yields per hectare are desired. A large portion of the water used in irrigation is lost through evapotranspiration and seepage, requiring that more water be applied to fields than that needed by the crops. Often less than half the water drawn for irrigation is wasted before it reaches the intended fields.

By 1988, over half of the land under irrigation in ASALs was in small-scale schemes which relied on water abstracted from permanent rivers arising in the highlands beyond the ASAL regions. This supply is being reduced as upper catchment land-use intensifies and utilizes a greater portion of the available river flow. Irrigation schemes in the ASAL regions are usually located in areas with the best access to water and more fertile soils and hence displace other forms of land use. The costs of developing irrigation systems, both directly in terms of financial outlays and indirectly in terms of social disruption and displacement of peoples, have been high and several schemes have failed. However, irrigation remains a major user of surface water.[6]

Water for livestock is also a significant and growing demand, particularly in ASAL areas. Sheep and goats require some five litres of water daily, cattle about 20 l, while camels consume almost 100 l once per week.[7] Recurrent droughts cause great loss of livestock in the ASALs. Water to support the livestock industry can be sourced from surface water, where available, or from boreholes. It is estimated that by the year 2010 livestock water demand will be equivalent to 20% of the domestic water use.[8]

Wildlife and tourism are important economic land uses in Kenya. About 95% of the land in the Kenya Wildlife Service (KWS) protected area system is in the ASALs where wildlife exert a considerable demand on water resources. In order to reduce the loss of wildlife during droughts, boreholes and shallow wells have been built in protected areas. However, provision of water to livestock and wildlife must be done with a good understanding of the social and ecological dynamics of the production system to avoid the problems encountered in the past. These have included such as devegetation around water points, overpopulation of animals and alteration of migration and herding routes.

Fisheries provide a substantial contribution to local lakeside and coastal economies, export earnings and national food supply. The fisheries of Lake Victoria, Lake Turkana and Lake Naivasha, as well as those of the Kenyan Indian Ocean coast, are all under threat from pollution, sedimentation and other factors which have disrupted the ecology of the resource.

Currently, hydroelectric power makes up about 75% of the total electricity generated in Kenya. The Kenya Power and Lighting Company plays a leading role in planning, designing and implementing hydropower projects in collaboration with river basin development authorities. The number of large dams and reservoirs for hydropower generation continues to increase. Major dams are owned by the river development authorities. The water held in these reservoirs may also be used for other purposes.

Many conflicts arising over land originate in competing demands for water. These may be between individuals wishing to use water for the same purpose, say among farmers over access to irrigation water, or between different uses and interests, such as an urban water supply or hydropower project against the interests of rural land users. Some of these competing uses may be played out as conflicts between government ministries.

Attempts to develop rural water supplies illustrate conflict which can arise between rural landowners due to the prevailing land tenure system. For example, the land tenure system in Kisii, a densely populated district, is predominantly private ownership with little public land. Landowners in Kisii have been concerned that when public water pumps or pipes are sited near or across their landholdings, then the government may acquire their land claiming a public interest. Agreements reached over piping may subsequently be abrogated by sons or other relatives of landowners, creating an inter-generational conflict. Property owners also fear that allowing construction of public facilities like hand pumps on private land will encourage encroachment on their property by outsiders seeking to use the facilities.

Another rural land-use conflict is over the use of riverbanks. The law provides for a buffer along river and stream banks to protect the water course from erosion and pollution. However, riparian landowners or land users frequently cultivate right up to the river edge. Land shortage, uneven or general lack of enforcement, and lack of understanding on the part of the farmers as to the purpose of the restriction contribute to the conflicts which result when enforcement is attempted.

Other conflicts arise when local communities are not involved in the decision-making process in matters directly affecting them. Around the world construction of large dams tends to cause conflict, and Kenya is no exception. Whether for water supply, hydropower, irrigation or other purpose in the interest of the national economy or urban populations, communities residing in the area to be flooded have little to gain and much to lose. Lack of participation in decision-making also creates conflicts between upstream and downstream users of river water. Where a river passes through an urban area, urban and industrial effluent may make the water unusable downstream. In the case of the Uaso Nyiro River, increased abstraction of water for small-scale irrigation in the upper reaches of the catchment has reduced the flow to the downstream users.

Overlapping interests of ministries and potential for jurisdictional conflict is exemplified by the Chyulu Hills. Here there is a water reservoir for Mombasa municipality administered by the National Water Conservation and Pipeline Corporation; a settlement scheme administered by the Ministry of Lands and Settlement; water conservation measures executed by the Ministry of Land Reclamation, Regional and Water Development; wildlife and tourism management by the KWS; and environmental protection measures being implemented by the Ministry of Environment and Natural Resources.

This brief review of types of water conflict raises a number of important points. First, introduction of change without understanding the prevailing land use and governance systems of the local population generally undermines the system which was in place. However, the new resource management system is unlikely to work as expected if it conflicts with the pre-existing systems or norms, or fails to take advantage of local knowledge. This suggests that change should emerge through consultation and shared knowledge of both the local circumstances and external imperatives. Secondly, the ownership of land confers certain rights to water which also entail responsibilities in relation to other members of society, both nearby and distant. These rights and responsibilities are complex and yet complementary. Unless the dual character is recognized in systems of reciprocal relations many types of conflicts may arise. The next section examines the origins of these rights and responsibilities.

Rights to land and water

Water resources and land tenure

The right to water under English common law was derived from land ownership in two ways. First, by ownership of the land under or over which water flowed, and secondly, by ownership of land adjoining surface waters, called riparian rights. While English common law provided the conceptual foundation for water rights in Kenya, important aspects were fundamentally changed. How water rights were derived from these types of land ownership is examined below.

Kenya has a diverse land tenure system with individual private property, group private property, state-owned land and land held in trust by the state. Customary tenure is practised in various forms within most of these categories. Ownership of water resources is vested in the state. However, the practice of water management cannot be separated from questions of land management since access to water in most cases derives from access to land. Control of access to water in the drylands, for example, is often a tenure-building mechanism, affecting land settlement patterns, disenfranchising the less powerful from access to water, and in the process creating conflict.

Inevitably, government decisions about the use of water resources will affect existing patterns of land tenure. Such decisions may encounter claims of rights of use or access based upon the nature of the existing tenure regime and cultural norms. As has been found in the case of land management, the presence or absence of tenure security affects whether people will take an active role in investing in developing the resource in question.[9] The same can be said for water.

In government irrigation schemes, the state owns the land and cultivators become lessees with temporary occupation licences which recognize only the alottee and his or her spouse, and allow the state to evict them. These arrangements are buttressed by large state bureaucracies which may control anything from the residential affairs of the irrigators to the conduct of transactions in holdings, crop planting timetables and marketing of the crops.[10] In such cases land tenure remains very insecure and a major disincentive for any investment by the cultivators.

In Kenya, the predominant form of land tenure in the high and medium-potential areas is individual private tenure. As defined in the Registered Land Act: "The registration of a person as the proprietor of land vests in that person the absolute ownership of the land *together with all rights and privileges belonging or appurtenant thereto.*"[11] In the italicized words lies the key to the relationship between land tenure and water resources in these areas since the most important of the "rights appurtenant" is the right to water.

However, customary land tenure predominates in many African countries. It still exists in Kenya to varying degrees, and influences many rural communities' perceptions of water rights. In Africa, the amount of land under customary land tenure is quite significant. For example, in Zambia, some 94% of the total country is under customary tenure and in Cameroon, the proportion was recently as high as 99%.[12] While the details of customary tenure will vary from case to case, there are certain distinct features which tend to distinguish it from other systems of tenure. Overall the customary system runs on the principle of the community interest rather than for the advantage of a particular individual. This has far-reaching implications in the way resources are utilized. African customary tenure arrangements are governed by kinship as the primary organizing factor. The rules of access to and use of land and water are predicated primarily on membership and status in the social group controlling a particular territory.[13] Individual families enjoy fairly clearly-defined rights of use over different parcels of cultivated land. Such family rights are transmitted to succeeding generations in accordance with the prevailing rules of succession.[14]

In Kenya on-going alienation of trust lands, where customary governance regimes are most active, undermine the security of tenure needed for local investment in water development. Another problem encountered by water development projects is that water management methods, technologies and rules introduced into areas where customary rights and norms prevail often meet with resistance. This is due to local people having different expectations, rules of access, decision-making processes and means of maintaining equipment. Local knowledge about hydrological patterns (e.g., flood levels, rainfall patterns, soil types) is rarely accessed and effectively combined with external technical knowledge such as microbiology or mechanical and technical specifications of technologies.

In contrast to the tenure system in Kenya, customary water rights in Japan are recognized by the main water law, the River Law, and considered to be rights permitted under the law. Customary water rights came about due to scarcity of water during droughts and increasing population density. "The concept of water right was born as an institution of conflict resolution in a social system at individual locality."[15] The first modern law statute to formally grant a water right was the Old River Law, enacted in 1896. Customary water rights were multi-purpose, including irrigation as the main use, but also drinking, domestic uses and fire-fighting. The rights included rules as to priority of uses according to both temporal and locational factors and the quantity of the water to be abstracted.

The right to water

The origins of Kenyan water law can be traced to English common law while the roots of English law can in turn be traced to Roman law. As has been noted in earlier chapters, Kenyan legal and constitutional provisions exhibit significant continuity with their colonial antecedents. However, in a number of areas the post-colonial Kenyan law provides for an overriding interest in state control; water is such an area.

Under Roman law, running water, light and air were considered *res communes*, defined as "things the property of which belongs to no person, but the use to all."[16] This basic principle is incorporated in the English Registered Land Act which characterizes these "natural rights of light, air, water and support" as *overriding rights* which, unlike other rights, would not be subsumed even by the registration of an absolute proprietor.[17] Similarly, under English common law, it is an elementary principle that running water cannot be the property of anyone, even of one who is the exclusive owner of the banks on both sides of a river. "Flowing water . . . is public and common in this sense only, that all may reasonably use it who have a right of access to it, *that none can have any property in the water itself. . . .* But each proprietor has the right to the usufruct of the stream which flows through it."[18]

Therefore, English common law does not recognize property in water, but rather, a "right to water". This right, however, is fundamentally qualified in three important respects: access, possession and use. First, right of access belongs only to those "who have a right of access" to the water. Hence "the right to the use of water arises . . . *from the right of access to it*" by virtue of owning the land abutting the water.[19] So first and most important, the right to water belongs only to those persons holding some proprietary interest in land, "for no one else can do so without committing a trespass."[20] Where there is only one riparian landowner, that owner's right to the enjoyment of the water is so exclusive as to be "akin to a proprietary interest."[21]

So far-reaching is the right of landowners of non-tidal, non-navigable rivers that they "could combine to divert, pollute or diminish the stream" and "no one could call them to account".[22] Hence the conservation of the water resource is dependent on the interest of the private landowner. As long as there is no riparian owner complaining, the various riparian owners may do as they please. Under English common law the public, in their capacity only as members of the public, have no standing to complain about the use or misuse to which riparian owners choose to put the water.

The second defining characteristic of the "right to water" under English common law is that the right of possession is a temporary one. When possession is abandoned, the water once again becomes *public juris*. Also, the first occupant may not, by diverting the stream, deprive the owner of the land below of the special benefit and advantage of the stream's flow. This means that flowing water may not be "hoarded" by individuals.

Third, is the right to use which combines two traits of water. The right is only to the *use* of the water, and the use must be "reasonable". A landowner's right to water only extends to the amount necessary for some useful purpose in connection with his or her land. It is not an absolute and exclusive right to the flow of all the water in its natural state. No riparian landowner may use the water to the prejudice of other landowners upstream or downstream. Each must use the stream in a reasonable manner so as not to destroy, or render useless, or materially diminish or affect the use of the water by other proprietors. Unreasonable and unauthorized uses are restricted. What amounts to "reasonable" use will depend on the circumstances of the case and may be difficult to define. Principles, under the name of "riparian rights", have been developed to deal with this difficulty. We shall return to these principles later.

The common law made one exception to its doctrine of reasonable user: it does not apply to water which is not in a defined channel. This is based on a division of bodies of water into two categories: that water which is flowing in a known "defined channel" above (or occasionally below) the ground, and that water which is sub-surface percolating water or surface water which "follows no regular or defined course." Under English common law the doctrine of reasonable user is applied to the former but not the latter.

Hence, most groundwater is seen to fall within that principle which gives to the landowner all that lies beneath the surface, as in the case of minerals or oil. So landowners may appropriate all the water that is beneath their own land and thus prevent it from percolating to their neighbour's land. Further, they may appropriate such water to the extent that they cause water which is under their neighbour's land to come to their own land when it otherwise would not have. They may then appropriate that too, such as through drawing from a well, to the extent that they absolutely drain their neighbour's land.

These principles are based on a lack of knowledge and the resulting uncertainty about the movement of unconfined surface water and groundwater. It is argued that there is no difficulty in enforcing the right to running water in a channel since it is "something visible, and no one can interrupt it without knowing whether he does or does not do injury to those who are above or below him."[23] In contrast, to prove an interruption of groundwater flow would require scientific evidence. The explanation for this distinction between surface water in a defined channel, and other dispersed or underground water is likely to lie in the abundance of water in Great Britain at the time. Land owners were able to survive well enough without quibbling over sub-surface water.

Water rights in the USA reflect the same division between water that is percolating, primarily groundwater, and that which is in a defined stream. The scarcity of water in the western USA led to the ownership of groundwater by the state and subject to appropriation for other uses. This modification became known as the doctrine of prior appropriation. Absolute ownership of groundwater (as under English common law) allowed water to be treated as any other sub-surface resource, such as petroleum. This position was modified by the courts to require the same criteria of reasonable use as was applied to surface waters, hence limiting the waste of water or its export to other land. Some states modified the groundwater rights of landowners still further by requiring them to take the needs of other users into consideration, known as correlative rights. "Where limited water supplies are available, overlying land owners share proportionately in the supply according to the amount of land owned."[24]

In a country faced with a shortage of water such as Kenya, the English common law position would not advance the wise use of the resource and could not be accepted without modification. Indeed, legislation in Kenya has made major inroads into the common law position as a whole. Exactly how will be considered later.

In summary, under English common law the landowner's right to running surface water is a right to a temporary usufruct, subject to the doctrine of reasonable user guided by the "riparian rights" principles. Landowners however, have the right to any and all sub-surface water which they may appropriate from their land.

Riparian rights

The rights of riparian landowners do not arise from their ownership of the bed over which the water flows. Rather, they arise from the *right of access* which such proprietors have to the water by virtue of owning the abutting land. The very word "riparian" is relative to the bank and not to the bed of the stream. Riparian rights belong *only* to riparian proprietors and hence to a small proportion of land owners. The riparian rights of the land owner comprise "the right to have water come to him in its natural state in flow, quantity and quality, and to go from him without obstruction . . ."[25] Thus, the riparian land owner has three rights: to the natural quantity of water; to the natural quality of the water; and of access and navigation.

In regard to quantity, under English law riparian landowners may abstract, divert or impound the water of the stream to which they have access. They could choose to use the water for ordinary or primary purposes such as drinking and cooking, cleaning and feeding their families and watering their cattle. Secondly, they could use it for some other purpose connected with their land, usually called an extraordinary or a secondary purpose. Third, they could use the water for purposes foreign to or unconnected with the land ownership. The rights to water in the first two cases differ from each other, and in the third case landowners have no rights at all.

In the ordinary (primary) use of water, a person owning the banks of a stream has no restrictions and may exhaust the water altogether. No other riparian proprietor can complain of that. But this must be limited to domestic use by the riparian owner. Any other use or user "will be wrongful if it *sensibly* affects the flow of the water by the land of other riparian proprietor."[26] This right to ordinary usage has been partially protected under Kenya's legislation.

Riparian proprietors may also use the water for extraordinary (secondary) purposes, provided they do not interfere with the rights of other proprietors either above or below them. The use must be "reasonable" and the water must be returned substantially undiminished in volume and unaltered in character. The riparian proprietors may use the water for irrigation but must return it to the stream with no diminution other than that caused by the evaporation and absorption expected from irrigation. In Kenya the right to extraordinary usage, as a right, has been abolished by statute and now may only be exercised with a permit.

The riparian proprietor's right to quality is a right to the flow of the water past his or her land, in its natural state of purity, undeteriorated by noxious matter discharged into it by others.[27] Pollution is judged by whether what is added would appreciably pollute the stream if it was otherwise unpolluted. So, it is no defense to show that the stream is already polluted from other sources. Two key features of this right merit further examination. First, as always, the right belongs to the riparian proprietor. A non-riparian owner generally cannot take legal action for an act of pollution.

Secondly, unlike the right to quantity, the right to quality is an absolute right which may itself limit the right to quantity. Pollution is, in itself, an unlawful act so that no one may, of common right, pollute water. Where it is impossible to separate the illegal pollution from a legal use, the wrongdoer must bear the consequences of any amount of prohibition even if, unavoidably, it extends to a total restriction of the use. This is a fundamental qualification of the rights of absolute proprietorship. It is significant that the qualification is in the interests of water resource conservation.

Where the pollution would injure public health, then there can be no right whatever to pollute water. In this situation, not even the state, let alone private individuals, can grant the right to pollute.[28] The restriction is based "upon the general illegality of the supposed grant and *the injury to the interests of the public.*"[29]

The English common law on the pollution of water is not based just on rights of property. It is based also on the principle of nuisance: "if filth is created on any man's land, then he whose dirt it is must keep it that it may not trespass."[30] Upon this principle, the owner of a well has a right of action against the person who poisons the water that the owner has a right to get.

Two factors are noteworthy here. First, the recognition of the fact that the management of water resources is not solely in order to enhance private proprietary interests in land. There is also a matter of principle involved, that is, the general concern about the pollution of water in the interests of the public. This inclusion was a logical consequence of the detachment of water management from private proprietary interests in land. These two factors are at the base of current legislative provisions in Kenya regarding water management generally.

It is quite clear that the private landowner in England occupies a very privileged position as far as the management of water resources is concerned. An unbridled exercise of these rights would be inimical to the conservation of these resources today. Therefore, it is no surprise that Kenyan statute has radically altered this position. However, it has done so in such a way that land tenure still remains central to water management.

Lastly, since the right of access does not depend on ownership of the soil beneath the water, it makes no difference that the water may have receded from the riparian land due to silting up or reclamation. It should also be noted that riparian proprietors are effectively precluded from championing the public interest under the guise of protecting their private interest. The significance of this for the conservation of water resources is that riparian owners would not be able to complain of a diminution of water where the ultimate loser is the public. In the dry western states of the USA, lack of sufficient surface water resources required limitations on common law riparian rights. As the lands were settled and population increased, the needs of non-adjacent land owners became acute. As a result a system to allocate water rights, the doctrine of prior appropriation, was developed which repudiated or severely limited the riparian doctrine.[31]

Water rights allocation in the USA

The United States provides an interesting comparison in the evolution of water law. Like Kenya, the USA derived its laws from English common law. Most land is held under private individual ownership. The regulation, control and use of water "is vested in the sovereign authority of the nation or its subdivision," in this case in the individual states. In the western states, which are far more arid than the eastern states, state constitutions and laws "declare that the waters within their boundaries are owned or belong to the public or the state. Flowing from the right of public ownership are the rights to use water. The character or nature of these rights may vary and problems of federalism occur where state's rights and the national interest may be in conflict."[32] Due to the arid and semi-arid nature of the western states, the departure from English water law has been greater and more authority has been vested in centralized state governments than in the eastern states. There is also an emphasis on *allocation* of water by the state. Under state ownership water rights are *usufructuary* only, although these rights can be protected as property under the law. However, a system of state ownership and control of water was put into place in the western states of the USA due to the scarcity of water and recognition of the vital public interest in water resources. State ownership provided a significant departure from the English common law and reflected both the scarcity of the resource and the development interests of the states.

State ownership required that an administrative system be developed which could allocate the right to use water to the intended users according to government policies and priorities.[33] The administrative water rights system required the identification of uses and users, quantification of the available water, setting priorities and balancing competing uses, and adjudication of use rights. Although costly to administer, this system had several benefits. It could be used to protect financial investments in water works and uses which could ill afford a reduction in supply (such as hydropower plants or irrigation schemes). It also enabled states to guide plans for such investments in terms of location and size. The process was usually administered by a state agency which accepted and reviewed applications, provided permits and inspected the use. Such a system was established in the State of California in 1914 regarding surface waters. Similar systems also allowed planning to avoid overdraft or pollution of groundwater, as in the case of the Ground Water Management Act of 1980 of the State of Arizona. This Act was designed to ensure sustainable use of water for agriculture.

Legal and institutional framework in Kenya

Legislation

The Water Act is intended to provide for the conservation, control and apportionment of and use of the water resources of Kenya. Ownership of all water bodies is vested in the state. The control of water is vested in the relevant minister, (currently the minister for land reclamation, regional and water development) whose duty is to promote the investigation, conservation and proper use of the country's water resources. These provisions make the management of water resources a public concern to be managed by the state. The usufructuary right to use water may be acquired only under the Act, obtainable by permit: "In all cases of proposed diversion, abstraction, obstruction, storage or use of water from a body of water . . . application must be made for a permit."[34] This is enforced through criminal sanction.

A permit may be required for some domestic uses, all public uses, minor or general irrigation purposes, industrial uses, for power generation and "any other purpose approved by the Water Apportionment Board." These purposes subsume all the uses of water which the common law would characterize as "extraordinary" (secondary) purposes. A permit is not required for the storage of water, or the abstraction of water from a dam constructed in any channel or depression which has been declared by the Water Apportionment Board not to be a watercourse.

A permit may be changed or cancelled under certain circumstances, including: changes in the weather such as a drought; an increased demand upon the water; the proposal, by any community, of a better system of water utilization; in consequence of a hydrographic survey; or failure to make beneficial use of the permit, among other reasons.[35]

These requirements effectively abolish the common law riparian rights to the use of water, which are equivalent to absolute proprietorship. There are defined exceptions to this position. A permit is not required where the abstraction or use of water from any body of water is by a person having lawful access thereto, for domestic (primary) purposes, if such abstraction is made without the employment of works. "Works" are defined to mean "any structure, apparatus, contrivance, device, or thing for carrying, conducting, or utilizing water." A person using a pail or a pot to convey water to his or her house for domestic use would not require a permit. This provides a highly circumscribed right of use for primary purposes.

Secondly, a permit is not required when the works for the development of groundwater are situated further than 100 yards of any body of surface water. This provision is designed to protect surface water from being unwittingly siphoned off through wells and boreholes. It is also intended to allow one to sink a borehole to utilize groundwater without obtaining a permit. However, it is prohibited to abstract water in excess of one's reasonable requirements and which one cannot use in a reasonable and beneficial manner from any well. This is a significant change in the common law position regarding the right to use groundwater. It extends the doctrine of reasonable user to this category of waters as well, hence limiting access to groundwater except by the permission of the state. Groundwater use is controlled by the ministry responsible for water through the Water Apportionment Board, which approves applications, lists boreholes, plots them on a base map and subsequently records them at the ministry's Groundwater Division.

The supplies of water undertakers, those specifically permitted to supply water to others, are protected by the Act by a prohibition against any others constructing a well within the limits of an undertaker's supply without the consent of the minister. Water undertakers are empowered to make regulations to protect any water belonging to them against pollution. Regrettably, Kenyan statutory law on pollution has not improved upon the English common law position. It is an offence pollute a source of water supply but only if the water supply is to be used for human consumption. Pollution which may have a negative impact on the environment is not considered. The only possible advantage of Kenyan statutory law in regard to pollution is that it makes the enforcement against water pollution a matter for public authorities rather than leaving it to the individual land owner.

The law on pollution apart, it is clear that the common law position has been substantially altered by Kenyan statute. However, land tenure still remains central for two reasons. First, because it is the land owner who applies for a water permit. Secondly, because those who may be exempted from the permit requirement (where there are provisions for exemption) are the same landowners. This puts the landless, those without title in land and those living under customary tenurial regimes at a great disadvantage relative to water supplies. These provisions make it virtually impossible for such people to take the initiative to develop or gain access to a water supply under statutory law.

Institutions

The Ministry of Water Development was established in 1974 to be the "principal agency responsible for the management, development, operation and maintenance of water supplies, sewage disposal and pollution control."[36] Its principal executive organ was intended to be the Water Resource Authority. The duties of the authority included investigating the water resources of Kenya, advising and making recommendations to the minister in regard to improving, preserving, conserving, utilizing, and apportioning such resources and as to providing additional water supplies.

Permits for the use of water are issued by the Water Apportionment Board. Applications may be inspected by the public at the offices of the board and objections raised by the public. Where the board is of the opinion that the permit applied for is likely to be in the public interest, or not adverse to it, it must conditionally approve the application. If any objection is lodged against the application a public inquiry must be held by the board prior to refusal or approval of the application. The approval is always conditional being "subject to the availability of flow."[37]

The administration of water resources under the Water Act provides for water undertakers to be designated at the local level. A water undertaker is an individual or corporate body with the authority to manage a water supply works and sell water. Selling water to more than five people is prohibited by anyone other than a water undertaker. This provision allows for private management and sale of water, considerably reducing the burden on government. It is also flexible in that the state can appoint water undertakers who may be NGOs, local government, individuals, associations or companies so long as they have the capability to maintain the infrastructure and supply to the defined client group.

Water users' associations were established in Kenya by the colonial government in order to improve local water supply management but were abandoned at independence due to their connection with the colonial regime. Recently, however, as with soil conservation, the idea has become accepted once again and associations are increasingly being established. Riparian landowners associations are also being established, as in the case of Lake Naivasha. Such associations are often more able to mobilize the labour and financial resources needed to improve the management of the water body through establishing and enforcing rules of access and the duties of the users. An association may be able to gather information and develop a management plan and invest in infrastructure improvements such as dam repair, fencing and access points, and prevent pollution of the water body.

It should be noted, however, that the basis of a riparian association is the ownership of land abutting a water body, hence the membership may be a more exclusive group than if the association were based on water use or need. In the case of Lake Naivasha, the town of Naivasha which has serious water shortages despite its proximity to the lake is not a riparian owner. Unless public access points or rights are provided riparian associations may also exclude the local rural population which does not own land abutting the lake but may require access to water for livestock and domestic use. Hence it should be noted that while the formation of formal natural resource-based associations may provide a significant step towards improved management systems, they are not necessarily equitable or representative unless positive steps are taken to make them so.

Given the government's focus on the formal institutions described above it is easy to forget the important role played by what are seen as "informal" institutions. Water resources in Africa have long been managed under traditional governance systems many of which still function at the local level. In many communities the development and management of water supplies is still governed by customary rights and responsibilities. Rural domestic supplies are also primarily used and managed by women.[38] Despite the attempts of government to provide large-scale, more technologically-advanced water supply systems, these have often proved unsustainable for technical, economic or social reasons and rural people may revert back to their customary practices. Hence informal institutions (they may be well-recognized at the local level) provide not only the backbone of current water resources management but also provide examples for future systems. In considering appropriate governance systems for water—those that are effective, equitable and sustainable—it may be more useful to facilitate the expansion and evolution of such informal systems rather than their replacement.

Special powers of the state

In addition to the fundamental changes made by Kenyan statute in the common law rights of the riparian landowner inherited from the English, the state has wide powers to act to conserve and utilize water resources under the Water Act. These powers affect individual water rights as envisaged under the common law and reduce the absoluteness of the proprietorship of the land owner. These special powers arise particularly in respect to protection of water catchments and groundwater resources and are vested in the minister responsible for water.

Where the minister is satisfied that special measures are necessary for the protection of the water resources in or derived from any area, he or she may declare the area to be a *protected catchment area*. The Minister may then proceed to require, regulate or prohibit any act by any person in the protected catchment area considered necessary for the protection of the area or for the protection of the water supply obtained from it.

In respect of groundwater specifically, where the minister is satisfied that in any area special measures for the conservation of groundwater are necessary in the public interest (whether to protect public water supplies or protect water supplies for industrial or other purposes), he or she may declare it a *conservation area*. Such an order has far-reaching consequences. First, every person who wishes to continue diverting or abstracting groundwater by mechanical means within any conservation area, must within six months apply to the Water Apportionment Board for a permit. Secondly, no person may construct or extend any well in a conservation area for the purpose of abstracting groundwater without having obtained a permit from the Water Apportionment Board to do so. The only exception is where the person is not using mechanical means to abstract the water.

Equally far-reaching are the powers given to protect the water supply of a water undertaker. Where the minister is satisfied that special measures are necessary to protect a catchment area providing the water supply of a water undertaker, the minister may declare it a *protected area*, and may require, regulate or prohibit any act within the area deemed necessary to protect the area or to protect the water supply obtained from it.[39]

Further powers obtain during a drought—or at any time in the case of small watercourses—whereby the Water Apportionment Board may require any person to allow to pass such proportion of the water in the watercourse as appears to the Water Apportionment Board to be equitable, whether or not the person had already obtained a license, sanction or permit. The board may also prohibit any practice which, in its opinion, causes undue reduction of the water in any watercourse.

Further reinforcement, if needed, is found in the Agriculture Act. Here the relevant minister may, with the concurrence of the Central Agricultural Board, make rules for any or all of several specified matters if he or she considers it necessary for soil conservation.[40] First, when deemed by the minister to be necessary for, *inter alia*, maintaining of water in a body of water within the meaning of the Water Act, the minister may prohibit or regulate: land clearing for cultivation; the grazing or watering of livestock; and the firing, clearing or destruction of vegetation including stubble. Secondly, the minister may require, regulate or control, *inter alia*, the drainage of land, including the construction, maintenance or repair of artificial or natural drains, gullies, contour banks, terraces, or diversion ditches.

Other statutes also provide enabling powers which can be brought to bear on the land owner for the purposes of water conservation, including the Forests Act, the Malaria Prevention Act, the Public Health Act and the Trust Land Act.

In summary, there are many legal means by which the state can regulate the use of land in the interest of protecting water resources. These measures override the private interest in land or water and certainly any customary rights as well. The broad scope and intersectoral nature of these special powers of the state provide a complete mandate and means for water resources protection by the state. However, it is clear that the opportunities provided in law to the central authority have not resulted in adequate or sustainable water resources development. Some of the reasons for this are examined in the following section.

Issues in water and land tenure

The question of ownership

We have shown that ownership and control of water in Kenya is vested in the state. Kenya has followed the anglophone tradition in Africa where English common law doctrines and statutory modifications before and after independence have firmly vested the ownership of most natural resources in the state.[41]

Even though the Water Act sets to protect rights of individuals with water in their private land holdings, this is limited by the provision that such persons have only *usufruct* rights over the water.[42] To utilize water in a water body they must seek a permit unless it is to be used for limited domestic purposes. In the case of groundwater a permit is also required unless the well is a prescribed distance from other wells and surface waters. Therefore, a permit is required for some domestic uses, all public uses, minor and general irrigation purposes, industrial uses, for power installations and any other purposes approved by the Water Apportionment Board.

As noted earlier, riparian rights of land owners are circumscribed by the Water Act. In addition, the law regulates the use of land within two metres of a water body in order to protect the catchment. However, this important rule is not well respected and land abutting streams is often used for cultivation and other more permanent activities including construction of buildings and walls. Consequently, the important functions of floodplains—flood and soil erosion control, prevention of loss of life and property—are being compromised. Evidently, property owners and land users do not feel constrained by this regulation. Furthermore, traditional land use included floodplain gardening which utilized fertile agricultural land in otherwise dry or unproductive areas.

Due to the increasing pressure for land for settlement and production, river banks and floodplains tend to share the same fate as wetlands—being seen as underutilized resources which should be modified and developed. Allowing low-impact uses, such as some customary land management practices or farming with soil and water conservation measures, may need to be considered while prohibition of high-impact uses, such as construction, should be enforced.

Associations of riparian owners are beginning to emerge to govern the uses of the waters to which they have rights by virtue of their land holdings. Such associations may be effective in protecting the resource for their own use, or for the public benefit or both. The state, however, retains ownership of the water body itself. As noted earlier, riparian landowners may have particular interests which are not held in common with the surrounding communities. Therefore the public interest in water resources—including local and intergenerational interests—should be taken into consideration in the formation and governance of associations.

Kenya's Constitution provides that holders of private property have the right to determine the use of their property, including the right to dispose of it.[43] These rights act as a buffer between the interests of the individual and those of other entities including the state and the public. However, the state has the right to establish easements on private land, which limits the rights of the landowner. Creation of easements involves taking from owners some of the rights to use their land in the public interest, as is done with zoning and other land use regulations.

The state has an obligation to pay full and just compensation when it deprives individuals of their property.[44] Fixing the amount of compensation is provided for under the Land Acquisition Act.[45] Generally, compensation must take into account inconvenience, disturbance, or damage caused by the interference with or acquisition of the property. This is what will amount to just compensation as distinguished from mere compensation. Just compensation will ensure that when property is taken, due process of law is followed which establishes the value of the property taken and specifies the conditions for such acquisition.

However, whatever the amount of compensation, the mental trauma and the loss of the satisfaction found in one's own property is irredeemable. For example, compensation made for displacement by irrigation schemes and reservoirs tends to ignore socio-economic considerations. Compensation is usually paid in cash rather than in the form of land of equivalent value, and is generally paid to the adult male in the household. As a result the family may become landless, with women and children being particularly at risk. In the case of irrigation, a substantial number of displaced people may be resettled within the scheme. Particularly where land was held under an indigenous tenure regime, those displaced tend to settle among their kin in the vicinity of the proposed scheme. This reduces the amount of land available per family in the scheme's catchment area.[46]

These considerations need to be taken into account when developing large-scale water projects which inevitably dispossess local people of their land. Approaches which have a lower social impact, such as small-scale hydropower and other energy sources in the case of energy, and rainwater harvesting in the case of agriculture, may provide better alternatives.

The Water Act provides for the establishment of easements, include the right of access "along a route approved by the Water Resources Authority . . . to any piece of land contiguous to the water of the operator in so far as may be necessary for the purpose of constructing, inspecting, maintaining, operating or repairing the works of the operator."[47] The actions of the operator should not harm the landholder, such as by flooding, accumulation of weeds, siltation or any other obstruction, and compensation must be paid for any damage caused. A closely-related provision is the right to transport water through land that is not one's own. Under the Water Act, a party can secure rights to another person's land for purposes of transporting water, such as through pipes or channels.

Easements provide an important function by providing access to water resources which would otherwise be prevented by private land ownership. This can be a particularly important mechanism in rural areas in order to provide access to surface water for wildlife or livestock, and for domestic purposes such as collecting drinking water or bathing for those people who are not riparian owners. It is also essential for the development of public water supply systems which require piping water across large distances from the source to municipalities, market centres and schools.

Conceptually, easements are also important because they disaggregate the bundle of rights associated with land ownership into distinct functions, such as the right to pass over private land. In Britain the right to walk across the countryside is a jealously-guarded public right which overrides the rights of private landowners. Since many natural resources are seen to be public goods their control cannot be fully privatized. This is recognized by customary norms in Kenya which permit the use of water and the gathering of wild famine foods (such as herbs and fruits) by any person in times of drought.

The palpable scarcity of natural resources such as water, woodfuel and land, and the ease with which increasingly dense populations pollute essential resources such as air and water, has increased awareness of the need for new mechanisms which recognize the public interest in environmental quality. Scarcity of water makes a strong case for seriously considering expanding the public interest in water rights whatever the prevailing tenure system. This points to an expansion of the public trust role, and a decrease in the role of private ownership, whether by the government or by individuals.

The public trust doctrine

The public trust doctrine originated in Roman law and has been given its contemporary interpretation by US law. Emperor Justinian provided that water, like air, is incapable of private ownership; the resource was seen to belong to everyone and therefore could be owned by no one. Under English common law, the king was held to have sovereign power in navigable waters and his sovereign power was paramount to private proprietary interests. In the case of the USA, after gaining independence, the king's sovereign control of waters was transferred to the individual states. The state's sovereign interests provided the foundation of the public trust doctrine, which recognizes that the state has unique powers and responsibilities over the waters, *and that they hold this in trust for the people*.[48] Thus under the public trust doctrine as understood in the USA, the state holds its navigable waters and underlying beds in trust for certain public uses, principally navigation, commerce and fisheries.

Some scholars regard the public trust doctrine as a form of state property in that it creates a public easement in navigable waters.[49] Others regard the doctrine as an exercise of sovereign state authority to which the state is entitled.[50] The public trust doctrine gained recognition following a US Supreme Court decision declaring that the state of Illinois held sovereign interests in lands underlying navigable waters and that such interests were held in trust for certain public uses.[51] This decision may have been based on the police power which allows a state to reasonably regulate private property for public purposes.

Kenya's Constitution, on the one hand, emphasizes private property, but provides for extensive state ownership and trusteeship on the other. The state can also acquire land in the public interest under the provisions of the Land Acquisition Act. Hence, a notable feature of the Constitution in respect of land is the triple functions of the state as public trustee, public landowner and a land banker for development interests. As a public trustee, the state is expected to protect the interests of the public in the vast trust lands. This raises an important question: In trust for whom? Under the colonial regime land was held in trust for other uses, primarily future settler development. Hence the state acted as a land banker. Since independence, it has generally been understood that the state holds land in trust for those people who have traditionally resided, and continue to reside, in those lands until they become able to manage such lands themselves. However, disposal of trust lands to individual parties indicates that this may not be the current interpretation.

Chapter IX of the Constitution lays down in detail a programmatic framework for the public trust in respect to land. Authority over trust land, which covers almost half of the country, is vested in the central government which may delegate its authority to local government (in particular county councils). Overall authority to regulate, distribute, manage and dispose of these lands rests with the government.

In trust land, customary land rights, privileges, grants and occupancy rights are null and void where inconsistent with written law. In fact, customary land rights are readily subject to qualification, and a person can be deprived of these rights by payment of compensation. With regard to water, the state can compulsorily acquire land for purposes of water undertaking and owns all water bodies whether on private, public or trust land.[52] This authority is based on the assumption that the state is acting in the public interest, and thus acts as a public trustee. As these legal provisions demonstrate, the state has such immense powers under the trust provision that it is difficult to distinguish between trusteeship and ownership. Given these powers, it could be argued that in Kenya trusteeship is only a slightly modified form of private ownership by the state since the government can divest itself of trust lands by redistributing them in such a way as to serve its own interests.

But more important with regard to water, the state retains both proprietary *and* regulatory interests and rights over landowners. The state has the right to define water rights as subject to its continuing regulation and control over the resource and therefore water rights holders can have no expectation that their rights will be free of such regulation and control. Ownership and trusteeship of land coupled with broad regulatory powers has enabled the government to have dominion over all water resources. In short, under the public trust doctrine, the government may modify land and water rights in such a way as to bring into question the concept of trustee as it is currently used.

Equity and gender

In the context of economic reform, the role of government is being redefined to move away from ownership and management of essential goods and services to creating an enabling environment for others to provide them. This is based partly on the growing evidence of inefficiency of centralized bureaucratic systems and the clear lack of financial resources which developing country governments can command in order to run such systems. The role of government as provider of essential goods and services included the expectation, and indeed commitment by most governments, to provide clean water to all their citizens. This promise, while based on an appreciation of the central role of water in development and a commitment to equity in access to water, no longer seems to be attainable. However, it must be asked whether the goals of poverty alleviation and equity must also be abandoned, or indeed whether they *can* be abandoned if sustainable development is to be achieved.

Women develop and maintain rural water supplies as an integral part of their agricultural and domestic management responsibilities.[53] As farmers, they require water for their agriculture, and in turn their land management practices affect water resources. The impact of water on family health is well known, and hence women have a particular interest in the supply of safe water for their children. However, the emerging approach of valuing water as a commodity to be put to productive use tends to minimize the interests of women in water resources management.[54] First, the most financially productive uses of water which can be quantified are in irrigation, livestock and industry. These are all areas which provide a cash output and are mainly managed by men. Where water is provided at a fee, women are less likely to be able to use it since they generally have less access to cash than men. In addition, where access to water is contingent on property rights in land (in terms of participation in decision-making, riparian access or in other ways), women are far less likely to compete successfully since land ownership by women in Kenya lags well behind that of men. The legacy of customary and contemporary exclusion of women from ownership of land is still evident today.[55]

Based on the foregoing, is important to strike the right balance between the past view of water as a free good to be provided to the public by the government, and the emerging view that water is a commodity to be controlled by private interests and sold to whomever can afford it. Clearly the latter view does not bode well for the poor, the landless, and women and their children. It would also undermine the local knowledge and governance institutions and mechanisms which are currently used to manage many rural water supplies. Neither is the former a viable solution, as experience has shown. What is needed are governance mechanisms which promote equitable access to water, and which foster the growth of diverse institutions to enable the development and sustainable management of water resources.

Options for reform

Development strategies and project planning have often assumed water to be a constant factor and thus neglect the need to protect and develop the resource. Those projects which specifically address water—whether for irrigation, domestic use, livestock or energy—have frequently failed to look sufficiently at the social impacts of water supply and its effect on sustainable land use. While the law recognizes the need to protect water resources, the centralized management of access to water has not succeeded in developing the resource to the degree needed. Yet this dynamic and pervasive resource is an essential component of economic development and ecosystems.

Water and the public trust

In Kenya, the state owns, controls and regulates water use. It is also a trustee of a large proportion of the land. State ownership and control over such vast natural resources is in itself an impediment to the management of those resources in part due to the physical and institutional distance between the owners and the users. The government also has the power to convert communal land or water resources to any use it deems fit. This may not take into account the interests and rights of landowners or customary users and hence give rise to conflict. Thus the importance of clearly defining who the "public" is. The fact that there is public interest in water resources which may subordinate individual property interests also engenders tension over water utilization. There is a clear need to develop reciprocal relations as a means of balancing private interests and the varied public interests in this scarce resource.

The multiple roles of the state regarding land and water have far-reaching legal implications. As we have already seen, one of the consequences is the existence of a complex system of licensing procedures administered by water authorities. Clearly some regulatory mechanisms are needed given the increasing competition for the resource and destruction of watersheds. However the locus, priorities and degree of regulation need to be re-examined.

It has been argued that water be privatized in line with economic liberalization and reduction of the government's role in resource management. Suggestions have been offered that the government respond to the need to increase efficiency of water development through giving the responsibility to abstract, distribute and allocate water to private individuals, associations and corporate interests. It is maintained that this can be done while retaining a measure of public investment and state planning and regulation in essential water development activities. Complete private ownership of water resources is neither likely nor desirable due to equity and strategic national development considerations.

The state's role as owner of water resources may need to be reconsidered in light of the overwhelming public interest in water. The role of public trustee may be more appropriate. However, trusteeship would need to be redefined to eliminate current inconsistencies and given a clear and acceptable definition of the public interests. Popular participation in decision-making will be essential to responsible trusteeship. The state is justified to intervene when the resource begins to be scarce. Equally, state intervention to regulate water use, especially to prevent adverse environmental impacts and ensure equitable access, will remain important.

In Kenya, irrigation can be expected to remain the largest of all water uses for some time to come. Water for irrigation is not suited to exclusive private ownership and control since the potential demand from this activity may substantially reduce the water available for other uses. An unregulated private regime would encourage indiscriminate consumptive utilization of water and lead to rapid depletion.

Conferring full private rights over water upon individuals or corporate entities directly, in the face of potential scarcity, would undermine the objectives of sustainable development. The potential for inequitable distribution of a delicate resource which is essential for life is not suited to experimentation. This requires a national policy, and legal and planning framework which specifically addresses the allocation of water between competing uses—domestic, public, industrial, power, irrigation, transportation—according to explicit development and equity criteria. In other words, there needs to be in place a water resource planning activity based on acceptable priorities and accurate assessment of the available volume of water in catchment areas and drainage basins and recharge rates. Consequently, one of the options for constitutional revision would be to encourage private (individual, community or corporate) water management while maintaining state regulation of the resource and enhancing state planning of its protection and use.

Innovations in rights and institutions

Since land tenure and water resource management are inextricably linked, most of the policy options governing water also relate to land. There is need for an over-arching land-use policy to integrate the various tenurial and sectoral arrangements that exist in the country. Currently, land-use is governed by laws and institutions established to deal with agriculture, forestry, wildlife, transportation, energy and trust lands. All of these sectors affect water resources. The current national Development Plan devotes a section to policies and strategies for water resources and development, stating that: ". . . the government will ensure that water resource conservation and management will form part and parcel of overall environmental conservation."[56]

Over the years, the government has recognized the need to review and develop a comprehensive land-use policy through the establishment of a Land Use Commission, as suggested in the national development plans of the 1980s and 1990s. One of the policy issues that such a commission would investigate is the protection of water catchment areas which must involve the land, forest and water sectors.

It is essential that governance systems impinging on water resources recognize the scarce nature of water in Kenya. This will require a departure from the English antecedents which were based on a plentiful resource, and focus on developing the water rather than just extracting and apportioning it. This would include emphasizing mechanisms to promote groundwater recharge such as revegetation, rainwater harvesting and continued investment in soil and water conservation. Sustainable management systems should also be promoted for water catchment areas so that they may both provide livelihoods and enhance recharge. Alternatives to large-scale interbasin transfers and dams should be developed in order to avoid major disruptions of the hydrologic systems which have serious ecological and social consequences.

As already indicated, the current Water Act is regulation-based, dealing largely with the procedures for responding to requests for water apportionment and fixing penalties for contravention of its rules. It lacks planning and priority-setting mechanisms and has inadequate provisions for assessing activities which may have adverse impacts on water supply and utilization. In essence the current legal regime concentrates on the distribution of water for consumptive uses to the exclusion of other environmental considerations.

In view of the government's calls for a review of land use policies, it is important to understand the underlying assumptions about land ownership. It is time to look into alternative resource tenure systems that reflect Kenya's diverse production and social systems. Governance regimes which allow the disaggregation of rights to enable multiple uses and security of tenure where needed (whether customary or statutory) should be considered. A coherent land-use policy covering all the key sectors with a co-ordinating mechanism to reduce conflicts is also required.

Clearly there is an urgent need for measures to harmonize the different sectoral activities in order to foster optimal land use and control environmental degradation. Comprehensive water and forestry master plans have now been drafted which have generated information on these sectors and on their relationship with other sectors. In addition, a national environmental action plan has been prepared which cuts across the sectors. These are steps in the right direction. But no matter how well these plans are prepared, since they address only policy and legal change they can only have limited impact as long as constitutional provisions inhibit sustainable resource management. Reform of the constitutional framework should therefore precede or be done in concert with the formulation and periodic review of new water law and policies.

Conclusions

Natural resource tenure systems define the ways in which resources are mobilized for economic development. They also define the equity of access, distribution of benefits and sustainability of resource utilization. For this reason, resource tenure systems must be clearly defined within the law and conferred security under the law. Kenya is somewhat unique in having a diversity of land tenure systems which align roughly with its diverse socio-ecosystems. Kenya has also gone further than many countries in Africa in experimenting with private property regimes. Historically, Western norms and laws providing rights to water have attempted to provide a set of rules for managing a dynamic public resource within the constraints of a fixed privately-owned resource—land. In Kenya the *de facto* tenure regimes governing land are diverse and evolving, providing an additional challenge to an already complex problem.

Since water is essentially a common property resource with an overwhelming role in the public interest, its sustainable use depends on how individuals, civil society and government relate to each other through the medium of governance. Water is also an extremely scarce resource in Kenya. Hence exclusive ownership, whether by individuals or the government, may not be the most suitable regime. Governance mechanisms are needed which allow water to be managed at different levels in the public interest. Thus, public trust status may provide the best governance framework if revised to reflect equity and participation concerns.

This requires that the public trust be conceived as government custodianship for the public, comprising both current and future generations. Key issues which should be embodied in the public trust include equitable distribution, enhancement of recharge, multiple compatible uses of water catchments, encouraging the operation of traditional resource management systems, and other issues which reflect the dynamic nature, the scarcity and the essential properties of water. It is also necessary to build capacity to enhance surface and groundwater supplies in institutions at the local, regional and national levels.

The land tenure system should also reflect the social and ecological links between land and water. This will need to be put in place in concert with a

clear land-use policy. Innovative measures which provide for different types
of rights for different resources should also be considered. For example,
zoning which allows certain uses in water catchment areas but regulates
those which may damage groundwater recharge could have great benefits.
Rather than attempting to exclude people from conservation and catchment
areas, zoning would permit people to earn a living from the land and only
restrict those activities which would be damaging to the particular
ecological functions of concern, i.e., groundwater recharge. Zoning based on
the population density which can be supported by the water resources, or
restriction of polluting industries from locating over aquifers or on certain
water courses are other options. Easements which would allow access to
surface waters by people who are not landowners, as well as to wildlife, may
also take on an increasingly important role.

Notes

1. Falkenmark and Lindh, 1993.
2. Republic of Kenya, 1992b. Main Report, Vol. II, Part 1, p. 2.
3. Republic of Kenya, 1992b. Main Report, Vol. II, Part 1, p. 2.
4. Republic of Kenya, 1992b. Main Report, Vol. II, Part 1, p. 5.
5. Republic of Kenya, 1992b. Sectoral Report(E), p. E–23.
6. Republic of Kenya, 1992b. Sectoral Report(E), p. E–28.
7. Baker, 1984, p. 10.
8. Republic of Kenya, 1992b. Main Report, Vol. II, Part 1, p. 9.
9. Bruce and Migot-Adholla, 1994; Mugabe *et al.* , 1994.
10. Okoth-Ogendo, 1988, p. 190.
11. The Registered Land Act, Sec. 27(a), (emphasis added).
12. William, 1985, p. 82.
13. See Cleaver and Elson, 1995.
14. Migot-Adholla, Place and Kosura, 1994, p. 122.
15. Teerink and Nakashima, 1993, p. 55.
16. *Liggins* v. *Inge*, (1831) 7 Bing. 682, 131 E.R 263 at 268 per C.J. Tindall.
17. Registered Land Act, Section 30(b).
18. *Embrey* v. *Owen*, (1851) 6 Ex. 353, 155 E.R. 579 at 585–6, per B. Parke (emphasis added).
19. Hobday, p. 97 (emphasis added).
20. *Race* v. *Ward*, 4 E. & B. 702, 119 E.R 259 at 262.
21. *Halsbury's Law England*, 4th ed., para 370.
22. *Lyon* v. *Fishmongers Co.*, (1876) 1 App. Cas. 662 at 673.
23. *Ewart* v. *Belfast Guardians*, (1882) 9 L.R Ir. 172 p. 194, per C.B. Pallas.
24. Teerink and Nakashima, 1993, p. 18.
25. *Chasemore* v. *Richards*, (1859)7 H.L.C37411 E.R. 140 p. 152.
26. *Ormerod* v. *Todmorden Mill Co.*, (1883) 11 Q.B.D. 155, p. 170 (emphasis added).
27. *Jones* v. *Llanrwrst Urban District Council*, (1911) 1 Ch.D. 393.
28. *Attorney General v Burridge, The Portsmouth Harbour Case*, (1822) 10 Price 350, 147 E.R. 385.

29. *Blackburn* v. *Somers*, (1879) 5.L.R. Ir. 1, p. 17 (emphasis added).
30. *Hodgekinson* v. *Ennor, (1963) 4 B&S 229, 122 E.R. 446* at 450, quoting *Tenant* v. *Goodwin*, 2 Ld. Raym 1098, Slak. 21 360.
31. Teerink and Nakashima, 1993.
32. Teerink and Nakashima, 1993, p. 10.
33. Teerink and Nakashima, 1993.
34. Water Act, Sec. 36(1).
35. Water Act, Part XIII.
36. Republic of Kenya, 1984a, para. 1.73..
37. Odero, 1975, p. 100.
38. Cleaver and Elson, 1995.
39. Water Act, Sec. 150.
40. Agriculture Act, Sec. 48.
41. Exceptions in anglophone Africa include Zimbabwe, Lesotho, Swaziland, Botswana and South Africa. This may be due to the influence of the South African regime which was based on Roman–Dutch law. See Okoth-Ogendo, 1988.
42. Water Act, Sec. 35.
43. Constitution of Kenya, Sec. 75(1).
44. Constitution of Kenya, Sec. 75(c).
45. See the Land Acquisition Act, schedule, Sec. 1–4.
46. Okoth-Ogendo, 1988, p.189.
47. Water Act, Sec. 110.
48. Walston, 1989, p. 586 (emphasis added).
49. See for example, Sax, 1990.
50. See among others: Ingram and Oggins, 1992; Wilkinson, 1989.
51. *Illinois Central RR* v. *Illinois*. The Illinois legislature had granted a fee interest in the Chicago Waterfront to a Railroad Company. The legislature later revoked the fee grant and the railroad company sued. The Supreme Court upheld the action of the Illinois legislature. For more on this and related cases, see *Natural Resources Journal,* 1992: 32(3) and 1990: 30(2).
52. Water Act, Sec. 148, also Part II, Sec. 2.
53. Khasiani, 1992; Sigot, Thrupp and Green, 1995.
54. Cleaver and Elson, 1995.
55. Gender equity in landownership has been hindered by the fact that women were not registered as land owners during the process of land adjudication, consolidation and registration of the 1950s. See Kabeberi-Macharia in Khasiani, 1993.
56. Republic of Kenya, 1994a, p. 199.

Land tenure and forest resource management

7

P. N. OKOWA-BENNUN WITH

ALBERT M. MWANGI

Introduction

This chapter examines the relationship between land tenure and forest resources management in Kenya. It reviews the various property rights regimes and outlines their implications for the sustainable utilization of forest resources. It argues that there is a need to create a balance between property rights and the need for conservation. In making this case, the chapter presents an overview of the values of forest resources. This is followed by an assessment of how the various property regimes affect forest resource management.

The chapter concludes with suggestions on what kinds of constitutional provisions need to be considered in creating a balance between private property interests and conservation requirements. In addition, the chapter calls for a review of the concept of trusteeship as used in the Kenya Constitution regarding trust lands and notes that such a review could go a long way in providing a sound constitutional basis for community-based management of forest resources.

The value of forests

Kenya's forest cover is estimated at 1.4 million ha, or nearly two per cent of the country. The gazetted forest area is about 1.7 million ha of which closed canopy forest accounts for 1.22 million ha (which include plantations).[1] In this discussion a forest is considered to be any natural vegetation in which the dominant species are trees, with crowns that touch each other to form a continuous canopy. Loosely speaking, almost any vegetation with trees, including plantations, would constitute a forest. The Forests Act defines a forest area as any area that has been declared to be a forest area by the minister responsible. Under Section 4 of the Act, some of the areas that fall within the legal definition of forests may not be forests from an ecological or production perspective.

Forests serve a number of critical roles. These functions include the prevention of soil erosion and the maintenance of the soil's fertility, the protection of water catchment areas and wildlife habitats, as well as the conservation of valuable gene pools of flora and fauna. In general, the maintenance of ecological integrity depends a great deal on the extent of forest cover. For instance, a study of the south-western Mau and Transmara forests, concluded that these forests are some of the largest tracts of indigenous highland forest remaining in East Africa (Figure 8). Within them are a number of rare or endangered species of fauna and flora, the loss of which cannot be replaced. The area also serves as a watershed for a number of rivers and their tributaries. Removal of natural vegetation in these forests without replacement would consequently increase soil erosion, the frequency of flash flooding in these rivers as well as the rate of siltation downstream. In general, the maintenance of ecological integrity depends a great deal on the extent of forest cover.

The other important functions of forests include supplying fuelwood, timber and traditional medicines for local consumption. Fuelwood is still the principal source of energy for the majority of rural households and for low-income groups in urban areas. The current annual supply of fuelwood is estimated to be 18.7 million tonnes of which about 28% comes from gazetted forests; 47% from family farms and 25% from rangelands.[2] About three quarters of the charcoal used in urban areas is derived from rangeland vegetation. These demands on forest and woodland resources can only be met without causing environmental degradation if the resources are exploited on a sustainable yield basis. That is, exploitation must be carried out in a manner that allows the regeneration so as to meet present and future needs. Unfortunately, this is not happening in respect of Kenya's forest resources.

Figure 8 Forest reserves in Kenya

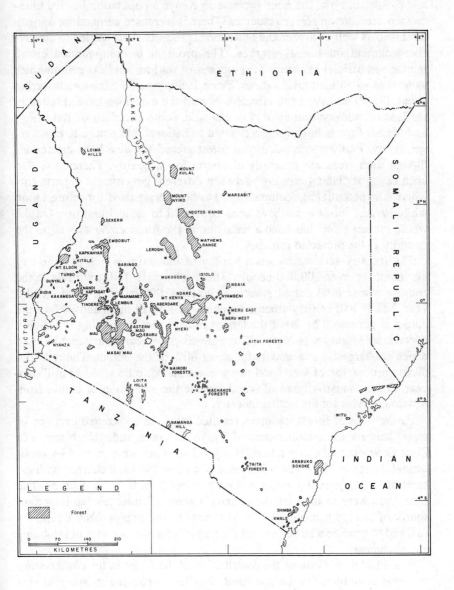

SUDAN

ETHIOPIA

LAKE TURKANA

UGANDA

SOMALI REPUBLIC

LOIMA HILLS

MOUNT KULAL

MOUNT NYIRO

MARSABIT

NDOTOS RANGE

SEKERR

MATHEWS RANGE

EMBOBUT

KAPKANYAR

LEROGHI

BARINGO

KITALE

MT. ELGON

TURBO

MUKOGODO

ISIOLO

BUNYALA

NGAIA

BUSIA

KAKAMEGA

NANDI

KAPTAGAT

NDARE

MT. KENYA

NYAMBENI

TINDERET

LEMBUS

MARMANET

ABERDARE

MERU EAST

MERU WEST

VICTORIA

L. VICTORIA

NYANZA

MAU

EASTERN MAU

EBURU

NYERI

KITUI FORESTS

MASAI MAU

NAIROBI FORESTS

LOITA HILLS

MACHAKOS FORESTS

TANZANIA

NAMANGA HILL

WITU

ARABUKO SOKOKE

INDIAN OCEAN

TAITA FORESTS

SHIMBA

KWALE

LEGEND

Forest

0   70   140   210

KILOMETRES

The depletion of Kenya's forests has also been aggravated by various social problems. First, the rapid increase in Kenya's population has led to increased pressure on scarce resources. There is increased demand for agricultural land as well as timber and other forest products. This has led to massive encroachment on forest reserves. The problem is compounded by an increase in official excisions for purposes of settling landless communities as well as establishing tea estates. Since 1986, over 33 excisions covering about 47,000 ha have been effected. Not all the excisions have resulted in the loss of conservation areas. For example, some excisions of Kakamega and Mrima forests have been converted to national and nature reserves respectively. Furthermore, additional forest areas have also been created although such areas are generally of poorer forest quality. There have also been cases of "land swapping" between different government departments where low potential agricultural land has been designated for reforestation while natural forest areas have been converted to agricultural use. On the whole the net effect has been a reduction in the forest cover as well as the integrity of the protected forests.[3]

The forestry sector supports a variety of industries which provide employment for over 100,000 people. There are nearly 450 saw mills in the country whose total output is estimated at 200,000 cu m of sawn wood a year. Nearly half of the output is accounted for by 14 mills and 80% of the output is generated by 20 of the largest mills. Paper processing is a highly concentrated industry in Kenya. There are six paperboard and paper mills of which the largest one accounts for about 80% of the output. The total domestic production of wood and paper is estimated to be US$100 million a year. Other industrial uses of wood include the extraction of tannin from *Acacia mearnsii* for the leather industry.

Further loss of forest resources resulted from the ungazetted excision of forest land for the establishment of Nyayo tea zones under the Nyayo Tea Zone Development Corporation (NTZC). The zones were created by presidential decree in 1986. The NTZC was created in 1988 and charged with the creation of tea growing zones around gazetted forests in 14 districts. The objectives were to increase the country's acreage under tea (an important source of foreign exchange), to provide a source of employment in rural areas, and to provide a buffer around the nation's forests as a way of inhibiting encroachment.

It is difficult to evaluate the contribution of the zones to the conservation of forest resources. On the one hand, they have provided meaningful employment to local communities, thus alleviating the problem of over-dependency on forest resources. On the other hand, much forest land has been lost through the creation of the zones. They have for example, led to the loss of over 15,000 ha of forest in the Mau and Transmara forests to date. There is also evidence to suggest that they have failed to act as a buffer against encroachment. It may be too early to evaluate the effectiveness of the zones as conservation agents. For the moment, it can be said with some certainty that their role as buffers against encroachment has not been realized.

Although it has been suggested that the state should relinquish its monopoly rights over gazetted forests, we have also indicated that there remain exceptional instances when the retention of such monopoly rights is the best way of conserving stocks or endangered species. The effectiveness of monopoly rights, however, presupposes the existence of an efficient state machinery able to carry out its duties. Unfortunately, the existing capacity of the Forest Department is inadequate and needs to be strengthened and used efficiently if it is to achieve this. Forest policy and legislation are frequently contravened owing to inadequate enforcement capability, and differences between local and national priorities. Other problems hindering effective policing of monopoly rights include labour shortage, lack of vehicles and inadequate funds to maintain those vehicles that are available. If the state is to effectively police forest areas under its exclusive control, the above problems must be addressed.

It is significant that much of Kenya's tree resources exist outside of gazetted forests in the extensive woodlands and on land devoted to agriculture. These trees are embedded in pastoral and agricultural land use systems and fall under a number of different types of tenure regimes.[4] They are also usually managed by the land users, and may be protected by social norms or physical barriers. Government policies and economic forces can have severe impacts on the management and exploitation of these trees. Charcoal prices, for example, will determine the tree offtake required to cover domestic needs of a dryland farmer, especially during a drought.[5] The government and other organizations concerned should actively promote the use of alternative sources of energy, to ease the present overdependence on fuelwood and charcoal. It is only when these related social and economic issues are addressed that one can expect the property regimes discussed in this chapter to realize their full potential.

It is against this background of rapidly declining forest resources that the imposition of legal safeguards becomes mandatory if depletion of forests is to be effectively controlled. Since forests partake the form of fixtures on land, any scheme for their conservation and management must necessarily impinge on entrenched property rights under existing property regimes. Conservation measures must therefore find legitimacy under a variety of property arrangements. Their efficacy, too, must be evaluated within the same framework.

Property rights in land

Land tenure and forests

Much has been written about the role of tenure rules in resource use and conservation.[6] There are three distinct tenure regimes in Kenya's legal system. It is necessary to examine the contents of each in some detail, since the conservation and management of trees is to a large extent determined by the legal attributes of the land on which they are growing. The first regime is characterized by the absolute proprietorship of an individual or a legal entity over a given parcel of land. It is derived from English property law concepts of individual tenure and is statutorily embodied in the Registered Land Act and supplemented by both the Indian Transfer of Property Act and the Registration of Titles Act. This absolute control conferred on individuals and other legal entities is however implicitly subject to superior rights (radical title) vested in the state.

One of the incidents of this absolute proprietorship is that proprietors *alone* have the power to determine the use to which their land can be put. This means that an individual farmer can impede the development and management of forest resources, if he or she refuses to take part in afforestation or agroforestry programmes for any reason. Fortunately, the state retains the power to regulate the use of private land, if such regulation is deemed to be in the interest of land preservation or development. It should however be noted that incentives to land owners may be more effective than legal sanctions in encouraging the adoption of agroforestry and afforestation.

The second property regime in existence is based on communal ownership of land. In property jurisprudence, this property regime is referred to as customary or communal land tenure. Customary tenure rules are complex and multi-layered. They vary spacially and temporally although certain characteristics and principles are held in common among communities across Africa. In theory this property regime is no longer significant with the advent of land adjudication and consolidation programmes. The property regime may, however, be functional at the local levels; it is significant here because it is linked to the application of indigenous knowledge to the management of natural resources.

It is indeed the case that in practice this regime continues to govern property relations even in those areas where individual tenure regimes are in existence. However, as a distinct legal category, the communal tenure regime applies only to two categories of land areas. The first are trust lands, formerly known as native reserves, where the land has not been adjudicated and consolidated. The second instance of its operation is in respect of the Land

(Group Representatives) Act. In situations falling within the scope of the Act, individual title is deemed an inappropriate arrangement particularly in light of the prevailing land use practices (predominantly pastoral) and other cultural considerations.[7] All members of the group have equal and guaranteed access to the resource in question. The management of the resource is vested in a team of representatives acting on behalf of the collective whole.[8]

The third property regime takes the form of state ownership. This is applied to gazetted forests subject to the state's monopoly rights. Under the Forests Act, land may be declared a forest area by proclamation in the official *Kenya Gazette*, and by the same mechanism any forest area may be declared as demarcated forest or nature reserve.[9] Although state ownership of forests has been widely criticized, it can be argued that private state ownership often makes the best sense where the plan is to conserve the forest for some reason rather than working it industrially. This may be the case where the purpose is to conserve the flora and fauna, watersheds, or where the aim is to ensure the conservation of tree stock and species.[10]

Unfortunately the state has proved to be an inefficient custodian of the monopoly rights vested in it. The system of state ownership of forest reserves is bound to fail unless it is intimately linked to the social context of its operation. It is precisely because this linkage is missing that the depletion of forests by communities neighbouring them continues on a grand scale, as the search for agricultural land and fuelwood resources continues. Forest reserves are viewed by local people clamouring for land as wastelands which can be exploited as a degraded common resource.[11] In this regard ". . . the future of . . . forests is inextricably tied to the future of the local population; the conservation of the forest depends upon the sustainability of local rural livelihood. Attention to human issues will therefore necessarily be part of any proposed ameliorative and management measures."[12] It is suggested here that if human pressure on land is not eased, no amount of repression or regulation is likely to be an effective mechanism for conserving and managing our forests.

Landlessness and security of title

The future of Kenya's forests is intimately tied to the provision of security of land tenure to landless communities. The acuteness of their dependence on forest resources has already been noted. The depletion of forests may be partially brought to a halt if local communities are made grantees of leaseholds in the neighbouring forests. That, however, must be viewed as a temporary solution since a lease is only an interest in land for a fixed number of years. It is therefore unlikely to offer the kind of security that most landless people are looking for.

In certain areas, the problem has been partially alleviated through excision of government land. However, it should be noted that providing adequate land for resettlement does not in itself remove all pressures on the forest. In situations where resettlement of landless people has taken place, settlers have found it difficult to establish themselves as farmers because they lack the financial resources to purchase seeds, and tools required for cash crop farming. In some cases, the settled people, have had to return to the forest in order to survive.

The relocation of these people, many of whom still depend upon hunting and gathering for their subsistence, is unlikely to be adequate on its own. Concrete support to enable the settlers to establish a viable economy is needed. Agricultural extension, loan possibilities and perhaps grant assistance with seeds and fertilizers to launch cash-cropping has been cited as an area of desirable assistance. The need for community education, for example, to encourage settlers to see the folly of selling their land in times of acute financial need has also been stressed. It has been suggested that a stock-repayment-by-progeny scheme could work well and contribute significantly to settler stability. In short, implementing means to induce a slow but sure rise in settler standard of living will prove critical to the success of the relocation exercise and to the success of government efforts to keep the forest clear of squatters.

In order to make the relocation exercise viable, the government should be prepared to provide more land for the activity. Although it has been noted that excision of land is both a necessary and useful exercise, it is also unfortunate that in its present form, it leads to very serious loss of forest resources. In this regard vast forest resources are lost through the formal excision of tracts of forest for human settlement and other uses.

Public tenure and its alternatives

State ownership and control of forests

The establishment of forest areas and the declaration of nature reserves are the two principal mechanisms used by the state to create and consolidate its monopoly right over forests.[13] It is a characteristic of this monopoly right that the state alone determines the use to which a state forest can be put. Crucial decisions on the delineation and management of state forests are left to organs of the state and parliament. There is limited room for public participation in the decision-making process. Under existing legislation, the following activities are prohibited in gazetted forests, unless licensed by the state: grazing, honey gathering, hunting, taking, damaging or setting fire to any forest produce, staying in the forest overnight, clearing land and constructing a road or path.[14]

Presidential decrees and orders from the provincial administration have also been used in exercising state control over forestry-related activities on public and private lands. A presidential decree prohibited all cutting of indigenous timber in 1986 and 1987, and district-level initiatives banning grazing and residence in forests have been adopted at national levels. In some districts such as Kericho and Nakuru, the district authorities have banned the production of charcoal within the forest and have ceased to issue permits allowing the transport of charcoal. Although the desired outcomes are sometimes not realized, these decisions often have good forest conservation intent.

In nature reserves, any removal of or damage to forest produce or disturbance of the flora and fauna must be conservation-motivated, and must be authorized by the chief conservator (now the director of forestry) while hunting and fishing are expressly prohibited. There are reasonable ecological reasons for these prohibitions. From a theoretical standpoint, the state appears to have put in place a fairly watertight mechanism for the management and conservation of forest reserves. The practical efficacy of this regime is, however, open to question.

State monopoly rights can be justified on a number of grounds. First, since forests serve a number of important societal functions that transcend individual concerns, their protection is best assured by a system of state control. Forests provide goods, services and amenities that are of a public nature and should not, therefore, be left entirely in the hands of private institutions whose principal goal is the maximization of profits. For instance, the private sector may not have a financial reason to protect forests for their roles in soil conservation, water catchment protection, climate amelioration, preservation of biodiversity or aesthetic values.

Secondly, proper management and conservation of forests presupposes the existence of expertise and financial resources that almost always lie beyond individual competence. In countries where private forestry is well developed, a lot of resources have gone into capacity-building through training of land owners and forestry extension staff. They are also supported by financial incentives and an elaborate infrastructure in all aspects of forestry. The training of forest officers as well as the policing and management of the remaining national forests are arguably, tasks that can only be efficiently performed by the state at the present time.

Finally, state ownership is important because it provides a framework for long-term planning and implementation of policies. It also allows for the establishment of an integrated approach to the conservation of forest resources. Since forest resources are the concern of different government ministries, it can be argued that only the state apparatus provides a mechanism for coordinating the works of the ministries. Such then is the strength of the case in favour of public ownership, at least in theory. The practice, however, provides a most gloomy picture, for the state has not been able to effectively assert its monopoly rights against forest dwellers, illegal squatters, contractors and even its own employees.

It has been argued here that conservation strategies that are insensitive to the social context of their operation are doomed to fail. The dependency of communities bordering forests on forest resources must first be alleviated if state monopoly rights are to serve their functions. The proposed new forest policy contained in the Kenya Forestry Master Plan addresses the question of traditional rights and states that: "When not in conflict with the principle of sound and sustainable resource utilization and management or national development priorities, the traditional ways of life of people living within and adjacent to designated forest areas, and the forest-related cultural values and religious practices of these people will be respected."[15]

The forestry master plan further notes that local people will be viewed as development partners and will be encouraged to participate in the management, utilization, and conservation activities of various forestry programmes such as indigenous forests, plantations, farm forestry, and plantation forestry.[16] It is thus hoped that current and future forestry planning will exhibit a genuine commitment to the needs of local communities. However, unless the related problems of dependency on forests for fuel, landlessness, and lack of alternative economic opportunities amongst communities bordering forest reserves are solved, the stated objectives of the Forests Act will not be realized.

It is against the background of state inefficiency in managing resources under its charge and addressing local community needs, that it becomes necessary to explore the possibility of replacing state control with alternative property regimes or transferring some state rights to local communities. It should be noted that a radical change in the tenure structure for state forest lands is likely to be a very contentious issue. Two alternative property regimes have been proposed. The first school of thought postulates that forests would be better managed if they were privatized. This would involve transferring state-owned forest lands to individuals or other legal entities who would then have absolute control over the mechanisms of exploitation and management. The second school of thought argues that an efficient management of forests must take into account the dependency of local communities on the same resources. Such a management system would incorporate the rights of local communities and also clearly state their obligations. State forests have often often failed to address local community needs because their goals and levels of output are centrally determined. Proponents of this alternative therefore suggest that forests can only be effectively managed if leaseholds were to be granted to communities dependent on state-owned forests. These leaseholds would be subjected to strict contractual terms designed to ensure that exploitation is only undertaken on a sustainable yield basis.

Privatization of state forests

The idea of private forests is not novel. In Britain, Austria, Scandinavia and the Mediterranean countries, farmers are the major owners of forests. In Latin America 50% of the forests are in private hands, as are the bulk of forests in Japan and Korea.[17] The merit of privatization lies in its ability to act as an investment incentive. It also results in effective control of the resource in question. On the merits of privatization, Commander has observed that there is "plentiful evidence . . . that forests can be maintained in a private ownership concept and that the privatization of rewards ensures the satisfactory enforcement of rights. The state, precisely because of its amorphous and disparate nature, is inherently a weak vessel for the physical, let alone psychological enforcement of exclusive controls".[18]

Despite its stated advantages, it is suggested here that the shortcomings of full privatization in the Kenyan context generally outweigh any merits it may have. It has been noted earlier that privatization introduces a profit interest in the management and conservation of a resource with public ramifications. There is little evidence in Kenya that privately owned forests have been managed with a long-term view. Secondly, whilst it may cure some of the weaknesses inherent in a system of state ownership, it will not solve and if anything it may compound the problems of local communities dependent on forest resources. Local communities are not likely to benefit from a privatization exercise, since they lack the capital and expertise which are essential prerequisites. The creation of private interests will also automatically extinguish any *de facto* secondary rights that local communities enjoy in neighbouring forests.

It is therefore the case that whilst privatization may meet some of the shortcomings inherent in state control, it is unlikely to solve the concomitant problem of dependency by impoverished local people on forest resources. It is therefore suggested that despite its merits, privatization is far from a feasible alternative. Privatization of forests in Europe and other developed countries may have succeeded because their economies have an industrial base rather than an agricultural one. This has minimized the local demand for agricultural land and fuelwood and the unfortunate side effects of privatization on local communities. Despite this feature, Clawson notes that in the USA, the most serious problem for private forestry has been ". . . the lack of incentive on the part of the private forest owners to upgrade or maintain the quality of the external benefits their forests provide."[19]

In the USA, 38% of the unreserved forests (forests that have not been withdrawn from timber use by legal or administrative rules) or approximately 112 million ha are under some form of public ownership.[20] In addition, reserved lands for national parks, fish and wildlife, defense and other uses contain extensive areas of forest lands. This extensive public ownership of forest lands is a reflection of the American society's "concern over the consequences of private ownership of forests."[21] In society's view, the value of public goods and the existence of many externalities is often so critical that state ownership has been preferred.

If the relevant social and economic considerations are not taken care of, privatizing state forests can lead to undesirable consequences. Whyte, for example, notes the following on a 1987 political decision to privatize New Zealand's commercial forests and to passively protect non-commercial forests: "having saved the forests of New Zealand for 70 years, they are now under threat again because of a lack of management input, while the commercial plantations have a far higher risk of being exploited for the benefit of individual firms rather than of the nation as a whole."[22]

In Kenya, gazetted forests (forests that have been surveyed, demarcated on the ground and legally declared to be forest reserves) cover 1.7 million ha while partially forested areas which are proposed for gazettement cover another 0.5 million hectares. This adds up to a total of approximately 2.2 million hectares.[23] In addition to their commercial use, these forests are critical for water catchment, preservation of biodiversity and the provision of many non-timber forest products that are highly valued by local communities. The fundamental challenges in this policy environment include properly defining society's interest and also reconciling short-term and long-term needs of the population.

One option is to move gradually towards the privatization of the commercial forestry sector (plantation management) while state ownership of forest land and trees are retained.[24] Projected gains from the proposed changes must be carefully weighed against the broader social costs. Given Kenya's limited forest resource base, it is crucial that the remaining state forests are managed in society's best interest.

Feasibility of leaseholds

It is suggested in this section that the state should relinquish some of its monopoly rights over specific areas and specific forest products and replace them with leaseholds, to be granted to communities neighbouring and dependent on forests. In this proposed arrangement all leaseholds would be subject to supervisory powers vested in the state. These leasehold should contain inbuilt contractual terms with regard to tree cutting, planting and the extraction of other forest resources. Under this arrangement exploitation must be carried out only on a sustainable yield basis. In other words this particular arrangement would tap most of the benefits of private tenurial rights while at the same time taking care of the related problem of dependency of neighbouring communities on forest resources. In return, the grantor of a leasehold will be required to adopt such land use practices that are likely to lead to the conservation and management of forests on a sustainable yield basis. This kind of programme would require careful monitoring evaluation to determine the exact nature of rights to be granted to local communities as well as the potential impacts of individual and social investment decisions.

Leasing is a partial transfer of rights over land and is one option under which state-owned forest land can be managed to encourage efficiency in use. All rights that go with ownership revert to the owner after the agreed duration of the lease. The final outcome of this tenurial arrangement depends on the conditions of the lease and how closely they are enforced. Other options short of transferring the forests to private ownership include renting, sharecropping and granting easements. These arrangements essentially involve trade in property rights over land.

The terms of the leaseholds would, for instance, regulate the type of forest cover to be maintained, density of planting and the felling cycle. In addition, the leasehold terms should stipulate the minimum as well as the maximum levels of permitted felling. Some forest management decisions are fairly complex and are guided by a series of technical notes and orders. Good forestry advise to leaseholders would therefore be necessary. Since the state would under this arrangement retain ultimate supervisory powers, it is suggested that it should also provide technical advice and other necessary services. In this way the state could ensure that ecological integrity is maintained while meeting the more immediate needs of forest communities.

Any new system would need to reflect the differential access to and control over forest products by women and men. Otherwise, women may lose access to products important for maintaining family welfare, such as medicinal plants, fuelwood and roofing thatch, as well as independent sources of income. It has been noted that where women make substantial investments in reforestation projects, such as caring for nurseries and transplanting seedlings, men may benefit disproportionately by being the ones to harvest and market the trees and hence control the proceeds.[25] Rocheleau and Edmunds suggest that policy and project interventions make "explicit reference to who disposes of tree products and help women to avoid situations in which their labor is exploited largely for the benefit of others."[26] Legal changes should also support women's rights to access to forest products.

Leasehold transfer of certain rights can go even further in supporting women's rights to access to forest products. First, they should be granted to women as well as men, particularly women heading households and others who lack other family support. Secondly, leaseholds can be designated specifically to "accommodate multiple uses and multiple users, including women's use and access rights on male private property, community property and property controlled by public officials."[27] For example, gathering or collecting forest products, usually a women's activity, can be given legal recognition and protection. Across Africa women commonly have rights to gather deadwood and fruits and fodder from trees otherwise controlled by men. These well-established customary rights can be legally codified and expanded to include having a say in choice of species for reforestation.

This proposed regime has its shortcomings, too. Indeed there is evidence to suggest that it has been tried before, on a small scale but without much success. Throughout British colonial Africa the *taungya* system (popularly known as the *shamba* system in Kenya) was in operation. In Kenya, the system was developed as a practical mechanism of getting vast areas of forest planted. Farmers were encouraged to rent forest land for cultivation and were required to plant and tend seedlings at the same time. After three or four years, the cultivators would be issued with other plots elsewhere and would leave the young plantations to grow without accompanying agricultural activities. A total of 170,000 hectares of plantations have been established in Kenya to date, and nearly all of them through the *shamba* system.[28] Unfortunately, the system did not work well for a variety of reasons. The *shamba* system as originally conceived ". . . had the built-in defect that the cultivators were allowed to reside in the forest, and so eventually to acquire squatter rights."[29] It led to an influx of tenants and workers on gazetted forests, and massive encroachment on forest land, thus defeating the very idea of conservation. Much gazetted forest land was being intensively cultivated and grazed. A study of the situation led to the dissolution of the *shamba* system in 1989.

It is submitted that the *shamba* system failed not because of any inherent defects in the idea, but because it was introduced without sufficient safeguards capable of meeting the ends of forest conservation. Existing evidence suggests that it operated in a fairly loose and informal way, and was, strictly speaking, not a legal regime capable of strict enforcement. It is, therefore, suggested that if applied effectively, the system of granting leaseholds can be an excellent way of managing production forests presently owned by the state. All the appropriate guiding mechanisms, however, need to be put in place to avoid past mistakes. According to the Kenya Forestry Master Plan, an important concern in plantation forestry development is to "find a workable and economically efficient alternative to the shamba system."[30] Leaseholds can serve both the ends of conservation and at the same time enable the state to meet its social obligations to its citizens.

Communal tenure and forest resources

The communal or customary property regime is premised on indigenous property systems that were in existence before the advent of colonialism. In practice, customary tenure retains an enduring influence in Kenya despite the "modern" legal framework. The regime does have some legal application, limited to two categories of land. The first category concerns the trust lands which were formerly native reserves, and especially in those areas where the land has not been adjudicated or consolidated. However, the constitutional provisions and laws that relate to trust lands are inherently biased against traditional rights and interests and have generally served as instruments for phasing out those rights and interests (Appendix I). The recent conflicts between county councils (as custodians of trust lands) and local communities over forest areas in pastoral lands illustrates this point.

The second concerns those areas in respect of which the Land (Group Representatives) Act is in operation. In these situations, the primarily pastoral land use practices and social structures make individual tenure an unattractive framework of ownership. The essential characteristic of communal tenure is the existence of diverse use rights by a group of people over the same piece of land and the complete absence of exclusive ownership. The property is usually managed by a number of individuals on behalf of the corporate whole.

Communal ownership of forests generally ensures access for all group members to tree resources. This access is generally defined by gender, season, state of the resource and other socio-economic and cultural factors. Communal regimes protect the sustainability of the resource by establishing closed seasons, bans on the cutting down of live trees, or particular methods of tapping the resource. These rules are designed to ensure resource use in perpetuity and are generally responsive to changing external circumstances. However, communal ownership has shortcomings as a means for conserving forest resources. First, it may not be able to withstand the demands accompanying severe resource scarcity and it becomes very vulnerable in the face of population increases. In this regard Shepherd has noted that as "land itself becomes short, security of tenure becomes more important. No long-term activity, especially tree-planting, will be undertaken without it. Shadowy usufruct rights . . . are too uncertain over the long term, so that tree tenure without land tenure gradually becomes an impossibility."[31] This is true for many parts of Kenya where communal tenure has now given way to various forms of private ownership. Important exceptions to this observation exist, however, where strong customary norms are in effect. This can be observed in the case of sacred groves (such as the Kayaforests in Kenya) where spiritual beliefs and practices add weight to customary norms.[32]

This change has been effected through the fiat of legislation. The undermining of traditional decision-making and social norms has also reduced the effectiveness of this regime where it still exists. This erosion of customary use has also undermined the rights of women. The right to trees, for example, is guaranteed in many African societies.[33] These rights, however, have been eliminated through the introduction of modern tenure systems, especially the granting of titles to land. The elimination, in turn, has often led to the failure of development projects. As Rocheleau notes, "the road to failure has been paved with good intentions, bad information, and inadequate treatment of women's access to one or more factors of production."[34] Trees and other vegetation are a basic form of natural capital for the local economies and restricting women's access to this resource often undermines community development.

But in order to restore the integrity of local practices, major changes would need to be introduced in the Constitution, particularly to remove those provisions which allow statutory law to render customary practices null and void. A positive constitution would give standing to traditional practices and allow them to evolve with time to become the basis for integrating indigenous practices into common law. The place to start in this effort is to revise the sections of the Constitution dealing with trust land by first defining and implementing the concept of public trusteeship in a manner that is different from the current usage in Kenya. Under the current usage, the state acts as a private owner of land which it allow the people to use. However, a genuine application of the public trust doctrine requires that the state holds the land in trust for the people.

Private property and police power

The manipulation of private tenure to serve the ends of forest management and conservation is problematic. Private ownership, whether created under the Registered Land Act or the Registration of Titles Act, generally carries absolute rights as regards use and abuse. There are, nevertheless, certain conditions imposed on this form of ownership to cater for public interests.

The specification of property rights associated with a particular form of land ownership is therefore very important. An adequate set of property rights is one that includes: ownership (a legal device that assigns the right to use), full specification of the rights (this provides information on rights, restrictions and penalties for violating them), transferability (allows the owner to transfer different rights to land that one owns), and enforcement (unenforceable property rights are no rights at all).

In matters of forest conservation on privately owned lands, the fundamental question to be asked is whether the state should retain any powers to regulate land use, and if so which ones. In simple terms, can farmers be legally compelled to conserve or grow trees? It is suggested that the answer to this question is in the affirmative. A case in point could be the Naivasha thorn trees (*Acacia xanthophloea*) near Naivasha town on the way to Nakuru. The trees are mostly on private land but there has been public outcry in the press whenever conservation-minded members of the public notice tree cutting in the area. Such appeals to conserve the trees are often directed at the government rather than individual land owners. It is therefore necessary to consider the legal basis of the powers of regulation and qualification. The Chiefs' Authority Act, for example, has wide-ranging powers and has been used to deny tree cutting rights to individual land owners or to compel them to plant trees. There are high transaction costs associated with the specification, transfer and enforcement (policing) of property rights and a policy decision regarding how detailed this process will be has to be made. Other things being equal, investments in specification, transfer, and enforcement of property rights should proceed to the point at which the marginal conditions for efficiency are achieved (when marginal costs are equal to marginal revenue).

The main legal instruments which provide the state with police powers over private land in Kenya are the Agriculture Act, the Chiefs' Authority Act and with more limited application, the Grassfires Act. The basis of powers conferred by the Agriculture Act and the statutes of various drainage basin authorities are examined below. Even in countries where private property interests in land are most highly developed, the state always retains the power to regulate and qualify, or even extinguish, private property rights in land. This normally happens when such qualification or regulation is necessary for the realization of a state objective or is deemed to be in the public interest. It has been observed that these powers emanate from the fact that as part of tenurial arrangements in society, the state holds the ultimate title over all parcels of land within its jurisdiction.[35]

The Agriculture Act contains such regulatory powers and provides the most secure basis for implementing agroforestry programmes. Agroforestry is a useful land use practice that protects the farmer's land from soil erosion, preserves or improves its fertility, and provides fuelwood, fodder, and other wood products. At the same time, it protects natural forests from depletion by reducing pressure on existing forest reserves. It was noted earlier, for instance, that 47% of the fuelwood used in Kenyan households comes from family farms. The potential for agroforestry and other forms of farm forestry in this regard is therefore high. The diffusion and adoption of agroforestry does not, however solely depend on legal provisions. Other important reasons for its adoption or non-adoption might include its profitability (real or perceived), land characteristics, extension education and socio-economic settings within which the land owners are operating.

Since agroforestry can be legally compelled under the Agriculture Act, a detailed examination of the provisions of the Act is necessary. The stated aims of the Act are to promote and maintain a stable agriculture; to ensure the conservation of the soil and its fertility; and to stimulate the development of agricultural land in accordance with accepted practices of good land management and husbandry. In view of the stated objectives, it is submitted that agroforestry or afforestation programmes on private land can only be legally compelled under the Act if such programmes serve the ends of stable or increased agricultural production. This is a great shortcoming of the Act as a tool for implementing multi-purpose forestry programmes on privately owned lands.

Section 48 of the Act empowers the minister to make rules for the preservation, utilization, and development of agricultural land. The rules may prohibit, regulate or control (i) the breaking or clearing of land for the purposes of cultivation, and (ii) the firing, clearing or destruction of vegetation. The section specifically empowers the minister for agriculture to make rules regarding the afforestation or reforestation of land. The Agriculture (Basic Land Usage) Rules lay down regulations for the protection of land from soil erosion and the protection of water courses by prohibiting cultivation on particular landscapes, the cutting of vegetation, the depasturing of livestock and by requiring the planting of trees. Various agencies are vested with enforcement powers. These are the District Agricultural Committee, the Provincial Agricultural Board, and the Central Agricultural Board.

Additional powers are conferred on the director of agriculture who is authorized to issue land preservation orders to occupiers and owners requiring the performance of acts deemed necessary for soil preservation and prohibiting activities that might degrade the land. Under section 56, the director of agriculture may enter any land and implement the requirements of a land preservation order. The Act authorizes the director to seek reimbursement from the owner or occupier. Under Section 64, the minister for agriculture is further authorized to issue land development orders. These orders may require the person to whom they are directed to adopt such systems of management or farming as are considered necessary for the proper development of the land for agricultural purposes.

These powers provide great hope for the implementation of forestry programmes on private land. Apart from the powers specifically conferred by the Agriculture Act, other ministries responsible for energy, arid and semi-arid lands, environment and natural resources have mandates that include the development of agroforestry. The Ministry of Environment and Natural Resources, particularly the Forest Extension Services Division (FESD) which was formerly known as the Rural Afforestation and Extension Services (RAES) Division has also initiated many successful afforestation programmes and heightened awareness on the need for tree planting among farmers.

The Forests Act is silent on forestry activities on private lands and the FESD has largely worked on the basis of Sessional Paper No. 1 of 1968 entitled *A Forest Policy for Kenya*[36] which in Section 8 explicitly supports government involvement in "the establishment and proper maintenance of private forests, including farm woodlots, not only for productive but also for protective purposes." The new proposed forest policy addresses farm forestry more explicitly and states that forests and trees on "farms and private lands will be managed according to the national development objectives and land owners' priorities. The State will provide financial support to the areas kept for soil and water conservation purposes as necessary and will vigorously promote all forms of farm forestry."[37] It is expected that current forestry legislation will be reviewed to incorporate these policy goals.

Unfortunately, it would seem that the ministries involved in encouraging the adoption of tree planting and agroforestry are operating without the backup of legal powers of enforcement. The success of their initiatives, therefore, depends on the co-operation and goodwill of the farmers and is not legally-binding. This is a major set-back and it is necessary that appropriate legislation is passed to give legal authority to their activities.

The Agriculture Act aside, the various provisions to be found in the constitutive instruments of the Lake Basin, Kerio Valley, Tana and Athi Rivers development authorities can also be legitimately used to implement agroforestry programmes. The instruments vest in the authorities extensive regulatory powers covering the design, initiation, planning and monitoring of development activities. They also have the power to co-ordinate the abstraction and use of natural resources in their areas of jurisdiction.

Finally, the respective authorities are conferred with broad general guidelines for conservation. They provide that the authorities shall have the power to ensure that land owners in the area undertake all measures specified by the authorities to protect the water and soils in their jurisdiction. These general powers provide scope for the regulation of private property rights in land. Particular latitude for state action is provided in the case in irrigation schemes where farmers generally have the status of tenants.

Agroforestry and afforestation programmes can legitimately be undertaken under the development authority acts. The Bura irrigation scheme, for example, has in collaboration with other agencies incorporated forest management and research in its programme. Serious fuelwood shortages in Bura made forestry development a major concern for the irrigation scheme when it was initiated. By the early 1990s, a total of 780 ha of trees had been planted under irrigation.[38] The regional development authorities have greater potential than the Agriculture Act, with regard to the implementation of forestry and agroforestry programmes. Under the Agriculture Act, any agroforestry or afforestation programme must be intimately linked to the goals of agricultural production. This means that trees cannot be grown or preserved as entities worthy of protection in their own right.

The most significant limitation of the powers vested in regional development authorities lies in the fact that those powers only apply in respect of the specific drainage basins over which they have authority. This means that if an afforestation programme cannot be justified under the Agriculture Act and the area in question is outside the jurisdiction of the authorities, then legally there is no power which can legitimate its institution. Unfortunately, there is little evidence to suggest that the drainage basin authorities have made effective use of the powers conferred on them with regard to forest conservation and management.

The provisions of the various statutes which allow the state to intervene on private property in the interest of environmental management show the need for a more coordinated approach to create a balance between private and public interest in forests. One of the options is to codify these guidelines into a clear constitutional provision on the place of public interest in the articulation of private property rights. One may even go further and suggest that the state should assume the role of a genuine trustee holding forests on behalf of the people. Where a state acts a trustee, it can make decisions on how to delegate authority to local communities regarding certain resources. Under such circumstances the state would cease to own forests but would retain the sovereign right to regulate their use in the interest of the people. This approach will require a different approach of trusteeship from the one applied in Kenya today under the Trust Land Act and the related constitutional provisions.

Conclusion

We have argued that although there is some justification for retaining state monopoly rights over specific forest reserves, there are currently forests that can be effectively managed by local communities under a system of lease-holds. State ownership and control has proved to be an ineffective mechanism in many cases. Any conservation strategy must be sensitive to the social problems of surrounding communities, in particular their dependence on forest resources. For this reason, it has been suggested that state monopoly rights in some forests should be replaced with a system of leaseholds, granted in favour of forest dependents.

Loosening of state monopoly rights should, however, be the exception rather than the rule. In most cases, private ownership of forests is profit-driven and land owners seek to maximize individual benefits. Measures should be made under such condition to balance between social and private benefits. Care should also be taken to maintain women's access to and control over certain forest products, as well as equal access to land ownership. Rocheleau and Edmunds explain the implications of privatization thus:

> Today, interventions in community forest management, farm forestry and agroforestry frequently invest *all* access rights in a single 'owner', partly for the sake of bureaucratic simplicity and efficiency, partly on the assumption that such 'owners' need exclusive rights in order to manage their land effectively. Unfortunately, because women's rights do not generally include the primary rights of disposal and control, interventions which invest exclusive ownership rights in a single individual undermine women's customary rights of access to trees, tree products and other vegetation.[39]

Where there is insufficient information on resource values and rights, it is prudent to err on the side of caution and support resource conservation under state ownership. However, even in these situations, the state should find a way of alleviating the dependence of the neighbouring community on the particular forest.

With regard to agroforestry and other afforestation programmes on private land, it would seem that the Agriculture Act still provides the most secure basis for their implementation. Unfortunately, it is difficult to determine whether or not the Act has been effectively utilized. Even when vigorously enforced, the provisions of the Agriculture Act are still a very limited means of realizing the wider objectives of afforestation. This is because any programme instituted under the Act must be primarily aimed at serving the goals of increased agricultural production. It is this linkage to agricultural purposes that has proved to be one of the greatest shortcomings of the

Agriculture Act. It follows that legally, there is no power to compel the planting of trees on land as entities worthy of protection in their own right.

The role of industrialization in reducing pressure on forests cannot be ignored when addressing the goal of sustainable forest management. Alternative sources of employment and energy would reduce the demand for agricultural land (and hence forest conversion) and fuelwood, respectively. Although this chapter has not attempted to discuss larger questions of economic development, these factors must be considered in strategic national planning for natural resource use.

Finally, it is suggested that in view of the limitations of the current laws described above, it is important that specific provisions be introduced in the Constitution that create a balance between private property and public interest. In addition, the role of the state as trustee of natural resources on behalf of the people needs to be articulated in a positive manner so as to restore the confidence of the people in public institutions. This should be accompanied by constitutional measures that recognize that local traditions and practices are the foundation upon which to build legal innovations into common law.

Notes

1. This excludes open canopy woodlands.
2. Republic of Kenya, 1989a.
3. For details on excisions and additions, see IUCN, 1995.
4. See Chapter 10 of this book on tree tenure in pastoral lands.
5. A. Field-Juma, pers. comm. Charcoal production has been banned by authorities and chiefs, with limited effect.
6. See Raintree, 1987.
7. Okoth-Owiro, 1988.
8. Land (Group Representatives) Act, Section 5(11)(b).
9. Forests Act, sections 4 and 5.
10. Shepherd, 1986, p. 10; See also Commander, 1986, pp. 9–10.
11. See Beentje, et al., 1987, p. 20; See also Republic of Kenya, 1990b.
12. Republic of Kenya, 1990b, 153–154.
13. Forests Act, sections 4 and 6.
14. Forests Act, Section 8.
15. Republic of Kenya, 1994f, p. 243.
16. Republic of Kenya, 1994f, p. 257.
17. Shepherd, 1991, p. 9.
18. Commander, 1986, p. 14.
19. Clawson, 1982, p. 292.
20. Ellefson, 1992, p. 434.
21. Ellefson, 1992, p. 434.
22. Whyte, 1994, p. 93.
23. Republic of Kenya, 1994f, p. 52.
24. Republic of Kenya, 1994f, p. 181.
25. Rocheleau and Edmunds, 1995.

26. Rocheleau and Edmunds, 1995, p. 22.
27. Rocheleau and Edmunds, 1995, p. 13.
28. Republic of Kenya, 1994f, p.165.
29. Republic of Kenya, 1994f, p. 166.
30. Republic of Kenya, p. 176.
31. Shepherd, 1985, p. 6.
32. Dorm-Adzobu and Ampadu-Agyei, 1995.
33. For a discussion of customary tree tenure see Chapter 10 of this book.
34. Rocheleau, 1987, p. 80.
35. Okoth-Owiro, 1988, p. 267.
36. Ministry of Natural Resources, 1968.
37. Republic of Kenya, 1994f, p. 232.
38. Republic of Kenya, 1994f., p. 69
39. Rocheleau and Edmunds, 1995, p. 32.

Land tenure and wildlife management

8

SIRI ERIKSEN, EVANS OUKO
AND NJERI MAREKIA

Introduction

The fate and state of wildlife has been one of the most controversial issues in land use management in Kenya. Wildlife conservation objectives in Kenya involve the natural environments and their fauna and flora, with an implicit emphasis on wild animals. This chapter looks at how land tenure is linked to the management and conservation of wildlife. It first examines the ecological and economic importance of wildlife. It then looks at how the conservation of this resource is integrated in different tenure systems, from the public tenure introduced by the colonial authorities along with the concept of conservation, to private tenure on land traditionally containing wildlife, and customary tenure that has traditionally been used to manage these resources. The sources of conflicts between wildlife and humans and how these relate to land tenure and land use are then identified. In dealing with such conflicts, the issue of environmental representation or the right to speak for the environment arises. These themes are exemplified in two case studies: the interaction and conflicts over resources between Akamba and wildlife in parks and reserves in the Tsavo area; and the controversy over rights to resources and land in the Tana River delta wetland. The chapter lastly outlines the implications these conflicts have for tenure reform.

The value of wildlife

The government of Kenya takes utilization of land by wildlife as a very important aspect of land use, tourism being the largest earner of foreign exchange. Although most protected areas are situated in low-potential dry areas, these contain important animals and plants as well as land forms, unique geographic and environmental phenomena, and a range of different habitats. As well as the economic value for tourism, wildlife conservation areas have important ecological values and harbour the last vestiges of unique habitats that have not been seriously affected by human interference.

The tourism sector benefits the most from the conservation of Kenya's biodiversity. The top two tourist attractions are the terrestrial game parks and the Indian Ocean coast. Tourism is the single leading foreign exchange earner for Kenya. Since 1987, foreign exchange earnings from the sector have been slightly more than the combined earnings from coffee and tea, the traditional major foreign exchange earners.[1] With the fluctuating prices of Kenya's major cash crops—tea and coffee—tourism will continue to be an important stabilizer for the economy. Total tourist arrivals have gradually increased from 65,400 in 1963 to about 814,400 in 1990. The figure dropped to 698,600 in 1992 but rose in consecutive years to stand at 832,000 in 1994. The number of visitors to the national parks and game reserves grew from 1,095,800 in 1988 to 1,427,800 in 1993.[2]

An indication of the growth of the tourism sector is the fact that national earnings rose from US$129 million in 1977 to US$450 in the early 1990s from gross receipts. The tourists come to see, within their natural habitats, large animals such as elephants, lions, giraffes, buffaloes, leopards, cheetahs and zebras. Kenya is also famous for its rich birdlife and many smaller animals within their terrestrial and marine habitats. About 27% of earnings in the tourism industry can be attributed directly to wildlife and another 26% indirectly.[3]

In recognition of the importance of its biological resources, a number of national parks and reserves have been gazetted. Of the total area of Kenya of 582,646 sq km national parks and reserves cover 44,562 sq km which is 7.65% of the country (Figure 9). Of this, national parks account for 5% and national reserves and sanctuaries for 2.65%.[4] These protected areas were established with the aim of preserving a natural heritage of great ecological and economic importance. Although estimates vary, there is agreement that the majority of wildlife resources in the form of animals and plants are contained outside protected areas. Therefore in planning for the management of the national parks and reserves this should be taken into account.

Figure 9 Wildlife conservation areas in Kenya

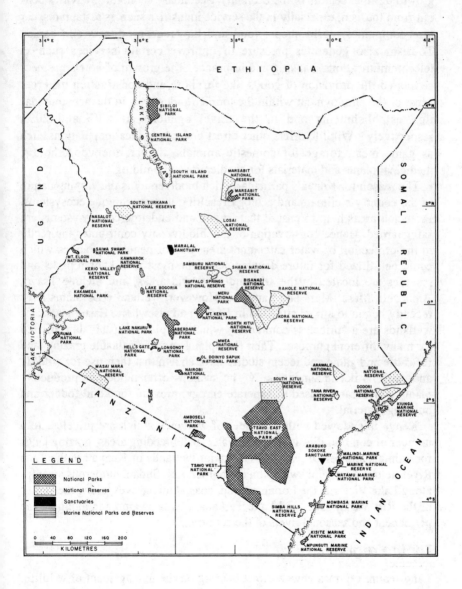

The tourism industry also generates employment and contributes to the growth of other sectors of the economy. Secondary economic activities benefit from tourism, especially in the service industries such as restaurants, car hire companies, curio shops, food and beverage producers and banks. Tourism also generates pressure to improve certain services such as telecommunications, banking and insurance. The growth of hotels has necessitated the provision of goods like furniture and construction material. Most of the employment within the tourism industry is in the accommodation establishments and in the travel agencies at 60% and 20%, respectively.[5] Wildlife offers other direct benefits to local populations such as game meat, forage for domestic animals, timber, fuelwood, honey, medicinal plants and materials for handicrafts and building.

The reason for Kenya's particularly rich biodiversity is the varying nature of the country's climate and ecology resulting in many unique ecosystems. Protected areas help to ensure that fragile and endangered ecosystems are safeguarded. Hence conservation of this biodiversity contributes indirectly to the protection of water catchment areas and of genetic resources which could be utilized for future development. The most well-known parks and reserves are located in the arid and semi-arid areas, and include Tsavo, Amboseli, Masai Mara and Samburu. However, wetland ecosystems have recently begun to attract attention in Kenya and elsewhere. Eastern Africa's wetlands are a "priceless commodity which should be sustainably utilized for many different purposes. Their floodplains provide valuable grazing land for cattle and game and recent studies have shown that their use for wildlife and cattle is not incompatible."[6] The swamps offer numerous productive plants which can be used to generate energy, provide food and fodder and building material.

Kenya is endowed with a number of wetlands which are priceless to a number of communities in terms of water, fish breeding areas, grazing lands for animals and for cultivation. The major wetlands of Kenya are the Tana River delta's Lotragipi swamp on the border with Sudan, numerous swamps along Lake Victoria, the Lorian swamp, coastal mangroves, along the shores of the Rift Valley lakes and Lake Turkana, Mwea swamp and along all the permanent and seasonal rivers of the country.

Tenure regimes

Land tenure regimes have a direct bearing on the management of wildlife. Rights related to wildlife are chiefly secured through public tenure. The question of wildlife and land tenure thus centres on the issue of public versus individual rights to land and natural resources. There are three systems of land tenure in operation in Kenya: public, "modern" and customary. The first system involves the ownership of land by the state through various laws. The essential characteristic of the "modern" system based on English common law is that it confers titles and rights on individuals for use as they please. The last system of tenure is based on indigenous property arrangements, often referred to as customary or communal land tenure.

Land encompasses a range of resources, whose scope and influence transcend private property boundaries. Statutory law regards land as a single resource to which there may be a variety of rights (use, alienation, etc.). Whereas customary law tends to recognize a bundle of aggregated rights to the many natural resources associated with land. These rights may apply to specific fodder, trees, ground water, particular forage areas or species, and may vary according to season and condition. Where customary tenurial systems have been replaced by modern tenure the flexibility and complexity of rights which can promote sustainable resource management as well as equity are lost.

Public tenure

The colonial government delineated boundaries of land ownership and land tenure systems across the colony based on findings of the 1933 Kenya Land Commission Report. Land was set aside as "Native Reserves" for individual tribes perceived to be occupying the land, and some areas were annexed for settler population. Thinly populated land was designated as state property or "Crown land". Soon thereafter conservation areas were established. This involved setting aside areas with exclusive public tenure, where the purpose of conservation of wildlife was paramount. This was to protect these from what was perceived as detrimental human interference, largely the result of over-hunting. The 1945 National Parks Ordinance stated that national parks were for "the preservation of wild animal life, wild animals and objects of aesthetic, geological, prehistorical, archaeological, historical or other scientific interest therein, and for incidental matters relating thereto." Economic gains from wildlife were considered incidental and economic consumptive utilization of resources by the public inside parks was not allowed. The first national park was gazetted as Nairobi National Park in 1946, followed by Tsavo in 1948. A large part of these areas fell on perceived unutilized Crown land already under state ownership.

At independence the native reserves became trust lands administered by the county councils. This chapter is concerned with two issues related to trust lands: the first is that of privatization through land registration; the second is that the government can decide to adjudicate trust land for a public purpose as it has the overall supervision of these lands. One such purpose can be gazettement of a national park. These issues arise from specific constitutional provisions which allow for the conversion of communal lands to other land uses.

Section 115 of the Constitution provides that all trust land is vested in the county council within whose area of jurisdiction they are situated and is to be held "for the benefit of the persons ordinarily resident on that land." The council is to "give effect to such rights, interests or other benefits in respect of the land as may, under the African customary law for the time being in force and applicable thereto, be vested in any tribe, group, family or individual. . ." However, privatization of trust land is permitted, declaring customary laws, and thus customary tenure, void. In addition, land can be acquired for public tenure by either the county council or the national government. Under Section 117 of the Constitution, parliament may empower the county council to set apart an area of trust land for use and occupation "by a public body or authority for public purposes" or by any person for a purpose which in the opinion of the council is likely to benefit the persons ordinarily resident in that area. This provision, which extinguishes customary laws in that area, has been utilized to establish national parks and reserves.

Section 118 of the Constitution provides for the vesting of portions of trust land in the government where the President is satisfied that such land is required by the government for purposes of the government; a body corporate set up by Parliament for a public purpose; an enterprise in which the shares are held by or on behalf of the government; or for prospecting for or extracting minerals or mineral oils.

An important and unusual aspect of land tenure in Kenya is that even on private land where the individual has precedence, wildlife is owned by the government. Hence, land owners and users could not kill wildlife which threatened or damaged their crops, property or families. After the Presidential directive banning hunting in 1977, non-consumptive use of wildlife for tourism, recreation and education became the only legal forms of wildlife utilization.[7] This ban was meant to protect their over-exploitation, particularly by curbing poaching.

The overall authority in ensuring rational conservation, management and utilization of wildlife resources in parks and reserves and non-gazetted wildlife areas is entrusted to the Kenya Wildlife Service (KWS) under the Wildlife (Conservation and Management) Act. Parks and reserves are declared (gazetted) by the minister for tourism in consultation with the minister for lands in the case of government lands, in consultation with the relevant county council for trust land, and the owner in the case of private land. The same stakeholders are involved in boundary changes or degazettement, in addition to approval by parliament. Generally, the local communities are not adequately consulted before gazettement is effected. It is the duty of KWS to ensure that no settlement or consumptive uses occur in the parks. KWS also advises county councils who manage national reserves, marine reserves and local sanctuaries. In these, some forms of human land use can be allowed, such as rearing livestock, according to the local formulation of rules, which in turn evolve from government policy.[8]

The police power of the state, through legislation restricting certain activities on the land, does not always provide for compensation. Where land is adjudicated, full compensation is to be paid when the land itself is alienated by the state. However, when resources are alienated, which occurs due to government ownership of wildlife on private land, compensation is not by right paid. Currently, no compensation is paid for the damage to livestock, crops and other property by wildlife.[9] In the absence of a right to compensation or efficient compensation system, property owners bordering wildlife areas are left on their own to bear the cost of maintaining wildlife on their land. Therefore wildlife is generally considered to be a liability to the landowner. This often leads to resentment and conflict between the government and local communities.

The aim of wildlife conservation is the sustainable management of the resource base in the public interest. Due to exclusive public tenure and management of wildlife, the local population has been denied access to and benefits from wildlife living on their land.[10] Expelling local populations through gazettement of parks and reserves means that their rights to resources inherent in traditional land use systems are lost along with the right even to live on the land. In the process of conversion to private land tenure, involving both public property acquisition and individual privatization, customary law and thus customary rights give way. Traditional knowledge on how to manage land and the resources on it as well as tenure systems are lost.

The provision in the constitution that ". . . no right, interest or other benefit under African customary law shall have effect. . . so far as it is repugnant to any written law" ensures that traditional norms and rules lose their effect.[11]

Insofar as economic returns can be seen as benefiting the public, a central question in exerting conservation authority is how directly it benefits local populations. Most of the money collected from national parks goes to the national treasury, from where it is allocated to different regions of the country. Presently, local communities benefit from non-consumptive tourist-related activities, employment and businesses. In the case of game reserves where local people are more directly involved in revenue sharing from wildlife protection through the local county council. Wildlife sanctuaries run by local county councils also exist in game reserves; local communities may practice their traditional cattle rearing in the wildlife sanctuaries. Proceeds obtained from tourism are paid to the county council, the body entrusted with sharing out the revenue among the local inhabitants adjacent to the game reserves.[12]

In 1989 Kenya restructured its wildlife management policy from the government-controlled Wildlife Conservation and Management Department to KWS, a parastatal institution. KWS is preparing new policies on how local people adjacent to protected areas can benefit more directly from revenue accruing from wildlife. One of the recommendations is that 25% of the income obtained from wildlife be allocated to local communities. The question of apportionment of this revenue vis-à-vis the extent of human-wildlife interaction and conflicts, is not yet clear. Through its Community Wildlife Service, KWS seeks to establish community projects such as health or education and improve relations and communication with the local community.

Recently, KWS has started granting use rights on wildlife to land owners. On an experimental basis, exceptions to the hunting ban are being granted to enable land owners to crop wildlife. There are also discussions on other forms of wildlife utilization with direct financial benefit to the landowner, such as trophy hunting and easing regulation in trade and marketing of wildlife products. The ban and other policies such as the removal of compensation for crop damage by wildlife are under review. Even if the ban on hunting were to be lifted and consumptive wildlife utilization was allowed on regular rather than exceptional basis, wildlife would remain primarily under public ownership, and strict management requirements would be necessary.[13]

The state, however, could adopt a different approach where it functions as a trustee holding the resources in the interest of the public. This would provide for the applications of different forms of wildlife ownership which would be regulated by the government to promote utilization while at the same time ensuring conservation. As a public trustee, the government would also be expected to intervene and protect the interest of the public in case the survival of wildlife is threatened by other land uses. It would otherwise to be difficult to promote the privatization of wildlife-based activities with the state retaining its present role as an owner of the resources.

Modern tenure

"Modern" land tenure in the form of absolute proprietorship by individuals is increasing in Kenya. This is partly a result of Kenya's strategy for economic expansion. The principle objective of the Kenya government in rural development has been to maximize the use of the country's agricultural resources for national needs, redistribute population growth, and ensure economic growth in all regions. This has led to the policy of land privatization, and to the introduction of modern agriculture and commercialization as a means of integrating each region of the country into the national economic system. As such, land tenure and land use development in some aspects conflict with conservation imperatives.

Privatization means the conversion of rights to land and its resources from the public or community to the individual. The state's expectation in land privatization is that not only would rights to land be clarified, but also that registered proprietors would become innovative, productive and entrepreneurial. Privatization is meant to achieve higher interest and investment of the individual in the resources on the land, and subsequent higher productivity. Individual title has also been criticized for leading to over-parcellation, over-exploitation of the land, and landlessness.[14] Privatization also leads to the subdivision of land, often for different uses and fencing, thus blocking the access of wildlife.

In the late 1960s, the government adopted legislation that would promote commercial livestock production in nomadic pastoral areas. In line with this, the 1968 Land (Group Representatives) Act was introduced. It made it possible for a group of pastoralists to register a block of land with fixed boundaries. It was hoped that this would help the pastoralists to think of herd management more in the commercial ranching sense. Although this was meant as a compromise between individual ownership and granting access to larger tracts of land, some of the implications were the same as for privatization, namely the paramount right of the corporate individual over the public.

Both customary and English property law are in operation in the rangelands, where much of current wildlife and protected areas are found. Land law in Kenya attempts to provide for customary rules within a statutory framework. This can lead to conflict as illustrated by the following example. With changes in land tenure among the Maasai, the people are divided into group and individual ranches which often have territorial implications at variance with traditional units and new administrative zones. Communal lands were divided into smaller units (group ranches) with officially registered members holding a group title deed, giving entitlement to the exclusive use of the ranch resources. Group ranches did not coincide with any level of traditional socio-political organization. Confusion regarding the locus of authority and lack of co-ordination have ensued, and movement across ranch boundaries remains a common response to dry conditions. There has also been pressure for subdivision of group ranches and thus further individualization of land.

Customary tenure

Customary land tenure gives access to land for a given community. The social unit sharing an area may be a clan as among the Samburu, a section or sub-tribe as among the Maasai, or some other locational grouping. Below the access group there are smaller groups controlling local resources.[15] Communal tenure is said to discourage individual initiative to invest in land and to manage it properly. On the other hand, communal tenure among pastoral communities allows migration following seasonal availability of resources. Communal tenure with customary laws regulating access and use has been confused with a regime of free access where customary laws and controls on use by individuals within a community have been removed.

Appropriation of range resources is achieved by the group in the context of the social relations they establish.[16] For example, most Maasai do not want to be seen monopolizing range resources, since they are meant to be shared. Elders are cautious of this and often fine individuals trying to usurp natural resources for their own use. In other pastoral communities such as the Gabbra, there were strongly developed legal sanctions to enforce selectivity in resource utilization. Deviants were punished in order to encourage soil conservation practices.[17] Land, under traditional pastoral arrangement does not belong to any particular person or family. It is collectively owned by the society with boundaries generally recognized by neighbouring sections. Some sections form alliances which permit them to graze on one another's land, making sectional boundaries less visible. Individuals and families have land-use rights which can be transferred to progeny, provided the family continues to reside in the locality. Among the pastoral Maasai, land is a resource that should not be owned, sold, or exchanged by an individual.

Customary tenure varies according to the ecological characteristics of the area. Within the Tana River delta, the homeland of the Pokomo, there is a system common to most agricultural communities of Kenya. Land belongs to the clan and the household and is distributed on that basis. Land is not a saleable commodity among the Pokomo. Away from the river and delta, in the interior where it is drier, nomadic pastoralists like the Orma and Wardei regard land as a common property. The delta provides the dry season and drought fall back grazing for most of the Orma community's livestock. The Bajuni community utilizes the area for fishing. Thus multiple uses can exist separated by time and regulated by norms developed to utilize specific niches. Although customary tenure practices still exist, officially customary land tenure has been replaced by statutory tenure through government, private, and trust land.[18]

Wildlife conflicts

Wildlife conflicts can be defined as situations where use by humans and wildlife affect or are perceived to affect each other in a negative way. The extent to which these interactions cause conflict reflects increased pressure for utilization of those resources in a restricted area, or decreased compatibility in uses. Conflicts take the form of illegal or excessive human use of protected areas or resources, and land use practices outside or bordering the protected area which affect wildlife interests both inside and outside the protected area. These conflicts represent people's interest in utilizing the resources of protected areas which are being denied to them.

Other conflicts occur when wildlife affects other land uses when they move outside the protected areas and consequently undermine people's livelihoods. Wild animals can, in turn, experience restricted range as their habitat is converted to human uses that preclude wildlife utilization. The two sources of conflicts are wildlife and human competition for land resources, and lack of access.

Conflicts between individual and public tenure originate in the fact that the local population is not allowed to utilize the natural resources to which they feel they have a claim. In addition, government property in the form of wildlife, whose management and conservation does not involve the local population, is seen as violating private property on which it does not have rights of access.

Source of conflicts

Tenure systems tend to reflect local strategies for resource utilization and distribution. The tenure systems and income from resource utilization outside protected areas are usually unrelated to conservation goals. Except for those local people who find direct employment in the tourism sector, it is very difficult for most people to perceive that they are actually receiving benefits from wildlife conservation. Instead wildlife may be interfering with their economic activities, for example through crop-raiding, killing of domestic animals by predators, transmission of disease and competition for pasture.[19] Wildlife is mainly perceived as a liability for those engaged in economic activities. Economic utilization and conservation are split spatially. Land users push for access to the land reserved for conservation and for access to resources on this land. The latter implies a change in tenure regime to disaggregate resource tenure from land tenure since some resources may be utilized with no detrimental effect on wildlife.

With growing population densities in the high potential areas in the country, more and more people are moving into the marginal lands to establish farms. Between 1967 and 1979, areas considered wildlife districts, such as Laikipia, Kajiado and Narok experienced a population growth of 7.3%, 5.6% and 5.3% per annum respectively.[20] Between 1979 and 1989, the same districts experienced population growth of 5.0%, 5.7% and 6.6% respectively. Expansion of agriculturalists into the higher-rainfall areas within these districts and agricultural development projects in riverine habitats have withdrawn these important areas from pastoral production and forced herders to graze their livestock on an ever shrinking range of inferior quality.

Privatization and fragmentation are also leading to land uses that effectively exclude wildlife. The emphasis on private ownership of land transforms the common property resources to private resources and breaks the ecologically designed migratory patterns of both livestock and wildlife. Since many species are characterized by localized distribution, a few parks and reserves will not suffice to protect the range of biotic diversity. An extensive and strategically planned network is needed. Even in protected areas covering several thousand square kilometers, some species have negligible prospects of survival. This is particularly true of three categories of species. The first includes those species which require large territories, so that even an extensive area includes only low numbers, as is the case with many carnivores such as the cheetah. The second category includes those species whose members have specialized habitat needs, with the result that, as in the first category, populations have few individuals. The third category includes species which are dependent on seasonal and patchy food sources and hence migrate. Some are inclined to undergo drastic fluctuations in population numbers, as is the case with flower-eating birds.

The status of wildlife and parks is related to the management and use of other resources with which they share an ecosystem.[21] This is particularly relevant in wildlife dispersal areas bordering parks and reserves. Most wildlife in Kenya is not confined in the parks and reserves. Estimates of numbers outside of protected areas range from 65% to 80%. This figure varies seasonally as many wildlife species migrate out of the park during the wet season and tend to concentrate within them in the dry season.

At present many wildlife dispersal areas surrounding parks and reserves (Amboseli, Tsavo, and Mara) are still unfenced, and are owned communally as group ranches or are trust land.[22] Livestock in these areas, like wildlife, depends for survival on flexibility of movement. However, with reduction in size of land available to pastoralists like the Maasai and Samburu, both wildlife and pastoralists and their livestock have had their traditional range reduced. Thus, sub-division and population expansion are likely to confine wildlife to parks which could contribute to animal over-population and environmental deterioration.

Customary law regarding resource utilization is being replaced by statutory law and emphasis on individual ownership. There is a perception that there are no restrictions to occupying new, "underutilized" land. Changes in land tenure have also resulted in a lack of land use co-ordination and insecurity of land tenure. As access of wildlife to land has diminished in the privatization process, police power in terms of restricting certain uses on private lands has increased. However, police powers cannot effectively co-ordinate land use in a process of rapidly changing land uses and commercialization. There is also a lack of co-ordination and clear channels of communication between the institutions and authorities dealing with different aspects pertaining to land. The rights of wildlife are inadequately represented as public land tenure and ownership of wildlife does not assure its survival on private land. Perceived free access to land on a "willing buyer willing seller" basis and free choice of land use combined with a single-use philosophy which discourages private wildlife utilization have exacerbated wildlife conflicts. These factors constitute a tenure regime that is effectively squeezing wildlife out of ordinary land uses.

Two case studies follow which illustrate the importance of developing land tenure systems which support the multiple uses of resources by multiple stakeholders. This, as will be seen, needs to take place within a clear and enforceable framework of institutions and rules which encourage reciprocity between different interests, particularly between wildlife and agriculture. The first case looks at land use change around Tsavo national parks, the second examines the development of the Tana River delta wetlands.

Mutual encroachment in the Tsavo area

The eastern side of the area traditionally inhabited by the Kamba, known as Ukambani, borders an arid tract of land (Figure 6).[23] This land was traditionally subject to non-intensive uses by several ethnic groups, among them the Akamba. Under the colonial government this area was designated Crown land. In 1948 the Tsavo national parks were gazetted, covering 20,812 sq km, or 3.6% of the land in Kenya. Later, several smaller national reserves were added, including Ngai Ndethya, South Kitui, and Chyulu Hills (now upgraded to a national park) in the same area. This case study focuses on how gazettement of the park and reserves and changes in land tenure systems in the Tsavo area affected both the Akamba and wildlife access to resources. The case demonstrates in particular conflicts emerging within the present tenure regime. The gazettement of parks largely eliminated traditional Akamba land uses on the land affected. The Tsavo area has a low agricultural potential with low soil fertility, low rainfall, the area getting increasingly arid from the Machakos and Kitui Highlands eastwards down the elevation gradient towards the coast.[24] Numerous accounts of the reasoning behind the gazettement of Tsavo have revealed that it was seen as a low-potential area and useful for little else apart from conservation.[25] In addition, it was a huge area which, it was hoped, could contain practically an entire ecosystem. The Akamba lost their access to the eastern and southern territories, which were traditionally used to support hunter-gatherers and pastoralists.

At the time of the Kenya Land Commission report in 1933, an area covering the north-western side of what later became Tsavo East National Park, the whole of Ngai Ndethya National Reserve, and the northern part of Tsavo West National Park and Chyulu Hills National Park were utilized by the Akamba. The report recognized that land could not support grazing if confined between boundaries, and recommended that movement of Akamba cattle to Crown land should be allowed through establishing grazing reserves.[26] Recommendations did not, however, entail any tenure rights as the government had exclusive authority over Crown land. The tenurial regime recognized land as a single resource, and did not disaggregate rights to the resources contained on it. Though the Tsavo game warden at the time had recommended to the Commission that the park could accommodate human settlements, instead hunting was outlawed, the rights of grazing and gathering were ignored and the people were evicted once the parks were established.

Over the following fifty years the Akamba experienced growing pressure to shift away from pastoralism and towards settled agriculture. Government programmes included forced destocking, grazing restrictions, hut taxes and land adjudication. Access to the grazing reserves on Crown lands was also eliminated. This process was accompanied by severe land degradation, later the focus of intensive government soil conservation programmes.[27] In higher potential areas of Ukambani unsettled land once used for communal purposes virtually disappeared due to the increasing population density. Arrangements of individual's use rights on land got more complex and sale of land increased from the 1930s. The introduction of modern tenure reinforced the process of individualization from the 1960s and also introduced private ownership in sparsely populated land.[28] This clan land is now increasingly being subdivided. The Ngai Ndethya as well as a few other pockets of high-potential land support settled agriculture and livestock. Ngai

Ndethya is subject to land speculation due to the high value placed on irrigation and tourism. Present land uses by Akamba close to the park and reserve boundaries involve a mixture of dryland agriculture, pastoralism and hunting. The extent of each depends on the rains each year, with agriculture being viable only in the good years.

The gazettement of Tsavo national parks initially closed off a zone for conservation within a larger area of similar physical characteristics. There were few differences in the land use inside and outside the parks as the whole area was very sparsely populated. Examination of demographic patterns in the Tsavo area from 1948 to 1979 revealed a dramatic process of land use intensification and population growth in Machakos and Kitui.[29] The areas of high population density (more than 50 persons per sq km) in Machakos and Kitui had expanded, the two areas almost joining by 1979. Population at lower densities had expanded to the southeast, "filling the previously empty area between the Chyulu Hills and the northwestern boundary of the Tsavo East National Park."[30] The areas supporting very low densities had decreased to about half of their 1948 extent. The immediate vicinity of the Tsavo parks had seen establishment of "significant" pockets of medium and high population density (more than 30 persons per sq km) during this period, constituting pressure around the immediate periphery of the parks. The 1982 Government of Kenya report estimated a threefold increase in the population density within 20 km of the Tsavo parks between 1948 and 1979.

Land use analysis from 1982 shows livestock rearing being displaced by other land uses near the park boundaries, and small holder agriculture spreading from the semi-arid to the more arid areas. Half the land within 20 km of the park boundaries was reported to support agricultural settlement although severely constrained by lack of water. Families living near the park boundaries have largely arrived the past decade, about 75% of whom are engaged in small-holder agriculture. Hence dry areas of traditionally low population density bordering the parks have experienced a significant increase in percentage cultivated land and a decrease in percentage bush and grazing land since 1948.[31]

The gazettement led to the eviction of people from the protected areas and banning of hunting and grazing. The Akamba were also denied access to their bee hives and worshipping shrines in the park. The only lawful use by the public became tourism and recreation. The Akamba were not consulted in the gazettement process. The resentment caused by this interference with economic activity and removal of traditional Akamba rights later undermined conservation efforts such as through their support of elephant poaching.[32]

As a result, both Akamba and the wildlife were marginalized through diminished access to land and resources. The perception of arid lands as wastelands and the need for a large area set aside for conservation secured tracts of land practically unaltered by human use. However, this approach neglected crucial wildlife resources contained in habitats outside the protected areas. The parks and reserves were meant to provide a large area within which movement of wild animals could take place more or less unrestricted. Yet the misperception of the closed and unused nature of the ecosystem is the basis for the main challenges facing the parks and reserves today.

The justification of the designation of the parks was not the wildlife resources in the area, but that the land was available for gazettement as Crown land. The precise reason that it was sparsely populated was its low agroecological potential. The boundaries thus delineated the areas naturally hosting the lowest number of species in the lowest density. With a few exceptions, higher potential zones are found outside the park, mainly in Kitui and Machakos, as well as the Chyulu Hills and Taita and Taveta. The wildlife densities are higher in areas both to the east and in highlands to the west of Tsavo. The agro-ecological zones dominating Tsavo have the lowest ecological diversity in terms of percentage of species of birds, amphibians, trees and shrubs, mammals and butterflies in the area.[33] The diversity in high potential areas is dependent on the survival of forest and national reserves, as well as practices promoting low intensity and high diversity of agricultural systems.

Intensification of land use in Ukambani over the past 50 years has changed the habitat, thus leading to loss of certain flora and expulsion of wildlife. In the areas of Tsavo national parks bordering Ukambani, this has meant that wildlife previously residing in those areas has been forced to move towards the national parks where such change in land use has not taken place. Wildlife originating from protected areas have also been cut off from migration routes and seasonal grazing outside the park boundaries. Private tenure close to park boundaries means conservation authorities have no control over these areas which are crucial grazing and migration areas. The choice of land use or fencing by one owner may block off access by wildlife to a much larger area. Thus wildlife populations are concentrated in much smaller areas than before. Only smaller wildlife populations can be sustained, and since smaller areas entail less space to move and less diverse habitat, wildlife populations are more vulnerable to environmental fluctuations. Ironically, a stable population therefore depends on human involvement through conservation monitoring and wildlife management (such as culling).[34]

The Akamba and other adjacent communities have encroached on both the land and resources under public tenure. One human activity that conflicts with existing regulations and conservation imperatives is charcoal burning, especially in the southern area of Tsavo East national park, at times on a commercial scale. Charcoal-burning involves collection of dead wood which would otherwise decompose, tracks left behind by lorries involved in collecting the wood and charcoal, and fires lit by charcoal-burners.[35] Uncontrolled fire retards the growth of young woody vegetation and the regeneration of young grass.[36] Human activities and settlement have encroached on the boundaries, where use of fire easily spreads into the park. Bush fires are sometimes started deliberately in boundary areas to clear bush and enhance grazing by livestock. Honey-hunters have traditionally used the area around Tiva River to collect honey; fires inadvertently started by honey-hunters spread to become bush fires.

Human encroachment has led to several cases of either temporary or permanent settlement within park boundaries. In the 1980s, an increase was noted in both the numbers of livestock and their incursions into the park. There have been repeated attempts at settling in the Gazi triangle of land jutting out from the north-west of Tsavo. This is partly politically motivated and spurred by "allocation" of this park land to clan members from the Machakos highlands, and partly by the need for access to water at Mwathe.[37] Small-game poaching is taking place near boundaries. Traditional hunting expanded into the park leading to Kamba participation in the devastating elephant poaching of the 1970s and 1980s, when about 26,000 elephants were killed.[38]

Antagonism among local communities has been growing due to crop-raiding and attacks by wildlife. Elephants do not constitute as great a problem in Ukambani, partly because the elephant population is very small. Around Taita, elephant raiding is a major reason why some land is not being cultivated. Akamba land does experience problems with wild pigs, buffalo, baboons and porcupine. There is also a perceived, though disputed, spread of diseases from wildlife to livestock.[39]

Population dynamics and changes in tenure have created two distinct regimes of land use which are becoming increasingly uncomfortable neighbours. The tenure regime has forced human land use away from integrating and conserving wildlife since local rights to economic consumptive utilization have been excluded by public ownership of wildlife. A long-standing resentment to their original eviction in addition to political and economic pressures spur Akamba claims to protected area resources. Responses to pressures have varied. KWS is planning to degazette most of Ngai Ndethya National Reserve, as it is already heavily settled and has low conservation value.[40] The government is in the process of resettling the landless people from Makueni on about 200 square kilometers of land in Ngai Ndethya National Reserve.

The KWS Community Wildlife Service engages in community projects in the area to enable people to benefit from wildlife conservation. Tolerance for certain uses of the parks has developed. Authorities do not always act on some practices such as honey-hunting, boundary grazing, gathering of herbs and wood, and the odd small game poaching. This is justified on the basis that wildlife is not threatened; that it may reduce crop-raiding, encourage the perception of direct benefits accruing from wildlife; and because it cannot logistically be controlled or avoided, particularly in times of drought. In effect, this is dismantling the perception of land as a single resource rather than a bundle of rights, and wildlife as public property. However, disaggregation of the rights to land resources has continued without the necessary legal support.

The contested Tana River delta

The Tana River delta, located at the mouth of Kenya's longest river, has for some years gained both local and international recognition from conservationists as a wetland harbouring rich biodiversity and offering a potentially lucrative opportunity for tourist investment ventures (Figure 6). The local population also consider the delta a very important resource in terms of their livelihood for it offers them not only a steady supply of water, but grazing lands for their livestock even during the driest months. In the early 1970s some sub-division occurred as group ranching was introduced in the area. It was this privatization of land within the delta that would eventually result in the sale of a particularly sensitive area by a ranching group to a private developer for shrimp farming. This led to an acrimonious row involving issues of public versus private land ownership regarding that parcel of land within the delta.

The Tana River delta controversy involved many interested parties, from the community level represented by a ranching group, to KWS and other government organs, like the District Development Committee and government ministries. Non-governmental organizations (NGOs) and foreign governments such the US and the Netherlands played key roles in the controversy. It involved court action and eventually required Presidential intervention to bring it to an end. The pace and the complexity of the controversy raised many questions especially regarding issues of land tenure.

The delta is highly productive, rich in plant and animal life and has therefore attracted a rapidly growing human population. The resulting pressure for more land has led to encroachment into the ecologically sensitive areas of the delta. This, compounded by the low agricultural potential of the surrounding areas, has often left the population with little choice but to acquire land in the ecologically-fragile ecosystem within the delta. The situation was exacerbated in the 1970s when in an effort to try and accelerate development, the communities were organized into ranching groups, which made token payments to acquire land within the wetland which was previously held as trust land. The ranching companies were intended to commercialize the previously subsistence cattle rearing activities of the local communities.

The wetland is especially valuable in the dry seasons for the cattle keeping communities in the area, often containing the last viable forage even in the driest seasons. Tana River as a whole is a semi-arid zone and the importance of such a reservoir to the enhancement of the social, economic and ecological development of the area cannot be overemphasized. Before the appropriation of the area by the government, the local communities had managed the area in a more or less sustainable manner. This was not so much due to a concern for the wider environment, but because of their need to receive a continuous return of benefits from the ecosystem.

One of the ranching groups that was formed in the 1970s was the Kon-Dertu Ranching Company. It was composed of 100 members who each made financial, livestock or in-kind contributions towards the purchase of land. The group applied for a parcel of land and went through the long legal process of registering the land under their name. The fact as to whether the land was public (government-owned) or trust land was never clearly established. The breakdown in administrative functions is reflected in the fact that when Kon-Dertu were receiving the title deed to the land, another company was also laying claim to the same piece of land and indeed had also received a deed. After protests from both sides, Kon-Dertu became the legal owners by acquiring the 20,000-ha parcel of land which was at the heart of the ecologically important but fragile area of the delta.

Two years before the granting of the licence to Kon-Dertu, the area had been earmarked as a wetland of international importance in accordance with the Ramsar Convention on Wetlands of International Importance which Kenya ratified in 1990. The proposal for a wetland park had been initiated by a group of professionals who included experts from KWS, the World Conservation Union (IUCN) and the East African Wildlife Society (EAWLS).[41] As one of the first global ecosystem-based treaties, the Convention had done much to focus the attention of governments and the conservation community on the international significance of wetland resources and the migratory birds which depend on them.

After the acquisition of the 20,000 ha parcel, Kon-Dertu sold off half of it to a Greek-owned company, Coastal Aquaculture Limited. Coastal Aquaculture planned to start prawn farming in the area. Herein the conflict arose as conservation groups led by EAWLS protested against the sale of the land to the company because, it was claimed, the negative environmental impacts to the delta would be too great if the venture went ahead. Coastal Aquaculture on the other hand, claimed that their initial studies had indicated that their actions would have no severe long-term consequences on the wetland. The company was supported by the directors of Kon-Dertu who indicated that the venture offered possibilities for long-term development of an area previously ignored in terms of development investment.

At the beginning it seemed that there was only one point of view within the ranching company. The directors suggested that shrimp farming would bring development to the area through infrastructural development. They criticized the conservationists who they claimed only began protesting when a foreign company bought the parcel of land but had previously not been interested. However, an increasingly vocal group of dissenting members of the ranch denounced the sale and claimed that the right channels were not followed and therefore the process was illegal.

A wide array of organizations support the conservation position, including NGOs such as the EAWLS, government organs such as KWS and the Tana and Athi Rivers Development Authority (TARDA) and private individuals. Foreign governments such as the US and the Netherlands also voiced their concerns through their embassies. In addition to local diplomatic interest, the local conservation groups also received considerable international support from institutions such as IUCN. This international interest turned what originally seemed like an isolated Kenyan issue into an international concern. EAWLS organized a series of meetings involving a wide range of Kenyan and international organizations at which the most recent scientific information was used to formulate positions for advocacy. The ability of EAWLS to mobilize scientific and technical knowledge and use it during the controversy that strengthened the case for sustainable development in the area.

The main argument of the conservation groups was that the delta was an important ecosystem offering numerous benefits to the people and should therefore be managed wisely. They were against the proposed large-scale commercial prawn farming because they claimed that it would adversely, and irreparably destroy the delicate ecosystem of the delta. Researchers and conservationists called for independent investigations into the environmental impact of the proposed development. They also challenged the legality of the sale and more specifically whether or not the right legal channels had been followed. There were claims by a member of the Kon-Dertu ranch that they had been granted a 45-year lease by the commissioner of lands in 1974 and that indeed the letter of allotment was available for public scrutiny.

The EAWLS indicated that the land that forms the delta had been proposed by a number of NGOs and government agencies to be converted to a national park and that allocation to Kon-Dertu was done improperly. EAWLS also claimed development would threaten the fishing industry and the water balance of the delta and consequently interfere with the setting up of the proposed national park.

Coastal Aquaculture and Kon-Dertu asserted that in various stages they had sought and been granted approval by TARDA and the District Development Committee (DDC); and also at several stages, the government departments responsible for fisheries, wildlife, lands as well as the Treasury were consulted. They also stressed that the deal was on a willing-buyer-willing-seller basis. They argued that their activities would not cause any major negative environmental impacts and that local people were opposed to the establishment of a park of any kind and might, like Kon-Dertu, be encouraged to view it simply as a conservation area. This argument was reinforced by an earlier relocation of people when another park had been established with unfulfilled promises of benefit to the local people. Hence local people were reluctant to participate in a similar venture.

The setting apart of trust land as provided in Section 117 of the Constitution and enforced by Section 13 of the Trust Lands Act was used as an argument against the sale of the land to Coastal Aquaculture. The process, as required by law, involves intricate hearings at different levels of government and the ultimate decision-making body is the county council. If the proposal is adopted by the county council then it must be published in the official *Kenya Gazette* before the setting aside takes effect. These details were not adhered to in the licensing of the Coastal Aquaculture venture. If the land had been under the jurisdiction of the state, then the state had the mandate to dispose of it as it so wished, but then an explanation of whether or not that disposition would be to the benefit of the public would be necessary. The basic question as to whether or not the land in dispute was going to be utilized for the good of the public remained the same, whether it was regarded as trust land or public land.

In the end the President ended the debate by declaring that the area be reserved as a wetland of international importance in the interests of conservation. One issue that was not resolved by this decree was whether all the group ranches that had been granted previously had become null and void. After the Presidential decree a national steering committee was formed, headed by TARDA who were to direct and oversee its workings. It consisted of a number of stakeholders including KWS, the National Museums of Kenya, IUCN, the National Environment Secretariat, the Permanent Presidential Commission on Soil Conservation and Afforestation and EAWLS.

The proposal to create a Tana delta National Wetlands Reserve, to protect a major part of the Tana River delta and its flora and fauna, has already been forwarded to the DDC. The proposal shows that the delta has the potential to become a model project for the compatible management of traditional human activities together with conservation. A management board is required to co-ordinate and integrate the various land-use practices in the whole delta in co-operation with the local people to ensure that it is compatible with their needs and contributes to improving their standards of living. It is also recommended that no group ranch or prawn farm should be established within the boundaries of the proposed Tana Delta Wetlands Reserve. Any new development project in the delta must be preceded by an environmental impact assessment.[42]

The lack of a clear land tenure regime and administrative authority were the major causes of the Tana River delta controversy. The contention that the area was trust land and the county council was therefore supposed to administer it in the interest of the community has never been resolved. Despite earlier requests by conservationists and KWS that the area be protected as a national park due to its rich biodiversity, group ranches were nevertheless established in the area. One of the reasons that was advanced by the opponents of the proposed park was that since the area is of importance to both the human and wildlife populations, inevitable conflicts between the two groups of users associated with such protected areas would arise. The Presidential decree ended the debate and the gazettment of the proposed park is expected although it is not guaranteed. The question now is whether or not the decision to establish a national park in the area will be implemented under a regime that will allow the communities in the area to still obtain the wetland's multiple benefits. The communities are not so much concerned with the wildlife *per se* but more with the other wetland resources such as water, forage, firewood, timber and fish. A system that disaggregates the rights to the resources of the area might be necessary. A clear and accessible decision-making process is needed to avoid a repeat of the break-down of governance witnessed by this case. It is also essential to ensure that local communities have a say in resource management as stakeholders with the same standing as governmental and non-governmental institutions.

If a park is established, it will consist of only that area that is considered most sensitive. Wetlands are open ecosystems and are liable to be affected by actions that might seem to be far removed from them. The current trend of privatizing group ranches and trust land portends a danger to the proposed national park because it could lead to personalized utilization of adjacent land to the detriment of the park. Therefore even with the changes occurring in the tenure regimes within the delta, the need for state regulation within the area surrounding the park, whether it is publicly or privately owned, cannot be overstated.

Another important issue that arises from the controversy is the need for conservation organizations to have the standing to represent environmental interests. In this case private, community and government interests were represented by the relevant institutions. The government, however, found itself in a position of having to represent several conflicting interests. It look the intervention of the President of the Republic, who holds considerable power regarding trust and government lands and is also the patron of EAWLS to make the necessary ruling. A more suitable constitutional position would be to allow *bona fide* environmental organizations to represent clearly defined environmental components in a way akin to the manner that directors represent the interests of private firms. This approach would be complemented by constitutional arrangements which enable the state to function as a trustee holding land and the related resources in the interest of the public.

Policy implications

Policy reforms should be centred around the alleviation of conflict between land uses promoting high mostly short-term productivity and longer-term sustainable ecosystems. They should be geared towards protecting wildlife, as a resource for the future. The exclusive rights of the individual and the public will thus need to be modified. In addition, the issue of environmental representation needs to be addressed, especially in situations where government may be expected to represent competing interests.

Interaction between humans and wildlife is presently problematic due to the arrangements of rights to resources inherent in the existing tenure system concerning protected and agricultural areas. This restricts the activities of both, and creates potential for conflict. Where it would not act to the detriment of the other, therefore, rights to resources could be transferred to or shared with the public and therefore accommodate both interests. This would be particularly important in the interaction zone around the boundaries of protected areas. With a sound land-use planning policy, encroachment by humans into protected areas can be controlled (although not necessarily stopped) and aspects other than agricultural values can be considered prior to allocation of land for different uses. Allocation of rights to resources on the land to reduce wildlife–human conflicts, can be summarized in the concept of integrated land-use policy.

Disaggregation of rights to different resources found on the land is needed. These rights include the ability of public institutions to utilize resources for conservation purposes, and of individuals, for private purposes, both inside and outside parks. For the individual, these include rights to undertake activities such as grazing or gathering inside the park, or wildlife utilization outside the park. This must be coupled with the duty to use these resources sustainably. If private landowners and communities bordering wildlife areas can generate income directly from wildlife, they will recognize its value on their land. They are then likely to take responsibility for conserving and ensuring their existence. This includes controlling their movement and cropping it both for sale and domestic consumption in order to maintain a sustainable population. Another right would be the right to deny wildlife access to private land, or the right to remove or kill animals interfering with private economic activities. This would dismantle the state's monopolistic ownership of protected area resources and of all wildlife. Rights to utilization of wildlife relate to management and harvesting of wildlife as a resource on ones land.

The local community could indirectly attain rights to some of the revenues from tourism inside parks. KWS has proposed a compensation system in which 25% of the revenue generated from wildlife-related activities will be vested in the local community. The issue of compensation relates to the ownership of animals. As long as the state is the sole owner of wild animals, one could argue that the damage caused by the animals on private property should be fully compensated. Similarly, the acquisition by the state of wildlife could warrant compensation to those who previously used them for their subsistence. Such compensation measures could be used to encourage the Tana River delta communities to support the proposed national park. However the state cannot always afford this type of compensation and previous compensation schemes were fraught with problems. The issue of determining and allocating compensation to individuals is notoriously difficult. Wildlife tend to migrate and the possibility of finding a solution through privatized ownership of wildlife is still complex. A compromise can be sought through rights of the individuals to utilize the resource, and manage it where it is permanently inhabiting private land. In some cases this may prove more profitable than agriculture, especially in dry areas.

Conservation authorities are losing influence over flora and fauna in agricultural and rangeland areas adjacent to protected areas, and within and around fragile ecosystems like wetlands due to increased privatization and subdivision. Greater efforts by conservation authorities in both the national and district-level could secure buffer zones and corridors that would be accessible to wildlife adjacent to protected areas. Such zones would have certain use restrictions but could otherwise be managed as private property. It should be noted that the trend in developed countries has been for the state or federal government to play an increasingly important role in environmental conservation through zoning and other means, in wetlands in particular.[43]

Ultimately a balance has to be established between private ownership and public interest. This could be achieved through the use of the police power in imposing certain limits on the use of private property. Various statutes, for example, can be used to prevent charcoal burning or clearing of vegetation on private land. The Wildlife (Conservation and Management) Act could be expanded to control other activities or practices such as fencing or restricting access by wildlife. Policing has been on the rise especially because of the increasing privatization of land and decline of regulation mechanisms through customary law. However, there are also other more comprehensive and positive mechanisms to ensure general public interest in the conservation of wildlife. The Land Planning Act, for instance, provides for evaluation and zoning of land uses and the allocation of land according to ecological parameters.[44] The local authorities and physical planning department could therefore prepare area plans on both private and public lands.

In the creation of interaction zones where public and private tenure are more and more intertwined, it is important that the local population attain influence in planning. Important strategies include representation in decision-making bodies and consultative organs charged with the management and allocation of resources and with land use planning. Any plans for establishing and managing parks or reserves should be developed in consultation with and in agreement with the people concerned. At the same time, it is important that integrated land-use does not become a catalyst for eroding the public interest in conservation. The state should essentially retain the fundamental authority to overrule other decisions and step in where planning and resource use are malfunctioning and therefore harming conservation efforts. Without clear boundaries setting apart wildlife areas, the escalating human population could take over these lands. The limits of authority and utilization levels of locally administered protected areas should be clarified and strengthened.

In order for the stakeholders to exercise their authority effectively, information and monitoring on the status and changes within wildlife ecosystems is crucial. Inventories on the status of wildlife and their ecosystems could provide a basis for decisions on land use planning and resource conservation in general. KWS is presently developing monitoring systems for wildlife in certain areas with the aim of determining quotas for cropping by individual land owners. In addition, individual rights to information must be enhanced for effective and positive involvement in the management of conservation. Extension could also be used to facilitate the identification of available land-use options by farmers.

Land-use conflicts can be minimized by a comprehensive land-use policy that allocates different ecological zones to suitable, and often multiple, purposes. For this to happen, there will be a need for co-ordinated land use decision-making that involves various ministries and departments, which are in one way or another concerned with wildlife conservation. Co-ordination is necessary in the allocation of rights and in developing proper channels of authority. This would seek to strengthen the mandate of wildlife in general development efforts and eliminate the insecurity and lack of clarity relating to land tenure that promote free access regimes and short-term uses. There is need for cross-sectoral co-ordination in policy-making, and a review of the impacts of food and agricultural policy on wildlife conservation. Planners within KWS need to increasingly work with other relevant sectors involved in land-use planning outside the parks to draw up land-use plans which incorporate national parks and reserves into surrounding areas.

There are also possible changes in the tenure system. In customary law, some resources, especially in marginal or low-potential areas, were controlled and managed by a political entity. Privatization in particular has undermined the authority of these entities resulting in intensive use of the resources in a bid to gain as much profit as possible from the land without due consideration for the wider ecosystem. The transformation of common property regimes into public lands has led to open access situations in some areas again, resulting in deterioration of the ecosystems. Acknowledging, formalizing and promoting aspects of customary land tenure could enhance traditional sustainable management systems and provide an alternative to privatization. Customary rules could be reconciled with or included as part of statutory law. For this to happen, customary rules will need to be understood and recorded for interpretation. The legal status of public agreements relating to management of natural resources, in particular wildlife should be clarified, and if possible enhanced. Finally, national park boundaries should only be altered by law to ensure consistency. As in the case of forest resources discussed in the preceding chapter, the finite nature of wildlife resources dictates that pressure on land for agricultural use be reduced by providing alternative employment opportunities.

Conclusions

The question of tenure and conservation of wildlife revolves around how well public interests in conservation are taken care of under a particular tenure system and how well the value and rights of wildlife are incorporated into the sphere of private interest and rights. We have argued that the present tenure system protects the biological resources within the national parks and reserves but neglects the rich biodiversity that lies outside the legal boundaries. The dominant conservation ethic has created a division between economic and conservation goals, where one precludes the other. The national goal for agriculture is inconsistent with conservation, exacerbated by a rigid division in forms of tenure. Rights of the public (through the government) are paramount in parks, and have sometimes been exercised with little consideration of, and to the detriment of, the local inhabitants and the customary land tenure that previously regulated sustainable use.

There is a lack of co-ordination between the various authorities and laws dealing with issues with a bearing on conservation outside national parks or protected areas. No paramount conservation concern is integrated in the tenure system of private ownership. This needs to be rectified in realization that privatization of land is the direction to which government policy has been leading in the decades since independence. A measure of government regulation will be necessary even on privately owned lands, and this is a matter that requires constitutional attention. This further argues a case for the interests of wildlife being represented through other mechanisms than public tenure alone.

Presently, wildlife is under public trusteeship through government ownership and management by KWS. Actions that break the laws inherent in this tenure arrangement can be stopped, but a case can otherwise not be raised on behalf of the environment. Transcending the tenure system, there is a need to enable *bona fide* environmental groups to represent environmental interests the way directors represent corporations. Such an approach could be seen as an extension of the public trust doctrine. The state as trustee of environmental interests could extend such trusteeship to environmental organizations under appropriate legislation and policies. The lack of effective representation of the rights of wildlife also stems from an implicit definition of wildlife as wild animals only. Outside protected areas, this is clearly manifested by public tenure of animals only, and not their habitats. Public trusteeship could therefore enhance the representation of not only wild animals, but also their habitats, including a wider range of species not currently protected. This ecosystem approach could ensure a more viable strategy for the conservation of the natural environments of Kenya.

Notes

1. Republic of Kenya, 1993a.
2. Republic of Kenya, 1993a.
3. KWS, 1990, p. 6.

4. KWS 1990, p. 8.
5. KWS, 1990, p. 5.
6. Denny, 1993.
7. KWS, 1990.
8. KWS 1990.
9. KWS, 1990.
10. Public tenure of wildlife does not guarantee the right of access to animals of privately owned land since land use is controlled by the individual landowner. However, the cost of keeping wildlife out is clearly prohibitive in most cases, and in many cases not physically feasible.
11. Section 115(2).
12. Marekia, 1991.
13. Pers. comm. with D. Bos, researcher from Wageningen University, the Netherlands, at Game Ranching Ltd., Athi River, Kenya, 1995.
14. James, 1971. See also Chapter 5 in this book.
15. Grandin, 1985.
16. Kipuri, 1989, p. 77.
17. Odegi-Awuondo, 1990, p. 35.
18 Republic of Kenya, 1993a.
19. It has long been debated whether significant disease transmission or grazing competition actually occur. See Grootenhuis, 1991.
20. Republic of Kenya, 1981.
21. UNEP and KWFT, 1988, p. 30.
22. UNEP and KWFT, 1988, p. 32.
23. "Ukambani" comprises the current Machakos, Kitui and Makueni districts in Eastern Province.
24 Bernard et al., 1989.
25 Such as Republic of Kenya, 1982.
26. Republic of Kenya, 1982, p.4
27. See Chapter 5 of this volume.
28. Tiffen et al., 1994.
29. Republic of Kenya, 1982. Machakos District included Makueni District during this period.
30. Republic of Kenya, 1982, p. 34.
31. Tiffen et al., 1994.
32. Oweyegha-Afunaduula, 1982.
33. Republic of Kenya, 1982.
34. About 6,000 elephants died in the drought 1970–72. Prior to the drought, there had been discussions on whether to cull the growing concentration and number of elephants in Tsavo, but no substantial culling took place. At the moment, the game warden is experimenting with burning of vegetation to create diverse habitats and open grasslands that are good for game viewing.
35. Hamilton, 1986.
36. Jensen, 1987.
37. Hamilton 1986; Ndung'u, 1995b.
38. Olindo et al., 1988.
39. Grootenhuis, 1991
40. KWS, 1990.
41. Ole Nkako F.M. 1992, p. 92.

42. Njuguna, 1992, p. 145.
43. Burhenne-Guilmin and Burhenne 1991, p. 53. This has been well established in the US, Britain and Germany in particular.
44. See Chapter 4 of this book.

PART III

CUSTOMARY RIGHTS AND SUSTAINABLE LAND USE

Land tenure in pastoral lands

9

ISAAC LENAOLA, HADLEY H. JENNER

AND TIMOTHY WICHERT

Introduction

The aim of this chapter is to examine the extent to which existing land tenure systems in Kenya affect the welfare and future of pastoral communities. Pastoralists are livestock owners who make use of seasonal pastures for the sustenance of their herds of sheep, goats, donkeys, cattle and camels. Pastoralism, however, is not solely a livestock regime. To varying degrees pastoralists engage in crop farming; commercial trading of animals; trading of craft articles of leather, metal and jewelry; supplying wage labour for farmers, town industries and government construction projects. The extent to which pastoralists groups engage in these activities varies by their location.

The chapter argues that the Constitution of Kenya contains certain provisions which are implemented through laws that undermine the welfare and future of pastoral communities. The constitutional provisions for trust land, while providing nominal protection for African customary law, also legitimize the continuation of the colonial land system that was designed to transfer customary rights from indigenous communities to settlers. It is through such a transfer programme that the interests, rights, values and practices of nomadic pastoralists are adversely affected. This chapter concludes that a revision of Chapter IX of the Constitution is needed to balance between development needs and the values, traditions, rights and practices of local communities, especially nomadic pastoralists. It proposes the overall adoption of the doctrine of customary use as the foundation for reviewing the Constitution and making the necessary amendments in this regard.

The ecology and economy of African rangeland

Africa contains a substantial portion of the world's arid and semi-arid rangelands, extending over three million sq km. These drylands support an estimated 16–22 million pastoral people and nearly 500 million head of livestock. These arid and semi-arid rangelands of the continent exhibit diversity in climate, land form, soil types, wildlife and vegetation. They are characterized by their high spatial and temporal variability in precipitation, receiving 250–750 mm of rainfall per year, and this directly affects plant and animal productivity.

Drylands account for a substantial area of the African continent. They constitute over 50% of tropical Africa, and cover 24 countries, varying from 100% of Somalia and Djibouti and 80% of Kenya, to just under 30% of Uganda. As a result of their extensiveness, they support a great number of people, many of whom are pastoralists or agropastoralists. As a proportion of national population in eastern Africa, drylands support rural human populations ranging from less than 20% in Kenya to over 95% in Somalia and Djibouti. Besides supporting human populations, they support the majority of goats, sheep and camels, and nearly half of the total population of cattle in eastern and southern Africa. Further, they are a home to a large variety of wild animals.

Some 80% of Kenya is classified as rangelands (Map 2). These are areas which are unsuitable for rainfed cultivation due to physical limitations such as aridity, poor soils, rough terrain and so on, and which support the natural vegetation that is a source of forage for both domestic and wild animals. Official definitions of drylands vary. The Food and Agriculture Organization of the United Nations (FAO), for example, uses growing days as the relevant criterion, and defines drylands as lands with a growing period of less than 120 days.[1] Within this range, arid lands might have less than 75 growing days, while semi-arid might have 75 days or more.

At the local level, the categorization of drylands will vary according to whatever local factors determine land use and productivity. Climatic factors will include not only the total annual precipitation, but also its seasonality and the probability of drought. Soil and vegetation quality will be another criterion, with particular reference to the prospects for moisture retention, erosion and nature of the natural vegetation. Land use and population pressure are also considered, such as the prevalence of pastoralism, agropastoralism and other forms of land use as well as the population density relative to the capacity of the land. Other features of local drylands might include topography, surface and groundwater availability, and the extent of land degradation.

The drylands in eastern Africa, and Kenya in particular, generally fall within two main types: dry croplands, and arid rangelands. The former refers to those areas of the rangelands which have been brought under cultivation. In such areas, dryland cropping is practised under a wide range of ecological and socio-political conditions. Crops are usually raised on the basis of subsistence, often in conjunction with keeping livestock. Agropastoralism makes use of the range grazing and insures against the climatic risks of dryland cropping. Expansion of agropastoralism into the more arid zones is often a response to population pressure, or in some specific instances of large-scale agriculture, due to mechanization. Although some of these initiatives meet with success, the associated costs may include land degradation and population displacement and impoverishment.

Within the arid rangelands, pastoralism is still the predominant form of land use, though it usually supports only a minority of the population. The Maasai of Kenya for example, occupy nearly seven per cent of the total land area, while constituting only one per cent of the national population.[2] In these zones, pastoralism often represents the only practicable form of human land use, since its essential feature consists of extensive livestock husbandry utilizing range grazing. Swift suggests that pastoral production systems are those in which 50% or more of household gross revenue, including both market and subsistence production, comes from livestock or livestock related activities.[3] Agropastoral systems, in this definition, are those in which 50% or more of household gross revenue comes from farming, with 10–50% from pastoralism.

Pastoralism requires the opportunity for mobility, with movements determined by the availability of browse resources and water. Since they are so dependent on the ecosystem, pastoralists form an integral part of it. The relationship is delicate, with increasing populations and overgrazing disrupting the integrity and regenerative capacities of the soils and vegetation when mobility is limited. Drought periods exacerbate the problem, and undermine the integrity further. Conflict may further limit mobility and make the ecological impact much worse.

Despite their fragility, drylands have for centuries supported indigenous pastoral people and their animals. For most of these societies, property relations entailed individual or household ownership of livestock and herds, and community control over access to pasture and related resources. Land ownership, to the extent that it has been articulated, has usually been one of "common property" within a defined group or community. Access to key resources, including water and the highly productive areas reserved for dry season grazing (such as wetlands and uplands) was regulated temporally and spatially.

Through this system of complex social structures and institutions, these traditional societies learned to cope with the generally poor soils and short-age of water. Their animal husbandry, hunting and gathering, and crop cultivation practices were well suited to sustainable use of the resource base. These practices were seriously challenged with the coming of colonialism to Africa. Much of the most arable parts of the drylands were alienated and turned into extensive livestock ranches, set aside as wildlife sanctuaries, or put under tillage. For the most part, these challenges were justified by the assertion that these lands were empty spaces with no individual resource owners, and that in any event the pastoral way of life represented irrational resource management.

While development action by independent national governments and international organizations varies from one country to the next, policy initiatives related to indigenous people of the drylands have in general been characterized by neglect or poorly informed misdirection, the latter often represented by the introduction of inappropriate technologies and by policies of sedentarization. These latter policies have usually been effected through comprehensive land registration programmes, involving a process which includes land claims, demarcation and adjudication with various legislative enactments facilitating the eventual registration. It is now being realized that initiatives, whether public or private, involving the transformation of property rights in land and other fixed resources, commercialization of pastoral economies, expansion of drylands cultivation, application of inappropriate technologies, increasing settlement of immigrant populations and sedentarization of the nomadic people have not only been unsuccessful (to the extent to which success can be measured), but have also created multiple problems for the people and the environment in the drylands.

In recent years, the drylands of eastern and southern Africa have continued to experience extended periods of drought, a net decline in productivity, the increasing settlement of immigrant and nomadic populations, and a dangerous level of environmental degradation. As a result, the people in these areas remain vulnerable to scarcity of resources, famine, land use conflict, wars and displacement. In short, their future survival is uncertain. The combined effect has placed the drylands environment and production systems in crisis.

It is estimated that nearly 59% of all ruminant livestock in Africa are found in arid and semi-arid lands (ASALS). The total value of livestock products is estimated to be 25% of the total agricultural output and is valued at over US$12 billion. This estimate, however, excludes other benefits of livestock such as manure and draught power. With these additional benefits, livestock products may account for 35% of total agricultural output.[4] The value of rangelands in overall economic output in countries such as Kenya should include the contributions of wildlife-based tourism. The regions that are often branded as marginal or of low potential support the bulk of dryland wildlife populations. In terms of ecological efficiency, these areas may be more productive than their high rainfall counterparts.[5] Clearly the commonly held belief that pastoral lands contribute little to national economies is false. Nomadic pastoralism is a rational land use system which has evolved over the years and is adapted to harsh and unpredictable environmental conditions. Under the prevailing level of investment, infrastructure and technological condition, nomadic pastoralism is the most viable economic system in most of northern and north-eastern Kenya and other dryland areas within and outside Kenya.

Pastoral nomadism is practised in ASALs and adapts to variable forage supplies and water distribution. The ability of nomadic people to survive in these marginal lands is attributed to their opportunistic mobility and diversified livestock husbandry. Grazing and browsing on sparsely and unevenly distributed vegetation, domestic animals need more extensive areas of forage as aridity increases. Thus, mobility and the size of the territorial domain utilized by a pastoral community increase with aridity. In this regard Galaty argues that land rights become more diffuse as occupation of a given region becomes more sporadic. He further adds the converse, that as mobility and the magnitude of the pastoral domain decrease in less arid regions and resource use becomes more constant, territorial claims become more concrete and specific.[6]

Another common characteristic of African rangelands is recurrent drought and famine. During severe droughts the herds of pastoral nomads are often decimated and accompanied by human suffering and environmental degradation. The impact of droughts is made much worse by sedentarization of formerly nomadic communities, water development without sound ecological considerations, exclusion of the nomads from vital dry season reserves and their compression onto smaller and more fragile land.

It is often argued that pastoralists keep too many animals, far above what the range resources are capable of supporting. Large herds are then unable to survive during periods of low forage production. However, given the large-scale fluctuations and patchiness of the rangeland ecosystem this practice is an effective means of spreading risks and ensuring continuity of the nomadic communities. Arguably therefore, the production system and ecosystem are intertwined, creating a complex inter-relationship between people, animal life, plants and the physical environment. Large areas of savanna and open woodland are sustained through dynamic interactions between human activity, mainly grazing and burning, and a diversity of wild herbivores as well as predation by wild carnivores.

African countries have realized the importance of protecting wildlife for economic gain. They have established national parks and game reserves, and maintained those created by colonial governments. These are mainly situated in the arid and semi-arid rangelands inhabited by pastoralists. The economic importance of these parks cannot be over-emphasized. For example, in Kenya protected wildlife areas are a major tourist attraction and tourism is the single largest source of foreign exchange for the national economy.[7] It is also to be noted that these rangelands are a source of important mineral resources. When these resources are exploited they are a major national income earner.

Ecology and land rights

Traditional resource management

Traditional resource management systems were characterized by a number of specific elements. First, indigenous precolonial society had a holistic approach towards managing and utilizing the various products and services which nature provided. The traditional systems were highly dependent on their environment; hence the local environment was not seen as dispensable. Secondly, traditional resource management was undertaken by generalists as opposed to specialists. The resource users combined the expertise of those knowledgeable about the environment, those who planned for its use, and those who in fact used it. A third element was that knowledge and expertize was gained through informal experiments and the accumulation of experience as opposed to formal education. Finally, traditional communities approached resource utilization with a special combination of the physical, the intellectual and the spiritual. By combining these various elements, indigenous communities, whether pastoral or agricultural, have developed norms, rules, beliefs and practices which achieve sustainable resource use within fragile environments.

It is for these reasons that traditional pastoralism is again widely regarded as the best use of pastoral rangeland, given the environment's extreme characteristics. Taking into account seasonal variations, it is clear that some parts of the drylands offer consistently better grazing grounds, while other parts may be better suited during other seasons. Particular groups have access to the most suitable grazing ground, as well as the most unsuitable. Under proper management the livestock feeding capacity can be maximized.

At another level, a benefit which accrues to such a system is that local governance systems may more easily be kept maintained, given that the land is occupied by an entire identifiable ethnic group, clan or family.

Customary pastoral tenure systems assign rights to different categories of resources, such as different types of water points, various arable field sites, transhumance routes, trees, riverine pastures, wet-season pastures. In a communal system, these categories of resources are generally not held by a single ownership unit. Rather, they are governed by an intricate system of organization. Thus, arable field sites might be controlled by households, riverine grazing controlled by a small group of co-resident households (i.e., compound or homestead), some water points and grazing owned by still larger kinship groupings (or neighbourhood units), while routes for movement of people are open to, or controlled by, ethnic or inter-ethnic confederations. Within these tenure regimes, there is a hierarchy of rights, which are divided between different "ownership" groups, ranging from the individual producer to the largest ethnic group. The regime is communal, since these ownership groups are not territorially distinct, thus mobility remains possible.

This system of "rights" and social structure implies a legal notion of "common property".[8] A common property regime is one which in effect represents private property for a group of co-owners or members. Within this regime, the management group, or co-owners, have a right to exclude non-members (which implies that the non-members have a duty to abide by this exclusion). Within the group itself, members have both rights and duties with respect to the use and maintenance of the property.

Along with ensuring effective internal use and management of resources, these traditional systems tend further to regard land as a collection of separate and distinct rights to resources which make up the land, often referred to as a "bundle of rights". These rights may include, or apply to, trees, ground water, particular forage and grazing areas, and are specifically flexible enough to take into consideration such factors as the change in seasons.

Common property must be distinguished from the notion of open access regimes, which are essentially "non-property" regimes; everybody's access is nobody's property. Open access may result from the absence, or breakdown, of a management and authority system. For example, a regime may become open access when institutional failures have undermined former collective or individual management regimes.

Colonial land alienation

Despite these highly developed and relatively complex traditional tenure systems, the colonial government in Kenya conveniently took advantage of sparsely populated customary commons to introduce Western jurisprudential doctrines. The land was treated as "ownerless", and colonial officials argued that "since Africans owned land only in terms of occupational rights, it followed that unoccupied land reverted to the territorial sovereign".[9] As a result, the British declared such land which had previously been shared under customary rules to be vacant, and subsequently designated as "Crown lands".

The British Crown was given power, by virtue of the Foreign Jurisdiction Act of 1890, for control and disposition over "waste and unoccupied land in protectorates where there was no settled form of government and where land had not been appropriated either to the local sovereign or to individuals. Her Majesty might, if she so pleased, declare them to be Crown Lands".[10] This power was extended to the East Africa Protectorate by the East African (Lands) Order-in-Council in 1901 and such designated Crown lands were vested in the Commissioner of the Protectorate (later the Governor) in trust for Her Majesty. By virtue of the Crown Lands Ordinance of 1915, these public or Crown lands were to include "all land occupied by the native tribes of the protectorate and all lands reserved for the use of the members of any tribe."[11] Thus the powers of alienation or disposal of all land was placed into the hands of the British governor.

Thus began a process of introducing a previously unknown notion of land rights. Described by Okoth-Ogendo as a "legal-structural authoritarianism",[12] it attempted to undermine, or de-legitimize, any notion of right based on customary law (such as rights of occupancy and rights to common property). By introducing, and then promoting, a land tenure system based on individualism, with a legal structure to offer protection, the non-indigenous settlers were able to obtain land for themselves and eventually political security.[13] The introduction of Western property doctrine at this stage ensured the establishment of a political system, a constitution and laws which would serve to guarantee the distinct rights of the individual.

At the time that independence became inevitable, the colonial government sought to retain the legitimacy and security of this property regime by encouragement and then co-option of an indigenous elite which had come to accept and benefit from it. The African sector that took over control of the country following independence were those who would also gain the most by the continuity of the economic and political colonial system. Through a variety of land-related policies, there were many Africans who not only acquired land, but with it a respect for property rights. Those who gained most from the opening up of the so-called "white Highlands" were "almost exclusively national level politicians, civil servants, businessmen, the managerial cadres in private industry and later, the armed forces."[14]

The emergence of this "landed oligarchy" was responsible for ensuring that the legal and institutional norms and structures of the colonial regime were not abandoned. They also offered some indication of how the land tenure regimes, including those of the drylands, were to develop in the post-colonial era. Because this elite had been able to acquire substantial property, and property rights, they had little interest in transforming colonial systems of land tenure which would jeopardize their control of land. Logically, they tended to support the argument that it is the absence of clearly defined property rights to environmental resources which is the main cause of environmental degradation. If property rights are defined and clearly and exclusively assigned, so the argument goes, then land users would have an incentive to take care of their land resources and use them in a socially optimal way.

At a basic level, this theory assumes a limited and simple comparison of clear, exclusive and enforceable property rights on the one hand, with a system of insecure, or even non-existent, property rights on the other. Hardin's "tragedy of the commons" concept has been used to argue that pastures open to all will eventually be overused and the carrying capacity of the land will inevitably be exceeded, generating tragedy through degradation and depletion; in essence, unbridled access to the commons can bring ruin to all. Statutory provisions therefore, attempt to ascribe rights which effect the exclusion of outsiders and others from claiming rights. More importantly, statutory regimes tend to regard land rights as a right to a single resource.

Increasingly, property rights analysis is recognizing that the relationship between property rights and land degradation, and the issue of tenure insecurity, is far more complex than a simple argument based on the tragedy or non-tragedy of the commons. It is becoming more acceptable to suggest that both common property regimes and private property regimes may provide viable solutions in appropriate circumstances. Increasingly, the traditional and modern aspects of land tenure and land use are attempting to coexist within similar terrain. Population pressures are forcing non-pastoralists into the drylands, where they make attempts at agriculture and demarcation of land. Pastoralists themselves are increasingly taking up cultivation, especially as a response to loss of grazing lands, poverty and loss of livestock and other outside pressures to diversify economically. Further, they are increasingly staking more tangible claims of rights to land as a means of preserving land which is in danger from outside encroachment. The history of Kenya, which has experienced and attempted to manage the simultaneous development of these competing regimes, has pointed to the potential for incompatibility and conflict.

Status of customary rights

It would appear from practical experiences that the "tragedy of the commons" described by Hardin has become a reality among Kenya's pastoralists. He spoke of the looming misery to be expected given a rising population coupled with individual unchecked access to the pasture "commons" by herders. So influential was Hardin's argument among academics, development practitioners and government workers that a variety of corrective treatments have been prescribed. These prescriptions fitted well with previous late-colonial and post-independence government schemes whose goal was to settle pastoralists and introduce private property regimes. These interventions were made under the assumption that the national economy would benefit as agricultural productivity increased due to the imposition of private tenure systems and the "rationalization" of the livestock economy. In effect, the pastoralists had to be saved from themselves for their own good. That this patronizing message, both blind to history and the realities of pastoral land use, has only recently been challenged attests to the power of the state and its supporters.[15]

Land tenure essentially defines the rules and social contracts whereby individuals and groups acquire, hold, transfer, or transmit interests and rights in land. The nature of land tenure in Africa is complex and could perhaps be best described as various points on a "tenure continuum". This continuum tends to be reduced at the national level to three essential types: customary tenure (usually communal), private tenure (usually individual) and state controlled land which may potentially be subject to either of the foregoing. Customary tenure, also known as common tenancy, is to be distinguished from systems of open access to resources stigmatized by Hardin in his classic paper referred to above. According to Bromley, under customary tenure, those in power ("the owners") exercise their right to exclude non-members, who in turn have a duty to respect that exclusion. The members ("the co-owners") are responsible for the exercise of both rights and duties related to the use and maintenance of the natural resources held in common by the members.[16]

Current land tenure in pastoral areas usually entails both a formal legislative framework as well as a less formal set of customary norms and practices. The customary tenure arrangements reflect shared community understandings about who holds what rights in which resources, privileges of settlement and movement and prerogatives of exclusion.[17] Under the customary systems, communities define the rights, privileges and prerogatives regarding land resources. Transformations in land tenure arise from changes in government policy, law, and changes in customary rights.

The government policies which pushed for the replacement of customary tenure in favour of private property systems, created a growing population of landless pastoralists with the wealth and power increasingly in the hands of a small, satisfied elite, resulting in discord and instability in the drylands.[18] These changes also restricted women's access to natural resources important for family welfare, such as medicinal plants, fuelwood and water points.[19] As a counter to these destructive trends, the World Bank and the Kenya government are beginning to think anew about land use policies in the drylands. It has been suggested that in the drylands, where resources are most suitable for livestock keeping, a form of land tenure is required which allows for common use of property, while at the same time securing land rights and defining responsibilities for conservation. Moreover, support from international aid organizations is growing for common property resource management and incremental tenure change rather than wholesale replacement of tenure systems.[20] The creation, restoration or re-emphasis of customary tenure as more suited to pastoralist realities may begin to reverse the negative consequence of state action which has directly or inadvertently led to the increasing misery and poverty throughout the drylands. Finally, a renewed pastoralism is a suitable, productive enterprise well-suited to Kenya's extensive dryland environments. Nevertheless, despite a dawning realization of the needs for land reform in the drylands, the beneficiaries of the status quo present enormous political difficulties to any meaningful change.[21]

In the face of these sweeping changes and growing pastoralist marginalization, is the budding awareness of the possibilities for pastoralist common tenancy by the Kenya government and international partners a case of too little, too late? Can, in fact pastoralist common tenancy, which once served so well, be reinvigorated and maintained? The next section provides review of customary tenure provisions within the law of Kenya will ascertain the relative legal importance of pastoral land rights. Both the opportunities and limits provided by this legislation will be probed followed by a brief case study illustrating the often contrasting reality between what is "on the books" and what is happening "on the ground". A concluding perspective, questions and new ideas for action are then offered.

Existing constitutional and legal provisions

Within the legal system of Kenya, land may be subject to any of a variety of specific laws, leading to a state of affairs which has created problems in both juridical and administrative terms.[22] There are two categories of land registration, registration of titles and registration of deeds, which are embodied in five registration laws: Registered Land Act, Land Titles Act, Government Lands Act, Registration of Titles Act, and Registration of Documents Act. In particular, the Registered Land Act makes provisions for "the registration of title to land, and for the regulation of dealings in land so registered." The Land Titles Act makes provisions for "the removal of doubts that have arisen in regard to titles to land and to establish a land Registration Court."

Apart from land which has been privatized (i.e., within the exclusive domain of an individual with a registered private freehold title), land within Kenya is known as either trust land pursuant to the Trust Lands Act, or as government land pursuant to the Government Lands Act. Trust land provisions may be the most significant in relation to communal land. The controversial aspect of this land is perhaps why specific provisions related to it have been entrenched in great detail within the Constitution. Legislation related to the relevant procedures governing the land includes: Land Control Act, Land Consolidation Act, Land Adjudication Act, and the Land (Group Representatives) Act.

It is clear from a reading of the legislation and the relevant literature that there is an explicit policy direction for the registration of land in Kenya. Registration is a process which includes claim, demarcation, adjudication and registration. Although this policy trend may be an explicit part of a process, there is some basis for communal land tenure claims within existing Kenyan law and a number of provisions exist which facilitate the erosion of communal land tenure rights.

As earlier indicated, trust land is likely to be the most significant legal concept related to communal land. Trust land is that which had been designated as Special Areas and was originally vested in the Trust Land Board, land which was formerly known either as Special Reserves, Temporary Special Reserves, Special Leasehold Areas and Special Settlement Areas and land which had been declared communal reserves under the Crown Lands Ordinance as in force on May 31, 1963. The control of the trust land shall, according to Section 115 of the Constitution, "vest in the county council within whose area of jurisdiction it is situated." The Constitution further provides that each "county council shall hold the Trust land vested in it for the benefit of the persons ordinarily resident on that land and shall give effect to such rights, interests or other benefits in respect of the land as may, under the African customary law for the time being in force and applicable thereto, be vested in any tribe, group, family or individual." This language would appear to grant relatively strong claim to customary tenure in these areas. The same words are echoed in Section 69 of the Trust Lands Act. However there are a number of other provisions in the Constitution which qualify the strength of the recognized customary law.

Firstly, and most significantly, the Constitution goes on to indicate that "no right, interest or other benefit under African customary law shall have effect . . . so far as it is repugnant to any written law."[23] Such a repugnancy clause in effect allows for the creation of any written law which may explicitly contradict and thereby supersede any customary rights. Since all other legislation must conform to the provisions of the Constitution the very fact that it has such provisions in effect extinguishes customary rights. To that extent, the strength and viability of customary law is clearly restricted. The issue is not that the repugnancy clause is necessarily bad, but the spirit of law as informed by colonial programmes, works against customary rights.

Further, pursuant to Section 113 of the Constitution, Parliament may grant rights or interests to prospect for minerals and oil. It may also set apart trust land for the purposes generally of the government of Kenya, for a public corporation, a corporation in which the government has shares, or for the purpose of prospecting for or extracting minerals, and in these situations customary entitlements are extinguished, though subject to compensation as provided in Section 118. To "set apart" in effect means to convey specified interests and rights in or over that land. Similarly, Section 116 provides that any other Act of parliament related to land may be applied to trust land, and when a title is registered under any such law other than in the name of a county council, it ceases to be trust land.

Finally, parliament may make provisions for the administration of trust land by county councils, and a county council may in turn set aside trust land for a variety of reasons. It may do so for use and occupation by a public body for public purposes, for prospecting for or extracting of minerals, or most significantly, for the use and occupation "by any person or persons for a purpose which in the opinion of that county council is likely to benefit the persons ordinarily resident in that area or any other area of trust land vested in that county council, either by reason of the use to which the area so set apart is to be put or by reason of the revenue to be derived from rent."[24] And where such land is set apart, "interests or other benefits in respect of that land that were previously vetted in a tribe, family or individual under African customary law shall be extinguished."[25] The only recourse for those with a customary entitlement is for "prompt payment of full compensation."[26]

The existence of these provisions which facilitate the erosion of customary rights is especially pertinent because of their existence within the paramount law of the land. Nonetheless, there are provisions within written legislation which allow for the recognition of customary legal rights. The notion of registration within the trust land areas was initially addressed through the Land Consolidation Act in 1959 (which had effectively replaced the Native Land Tenure Rules of 1956). The Land Consolidation Act provided a legal and administrative mechanism for ascertaining rights and interests in, and the consolidation and registration of title to, land within special areas which formed part of what was known as trust land. Pursuant to subsidiary legislation, the minister could "where expedient" apply the procedures of the Land Consolidation Act to adjudication areas. For each of these areas an adjudication officer would be appointed, who would subsequently clarify the rights and interests in land within a smaller "adjudication section". Within a fixed period of time, any individual person claiming a right or interest in the land within that section was required to present a claim to a committee appointed by the adjudication officer from amongst persons resident within the adjudication section.

Such claims could of course be based on African customary law, and could be made in person or by representation according to such law. In fact, the committee appointed for an adjudication section was to adjudicate and determine such rights and interests "in accordance with African customary law." These rights and interests would then be recorded in a Record of Existing Rights. The record would include a description of every person whose right was recognized as ownership, together with a description of the land, as well as any interest or right of occupation affecting any land which someone might be entitled to by virtue of African customary law. When such a record was completed and certified a demarcation officer would demarcate the boundaries within the section based on the Record of Existing Rights. These would be compiled within a demarcation plan, which together with descriptions of landowners, parcels of land, and interests in land pursuant to customary law, would form an Adjudication Register. This register was the formal registration of the rights and interests in the land pursuant to the Land Consolidation Act.

In 1968, the Government of Kenya refined the process of adjudication by enacting the Land Adjudication Act, which provides for "the ascertainment and recording of rights and interests in Trust land." In most respects, the Land Adjudication Act provides merely a parallel process to that of the Land Consolidation Act. Adjudication officers designate adjudication sections within adjudication areas within which rights and interests are recorded within an adjudication register. The Land Adjudication Act does however provide for some additional provisions. For example, these provisions may be applied to an area when a county council in whom land is vested so requests. Also, where a Record of Existing Rights has not been completed and certified pursuant to the Land Consolidation Act, the Land Adjudication Act may be applied to that area, even though the Land Consolidation Act also applies thereto (in all other cases the two may not both be applied to the same area). Further, the Land Adjudication Act dispenses with the notion of a Record of Existing Rights, and claims are made directly to a demarcation officer. The adjudication committee within a section, made up of local residents, is required as necessary to either adjudicate, decide upon, or advise as the case may be, "in accordance with recognized customary law." In addition, it is required to safeguard the interests of absent persons, and to bring to the attention of the relevant officers any interest in respect of which no claim has been made.

The most significant addition within the Land Adjudication Act is the provision for recognition of ownership in groups. If any group has, under recognized customary law, exercised rights in or over land which should be recognized as ownership, then pursuant to the Act, that group shall be the owner of that land. Group is defined as "a tribe, clan, section, family or other group of persons, whose land under recognized customary law belongs communally to all persons" who belong to such a grouping. Where a group is recorded in the Adjudication Register as the owner of land, or entitled to an interest not amounting to ownership, they are then eligible to have their group representatives incorporated pursuant to the Land (Group Representatives) Act, which provides for "the incorporation of representatives of groups who have been recorded as owners of land under the land Adjudication Act." As with the Land Consolidation Act, an individual may also be declared an owner of land where he has exercised rights over land under "recognized customary law." And as with groups, interests or rights falling short of ownership may also be recorded where they are granted pursuant to customary law.

Finally, the Government Lands Act makes provisions generally for "regulating the leasing and other disposal of Government lands, which are lands which have been vested in the Government." The Government Lands Act is important to the discussion of communal tenure rights, because in some pastoral areas land used pursuant to communal tenure systems is in fact government land, usually what is known as "unalienated government land". This is land which is not presently being leased to any other person, and for which the commissioner of lands has not issued a letter of allotment. There are no specific provisions within the Government Lands Act related to the granting of communal tenure rights, but those rights could potentially be obtained through the general provisions of the Act related to either leasing, disposal, or licensing for temporary occupation. Those granted a lease over government land are entitled, after paying rent and fulfilling all requisite conditions, to "quietly hold and enjoy the premises without lawful interruption." Leases may be for a period up to 99 years. Licenses on the other hand imply a more temporary use of occupation, and are granted specifically "to occupy unalienated Government land for temporary purposes." As with leases, they are subject to rent and conditions. Given the nature of communal tenure regimes, it is unlikely that pastoralist communities organized within such regimes will enter into formal relationships with the government which entail legal formalities such as licenses and leases. Nonetheless, these provisions do in fact exist, and there would appear to be no hindrance to pastoral communities taking advantage of them, though in the short term they may see no reason for entering into leases or licensing arrangements in situations where they may in fact be using such land in remote areas of the country unimpeded.

Disposal of government land offers more likely prospects for pastoral communities. However the disposal of government land is subject to a number of specific provisions which place the control of such disposal almost exclusively within the office of the president or the commissioner of lands. For example, the president generally may "make grants or dispositions of any estates, interests, rights in or over unalienated government land." This broad discretion could conceivably be exercised in favour of pastoral communities. The real question remains, however, as to whether pastoral communities intent on preserving communal tenure practices would have the political strength necessary to have such a clearly political discretion exercised in their favour. As an example of the relative bias of the disposal provisions within the Government Lands Act, the commissioner of lands (subject to any general or special directions of the president) may cause land available for alienation for "agricultural purposes" to be surveyed and divided into farms. As of February 1990, there were 302 settlement schemes in the country covering some 2,182,360 acres, through which land is given as "freehold subject to conditions." Despite other general provisions, it is unlikely that a government with a general policy direction tending towards the registration of individual rights will offer many possibilities for pastoral communities to acquire communal rights through such provisions. Nonetheless, while not referring specifically to the notion of customary tenure the way other legislation does, the Government Land Act offers provisions which could potentially be exploited by pastoral communities to obtain communal tenure rights, either through leasing, licensing or disposal.

Limits of legislation

The preservation of customary or communal land tenure rights would appear to have some basis in the primary language of the existing legislation. However, it is also clear that the exceptions to the rule clearly allow for the erosion of those rights. Specific provisions, as outlined above with respect to the Constitution for example, place limits on legislation as an effective means of preserving communal tenure rights. While the Constitution simultaneously grants customary communal land tenure rights (with regard to pastoral peoples) and erodes them is a clear indication that there is a deliberate policy through legislation to ensure that communal land holding is eliminated. This policy, firmly entrenched in the Constitution, is reflected in all other pieces of legislation which have operative powers within pastoral lands. The implementation of this policy is thereby achieved. It is interesting to note that while Kenya has strongly held onto the repugnancy clause in the Constitution, other African countries, realizing its counter productiveness, decided to drop it. Ghana, for example, dropped the phrase in 1960 and Tanzania omitted it in its 1963 legislation. While the debate is not concluded as to whether this has changed the status of customary law rights flowing from it, it is undoubtedly clear that they may well be better without it. Meanwhile, there are a number of other barriers for pastoral communities and others intent on preserving a rapidly disappearing tradition, which will be examined as follows: the unfavourable political climate, the confusing context, and the difficult access to the legal system.

The political climate

Where issues relating to customary law have been codified in legislation, they become subject to the "modern" legal regime. For the most part, this offers access to a court system which has traditionally emphasized the sanctity of private property, serves a government which tends to encourage exclusive ownership of private property as a way of developing the rangelands, and tends to be presided over by magistrates who are not influenced by traditional assumptions of structural equality and local harmony.[27] Customary aspects of law remain merely an option within a context biased towards the western notion of property rights. Individuals interested in individualized tenure are able to seek out favourable interpretations of provisions which best serve their interests.

The Group Ranch initiative, for example, despite a stated intention to provide for ownership in groups, offers the option of exclusive individual control of rights to occupation. Although the group representatives are to hold the land and other assets for the collective benefit of all members, disposition of any of the group land may be made simply with approval of the group representatives. Further, informal presidential pronouncements and unclear political statements contribute to blurring the apparent intent of the legal provisions. Thus, in 1989, the President of the Republic directed the civil service to send a team of surveyors to Kajiado District to demarcate land so that the owners of the group ranches could get title deeds for their land. He said "the issue of having group ranches will create problems in future."[28] Many group ranches have been subdivided, and new owners are able to deny access and use to what were formerly communal resources. In some cases they have decided to continue respecting community rights of general access. Despite what might appear to be an attempt to cater for collective benefit, there is in effect an unfavourable political climate which ensures that there is support for opting out of customary systems.

Nonetheless, the presidential pronouncement in Kajiado did not in fact result in the total collapse of group ranches there. This was because people became aware of their own rights through the legal system. Those intent on preserving communal rights are able to do so with some success because they too can take advantage of the "letter of the law", despite what might sometimes appear to be a rather hostile "spirit of the law".

The legal context

As indicated above, within Kenya land may be subject to any of a variety of specific laws, leading to problems in both juridical and administrative terms. This confusion is exacerbated by the bias within the legal system against communal tenure.

The Land (Group Representatives) act provides an example regarding the not insignificant aspect of disposition of land. Although the group representatives are to hold the land and other assets of the group for the collective benefit of all members, disposition of the group land may be made simply with the approval of the group representatives themselves. This provision not only places the authority for such transactions within a small group of individuals, but this is also one of many provisions which are "deemed to be contained in the Constitution of every group".[29] Further, the group representatives need do no more than consult the members of the group in a general meeting before disposing of any land held in their names, but such requirements may specifically be excluded or modified pursuant to the Land (Group Representatives) Act subsidiary legislation. There are numerous other provisions within the Act and the various schedules which provide a confusing and difficult context for communities which often have a distinct lack of formal education, let alone the necessary legal education to understand and safeguard their legal interests.

At another level, the administrative tribunals and committees which effect much of the legal decision-making within the contexts of the relevant Acts have very few specific guidelines that govern their processes. The broad discretion granted to them can quite easily be subject to both abuse and political interference.

Access to the legal system

One of the most practical limits placed on those who would wish to take advantage of the legal system in order to enforce communal legal rights or measures is the difficult access to the legal system itself, especially the courts. This requires capacity within the individual to pursue a legal right, and to do so that person requires the knowledge of the legal right, the resources necessary to pursue it through appropriate legal channels, and the commitment to pursue the matter to its conclusion. There is also the matter of legal standing required to present a case within the court system.

The lack of individual capacity to pursue a legal claim is often the initial and most basic hurdle faced. The lack of knowledge of legal rights and remedies frequently encountered, exists for a number of reasons. Education about the law and one's legal rights is difficult to convey within a system where even basic education is becoming increasingly difficult to maintain. Further, even when programmes for legal education may be in place, there is a confusing and difficult array of legislation which governs issues within communal tenure systems, as indicated in the previous section. Even where basic legal rights are appreciated or understood, the individual seeking to pursue those rights within a court of law is faced with a costly venture. Those wishing to seek the enforcement of legal rights related to communal tenure are most likely to come from communities which do not have the necessary disposable income available to pursue those claims.

Lack of financial resources undermines the commitment a person or group may have to pursuing those claims. Individual commitment to such a process may also be affected by the difficult legal or political climate referred to above. Where individuals are faced with enormous challenges from a legal system which tends to recognize individual rights over communal rights, they may not have confidence in their case succeeding. A political system which does likewise, and also has the inherent capacity to make the pursuit of communal tenure claims difficult if they are likely to upset the status quo favoured by certain political elements, can further undermine commitment to the case. Moreover, the corruption of advocates and judges when powerful interests are at stake is a significant barrier in pursuing such claims.

There is also the issue of legal standing or capacity to pursue a legal right. Courts in Kenya have been reluctant to grant standing to individuals making public claims, and have defined narrowly the situations in which individuals may have a legal interest in a matter. As a result, it is necessary for individuals interested in pursuing communal rights to mobilize interest and commitment within the community at large. This can often be a lengthy and difficult process, and will inevitably require the education of other members of the community by raising awareness and increasing knowledge regarding the relevant issues. A further element might include the need to convince other members of the community that the matter is pertinent enough to warrant the use of financial resources which may be scarce. The following two cases illustrate how these factors are played out on the ground.

Conflicts over sub-division of group ranches

The government programme to transform nomadic pastoral areas into settled agricultural regions has been marked by conflicts over the subdivision of group ranches. At Ndoto group ranch adjacent to the Ndoto Hills in Samburu District in northern Kenya, an interesting scenario has unfolded over the years (Figure 6). On September 2, 1981 nine prominent individuals in the district presented themselves to the then land adjudication committee and sought to be allocated plots of varying sizes within the 54,000 acre adjudications area. At the end of the meeting a total area of 14,350 acres had been given to the nine so that they could initiate development in the area. Inhabitants of the area had no idea what went on until late 1993 when they sat as a group to deliberate on whether to subdivide the area or not to. The people for whom land was to be subdivided numbered about 14,000. The total acreage left for them was 39,650 acres, about 2.83 acres of arid land with no viable economic use. It was then that the land adjudication committee which had remained unchanged since the allocations of 1981, realized the absurdity of their unanimous decision then to "initiate development." They resolved to reduce the acreages of the nine individuals from an excess of 1,000 acres to 20 acres each. The matter remains unresolved today. This situation brings to mind the resigned statement recorded by Galaty, that has become common among pastoralists with regard to subdivision: "It is no good but we still accept it as it has been done already . . . maybe in the highlands would have been better, but arid lands . . . it's no good."[30]

The arguments for and against subdivision of group ranches have brought out two diametrically opposed camps within a majority of the pastoral areas. On one hand are those who believe that real estate is a more economically viable enterprise than pastoralism. They are supported by government policy towards privatization of group land holdings. On the other hand are the "conservatives" who because of their belief in the traditional system, and to some extent for lack of an alternative economic pursuit, have stuck to a pastoral economy and therefore to a continued common ownership system of land holdings. The effect of this divide has been dispossession of group ranch members. In some group ranches where subdivision has taken place, yet not all members are prepared to go for subdivision, land sales by those unsure about the wish for title deeds have been on the increase, particularly in the 1980s. For example, Kajiado Maasai have been lured with ready cash in exchange for a thumb-print on a transfer form they may not understand. They believe that leaving their title deed behind does not disentitle them to their land and are surprised to discover that they have actually lost all rights to the land or portions of it. Even as group ranches are sub-divided and as registers are being compiled, it has not been uncommon for outsiders to find a way to be allocated parts of the group land. The infamous story of Mosiro group ranch illustrates this point where almost half of the people allocated land at the group ranch were outsiders.[31] It took the intervention of the vice-president and other high government officials to nullify the allocations.

In scenarios such as these, it has been asked many times why throughout the history of modern Kenya, the pastoral peoples particularly the Maasai have so easily been dispossessed of their land. The question does not have an easy answer, but it has been long established that the Maasai, for example, do not understand the value of land in the capitalist sense. To them land is much like air which no one can claim as his, nor any subdivision of it. Their dispossession has therefore been so easy, both by their own and others, because it is impossible in their context for anyone to partition off a piece of "God's land" as his or her own.

With the subdivision of group ranches it has been the practice to reserve portions of land for specific public functions. In the former Ntashart group ranch of Ngong Division, Kajiado District, one tract was so reserved including a large dam and its water catchment area for community use in watering their livestock (Figure 6). The community understood that the Olkejuado County Council held this land in trust for the benefit of the local residents.

In the political turbulence of preparing for Kenya's first multi-party election in decades to be held in 1992, a local politician began to act unilaterally regarding the subdivision and disposal of this water catchment tract. The politician claimed that some "big man" was going to grab all of the land. He proposed action to forestall such initiative through subdivision and distribution of this land to several owners who would "protect" this tract and prevent such grabs. Others regarded this politician's actions as simply the political expediency of one attempting to enlarge his power base by dispensing favours. Moreover, many people came to see a direct threat to the integrity of their major water source, one on which their livelihoods depended. The fact that such subdivisions could be legally made only by the county council and then only for some "public good" was seemingly irrelevant. What counted was the exercise of political power and the access to that power.

Or so the political leaders thought. A group of younger Maasai men, however, took action which has thus far blocked the subdivision of this tract. Had a "traditional" Maasai common tenancy applied, the action-counteraction of political leader versus young Maasai men might not ever have arisen. But existing law has truncated the functions of common tenancy by allowing land remnants to survive as a commons but under the stewardship of the county council as in Ntashart Adjudication Section. The normal checks and balances existing in traditional discourse through the council of elders (*enkiguana*) have been eroded. Little room is allowed for such social mechanisms under current circumstances with the consequence that political power has moved from the elders to the politicians who often act unchecked by the communities they represent. Moreover, the inherent respect that elders or older politicians command works to reinforce the control that such politicians exercise, even when their actions, such as the subdivision of lands, are perceived by many as detrimental to the community.

Extraordinary actions are required to counteract these tendencies. The young Maasai men conferred about these developments and sent out several investigators. Facts were gathered disputing the politician's story. More meetings were held where this information was more widely shared. An alternative power base began to emerge. A lawyer was engaged and a "caution letter" sent to the Kajiado lands office which had the effect of freezing further action relative to Parcel 5.

Within the community a previously scheduled seminar featured a visiting group of Maasai from Narok District who spoke about their experiences in community organization and the importance of land. A highlight was the showing of a video in the Maa language (spoken by the Maasai and other related groups) on their generator-powered television concerning Maasai land rights. Based on a true story from their area, it described how some leaders can do harm to a community through land subdivision. The timing for this presentation could not have been planned better. The women's groups, who had become aware of this issue, were now galvanized as a result of the video. They unreservedly opposed subdivision and spoke to the men saying that if the men remained silent, they would speak out to defend their community.

The issue became quickly politicized, drawing increasing numbers either opposing subdivision (virtually the entire community of Olosho-oiber) or supporting the efforts of the politicians to subdivide, largely from more distant communities. Neutrality was becoming more difficult. At last the senior chief convened a *baraza* (public meeting) at which representatives were each to be given the opportunity to state their case. In this way it was hoped that the truth and a corresponding course of action to resolve the matter would emerge. The meeting date was scheduled and rescheduled several times. Those leading the opposition to subdivision understood the consequences. If further subdivision were stopped unpleasant results could be exacted by the politician and his allies upon either the opposition or the community (such as withholding development assistance). Finally the *baraza* was held with over two hundred people in attendance. Interestingly, this event built on Maasai traditional practice of public meetings where the objective was truth and conflict resolution.

After a long process of statements, oratory and questions, the politician publicly apologized to the community for his actions. Moreover, a pledge was made by the politician that if the community desired that Parcel 5 remain unsubdivided, he would work to ensure this. The opposition had hoped to raise several specific questions about the conduct of the councillor but were given only a short time to present their case. The broader questions of political leadership they desired to raise were untouched. And yet the spectacle of a politician apologizing and agreeing to correct his actions was more than sufficient validation of the worth of the opposition's cause.

Most telling is the communities' confidence-building measure of being able to effect political change. People began to remind themselves that they need not wait for development (whether positive or negative) to happen as if it was a phenomenon somehow independent of them. It became clear to many that the key to change was their own action and initiative in understanding and analyzing their plight and the choices they could make together. A leader's words and actions need not be accepted and could in fact be changed. The people together could take action by themselves to improve their community. That continues to be the empowering lesson of this incident.

Policy options for pastoral lands

Traditional societies in Africa, such as the pastoralist peoples of Kenya, have over the centuries adopted elaborate governance systems regarding the allocation and use of land and natural resources. These systems govern their legal relationships as well, to the extent that they define situations whereby individuals and groups may acquire, hold, transfer or transmit interests and usufruct or land rights. Yet today, these pastoral communities are being increasingly influenced and informed by state notions of legal and social ordering rather than by their own traditions. And it is these dominant, usually quite different state notions of law which now guide the allocation and use of land.

Despite the current legal and political climate, which is generally unfavourable to the recognition of customary legal claims, there are nonetheless numerous opportunities within the current array of statutory legislation which gives credence to these rights and allows for a certain degree of protection. It is precisely because of the fact that there are provisions for communal tenure rights, however nominal, within the statutory regime that those who wish to continue maintaining such rights must claim the opportunities which exist to do so. The example from Olosho-oiber illustrates what may result when a committed local group acts to realize these rights. But it must be stressed that the key to success in the Olosho-oiber case was the twin aspects of legal redress and community action. One without the other would probably have been inadequate.

By gaining knowledge and understanding of the existing legislation, coupled with a commitment to community-wide education and mobilization for appropriate action when warranted, those most directly interested in preserving communal tenure rights will have crossed the initial hurdle. Thereafter, the commitment necessary to negotiate the maze of confusing legislation and an often unfavourable legal and political climate may come more easily, and others may be increasingly interested in providing the necessary commitment and financial support as well.

Many questions related to the application of existing legislation present themselves. We have shown that customary law is recognized both in the Constitution and other legislation and therefore that there is legal worth in African communal tenure, yet the very same Constitution has provisions eroding interests under customary law. A revision of this situation is the first step towards a recognition and entrenchment of African customary tenure within the legal framework of Kenya. Specifically, it may be appropriate to reconsider and remove the repugnancy clause in Section 115, as other African countries have done. There should also be limits placed on the ability of the government and county councils to set apart land, and appropriate checks and balances to safeguard indigenous interest when they do so. Legislation which provides for contradictory procedures, such as the Land Consolidation Act and the Land Adjudication Act, should be made consistent. When discretion is placed in local communities and group representatives, there should be appropriate procedures for reviewing their decisions and safeguarding indigenous interests.

Section 118 of the Constitution which as we have argued is the basis of customary tenure, needs to be revised to enable the state to function as a genuine trustee of indigenous rights, interests and values. It is equally important that following any changes in the Constitution related legislation should be amended to give greater recognition to African customary tenure.

The Trust Lands Act, for example, needs clearer provisions as to the role and importance of customary tenure. Related issues such as where to obtain basic information regarding land status under different legal regimes will need to be resolved.

A critical question which remains is how legal education may best be carried out, and how legal avenues which may offer protection for communal tenure rights may best be pursued. Currently, there is a dearth of information available to pastoral communities regarding legal rights they may claim within existing legislation. Further, there are few public institutions which offer legal services so that they may pursue these rights once known. As such, an organization concerned with pastoral land rights which could assist with legal education as well as with necessary legal assistance could be an important initiative. Legal education could be undertaken through personnel who have been trained, and could in turn disseminate information at the community level through local organizations and institutions, as well as through traditional community networks.

Objectivity would need to be maintained to ensure state support for such an initiative. It would need to be seen as a tool for educating people regarding their existing rights, as opposed to a forum for advocating that potential rights enacted. Legal assistance could take the form of research, preparing legal opinions and participating in relevant discussions and negotiations with affected stakeholders. Assisting with conflict resolution strategies which allow for disputes to be settled through alternative channels such as mediation or arbitration would be important, as well as assisting with litigation as necessary by providing legal support and counsel for court cases.

The creation of a pastoral land rights institute is merely one link in securing communal tenure rights in Kenya. With the linkage of such an institute and local pastoral groups engaged in community education, analysis and action, the securing of pastoral land rights is greatly strengthened. Meanwhile, those communities most directly concerned with securing those rights bear the burden of ensuring that they themselves develop the capacity to claim such communal tenure rights.

Conclusion

This chapter primarily addresses pastoral lands and the issues of law and fact that arise from the applicability of customary tenure thereto. The existing "modern" legal regime *vis-`a-vis* African customary regimes and the erosion of provisions giving credence to the latter by the former are also

I. LENAOLA, H.H. JENNER AND T. WICHERT

addressed. It is our view that practical examples have indicated that customary land tenure especially in pastoral lands cannot be wished away. Indeed the application of "modern" tenure has met resistance from existing customary rules. This points to the starting place for any future revisions of the modern regime.

Constitutional reform should be the first step towards recognition and greater understanding of the place of African customary tenure in Kenya. Customary pastoral land tenure is still strongly exercised in Kenya. Failure of codified legislation has led to a rethinking and re-emphasis of the values and worth in African customary tenure. Hence codification of traditional practices on the basis of the doctrine of customary use will be an essential aspect of any meaningful constitutional change in Africa.

Notes

1. FAO, 1993, p. 53. By using growing period as the relevant criteria, FAO reveals its bias in favour of crop production, despite the fact that the drylands primarily support pastoral livestock production.
2. Kituyi, 1990, p. 28.
3. Swift, 1988, p. 1.
4. Scoones, 1995, p. 2.
5. This observation is based on the high economic contribution per unit rainfall.
6. Galaty, 1994.
7. Republic of Kenya, 1993a.
8. This discussion of property rights and resource management regimes is based on Bromley, 1991, p. 21–34.
9. Okoth-Ogendo, 1991, p. 11.
10. Okoth-Ogendo, 1991, p. 11.
11. Section 5 of the Crown Lands Ordinance of 1915, quoted in Okoth-Ogendo, 1991, p 41.
12. Okoth-Ogendo, 1991, p. 170.
13. Okoth-Ogendo, 1991, p 169–172.
14 Okoth-Ogendo, 1991, p. 163.
15. See, Kituyi, 1990.
16. Bromley, 1989.
17. Galaty, 1994.
18. Salih, 1990; Rutten, 1992.
19. See Rocheleau and Edmunds, 1995, for a discussion of the impacts of privatization on women.
20. Bruce and Freudenberger, 1992.
21 Rutten, 1992.
22. Okoth-Ogendo, Oluoch-Kosura and Wanjala, 1991.
23. Section 115 (2); see Appendix I.
24. Section 117; see Appendix I.
25. Section 117(2); see Appendix I.
26. Section 117(4); see Appendix I.

27. Kituyi, 1990.
28. *Daily Nation*, April 15, 1989.
29. Land (Group Representatives) Act Subsidiary Legislation, Second Schedule.
30. Galaty, 1994, p. 193.
31. Galaty, 1994, p. 195.

Customary tree tenure in pastoral lands

10

EDMUND G.C. BARROW

Introduction

Recent concerns over sustainable development have resulted in the questioning of the role of private property regimes in environmental management. The questioning is not an idle academic effort but a serious undertaking to reform relationships between people and nature. The way property and property-related institutions are conceptualized and organized is central to the success of reform measures. This chapter argues that many of the basic principles needed to create a balance between property rights and natural resource management can be derived from customary practices. To illustrate this point we shall examine in detail the case of customary property rights among the Turkana of north-western Kenya.

The case of the Turkana shows that property relations in the area have been organized in such a way as to ensure the conservation of the natural resource base in general and biological diversity in particular. The Turkana customary rights system aims largely at maximizing ecological efficiency and sustainability. The case of Turkana (and indeed of many of other pastoral communities in Africa) underscores the need to give legal standing to customary practices provided that the practices offer a sound basis for the effective management of natural resources.[1] It should be stressed that the case for adopting the customary use doctrine is not an appeal to an idealistic past. The argument in this chapter is based on the conformity of customary practices to ecological principles. In a way, these practices have long anticipated modern ecological problems and created institutional arrangements that create a balance between property rights and conservation. These institutional arrangements are a reflection of an ecological outlook that deserves to be given due recognition in a legal framework that seeks to accommodate environmental conservation. The starting point for such a legal framework is the Constitution of Kenya.

Rangeland tenure and biodiversity

The general view that pastoralists operate a system of open access which inevitably leads to environmental degradation has given way to a more sophisticated view of rangeland tenure. Recent reviews and studies have revealed a nested hierarchy of relationships between different social entities using particular ecosystems or resources. This systemic approach allocated rights at different levels and to different groups in a manner that is consistent with the ecological requirements for recovery, optimal productivity and overall resilience. "In general, natural resources are usually owned by the highest social level . . . recognized in the group, and are then allocated down the hierarchy to lower levels of social organization through intricate systems of distribution."[2] The ownership referred to here is not the same as private property ownership. It is largely a system of public trusteeship and stewardship.

As one moves to lower levels of the hierarchy, communal, household and even individual user rights are granted. For example, the rights enjoyed by herbalists in some communities are akin to the rights enjoyed by patent holders under Western intellectual property regimes. Evidence from pastoral communities in a number of African countries shows that "the highest social level . . . retains formal ownership of the land, giving only usufruct to the lower levels. In some cases, the tribe can theoretically change the land distribution pattern, but in most cases, the rights of the lower levels are known, constant, inalienable, and based on historical precedence."[3] In essence, therefore, traditional rangeland tenure is based on two doctrines: public trust and customary use. It is the interactive application of these doctrines that enables pastoral communities to maintain their private interests as herders and guarantee the public good in the form of biodiversity and biomass.

Pastoralists know what biodiversity is and understand the necessity for maintaining it in terms of risk spreading and resilience in their production systems. On the other hand, outsiders usually do not understand the importance of maintaining a diverse and varied genetic resource base, and want to see such systems replaced. The outsiders emphasize, for example, settled agriculture with a reduced biodiversity, thereby precipitating the many and varied problems that pastoralists now face.[4] Problems have resulted from outsiders' attitudes about the relationships that exist between pastoralists, their livestock, the environment in which they live and external influences over which they often have little control.

A literature review reveals two differing positions. Some maintain that pastoral nomadism is caught in the cycle of livestock accumulation which leads to overgrazing, environmental degradation and famine.[5] Others hold that pastoral nomadism is environmentally sound and that the disruption of the normal system has caused the environmental problems.[6] This lack of understanding of traditional pastoral systems has been cited as a major reason for the failure of development programmes in pastoral areas.[7] Pastoralists have survived despite development schemes, not because of them.[8] However, their survival has been often at the price of ecological sustainability as pastoralists become increasingly marginalized in terms of their land, governance systems and loss of biodiversity.

Studies on tenure and natural resources have emphasized mainly the range resource (grasses) and, to a lesser extent, water resources. The importance of access rights to trees in pastoral areas has not been given the attention it deserves given the relative importance of woody species in dry environments. The example of usufruct rights to trees in Turkana District, Kenya, shows the importance the pastoralists place on trees in the natural resource system, and how important it is to understand traditional management systems before suggesting change. Such change has to be seen not only in its sociological, technological and legal contexts, but also from the point of view of maintaining biodiversity and the access rights or indigenous property rights that are implicit.

Very little systematic knowledge exists concerning tree use and tree planting among pastoralists and many questions need to be addressed.[9] These include: What are the rules regarding tree rights? What are the rights of individuals *versus* groups? For instance, it is common in Maasai group ranches to allow herders from neighbouring ranches to graze on the outer fringes of one's territory. However, visiting herders may be prohibited from actively shaking an *Acacia tortilis* tree for its pods by the group ranch members, especially in dry periods. This kind of measured response to a drought suggests more sophisticated management of tree resources than is commonly ascribed to pastoral groups.

However, groups seem to survive if they have clear-cut rules that are enforced by both users and officials, internally adaptive institutional arrangements, the ability to nest into external organizations for dealing with the external environment and decision rules for different purposes. Their chances are also better if they are subject to slow, exogenous change. Four areas need special attention: (1) how tenure of land and trees affects the surrounding ecosystem; (2) how access to land and forest resources under different tenure schemes affects the standard of living of people who depend on those resources; (3) how rules of tenure affect the preservation, protection and planting of trees; and (4) how the prevailing system of tenure determines the beneficiaries and victims of forest policies and forestry projects, and so sets the framework for conflict over benefits.[10]

In this respect, the system of Turkana usufruct rights to riverine trees is part of a broader natural resource management system which helps to spread risks inherent in an arid environment. It is also an important means of conserving—and to a degree manipulating, through management—the biodiversity that exists in areas of woody vegetation. In this case, property rights are an instrument of social policy and particular property regimes are chosen for particular purposes.[11] However, such indigenous property rights are neither unique to the Turkana, nor are they simple. They include such issues as "what rights" (for example, to own or inherit, to plant, to dispose of and to exclude), and "whose rights".[12]

Customary rights recognize the need for predictable and secure tenure over land and trees, or clear rights to their use. This serves as an important incentive for rural people to manage and maintain their resources. Such rights are, however, complicated by being three dimensional, in terms of people, time and space.[13] Furthermore, they are dynamic due to a complex social structure and changing social and ecological conditions. The rights to access to trees can depend on various factors, including the trees' origin (for example, whether self-sown or planted), the encompassing production system, (for example, whether private or communal land holdings), and the use made of the trees.

Thus the importance of trees in pastoral natural resource management is reflected in a variety of social controls relating to access, usage and maintenance of diversity. This has implications in terms of maintaining biodiversity in a production system where it is vital, and showing that indigenous property rights to such biodiversity are essential to sustainable natural resource management. However, in the case of the Turkana in Kenya, the statutory legal processes have not adequately tackled access and tenurial issues in the pastoral lands, either in terms of group management or individual rights of usage.

All governments now recognize the importance of promoting greater public participation in forestry activities. Yet if the policies are to succeed, pastoralists, farmers and communities will need stronger assurance that they will benefit. The current system of control provides uncertain and insecure rights, and conflicts between tenure systems are common in Africa, particularly between local customary and national statutory law. Where two systems exist together, each with a fair degree of credibility, uncertainty is created and customary rights may be eliminated.

Kenya land laws and trees

In Kenya there are many laws and regulations which govern the use of land. It is important to gain a brief insight into these legal instruments in order to understand the legal context of pastoral tree rights and biodiversity. Land tenure refers to the possession of the many rights associated with each parcel of land, referred to as a bundle of rights.[14] However, not all rights comprising the bundle may be held by the same person. Any system of land tenure is dependant upon the historical and cultural circumstances within which the given community has evolved and the legal and philosophical content of that community's conception of land.[15]

Thus, "land" can have at least two meanings. First, it can mean the land and all things attached to it, as reflected in the Registered Land Act of Kenya and where land becomes a commodity. Second, land without the various material objects (such as trees and buildings) which are legally severed from the concept of "land".[16] This is reflected in customary and communal land tenure. Here, the context of communal tenure is very complex but has two essential elements: equal access to land, and the legal and economic fact that land is not a commodity.

In Kenya, both forms of land tenure exist. The Registered Land Act governs land formerly held under customary law, and replaces what was essentially communal continuous law with that of individual ownership. This mainly applies to the trust lands (before independence referred to as 'reserve areas'), which fall under the jurisdiction of county councils and can be adjudicated, consolidated and registered. However, there are many parts of the country where this is not so easy, in particular the pastoral lands which are still governed and managed on the basis of customary law. At present, for sociological, ecological and management reasons, it is very difficult to successfully replace customary law with individual tenure.[17] Attempts are being made, however, often as a result of political pressure.

The Land (Group Representatives) Act recognizes some element of traditional law by giving a group title deed to a communal area of land on a cooperative basis. However, this approach is being modified and private title deeds are being given in such areas. For example, during a land adjudication exercise in Mosiro, Kajiado, it was discovered that out of 1,000 Maasai families who should have benefitted, some 459 plots were to be allocated to non-Maasai people.[18] This example illustrates how allocation of private title deeds in pastoral areas has benefitted non-pastoralists as well as the more powerful and rich pastoralists while the ownership status of the poorer people is further eroded.

Since land ultimately belongs to the state; the question is whether it is possible to balance the interests of the rural population and the government in terms of tenure. At present, customary law is largely unwritten and probably out of step with the wider development process. The development process does not attempt to understand such customary law and its regulations, whether they be of an individual or communal nature. Since communal tenure in Kenya derives from customary law, it is important to understand how communal tenure can be better understood, articulated and used as a basis for land management, even alongside individual tenure. Where the statutory law recognizes group, family or co-operative rights to land, the rules governing these rights under customary law in the various ethnic groups should be identified, understood and written into the statutory law.[19]

Statutory law basically operates on the principle of *exclusion* from land while customary law lays a greater emphasis on *inclusion* through communal access and usage. This issue of inclusion and exclusion is of integral importance in understanding customary law, especially in the more expansive pastoral systems. In pastoral communal law, the principle of inclusion is linked to the pastoralist's ability to retain relationships with those around him or her to continue having access rights, for instance to trees.[20]

Land tenure cannot be separated from land use. Land tenure rules emphasize issues between humans and the regulation of competing interests in the use of land. Land use rules emphasizes human-*versus*-environment, and aim to promote acceptable methods of husbandry and conservation. Thus, the holder of tenurial rights has the opportunity and duty to realize the objectives of land use. Land use decision-making therefore becomes a tenure issue. This raises the important question of who defines the objectives of land use. This point is important in considering tree tenure and the management of trees to sustain biodiversity in such fragile and risk-prone environments.

Direct regulation of the tree component in land use is one of the most important variables affecting the extent and type of tree usage. This is governed by a wide range of legislation and regulation on, for example, soil conservation, protection of indigenous trees, land use management, public forest management, cash crop and rangeland management.[21] Some of these regulations have features which may work to the detriment of the user and the environment.

In general, land and tree tenure can affect: (1) rights to trees, their protection and harvest; (2) site selection; (3) species of trees; (4) management of trees; (5) the right to own and inherit trees; (6) the rights to use trees and tree products, to gather honey, use trees as bee hives, cut all or part of living trees, use produce under trees; and (7) the rights to dispose of trees—destroy, lend, lease, mortgage, pledge, give away or sell.[22]

In most traditional herding societies in Kenya, communal land management practices encouraged the use of protected seasonal grazing reserves, clan rights to water and, in some cases, specific rights to trees. In such areas where the authority of the elders has been reduced, customary management rules are increasingly difficult to enforce. Where some authority remains, however, such rules can have a significant beneficial role in development and so should be fostered and built upon. In terms of traditional tree rights and regulations, some dryland social forestry programmes have usurped, and so weakened, the traditional rights and rules. Failure to recognize the relationship between property in trees and property in land has led to failed development interventions since national legislation, which development projects must conform to, tends to emphasize soil and land, whereas customary law takes more account of trees.

Likewise, certain—often well-meaning—policies can undervalue the management of trees by the people. For instance, nationalizing trees and rules prohibiting the cutting and use of certain trees undermines customary rules unless such rules are taken in the specific context of the users and not as a national decree.[23] Tree species that belong to the national government are not likely to be protected by farmers. In such cases, rules of land and tree tenure may provide positive incentives for destroying existing trees.[24] A combination of strong customary laws based on the grazing associations of the Turkana and private customary ownership of important rich patch areas of trees mutually reinforce a system that was traditionally sustainable. The grazing associations (*adakar*) regulate the use of trees in dry season grazing reserves, conserving important genetic resources there.

However, this system is threatened by the pervasive influence of government rules and regulations regarding land and resources that, at present, do not allow for such customary rules. This not only threatens the existing customary governance of trees and natural resources, but the very biodiversity that exists in such risk-prone areas on which pastoral production systems are based. Government policy-makers need to recognize the importance of customary law in risk prone environments not merely as a legal imperative, but also in the context of environmental sustainability, ecological diversity and land use management. Statutory law and government regulations should reflect these values.

Trees and the Turkana silvo-pastoral system

Turkana is a semi-arid and arid district of 72,000 sq km in north-western Kenya (Figure 6). It has a population of about 225,000 people and a low and highly variable rainfall, varying from 150 to 200 mm in the dry central areas to over 400 mm in the south.[25] The district is bordered on the east by Lake Turkana, on the west by the Ugandan escarpment, on the north by the Sudan and Ethiopia, and on the south by West Pokot and Baringo districts of Kenya. The topography consists of low central plains (600 m altitude) lying close to hills and mountains (1800–3100 m altitude). There are numerous ephemeral streams and the Turkwell and Kerio are the two most important rivers. The vegetation is related to moisture availability and so linked to elevation and proximity to ground moisture in the rivers.

The people of Turkana have evolved well-managed and sound ecological strategies which enable them to utilize the vegetation on a sustainable basis. They exploit different economic niches by having grazing livestock (cattle, sheep and donkeys) and browsing livestock (camels and goats) and diversified food procurement strategies.[26] The Turkana silvo-pastoral system makes best use of the vegetation both in time and space through a transhumant system of wet and dry season grazing combined with setting aside specific dry season grazing reserves (*epaka* or *amire*). Such complex, broad silvo-pastoral systems have worked in the past but are now threatened by externally-driven interventions such as settlements, irrigation schemes and health and education facilities. The indigenous system often cannot cope with the speed of change which such interventions bring.

The Turkana have a well-developed knowledge of their flora and its uses. Within this, woody species are especially valued since they can survive and produce well even through the long dry seasons, though some species are considered more important than others. Their knowledge reflects their life styles and the extent of their dependence on the woody vegetation. Specific species are used as dry wood for fuel; building timber for houses, fencing and thatching; food for livestock, particularly in the dry season; food for people; human and veterinary medicines for a variety of diseases; material for household utensils; amenities such as to provide shade and act as a meeting place; and a variety of cultural values, water purification and ceremonial purposes.

Indeed, the woody vegetation constitutes the district's most valuable resource of which the Turkwell riverine forest and the Loima mist forest are key. The value and distribution of the woody vegetation is described by Ecosystems Ltd.:

In 23% of the district woody vegetation virtually is confined to riparian strips. These areas coincide with the driest eastern parts of Turkana and dry season grass cover was found to fall consistently along a gradient of increasing importance in the riparian component . . . . Despite the acute shortage of grass, areas of exclusively riparian woody vegetation supported over 30% of all livestock in the district during the dry season, underlining their extreme importance as a dry season forage resource.[27]

Understanding this, the Turkana have developed the management of their trees a step further, especially in the drier areas. The herd owners within their *ere* (that area of permanent settlement where old and young stock may remain all year around)[28] may have ownership rights to particular resources which may include fodder, trees (*ekwar*; pl. *ngikwarin*), dry season wells and sorghum gardens. These resources are owned by the herd owner and his close family relatives and outsiders are allowed to use them without prior permission.[29] Although *ekwar* literally means that area beside the river bank—indicating the importance of the riverine vegetation—the term reflects the usufruct rights to the trees that grow beside the rivers. It also reflect *de facto* land ownership, although this is not explicitly stated in Turkana customary law. For the herder, the woodland is his farm in the sense that it is even more essential to his livestock than it is to the farmers crops.[30]

It is difficult, therefore, to give an exact definition for the word *ekwar* since it also implies a degree of flexibility that is hard to quantify. An *ekwar* is strongly associated with ownership of the trees (or more particularly their produce) beside or near a river (or in some instances, lake). It is of particular importance during the dry season when the *ekwar* provides the family with valuable dry season fodder in the form of pods and leaves from the various trees, in particular *Acacia tortilis*.

Given the key role that the riverine woodland plays in the district, the *ekwar* is an integral and vital part of the *ere* and thus of livestock and natural resource management. The importance of hill areas as dry season fodder reserves is recognized in terms of the "grazing group" which has rules and regulations governing their usage. The Loima mist forest is the most important of the dry season grazing reserves in the district.

Why have people such as the Turkana, developed such customary tenure and usufruct rights to trees? Trees provide a continuous flow of products throughout the year and are therefore important to risk management, especially in the arid and semi-arid lands. They can also be used to meet contingencies, such as by generating cash by selling firewood and providing and storing food and fodder during droughts. In such cases trees in the drylands can perform the function of a savings bank where the "interest", can be sustainably utilized.[31]

The system of *ekwar* is strongest along the river courses in the driest, central parts of the district. However, not every household has an *ekwar*. People own their *ekwar* for long periods of time, often in excess of two generations. The boundaries vary considerably but usually relate to a river bank or a prominent tree or trees, in particular *Acacia tortilis, Hyphaena compressa* and *Salvadora persica*. Wet season use of the *ekwar* is not considered as important as dry season use. It is in the dry season that the *ekwar* provides livestock food from trees such as *Acacia tortilis, Cordia sinensis, Salvadora persica, Hyphaena compressa* and *Zizyphus mauritiana*.

In this case, it is difficult to define the term "importance" since in addition to implying both quality and quantity of produce, is also related to what is available in the dry times, and how guaranteed that availability is. Therefore the importance of the dry season fodder is primarily related to spreading risks and retaining resilience. The relative importance of the different trees also relates to their abundance in the *ekwar* area. Qualitative variation is recognized within species where higher yield or better-tasting fruits can be recognized, and between species as a means of spreading risk through the harvesting of different tree products at different times.

Why should an essentially nomadic pastoral society develop a system of individual land ownership, or more particularly, user rights to an area and to trees in particular? The primary reason for such ownership relates to the dry season utilization of the trees in the *ekwar* to produce food for people and livestock. The *ekwar* system is generally absent from areas where trees are not common or occur sparsely. Furthermore, in the wetter areas of the district (in the south) where the vegetation is richer, the *ekwar* system may exist but is weaker because of the relative abundance of vegetation.

On this basis, the *ekwar* appears to be part of a land use management strategy for the Turkana that includes wet and dry season grazing combined with reserved grazing areas (*epaka, amaire*) and dry season fodder reserves (*ekwar*). The *amaire* are managed in a similar way to the *ekwar*, but are communal, and primarily for fodder and browse. Relating this utilization to ownership values serves to show how important the people consider trees to be in general, and the riverine forest in particular.

Storas states that "[p]roperty ownership among the Turkana pastoralists is not definite, but intimately related to the social organization of the people."[32] In this context, it is likely that *ekwar* ownership is some what flexible and not strictly defined, and will depend to a great extent on the way people use their riverine forest area. Where an *ekwar* owner is absent for a period of time and not using its produce, it is likely that someone else will take it over so that the produce can be used efficiently.[33] Such flexibility of *ekwar* ownership reflects reciprocal relations which provide another method of risk reduction, which makes the Turkana production systems more sustainable. This social organization therefore has important ecological implications in the way it enables people to regulate the exploitation of the natural resources.

The importance of access to natural resources is often judged according to the relative abundance and diversity of those resources. Recurrent confrontations over land use are intimately linked to a territory, such as an *ekwar*, whose holder has to maintain communal agreement that his rights are established by usage. These rights form the basis for extending and reinforcing the web of relations to people on whose support the agreement depends. This has important links to maintaining flexibility in resource management both in space and time and in relation to other users.

Tree access rights and pastoralism

Although the system of *ekwar* in Turkana relates primarily to usufruct rights to the produce of the riverine forest, it is almost impossible to separate this from tenure rights. Currently all land in Turkana District, like most of the communal rangelands in Kenya, is county council trust land held in trust for the people of Turkana. Where development has taken place such traditional rights appear to have been ignored. This has occurred at the irrigation schemes along the Turkwell River, settlements along the rivers and a fisheries project on Lake Turkana, among other cases.

The Trust Land Act (Section 8(1)) states:

> Where land is set apart under section 7 of this Act, full compensation shall be promptly paid by the Government to any resident of the area of land set apart who:
>
> (a) under African customary law for the time being in force and applicable to the land has any right to occupy any part thereof; or
>
> (b) is, otherwise than in common with all other residents of the land, in some other way prejudicially affected by the setting apart.

Yet none of the above provisions were adhered to when the irrigation schemes were formed, or the fish farm at Kalakol or the ever-expanding need for land in the settlement areas. By ignoring traditional access rights to such areas, the local land management strategies are being undermined to the detriment of the environment and the pastoral system. Further, and more insidiously, the biodiversity of the existing system on which pastoral land use management is based is threatened because the indigenous property rights are being ignored. This reduces the system's effectiveness in coping with the periodic drought and other natural or man-made disasters, and results in their increasing in frequency.

The irrigation schemes provide another example. In impinging on traditional Turkana sorghum gardens and tree ownership rights, those implementing these agricultural schemes have shown ignorance of traditional land use rights. This is exemplified by the conflicts and disputes that have arisen between the irrigation scheme and traditional cultivators. As a result, trees on both irrigated and rainfed areas have been cleared without any reference to their traditionally-defined values or rules governing their usage.

Ekwar ownership is not definite, but is based on the owner's ability to use his *ekwar* over time and his social network to support his rights. These social ties are the basis for Turkana land management through grazing, *ekwar* ownership and browse utilization. However, expectedly there are confrontations in such a system because such rights are often not clear cut, and these are usually brought before the elders for settlement.

Sustaining such indigenous property rights systems in the face of externally-generated pressures for change is a challenge, not just to the Turkana's *ekwar*, but to the future of pastoralism as a land use system into the 21st century. Given a realistic attitude to land demarcation in the drier areas, it could, eventually, be possible to combine a system of individual ownership (for instance based on the *ekwar*) with a group ownership to the wet and dry season grazing lands (including such reserves as *epaka* and *amaire*), based possibly on the *adakar*. Such a system might help to reinforce the conservation and biodiversity of the vital riverine forest lands and allow for flexible communal management of the rangelands based on mobility and risk spreading. Articulating Turkana indigenous property rights in present day policy, hence retaining the biodiversity would make the existing system more ecologically stable and environmentally sound. This could then form the basis for improved economic modelling of such systems.

The system of *ekwar* is important to the development process especially for the forestry and range management sectors in their conservation and extension activities. The *ekwar* owners represent a discrete and known target group with which to work. This is important for all concerned with the sustained utilization of the vegetation in the district. Reinforcement of such indigenous natural resource management strategies could serve to increase the woody resources available and make the system more sustainable in the long term through individual and communal responsibility. However, interventions that weaken such environmentally-sound management systems can serve to reduce the systems' resilience and therefore make them more susceptible to increased pressures and drought. It has been noted that,

> Development interventions that alienate land from existing usage will have serious consequences on the diversity of the existing subsistence economy. Thus such interventions should seek to reinforce and improve existing man-

agement systems for such areas, e.g., through multiple use management, reducing risk in sorghum farming and therefore enhance the environmental ethic inherent in the *ekwar* system. Where traditional uses of property rights (usufruct) ensure proper management, then the system should be provided with legal protection.[34]

Given current development attitudes to such traditional management systems, the effectiveness of the system of *ekwar* as a means of land ownership and, *de facto*, land management must be brought out. History shows us that where development has taken place in such areas, traditional ownership rights have been ignored. Therefore any threat to such systems, real or perceived, should be considered seriously. Traditional ownership rights should be recognized even if the land is held in trust for the people of Turkana District. In more practical terms, mechanisms are needed which can protect trees which may only be used periodically by pastoralists when the pastoralists are not present.[35]

Rich patch vegetation and marginalization

In many pastoral societies—and the Turkana are no exception—areas of richer vegetation, such as riverine forests and dry season grazing areas, are being excised from the pastoral production system and incorporated in other land use systems, such as irrigation schemes, settlements and dryland farming. The legal basis for such encroachments is usually flimsy. Customary laws are ignored in favour of increased national food production and housing settlements. This provides the ingredients for further land degradation, erosion of biodiversity and loss of customary governance systems.

In Turkana, expropriation of forests from the traditional system has brought visible signs of environmental degradation. The traditional controls and structures have broken down in favour of an essentially alien system for which no adequate controls have been developed.[36] Similarly in Tanzania the Barabaig pastoralists were forcibly removed from their vital dry season grazing for the development of large prairie-like wheat farms which accrue little or no benefit to the pastoralists. The farms are nationally perceived as priorities for wheat production (though wheat only accounts for 2–3% of the food intake, and that is mostly urban).[37] This significantly reduces the effectiveness of enforcing customary land management rules which leads to chaotic "open access" to the remaining natural resources, resulting in the degradation that is characteristic of the "tragedy of the commons" scenario.

Historically and up to the present day, Maasai dry season grazing, where rights to grazing are obtained by virtue of membership in a social unit,[38] has been taken out of the pastoral system by agricultural encroachment, large-scale wheat farming and settlements. This impoverishes the pastoralists and substantially increases the pressure on the remaining, usually more fragile and less fertile, grazing lands with the related threat of increased degradation. There are many other similar cases in West Africa. For example, the effects of large-scale cash cropping on subsistence agriculture and its effects on the dry pastoral lands bordering such lands in Mali, Niger and Senegal.[39] One way to help prevent this process is through an increased respect for the existing customary regulations governing resource use. Such rules and regulations should be articulated in terms of environmentally-sound development programmes that sustainably utilize biodiversity and respect indigenous property rights and are fully integrated into current policy and legal frameworks.

Forest governance options

In Turkana most of the traditional grazing controls are still in place and help to conserve the dry season fodder resources. The Loima hills mist forest area and other richly vegetated hill areas can be considered in a similar light to *ekwar* ownership. The pastoral people who communally use these area during the dry season have shown rational and sustainable management strategies by only utilizing the resources in the Loima hills during the dry season, which gives the grass and ground cover time to recover and set seed well during the wet season. In addition, they only utilize dead wood for cooking, and use bush species for building of temporary livestock enclosures. Nor do they cut large or important trees since the people do not use them directly. They may, and do, harvest wild fruits and other such produce which does not involve a destructive clearing of trees, and rationally use the water supply.

It is vital to the local livestock economy and social system that the important tree species be preserved as a genetic resource, and that the area remains accessible as a dry season range. Any severe restriction of access to the dry season grazing area would expose the pastoralists to a much greater risk of drought and famine.

There must also be a realistic means of preserving the genetic resources (mainly the tree species) while allowing continued access to the dry season grazing (combined with access to water, dead wood, wild fruits, bees and other traditionally-used produce). At present there are fears that should this resource be preserved as a forest reserve, then the pastoralists who depend on the area would no longer have free access to it. Such fears have to be allayed to ensure that the traditional pastoral rights to the area are respected and legitimized. Thus it would be unwise to remove woodland management by local people from the matrix in which it exists, be it farming or herding, and treat woodlands like a forest preserve resource.[40]

Changes in woodland management can only be done through participatory dialogue with the pastoralists, where all the issues are discussed openly and a plan is devised jointly. This plan should preserve the genetic resources and allow continued access to and use of the land within the laws of Kenya. This could then form the basis for the area to be gazetted as a forest reserve by the government but with a blend of customary and national laws governing its use. The people of the area should not be forced into decisions that they do not fully agree with or fully understand, nor should such decisions be made on their behalf as this would result in conflict at a later date.

The best option for the conservation of the unique genetic resource in the Loima mist forest would then appear to be under the Forests Act; with the area gazetted as a forest conservation reserve with its own rules and regulations tailored to govern the utilization of the gazetted conservation area. Such rules would be made jointly by the local pastoralists, the Forestry Department and the local government administration. Such an option would allow the Turkana to continue using the area as they have always done, and would introduce an important dimension in making the conservation of the area legally binding under current Kenyan law. The merging together of customary and statutory rules and regulations should allow for legal recognition of existing rights combined with legally sanctioned sustainable land use.

A similar process could be used in recognizing customary individual rights in *ekwar*. Such areas of individual rights could be the basis for individual tenure under the Registered Land Act. However, this is complicated by other customary social regulations that ensure that the resource is efficiently used and the need for the individual *ekwar* owners to be able to defend their rights of tenure to others around them in terms of efficient use of the resource.

These issues have to be related to rights over land and control rights.[41] Control rights are used to guarantee access and to respond to the changing needs of society. Rights of access are also related to membership in a society or group to enable these rights to be maintained—be they individual or group. Different people or groups may have different rights of access. This issue complicates the argument of ownership such as to an *ekwar*, or group ownership of dry season grazing reserves, in terms of present day law.

Implications for the future of pastoralism

If the legal process does not attempt to fully understand the customary laws, rules and regulations that govern the usage of land in pastoral areas, the result will be the erosion of local customary responsibility and biodiversity. This will serve to increase the likelihood of degradation and famine due to a now real tragedy of the commons, a free-for-all. Customary law in such areas, developed over long periods of time, helped provide the framework for sustainable land-use management that was environmentally sound in the traditional situation. This does not say that such systems were perfect in terms of current development perceptions. Obviously, there is room for improvement through the use of improved management practices. But such improvement should build on, and not replace, existing customary regulations and responsibility.

Unfortunately, many people are ignorant of these rules and regulations, whether customary or state. The two are not necessarily mutually exclusive, but more often than not, the state judiciary is used as an instrument to erode customary rights and regulations. This is especially so if it is seen to result in change that is an "improvement", such as turning rich patch pastoral land into an irrigation scheme or settlement. In general, research and development programmes, by their relative inaction in this field, condone the continuation of such "improvements".

Tenure in terms of forestry, and more so access rights to trees, has not been seen as an important issue. Development programmes often shy away from tenure issues since they have strong political implications. Research favours work on technologies, and not the attitudinal process of change that requires a solid understanding of existing land use systems. Development efforts often add to the pressures on indigenous tree management by neglecting its existence and undermining it with incompatible interventions which often lead to project failure.[42]

Clearly, neither research nor development can take place in a political vacuum. Nor can they blithely ignore issues of tenure and access. Yet, all too often, this is attempted. Research looks at issues from a technological, sociological or anthropological perspective, not from a governance perspective.[43] Therefore research findings, important as they may be, lack a policy and legal framework through which they could gain more definitive acceptability. Development programmes, on the other hand, concentrate on the sectoral disciplines they are working with and often do not see the work in terms of policy intervention and legal redress. Therefore the benefits of the work may be lost, or not acceptable locally.

This combination erodes customary law, indigenous property rights, genetic resources and biodiversity in favour of other land use systems. These land use systems have already been shown to be unstable in such high risk areas where management of risk and maintenance of resilience rather than economic production, were traditionally the primary objective. It has been noted that local efforts to find solutions should be encouraged. In this connection, customary tenure law is not rigid as it is often portrayed, but flexible and innovative.[44] Local people should be helped to find ways of accommodating traditional tenure systems to new and more productive patterns of land use that are ecologically sustainable, maintain biodiversity and respect indigenous property rights. Much of the requisite information is held by the local people yet project planners are rarely able to take the time to get an adequate appreciation of local knowledge and preferences. Similarly, many donor-funded natural resource management programmes, like many colonial programmes, fail to build on or even acknowledge, local practices and knowledge.[45]

Yet it is possible to see both research and development successfully undertaken on governance issues. This will require a better understanding of the existing policies and laws. When having such an understanding, research and development processes can visualize a policy and legal setting for their work. This makes the work more acceptable, and more importantly, can provide guidelines for improving existing laws and policies.

Most of the laws and policies in Kenya affecting land relate to the high-potential lands and are based on individual title deeds. This framework does not comprehend the customary rules and norms pertaining to the pastoral systems and may actively undermine and weaken them. Pastoral customary governance systems are the result of hundreds of years of managing and thriving in a high-risk environment. In such cases, risk management and resilience are the keys to sustainable land management and therefore the integral objective of customary law in these areas. Once these laws are degraded, ignored or destroyed, without similar compensatory measures, increased risk, loss of resilience and degradation are likely to occur. This has been visible in many pastoral societies all over the world: dry season grazing or rich patch vegetation has been excised for farm land, irrigation schemes and settlements. Likewise land, for example in Maasai areas, is being subdivided into individual holdings which are not likely to be environmentally sustainable in the long term. These aspects have a common theme: that of sub-dividing communal land into individual title deeds whether or not they are ecologically or sociologically viable. Land tenure has become a political and administrative issue which is not based on ecology, environment or sociology.

In the dry lands, tenure can therefore be seen as another tool to marginalize the pastoralists. But this need not be so. First, the role of pastoralism has to be understood in the light of sustainable land use management and in terms of present day development and economic aspirations. Customary practices epitomize the former and can be used as the basis for bringing pastoralism into the latter. There is, however, no room for romanticism; it has to be based on pragmatic reality which implies change so that pastoralists fully participate in local and national development. Likewise, pastoralism has to be seen not only in ecological and sociological terms, but also as having an important economic role to play in local and national development. For this to be fully realized customary rules and regulations have to be adapted and given state backing, thus building on—not replacing—the existing system.

The examples cited in this chapter provide an indication of how this could be achieved through a better understanding of both customary and statutory law, and how customary law can be adapted and incorporated into the statutory framework. Management of natural woodland and forests, by communities or individuals, is practiced by those to whom it belongs, so the understanding of ownership must be the initial focus of attention. It is important to understand existing group and individual rules and regulations, as a basis for land use improvement and also for looking at such issues in a policy and legal context. It may, in simple terms, be possible to confer group land rights on the grazing associations and allow for individual title deeds to people's *ekwar*. While such an approach is simple to write down here, in reality it would be much more complex.

Where risk and resilience are dominant themes in sustainable natural resource management in a harsh environment, research and development, policy and the legal systems cannot afford to effect change that increases risk and reduces resilience. To do so provides the ingredients for ecological degradation and disaster during drought. Too many examples in Africa provide testimony to this.

In general, agriculture and forestry are planned and managed on the premise of cultivation and individual tenure. Yet now, there is evidence showing the basic environmental and social soundness of natural resource management in the pastoral areas. The challenge is to translate this into policy and use it to adjust the legal basis for tenure where it already exists in terms of customary rights. State policy and laws and the Constitution need not only be determined by distant national planners and lawyers. We need to use the existing framework better to enable important customary rules and regulations to have a legal voice.

Conclusion

This chapter has shown that the customary property rights system practiced by the Turkana of north-western Kenya have evolved over the years to enable communities to cope with the fragile ecosystem. It has separated land from its derivatives such as trees and vegetation. This separation provides a basis for the management of natural resources without requiring exclusive ownership of the related land. It is a system that provides conservation incentives through regulated access to the resources found on land.

The case of the Turkana signals the importance of giving legal recognition to customary practices as a source of viable conservation approaches. To further this objective, it is important to re-examine those provisions of the Constitution which directly or indirectly erode customary practices and bring them in line with the doctrine of customary use. A more positive view is to introduce into the Constitution provisions that explicitly recognize customary practices as the starting point in contributing to a more relevant common law. In addition, the customary practices already embody a public trust doctrine under which land and other natural resources are held in trust for members of the community. The combination of these doctrines and their recognition in Kenya's constitutional law would be consistent with traditional practices as well as common law.

Notes

1. See Niamir, 1990 for a detailed review of the community management of forests by pastoral communities across Africa.
2. Niamir, 1990, p. 51.
3. Niamir, 1990, p. 51.
4. Sandford, 1983.
5. Picardi and Siefert, 1976; Ingold, 1980; Brown, 1971; Lamprey, 1983.
6. Hogg, 1987; Sinclair and Fryxell, 1985; Swift, 1977.
7. Sanford, 1983; McCabe, 1985; Fry and McCabe, 1986.
8. Baxter and Hogg, 1987.
9. Okoth-Ogendo and Brokensha, 1987.
10. Bruce and Fortmann, 1988.
11. Bromley, 1991.
12. Fortmann and Riddell, 1985.
13. Leach and Mearns, 1988.
14. Riddell, 1987.
15. Okoth-Owiro, 1988.
16. Fortman, 1987.
17. Wanjala, 1990.
18. *Weekly Review*, 1991.
19. This can reduce the adaptability of customary law, however. Such revisions should include highly accessible mechanisms for public input and oversight and periodic review.
20. Storas, 1987.
21. Scherr, 1989.
22. Fortmann and Riddell, 1985.
23. Scherr, 1989.
24. Bruce and Fortmann, 1988.
25. Ecosystems Ltd., 1985.
26. Brainard, 1981.
27. Ecosystems Ltd., 1985, pp. 3–4.
28. Hogg, 1986.
29. Rev. Tony Barrett, Catholic Diocese of Lodwar, pers. comm.

30. Shepherd, 1991.
31. Chambers and Leach, 1987.
32. Storas, 1987.
33. Burke, 1987.
34. Oba, 1989.
35. Okoth-Ogendo and Brokensha, 1987.
36. Norconsult Ltd., 1990.
37. Lane, 1990.
38. Grandin, 1987.
39. Franke and Chasin, 1980.
40. Shepherd, 1991.
41. Okoth Ogendo, 1987.
42. Mathias-Mundy *et al.*, 1990.
43. Lane and Swift, 1988.
44. Okoth-Ogendo and Brokensha, 1987.
45. Little and Brokensha, 1987.

Property rights, medicinal plants and indigenous knowledge

11

ARTHUR OKOTH-OWIRO

WITH CALESTOUS JUMA

Introduction

The last few decades have witnessed a revival of interest in traditional medicine in Africa and the Third World. This interest has not been confined to health planners, but has included pharmaceutical companies and conservationists. Scientific advancements, especially in the field of biotechnology, have stimulated interest in medicinal plants and the related indigenous knowledge. As a result researchers have had to reflect on the importance of links between property rights, medicinal plants and indigenous knowledge. At the centre of conservation efforts is the troublesome reality of property rights, and how these impact upon conservation efforts. It is assumed that property rights have an important influence on genetic conservation and the conservation of indigenous knowledge. And so a complete interaction can begin to emerge between property rights, genetic conservation, traditional medicine and indigenous knowledge.

The purpose of this chapter is to discuss this interaction from a legal perspective. The chapter reviews the legal institutions which sustain the interaction, and attempts to record the problems which result from the operationalization of the various regimes of the law. It also points out limitations and dogmas in legal institutions and normative frameworks while suggesting policy innovations and alternative legal regimes. The overall focus is to review current legal regimes and to propose options for creating a balance between private property interests and the sustainable use of medicinal plants. It is suggested that the starting point in conserving medicinal plants and the related indigenous knowledge is the recognition of the role of customary practices.

Technological advances and medicinal plants

Trends in the pharmaceutical industry

In order to appreciate the magnitude of potential interests in and profits from medicinal biotechnology products derived from medicinal plants it is useful to review the growth and structure of the pharmaceutical industry over the past few decades. The pharmaceutical sector is one of the most profitable industries in the world, with many of the leading firms achieving profit margins of more than 20%. Five of the most profitable firms in the world are pharmaceutical companies. The sector's total sales in 1994 was estimated at US$200 billion, of which western Europe accounted for 30%, the US for 25% and for Japan 30%. The rest of the world accounted for less than 30% of sales. Of these sales, patented prescription drugs, or "ethical pharmaceuticals" were valued at US$130 billion; the total sales for over-the-counter medicines was US$20 billion. In the 1990s, however, these margins have been under pressure as it has become technically more difficult to develop new drugs.

Only about 50 firms account for two thirds of the world output, with nearly a quarter of the world output being provided by just 15 firms. All the top 100 drug firms in the world are based in the US, western Europe and Japan. World sales in this industry grew by 10% per year in the 1980s but they are expected to grow by five per cent per year in the 1990s. The projected growth in the developing countries is higher than five per cent per year but other economic factors may inhibit such growth. Cost-awareness is forcing state health agencies and insurance groups to limit any major increases in pharmaceutical prices. Firms, especially in the US, argue that high health cover costs for employees reduces their competitiveness on the international market. Measures that would reduce pharmaceutical prices, especially through research and development (R&D) in new products become important aspects of corporate strategies. This has added to the attractiveness of biotechnology.

The pharmaceutical industry is dominated by large multinational firms and is characterized by major entry barriers, especially in relation to the development of new products. It depends on the development of high value-added products and is highly regulated. The major firms are vertically integrated and control all aspects of the business (including R&D, production and marketing). Their major drug types include cardiovascular, anti-infective, internal medicine, pain control and respiratory medicines.

Merck, the largest drug firm in the world, accounted for about one quarter of the share of the profits of the top 10 drug firms in the world. It accounts for five per cent of the world's market for prescription drugs and is responsible for six of the 50 best-selling drugs in the world. Merck's best selling drug is Vasotec, a heart medicine which fetches some US$1.5 billion a year. It is the world's second largest selling drug after Zantac, an ulcer drug manufactured by Glaxo of the UK which sells US$2.8 billion a year. Merck invests heavily in R&D and marketing. Its annual R&D budget is over US$600 million and it employs over 6,000 people in this activity.

The biotechnology industry is seen as a new source of economic growth and its value is projected to increase considerably. Recent studies of the biotechnology market show that its growth is shaped by the biotechnology firms themselves which help to stimulate demand for their products. Other factors which usually stimulate demand such as public procurement have been less prominent in this industry.[1] In this respect, market size projections have to be directly related to the co-evolving composition and structure of the industry. Product sales in the US biotechnology industry, for example, stood at an estimated US$10 billion in 1994 and are projected to hit the US$50 billion mark by the year 2000. This is a ten-fold increase in just under a decade. Similar rates of growth in product sales are also projected for the other industrialized countries.

The future of the biotechnology industry is currently being shaped by the high growth in R&D expenditure. In the US, for example, R&D expenditure on biotechnology-based pharmaceuticals in 109 major firms increased by 71% over the 1991–92 levels to a staggering US$1.9 billion (or an average of US$17.4 million per firm).[2] The increase in the US R&D expenditure is associated with the expected new biotechnology products. In 1991, for example, there were 135 biotechnology-derived products in clinical trials, 23% more than the previous year. In the same year, biotechnology firms filed 290 investigational-new-drug applications, a 26% increase from the previous year.[3]

Financial projections on the potential value of biotechnology products are influenced, to a certain extent, by the current value of plant-based products. The pharmaceutical sector has been the source of such information. It is estimated that every fourth drug prescribed in the US is derived from plant extracts. The value of such sales was estimated at US$4.5 billion in 1980 and stood at an estimated US$18 billion in 1994. In the mid-1980s, the annual over-the-counter and prescription drug value in Europe, Japan, Canada and the US was estimated at US$43 billion.[4] The annual worldwide sales of the pharmaceutical industry are expected to reach US$500 billion by the year 2000, of which the industrialized countries will account for nearly 75%. This is equivalent to the annual GDP of the UK or France.

Plants, drugs and indigenous knowledge

The plant-derived prescription drugs in the US originate from 40 species, of which 20 are from the tropics.[5] Given the sales value of these drugs, the average value per species utilized is US$200 million, bringing the value of the contributions of the tropics to US$4 billion for the species utilized. This, of course, is not the value of the species in their natural form because it covers all the costs of R&D, manufacturing and marketing. In addition to these drugs, more than 60 plant species yield prescription drugs which are used in the US for research but which have not been recognized by the US Food and Drug Administration (USFDA).[6] The 1990 estimate for the US market for "unconventional therapy", most of which is based on plant-derived medicines, was US$13.7 billion.[7] Over 300 species are sold as herbal teas in the US alone.

Africa has added considerably to the collection of clinically useful plants. Its contributions include *Catharanthus roseus* (anti-tumor), *Centella asiatica* (vulnerary), *Gossypium* (male contraceptive), *Pausinystalia yohimbe* (aphrodisiac), *Ricinus communis* (laxative) and *Stophanthus gratus* (cardiotonic). African countries, however, are not major sources of cultivated medicinal plants. Notable exceptions include South Africa, Namibia, Lesotho and Botswana which produce *Harpagophytum procumbens* as an unrefined drug; Sudan and Egypt which produce *Hibiscus sabdariffa* also as an unrefined drug; Cameroon, Nigeria and Rwanda which export *Pausinystalia yohimbe*; Zaïre which exports *Peumus boldus* and Zaire, Madagascar and Mozambique which produce *Rauvolfia vomitoria*. African material is also being used in a wide range of health-related activities. One of the most notable is *Phytolacca dodecandra* (*endod*) whose extract is an effective molluscicide and is now used in a number countries to control schistosomiasis (bilharzia).[8] This option is cheaper than using Bayluscide (niclosamide), which is marketed at US$30,000 a tonne by Bayer Company.[9]

Figures of sales of single products show that biotechnology products could result in large sources of income for the countries providing biological material. For example, Elli Lilly earns some US$100 million annually from the anti-tumor vincristine and vinblastine which are derived from the Madagascan rosy periwinkle (*Catharanthus roseus*).[10] Such a figure, however, is often mistaken to be the value of the plant.

Another way of looking at the value of plant-derived drugs is to estimate the economics of cancer, which costs US$14 billion annually in treatment and lost work days in the US. In the US alone, cancer is estimated to take 500,000 lives annually. At an estimated value of US$1.5–8 million per life (based on on-the-job risk analysis for purposes of public policy), their total value is between US$750 billion and US$4 trillion.[11] Anti-cancer drugs save an estimated 75,000 lives annually and some 30–50% of the drugs are plant-based. These estimates indicate that plant-based drugs save up to 35,500 lives annually. This implies that the economic value of plant-based anti-cancer drugs in the US alone is between US$34 billion and US$300 billion.[12]

Yet another approach is to estimate the value of the contribution of each species to the pharmaceutical industry. It is estimated that over 5,000 plant species have been examined in detail for medicinal effectiveness and yet only 40 species have yielded prescription drugs for the US pharmaceutical industry. An assumption of randomness would suggest that only one in 125 species would lead to new drugs. At an average retail value of US$200 million per drug, the world loses the equivalent of US$1.6 billion in retail value for every 1,000 species that become extinct. This assumes that in every 1,000 species, there are eight potential plant-derived drugs. The figure, however, is likely to be lower given the fact that plants with potential medicinal value are not chosen at random but carefully selected on the basis of research and indigenous knowledge.[13] This would suggest, though, that the potential value of plants increases with time as pressure on the resource base increases.

Such figures indicate that there is enormous value in developing new drugs and conserving the biological resources that could lead to such drugs. Equally important is indigenous knowledge that could lead to the discovery of medicinal properties in plants. Such knowledge has become an important aspect of biodiversity prospecting.[14] But developing a new drug requires extensive investment in research infrastructure, human capacity and organizational competence. It takes an average of 12 years to develop a new drug at the cost of over US$231 million.[15] The costs cover the screening of candidate compounds, identifying and isolating active compounds, testing for toxicity and doing clinical trials. The figure includes the costs incurred in pursuing "dead ends". The chances of getting a new drug are extremely low. It is estimated that only one in 10,000 chemicals provides a promising "lead", and less than 25% of the candidates reaching clinical trials get approved as a new drug.

The high risks associated with developing new drugs have resulted in novel institutional arrangements and alliances whose main aim is to reduce the high costs of R&D and the related uncertainties. Measures such as limited partnerships have been widely used. Major pharmaceutical firms are forging such alliances with specialized research institutions as well as with other drug firms. Sandoz Pharmaceuticals, for example, recently entered into a 10-year R&D deal with Scripps Research Institute in California worth US$300 million. In 1991, Sadoz entered a similar deal with Harvard University's Dana Farber Cancer Institute worth US$100 million over 10 years. Sadoz already has R&D alliance with US firms such as Magainin Pharmaceuticals, SyStemix, Cytel and Repligen. The alliances are aimed at bringing together a wide range of state-of-the-art intellectual resources in other institutions and firms. In the case of Sandoz, the alliance with Scripps enables it to have access to results of research supported through other sources of funds at Scripps (for example from the National Institutes of Health). Large firms also enter into alliances with academic research institutions to reduce costs since overhead expenses are lower in such institutions than in private firms. It is estimated that the average cost per patent for research carried out in a drug firm is US$5–10 million while the average cost for research through academic institutions is US$2.5 million per patent.[16] The scope for forging such alliances and being able to leverage local support in the developing countries is limited and thus requires even a greater degree of institutional innovation.

The uncertainty in drug development is illustrated by the work of the US National Cancer Institute (NCI) which has signed specimen supply contracts with over 25 countries worldwide. The institute had, by 1991, screened over 50,000 extracts for anti-HIV activity of which only three were likely to reach clinical trials. Only five of the 33,000 extracts screened for anti-cancer properties are undergoing further study.[17] Tropical plants with unique anti-cancer compounds include *Tabebuia serratifolia*, *Jacaranda caucana* and *Croton tiglium*. Over the 1960–81 period, NIC mounted the largest screening programme under which 114,045 individual extracts from up to 35,000 plant species were tested. Of these, some 4,897 extracts from 3,394 species exhibited biological activity. About 40 of the active compounds were considered for further development.[18] Much of the screening attention has turned to anti-HIV extracts. There are already some promising indications although it may take up to a decade before a drug is developed. An extract from a species of the vine genus *Ancistrocladus* found in Cameroon shows strong anti-HIV activity in the test-tube.[19]

The prospects of generating large incomes from the sale of extracts from plants are limited by the high rate of uncertainty and the long periods involved in drug development. The value of supplying extracts to pharmaceutical firms is relatively low given the low royalty rates (one to five per cent of net sales) and the long periods of product development. A royalty payment of three per cent for an extract that leads to drug with an annual market value of US$10 million would yield only US$52,500 in royalty payments.[20]

But there are ways of increasing the probability rate of getting a new drug, mainly by enhancing the local scientific capacity.[21] These include raising the local capacity in screening, greater knowledge of the physiological aspects of the disease, cumulative knowledge of the molecular structures of different plant extracts, and competence in bio-informatics. Such knowledge-intensive approaches could increase the chances of putting a new drug on the market ten-fold and thereby raise the royalty income to US$461,000 per year. Thus, a drug with an annual net value of US$1 billion—which is quite unlikely—would earn the supplier of biological material US$461,000 annually.

When a viable product has been developed, the sales turn-over can be high and investments in research can be recovered quickly. This is illustrated by the case of shikonin, the anti-bacterial and anti-inflammatory extract from the roots of *Lithospermum erythrorhizon* used in lipstick. Shikonin, which is also a dye, is extracted from roots. It takes at least seven years before the tree reaches commercial value and therefore an alternative way of producing shikonin was needed. The annual world market for shikonin was US$600,000 in 1988 but some US$50 million had been invested in biotechnology R&D. Although this figure looked excessive, it was subsequently justified by the sale of biotechnology-based shikonin lipsticks. When a biotechnology product was developed (costing US$500 less per kg to produce than using conventional extraction), its manufacturers, Kanebo, realized a turnover of US$65 million in two years in Japan alone. The five million lipsticks sold for US$13 each.[22] This case also illustrates how a technology can drastically alter the size of the market and create conditions for further expansion.

The approaches adopted in biodiversity prospecting, rely on isolating the active substances in plants. This poses problems for formulations which rely on a combination of different plant extracts as in the case of much of Chinese herbal medicine. However, some movement has been noted in bring such knowledge into conventional medicine. The NCI, for example, introduced a US$20.5 million programme to identify naturally-occurring foods which can be concentrated into preventive anti-cancer concoctions.[23] Medicinal plants and the related indigenous knowledge are intricately linked to land rights. In this regard, their fate is tied to land conservation and the related rights as discussed in the following section.

Property rights and genetic resources

Property and property rights

The essence of property is in the relations among people arising out of their relations to things. Objects over which the rights of property extend are objects conceived of as taken out of the mass of free goods and brought under the exclusive control of a person, and this control is called property. In this sense, property may be thought of as referring to the exclusive rights which extend over a thing. Indeed, a popular definition of property holds property to denote the exclusive relationship of a person or a group of persons to an object or complex of objects of material value.[24]

In terms of classification, property is either "corporeal" or "incorporeal". Corporeal property refers to rights in material things, while incorporeal property refers to "any other proprietary rights". In English and Kenyan law, corporeal property is divided into land and chattels, the latter term being sometimes referred to as personal property. Incorporeal property consists of rights in immaterial things (for example patents, copyrights and trade marks) and rights over the property of others (for example leases, tenancies, servitudes, securities and trusts).

The classification of property is usually a theoretical exercise in jurisprudence, as it does not alter or define the content of property rights embodied in the property itself. The conceptions of classification which are common in modern legal systems have an important correlation with the history of the evolution of property law and property rights. For instance, the common law to this day retains the rigid differentiation between real property (freehold interests in land), and personal property (all the other categories of property rights). This is because the law was first concerned with land, before other property rights became important.

Property only exists because there is law. This is because law defines and underwrites the mode and method of exercise of property rights. In its most developed form, this legal arrangement takes the form of a guarantee of rights to property.[25] The content of property rights is defined by legal concepts which indicate the variable strength of the relationship between holders of property, and their property objects. The holder of property exercises certain rights over the property object which are protected in law. The highest form of these rights is defined by the legal concept of ownership. This concept confers a bundle of rights over the property object.[26] These rights include enjoyment (the right to use, to appropriate yield, and even to destroy the object), possession (the right to occupy, physically control, and exclude others) and transfer (the right to donate, sell or bequeath).

Other legal concepts which articulate the content of the relationship between the holder of property and the property object include "possession", "detention" and "custody". These concepts represent a continuum of decreasing strength in the holder-object relationship.

There are legitimate and illegitimate methods of acquiring rights in property. Under English and Kenyan law, only three methods are considered legitimate. These are: originally; derivatively and by succession.[27] The other methods of purported acquisition of property rights are considered illegitimate, and the law does not protect rights so acquired. These methods include theft, coercion, conquest and extortion.

An important modern legal problem relates to the acquisition of rights over new forms of property. As society develops and becomes more complex, new forms of property are discovered or developed. Every modern society encourages innovation and seeks to protect the products thereof. The law attempts to offer protection of these new forms of property rights by deliberately restricting its classification of property to mere examples of those forms of property which fall in any given class. Any new property terms automatically fit in the relevant class without the need to re-define the concept and categories of property. But sometimes a new form of proprietary interest arises which does not fit in the accepted scheme of classification. A good example is the modern interest which human beings are recognized to have in a wholesome environment. It would appear that legal debates relating to the problems of *locus standi* in environmental matters do actually mask the real problem, which is whether such a legitimate interest in a wholesome environment constitutes a legally protectable property right.

More frequently, a legal interest arises, or is asserted, which is seen not to meet the defined criteria for legal protection. In labour relations there is the controversy surrounding "job-property", with the majority of trade unions purporting to see a protectable interest in it. In patent debates there is the problem of biological innovation, which is still held in most countries not to constitute a protectable interest. Then there is the problem of communal or traditional knowledge, and whether this can be protected as property.

The two legal problems cited here exemplify the limitations which may exist in the legal arrangements for the protection of property rights. In Kenyan law at least, it would appear that there is no legal procedure or instrument for the conversion of a legitimate interest into a property right, unless a specific statute makes provision for such. A statute with such a provision is the industrial Property Act of 1989.

A. Okoth-Owiro with C. Juma

Land rights and chattels

In the eye of the law, land includes the surface of the land, everything beneath the surface, and everything affixed to the land. And the right to land carries with it rights of property over the airspace above the land. Property rights in land are vested in the owner, in the private sense in which a legal person may have a bundle of rights over an item of property. These rights are, however qualified by the state which retains, and on occasions "creates" overriding rights over the land.

To fully appreciate the nature and content of the rights of land owners over their land, it is important to explain the types of relationships which a person may have with land under Kenyan law. These relationships give rise to different sets of legal rights. The subject-matter of concern here has commonly been discussed under the title of land tenure. It would appear that the nature and content of the relationship between a legal person and land depends on the system of land tenure under consideration, because tenure refers to the manner in which individuals or social groups hold or secure access to land including the terms under which such land is held. Land held under communal tenure is not owned privately in the sense in which land held under individual tenure is. The latter is regulated by the common law and the property legislation introduced, or copied from England. The former is also regulated by law, but the content of rights involved is more variable.

It may be suggested here that communal land tenure, by its very nature, strongly emphasizes conservation, as the land is to be used by present and future generations. Holders and users of land under any communal system have a legal duty to utilize the land in a manner that is consistent with its conservation. The situation is necessarily different when one considers individual land tenure. Here, the relationship envisaged by law is an exclusive one: a land owner acquires exclusive rights.

In Kenya today, there is a strong presumption in favour of individualized tenure. The property statutes, namely the Registered Land Act, the Indian Transfer of Property Act, and the Land Acquisitions Act assume that individual exclusive ownership of land is the system for the future in Kenya. At the same time, policy and legal measures are being strongly pushed to convert communal land to be registered and held individually. This transformation programme is given legitimacy in Chapter IX of the Constitution of Kenya on trust land and the related Acts of Parliament.

Property rights in land under the individual tenure system derive from the common law, and include what the modern property statutes have introduced. A proper reading of these rights would seem to suggest that land is a commodity over which the holder (at least the holder of absolute proprietorship) has exclusive rights and freedoms. Therefore unless there are legal provisions to the contrary, the owners of land are free to use and abuse their land as they please. In common law jurisprudence, this is what is sometimes referred to as "the doctrine of waste"; and the land owner has a right to commit it. Property rights in land under the laws of Kenya do not carry with them an automatic obligation to conserve the land. And this extends to fixtures on land, such as plants. Nor is there any obligation to regulate or otherwise restrict introductions or accumulations of any substance on the land.

However, there are common law limitations on the freedom to use and abuse land. The most important limitations are imposed by the tort of nuisance. The common law insisted that the full right of enjoyment and exploitation of land was subject to some limitation, in order to preserve the enjoyment and exploitation rights of adjoining occupiers. Another limitation is imposed by the doctrine of enforceability of restrictive covenants between freehold owners.[28] But it can be seen that although the common law regulated private rights, it recognized no supervening public or governmental interest in the private use of land.

Private property rights over land are enjoyed subject to the qualification that the state retains superior overriding rights over the same land. The most important of these powers are expropriation and supervision of use. The power to expropriate the land owner is defined in the doctrine of eminent domain, and entitles the state to nationalize land and assume its direct ownership. In the Constitution of Kenya, protection from deprivation of property is provided for in Section 75. But this is made subject to the exception that property may be compulsorily acquired in the interests of defence, public safety, public order, public morality, public health, town and country planning, or the development or utilization of any property in such manner as to promote the public benefit. A legal regime regulating land acquisition is then provided under the Land Acquisition Act.

Supervision of use of land is Usually considered as falling under the doctrine of "police power". It entitles the state to direct land owners as to how, and for what purpose they shall use the land which is otherwise their private property. In Kenya, two areas in which this has been most often done are agriculture and land use planning. The Agriculture Act and the Land Planning Act are replete with provisions which can be used to require land owners to use their land for purposes, and in ways that may be inconsistent with their wishes as land owners. Other statutes with similar provisions include the Local Government Act, the Town Planning Act, and the Chiefs' Authority Act.

Both eminent domain and police power are doctrines which hold great promise as potential legal strategies for effective conservation of the environment. In fact, environmental conservation through land use planning is a well-developed conservation arrangement in environmental science. thus, land may be nationalized for purposes of its planning, and police powers can be used to direct conservation measures on private land. Another strategy involves the retention of direct ownership by the state over public land for purposes of its conservation. In Kenya, only this last strategy has been exploited to create public forests, wildlife conservation areas and marine parks.

Chattels are moveable corporeal property not attached to land. The relevance of this category of property to conservation is not at first obvious. But if it is remembered that human beings have asserted ownership over a great variety of natural objects, then the key to conservation of resources, environment or knowledge often lies in the control of chattels. For example, plants are attached to land, and as fixtures, they are considered to be part of the land. But the moment they are severed from the land, they are chattels over which separate and independent rights of ownership may be asserted. These rights of ownership may then be enjoyed at the expense of the larger interest in conservation of genetic resources and the environment.

The law's protection is more directly concerned with possession than with ownership; this is because ownership is intrinsic and cannot be seen easily. The possessor of an object must be protected in the first instance. In relation to the environment, the possessors of a plant, or seed must be protected, even though they cannot assert ownership over the forest where the plant or seed is to be found. If they have "stolen" the plant or seed from land which is not owned by any individual, or whose owner does not mind the possessors' taking of the seed, Kenyan law protects the rights of the possessors to assert ownership over their seed, unless some statutory provision can be found which disqualifies the claim. There are exceptions to this, for example, in some provisions of the Forests Act.

The situation may be illustrated by a more complex connection. Plants and their seeds are not circulated for no purpose. Every plant and seed has its uses, and the exchange process is packaged with the full information on the utility of plants. Through observation, inquiry, purchase or theft, it is possible to discover the use or uses to which just about any plant is put by the members of the community which uses that plant. Most of this information is given innocently, and for no reward. But its impact on conservation of resources and knowledge can be very extensive. Kenyan law strongly emphasizes the protection of property rights in chattels. But the law is ill-equipped to protect either the national interest in conservation, or the private interest in reward for information and knowledge.

Rights in incorporeal property

The aspects of incorporeal property which are best developed in Kenyan law relate to rights over the property of others. Leases, tenancies, servitudes, securities and trusts are all very clearly articulated in property and commercial statutes like the Registered Land Act, and in the applicable rules of the common law and doctrines of equity.

Aspects of rights in immaterial things have also been developed in the legal system. Thus, copyright law is enacted in the Copyright Act, which lays down a legal framework for the protection of copyright in literary works, musical works, artistic works, cinematographic films, sound recordings, broadcasts and programme-carrying signals. Trade marks are also protected by statute. However, the most developed legal regime of incorporeal property is the law on patents, which in Kenya is to be found in the industrial Property Act of 1989. Inventions are protected through the device of patenting, and the Act provides that an invention is patentable if it is new, involves an inventive step and is industrially applicable. The definition of an invention is also broad enough, in that it means a solution to a specific problem in the field of technology. Clearly, the act contemplates the patenting of products of biotechnological process.

An analogous regime for the protection of rights in incorporeal property is the Seeds and Plant Varieties Act, which establishes a legal regime for the protection of property rights in plant varieties. All the above are examples of rights in incorporeal property. But there is no conceptual or jurisprudential delimitation as to what amounts to a category of "incorporeal property".

Traditional property rights systems

When English law was imposed on Kenya at the beginning of the twentieth century, the result was a plural legal system. This is because the imposition of English law did not extinguish the existing customary legal systems. In independent Kenya, legal pluralism has been legitimized by providing for the applicability of the several bodies of legal rules contemporaneoUSly.

thus, the Judicature Act provides that: "The High Court, the Court of Appeal and all subordinate courts shall be guided by African customary law in civil cases in which one or more of the parties is subject to it or affected by it, so far as it is applicable and is not repugnant to justice and morality or inconsistent with any written law . . ." Legal pluralism in Kenya means that traditional systems of property rights are relevant, and possibly applicable in present-day Kenya. But while the law envisages the applicability of traditional legal arrangements relating to property, neither the actual legal regimes, nor the institutional integration with the imposed regime of English property law, is clearly articulated.

The extent of applicability of traditional property rights is discernible by comparing traditional conceptions of property rights with the recognized classes of property under English law. First, this reveals the aspects of traditional property rights which are inapplicable because English and statute law have overtaken them. Secondly, and more importantly, this will lend support to the argument that for those aspects of traditional property rights which have no corresponding norms in English law, explicit legal recognition and application is required.

Proceeding on the basis of the above, land ownership and use, chattels (although what is capable of being owned may present problems) and privatized intellectual property find expression in imposed law. Yet there are aspects of traditional property rights which lack a parallel in the scheme of rights of the English property law. These include traditional or indigenous knowledge and communal intellectual property (for example of herbs, crops and ecology).

The dominant emphasis in the legal arrangements for the protection of property rights is the English common law notion of sanctity of private property: private owners have exclusive rights and should be free to use and abuse their property as they deem fit. This presents two problem scenarios in attempting to use the law for the ends of conservation. First, a conservation ethic cannot be read into the law. External legal sources for conservation have to be found outside the institution of property. Second, where property does not fit neatly into the scheme of private ownership, the law leaves a hiatus which can be misused by forces and interests which are opposed to conservation or to national economic sovereignty. For example, resources which are severed from the land like plants, or intellectual property which does not inhere in individuals like indigenous botanical knowledge, tend to be plundered in an unregulated manner. And the law cannot even begin to be used to control this situation because its methodologies are not adapted to this challenge.

It is also noteworthy that a holistic conception of the idea of property, and a delimitation of its province is still lacking in Kenya. The law holds out the potential for extension into legitimate interests that can be defined as property. The problem at this stage in the development of Kenyan law is that no system or procedure exists for converting legitimate social or economic interests into legally recognizable and protectable institutions of property.

Legal aspects of genetic resource utilization

The value of biological diversity

Biological diversity is an essential requirement for the continued survival of human civilization and for continued evolution. Plant and animal species are a source of many of the basic necessities of human life, including food, energy, industrial chemicals and medicines.[29] In addition, immense opportunities still remain open for future scientific research into the interrelationships between ecosystems, and the development of many practical applications of biodiversity.[30] These applications could include: (a) new domestications; (b) the extraction of new substances to be used as materials, food or drugs; (c) the discovery of new biological processes applicable in the medical sciences or in industrial operations; and (d) the identification of genes capable, when transferred to domesticated organisms, of providing them with certain desired characteristics such as resistance to particular disease.

Wild species also play essential roles within ecosystems as pollinators, seed dispersers, predators controlling the proliferation of other species or decomposers of organic matter.[31] In addition, ecosystems themselves provide mutual services to one another thereby ensuring ecological integrity. For these reasons, biological diversity must be maintained and conserved. Of the three aspects of biological diversity—genetic diversity within each species, species diversity and ecosystem diversity—the last is the main focus of our attention.

The main threat to biological diversity is the destruction, alteration or transformation of natural ecosystems by human beings. Such activities as the conversion of natural habitats for agricultural production, human settlement, and the unregulated exploitation of genetic resources are the major threats to biological diversity. These activities are almost always a function, or a by-product of the enjoyment of property rights over land. For example, the conversion of natural habitats for agricultural production on private land is an incidence of enjoyment of rights of ownership over land which cannot be regulated except by superior powers of the state over land.[32]

Along the same lines, conversion of forest land for human settlement is usually a result of pressure on available land allocated for human settlement. This pressure, variously categorized as landlessness, squatters or trespass, in truth means the legal and physical separation of a section of the population from ownership rights over land. The operating system of property relations is the most common cause of pressure on land. Urban sprawl and deforestation due to wood-cutting and the destruction of catchment areas are the result of pressure on rural populations which are unable to survive without interfering with the natural environment. This pressure results from the marginalization of the rural areas which, according to the dictates of the property relations in society, must be made dependent upon the urban areas. Legal regimes and policies to develop the urban areas by underdeveloping the rural areas commenced under colonial rule and continues today.

Property rights and their enjoyment affect negatively biological diversity generally, and genetic conservation specifically. Legal controls are therefore necessary to ensure that these negative impacts are minimized.

Conservation of genetic resources in Kenya

Under the existing legal arrangements in Kenya, there is no general duty placed on citizens, state organs or agents to conserve genetic resources. At the same time, there is no comprehensive legal framework for the conservation of genetic resources.[33] In effect this means that utilization of genetic resources takes place outside any system of legal regulation. It also means that an institutional framework for the management of the utilization process is lacking. It is nevertheless a fact that legal instruments exist in Kenya that affect the conservation and utilization of genetic resources. These instruments either create sectoral regimes for conservation of genetic resources, or restrict freedom of access to and utilization of property, with conservation as the objective. These legal instruments are discussed below.

First, Section 75 of the Constitution, in outlining the purposes for which property may be compulsorily acquired by the state, refers to "the development or utilization of any property in such manner as to promote the public benefit". In our view, public benefit should include the conservation of genetic resources, and therefore the Constitution should provide for compulsory acquisition of property to facilitate biodiversity conservation. However, environmental conservation has not been fully integrated into the political ethos or public awareness as a public interest in the way the Constitution uses the term. Moreover, the legal system grants standing to those who seek to protect their private interest and the protection of the public is left largely to the attorney-general.

Second, the conservation of aspects of plant resources is provided for in the Forests Act.[34] The object of the act is the establishment, control and regulation of forest areas. The Act empowers the minister responsible to declare any forest areas to be a nature reserve for the purpose of preserving their natural amenities and flora and fauna. Section 6 states: "In a nature reserve, no cutting, grazing, removal of forest produce or disturbance of the flora shall be allowed except with the permission of the chief conservator, and permission shall only be given with the object of conserving the natural flora and amenities of the reserve". A related, if less important statute, is the Plant Protection Act. The Act provides for the prevention of the introduction and spread of disease destructive to plants.

Third, the conservation of animal and plant habitats is also provided for in the Wildlife (Conservation and Management) Act. Under section 9(2), the director of wildlife management may set aside a section of a national park for use as a breeding place for animals, or as nurseries for vegetation. Section 15(1) further provides for the protection of animals and vegetation in areas adjacent to national parks, national reserves or local sanctuaries. This is a most useful provision as it can be invoked to protect areas that do not fall under the direct jurisdiction of the wildlife and forestry legislation.

Fourth, the conservation of aquatic genetic resources is provided for in the Fisheries Act, The Maritime Zones Act, and the Wildlife (Conservation and Management) Act. The objective of the Fisheries Act is to provide for the development, management, exploitation, utilization and conservation of fisheries in Kenya, in both inland waters and waters of the maritime zones. The minister in charge of fisheries and the director of fisheries are enabled by sections 4 and 5 to take appropriate measures to develop fisheries and manage the same to achieve the objectives of the Act.

One of the objectives of the Maritime Zones Act is to provide for the exploration, exploitation, conservation and management of the resources of maritime zones. Maritime Zones are defined by Section 2 to mean the exclusive economic zones together with the territorial waters and the air space above the exclusive economic zone. Section 5 of the Act provides that within the exclusive economic zone, Kenya will exercise sovereign rights with respect to the exploration, exploitation, conservation and management of the natural resources of the zone. These legal arrangements apparently affect aquatic genetic resources, which can be conserved using the framework of this enabling legislation. The Wildlife (Conservation and Management) Act, in addition to its other objectives, has been used to confer protection on marine habitats through the facility of marine parks.

At a more general level, there are items of legislation in Kenya which are useful as legal bases for the conservation of genetic resources. A good example is the Agriculture Act, which is at least as much a crop production statute as it is environmental conservation legislation. Section 48 of the Act empowers the minister to make regulations governing a great variety of land use activities on private land, including control of ploughing on slopes, protection of water catchment areas, the felling of trees and establishment of forests on private land. Also of interest is the Antiquities and Monuments Act which defines a monument to include "a specified site on which a buried monument or object of archeological or palaeontological interest exists or is believed to exist, and a specified area of land adjoining it which is . . . required for maintenance thereof . . ." These are extensive enabling powers, which can be applied to genetic conservation.

The laws affecting the conservation of genetic resources in Kenya, like all laws affecting the environment, developed piecemeal over a long period of time. And conservation was generally not the main purpose for their enactment. Inevitably, many gaps are discernible in the legislation and the implementation arrangements are not streamlined. The situation is exacerbated by the absence of a comprehensive national policy on genetic resources, which in practical terms, means that there is no policy focus for legislation. In the circumstances, it is obvious that the law on conservation of genetic resources is gravely wanting in scope and coverage.

A number of specific limitations in the law are considered to be the more serious omissions in legislation. First, Kenya lacks a legal framework for asserting national economic sovereignty over genetic resources. Legal requirements that purport to define rights and obligations over genetic resources are undermined in their operation by the free flow of resources across national boundaries. Second, there is not a single legal instrument for regulating the conservation of domesticated animal genetic resources. The utilization of these genetic resources takes place in a legal vacuum. Third, there is no law on human genetic resources. Fourth, there is no law to regulate the collection and marketing of plant genetic resources. The moment plants are collected, they are subject to the general law on personal property, and the international laws and treaties on plant resources. In fact there is no mention in the laws of *ex situ* arrangements for conservation anywhere. Fifth, agricultural legislation emphasizes utilization, and so operates to encumber conservation ideals.

Herbal medicine as intellectual property

It has been asserted elsewhere in this chapter that the knowledge that a plant possesses medicinal properties is a kind of intellectual property which is capable of being owned. It will be shown further on that this knowledge is shared by members of any given community (who collectively command part of the knowledge), and specialists in the same community (who command a more thorough specialized knowledge of plant life in their environment).

It is submitted that medicinal plants, as intellectual property cannot be protected using either the patent system, or plant breeder's rights legislation. The industrial Property Act, Kenya's patent legislation, excludes plants varieties from patentability unless they are products of biotechnology. The Seeds and Plant Varieties Act confers plant breeders rights only on persons who have "bred or discovered the plant variety concerned." Those with a knowledge that a plant has medicinal properties can neither be said to have bred or discovered these plants. There is no law to protect the proprietary interests of those with a knowledge that plants are medicinal.

Hence the following matters require legislating upon. First, the knowledge that plants can be used for specific purposes (i.e., indigenous botanical knowledge) should be recognized as property. Second, the legal person or group of persons in which this right should inhere should be identified; and here the choice seems to be between the state, farmers or herbalists, and individual citizens. A legal regime must be developed to protect rights of herbalists in the context of their knowledge of the plants they use. Third, a legal and institutional framework for restricting the transfer of this indigenous knowledge to non-Kenyans is required.

Medicinal plants are the important resource needed for the continued viability of traditional medicine. indigenous knowledge is the social and legal form in which its propagators are able to define their interest in medicinal plants.

Traditional medicine in Kenya

Importance of traditional medicine

Traditional medicine, sometimes referred to as ethnomedicine, has been described as: "the totality of all knowledge and practices, whether explicable or not, used in diagnosing, preventing or eliminating a physical, mental or social disequilibrium and which rely exclusively on past experience and observation handed down from generation to generation, verbally or in writing".[35] Traditional medicine is practised by specialists who are variously referred to as traditional healers or therapists, practitioners of traditional medicine, herbalists, etc. A traditional healer is a person who is recognized by the community in which he or she lives as competent to provide health care by using vegetable, animal or mineral substances, and certain other methods based on the social, cultural or religious background. The healer will also draw upon the knowledge, attitudes, and beliefs that are prevalent in the community regarding physical, mental and social well-being, and the causation of disease and disability.[36]

At least one study has attempted to classify healers into categories.[37] By focusing on the type of treatment administered, it was possible to classify traditional healers into four categories, namely: (i) pure herbalists; (ii) herbalist-ritualists; (iii) ritualist-herbalists, and (iv) spiritualists. The first category of traditional healers use plants for their healing. The second and third use plants and rituals either simultaneously or alternately, with the healers in the second category treating the ritual as peripheral to the therapy, and those in the third building the therapy around the ritual. Healers in the last category do not use plants, animal or minerals at all. It is clear that the vast majority of traditional healers use plant material to effect the treatment of their patients. This probably explains why in common Usage, the term traditional healer is used synonymously with herbalist.

Traditional medicine has attracted a lot of interest among policy-makers, researchers, the pharmaceutical industry and the World Health Organization (WHO). There are many reasons for this interest. First, in the majority of developing countries, modern sector health services are grossly inadequate. It has therefore come to be recognized that traditional medicine is an important supplement to modern health sector delivery arrangements. The recognition and incorporation of traditional medicine into the main stream of health delivery arrangements is considered a prerequisite to its meaningful exploitation as a supplement.

Second, as a matter of statistics, the vast majority of developing country residents depend on traditional medicine for their health care. It is estimated that three billion of the people in the developing world fully depend on traditional medicine to meet their pharmaceutical needs.[38] In many African countries people are reverting to traditional medicine in response to the declining accessibility of modern health services and the rising costs of medical care. It is thus the most important health sector in terms of accessibility for a large section of the developing world.

Third, traditional medicine has been shown to hold great potential for pharmaceutical development.[39] Traditional medicine makes use of various substances of animal, vegetable and mineral origin. Many pharmaceutical substances have already been extracted from them by making use of modern techniques.[40] Others could be produced in the future, if traditional medicine is better understood and more thoroughly researched. It is also recognized that traditional medical pharmacopoeia contain certain therapeutic methods and approaches which are as yet little known. Once they have been mastered and knowledge of them deepened, these therapies could revolutionize the diagnosis, prevention and treatment of certain diseases.[41]

Fourth, plants and their constituents hold great economic potential for the countries in which they are found, or for those who care to collect and preserve them. A key to understanding the uses to which plants are put is traditional medicine, and this explains the revived interest in the subject. Most of what is now known and accepted about traditional medicine was, until recently, suppressed or ignored due to cultural prejudice and bias on the part of policy-makers and researchers.

Traditional medicine and health policy

Before the advent of colonialism, health practices rested exclusively on ethnomedicine. The practice of ethnomedicine in pre-colonial Kenya is not properly documented. However, the following generalizations can be made. Traditional medicine existed as a holistic system of health delivery, and no alternative system had developed by the advent of colonialism. The province of traditional medicine was defined to exclude sorcery, witchcraft and negative forms of magic. The practice of traditional medicine was hereditary and/or through apprenticeship. It was therefore possible to evolve a social sub-class of professionals through the normal social division of labour. In addition, traditional medicine was practised for gain by those who had mastered the art. But the system of property relations in traditional society was such that every member of the community could gain access to and receive the services of a healer.

Another characteristic of traditional medicine relevant to our discussion is that the community within which the traditional healers practised recognized property rights inhering in the healers with respect to plant, animal and mineral materials used in healing, and their therapeutic knowledge. Access to medicinal information and materials was regulated by customary legal rules, enforced by accepted sanctions like ostracism, curses and physical punishment. Notably, although the traditional healer was the specialist, all members of the community participated in the healing process, especially at the primary health level. To some extent, technical knowledge of the healing properties of plants was socialized. Most members of the community commanded at least some aspects of this knowledge and used it on occasions. The art of healing, and knowledge of the materials needed, was not a completely privatized knowledge.

The official health policy from the beginning of colonial occupation was the active suppression of traditional medicine in Kenya, coupled with the introduction of "modern" sector health services. Cultural imperialism, the need to destroy independent centres of power that could serve as rallying points for resisting colonial authority, the introduction of Christianity and the fear of the unknown all contributed to the negative policy disposition towards traditional medicine.

Two main methods were used to crush traditional medicine: orchestrated campaigns of a cultural-imperialist variety, and the criminal law. The law was used to criminalize traditional medicine and to discredit its practitioners, by equating such healing with witchcraft, and then outlawing it. Throughout colonialism, therefore, traditional medicine was unlawful, and this contributed to its marginalization as a system of health delivery in Kenya. It should be noted however, that not all aspects of traditional medicine could be criminalized. For example, the institution of traditional birth attendants was merely ignored. It is therefore more accurate to suggest that during colonialism, traditional medicine was either neglected or suppressed. But traditional medicine did not disappear. It merely went underground.

In the post-colonial era, there has been a remarkable policy shift with regard to traditional medicine. The first decade following independence in 1963 was marked by official indifference. Then in the late 1970s there was a decisive shift by health and economic planners in favour of traditional medicine—a shift which was first comprehensively documented in the 1979–83 development plan. From this time it was accepted that traditional medicine was not illegal. It was also accepted that its contribution to health delivery arrangements was positive, at least potentially. Perhaps it was the attempt to translate this policy position into action that led to the introduction of administrative regulation of traditional medical practitioners in the 1970s. Recent interest in the subject has been reinforced by the reduction in public health expenditures and research into traditional medicine.

Legal limitations

The case of medicinal plants demonstrates the weaknesses of and challenges to the law, with regard to genetic conservation. Medicinal plants form the nexus between genetic conservation and traditional medicine. Medicinal plants pose three separate challenges for policy and law. First, like most plant resources, they are under the threat of genetic extinction, and appropriate arrangements must be made for their conservation. Second, medicinal plants are a very valuable economic resource, and national economic sovereignty should be exercised over them. Many pharmaceutical companies are now known to be involved in natural plant screening. For this purpose they organize collection expeditions to developing countries, where they obtain the medicinal plant resources. The country of origin should benefit from its plants, not least to encourage their conservation. Mechanisms for compensation and regulation of exploitation must be identified or developed.

Third, the knowledge that a particular plant has medicinal property is a form of intellectual property which reposes in private hands. This property right must be protected, and a legal regime for this purpose should be identified or developed. The protection of this peculiar form of intellectual property is compounded by the fact that it is a species of indigenous or traditional knowledge which has not been fully expropriated by private ownership interests. The communal end of the knowledge is not protectable under the current regimes of property law. Other regimes more appropriate for the purpose must be developed.

Medicinal plants can be conserved, in the first instance, by the same institutional and legal arrangements that are used to conserve other plants.[42] The legal arrangements consist of legal instruments directed at the protection of certain types of plant habitat and legal instruments directed at the protection of particular species of plants. In the second instance, legal arrangements specifically intended for the conservation of medicinal plants can be developed for their protection.

In Kenya, the law neither provides a comprehensive legal framework for the conservation of plants, nor addresses the imperative of conserving medicinal plants. Nevertheless, protection of medicinal plant habitats is possible under a number of legal instruments. The Land Planning Act and the Land Acquisition Act, as land use planning laws can be used to compel the protection and preservation of certain forms of habitats, as well as to police the use of private land. The Forests Acts can be used to establish nature areas for the conservation of the habitats thought to contain medicinal plants. The Agriculture Act can be used to establish forests in private land and thus encourage the survival of medicinal plant habitats.

Particular species of medicinal plants are more difficult to protect. In particular, it is difficult to think of the kind of legal instrument in Kenya that could be said to create botanical gardens. But for whatever it is worth, administrative authority, legitimately bestowed by legislation, can be used to direct and order citizens and landowners to conserve species of medicinal plants. The legal basis for this form of power is to be found in the doctrine of "police power". The legal instruments for administrative directives can also be used including the constitutional powers of the president. Section 23(1) of the Constitution provides that "The Executive authority of the Government of Kenya shall vest in the President, and, subject to this Constitution, may be exercised by him either directly or through officers subordinate to him". In exercise of such authority, the president of Kenya, in 1986, decreed that the *Aloe* was a protected plant, a measure which was prompted by extensive exploitation of some species of the genus for commercial purposes.[43]

The Agriculture Act, Section 48, empowers the minister for agriculture to take measures and issue orders which are Usable in directing the conservation of particular plant species. The Chiefs' Authority Act can be an important conservation statute; it empowers the chief to give orders on conservation matters, among other things. An example of the kind of orders which a chief can issue is an order prohibiting the cutting of trees, or the breaking of land for planting purposes. These broad powers can be used to require the protection and conservation of plant species.

Medicinal plants are property (i.e., things capable of being owned) both as things attached to land, and as personal property not attached to land. The ownership of medicinal plants is governed by the general law of property, at least in the first instance. According to this scheme, medicinal plants belong to the owner of the land on which the plants happen to be growing and any person who may have obtained possession of individual plants which have been severed from the land.

This regime of property law, in its generality, is inadequate to regulate ownership of medicinal plant resources. In particular, it does not provide for the exercise of national economic sovereignty over the resources.[44] Access to medicinal plants is regulated by only two considerations: consent of the owner where on private property, and knowledge that the plant has medicinal properties. Plants may be collected without knowledge or authority of the state. Neither such collections, nor possessions in gene banks are public property, and may therefore be exported. The basis for regulating access to genetic resources now exists under the Convention on Biological Diversity. Although there are no model laws on this subject, a number of existing laws provide elements that can be consolidated into a law on access to genetic resources.[45]

Legal protection of indigenous knowledge

The concept of indigenous knowledge

Every society is possessed of a domain of knowledge of a technical and yet common character which most members of that community is socialized into, in order to lead an endowed life, in some respect or other, within that community. Social division of labour dictates that not every member of the community will have uniform command of all aspects of this knowledge, but the knowledge is characterized by its public, or communal character. This knowledge is transmitted downwards from one generation to the next, through established systems of apprenticeship, socialization and transfer. This knowledge constitutes the cultural heritage of a community, and enables individuals to adapt to their environment, acquire techniques of self-protection, food production, shelter construction, disease control, and technology.

This knowledge may be referred to as indigenous or traditional knowledge, and can be distinguished from modern, formal knowledge acquired in school or through formal systems of technology transfer from one society to another.

In order to place the problem of conservation and protection of indigenous knowledge in context, three separate categories of knowledge may be identified in society. The first is traditional or indigenous knowledge which all members of a community (or selected segments thereof) acquire as part of the cultural heritage of the community. The second is basic social knowledge learnt by the individual in school and other formal institutions, the purpose of which is to socialize that individual to lead a productive social and economic life in a modern society. This knowledge is restricted to information within the purview of the general public. The third is specialized knowledge possessed by individual experts who have developed the knowledge, or appropriated it with the intention of asserting property rights over it. This category of knowledge amounts to intellectual property.

In Kenya's legal system, specialized knowledge is protected as private property; while basic social knowledge is knowledge which is held to have passed from the private into the public domain. Ownership rights cannot therefore be asserted over basic social knowledge. As for indigenous knowledge, modern legal regimes on property are largely inappropriate for its protection. This is not surprising as the law of property did not have traditional knowledge in mind, nor did the communities with traditional knowledge intend it to be legally protected as private property.

The legal challenge

Aspects of indigenous knowledge hold much potential for appropriate technological development in areas such as medicine, conservation of the environment, building technology and agriculture. Unfortunately, traditional knowledge rarely exists any more in organized systems or community life, most traditional social systems have been transformed by forces of modernization. And where the knowledge still exists, it has become so rare as to be perceived as specialized knowledge.

It can be assumed that traditional knowledge will be required in certain areas of "modern" life. The two examples which have emerged in Kenya are the conservation of genetic resources, and traditional medicine. It has also been seen that knowledge derived from traditional skills—like the case of medicinal plants—is privately appropriated for gain, and yet is today still freely obtained. It is suggested that an incentive system is needed to encourage the conservation of traditional knowledge, and to stimulate its transfer into the modern domain of specialized knowledge.

Legal innovations

A regime of rights for those who possess or control indigenous knowledge appears to be the logical approach to protecting the society's interests in indigenous knowledge. The idea of farmers' rights for the communities with ethnobotanical information has already been mooted. This approach aims to protect the interests of farmers whose knowledge ends up benefiting collectors of *in situ* genetic resources.

The basic proposition here is that since the appropriators of knowledge are going to privatize it, those from whom it is taken should be paid for it.

But this scheme is not just intended to ensure fair procedure for acquisition of knowledge. The other advantage in the arrangement is that indigenous knowledge must be transferred either into the public domain, or the domain of specialized private knowledge, if it is to be conserved. Otherwise it will be lost. An incentive mechanism will encourage those with the knowledge to part with it.

In addition to farmers' rights, therefore, healers' rights may also be mooted, for those with a special knowledge of medicinal plants. They too must be rewarded for their peculiar knowledge, in order that conservation of medicinal plants may be better carried out. Already suggestions to this effect have been deposited in the Industrial Property Act which defines utility models in such a way as to include herbal and nutritional formulations. However, the application is limited to formulations previously not available in Kenya. This provision has the potential to be expanded to cover certain aspects of indigenous knowledge.

Conclusion

The most important inference to be drawn from this chapter is that the current legal arrangements are not conducive to the survival of indigenous knowledge, and are ill-adapted to protect the legitimate interests of communities in traditional medicine and genetic conservation. The law may also be said to place strictures on conservation efforts through an over-emphasis on individually-held property rights in land. Customary practices and the indigenous knowledge which they embody are not threatened with extinction. This is due to the steady undermining of traditional resource management systems by the bias of colonial and post-colonial legal regimes towards exclusive private ownership of land. While revision of intellectual property laws to accommodate indigenous knowledge will be an important step, the first concern should be to ensure that the traditional natural resource management systems in which indigenous knowledge has life and meaning are strengthened.

Given the fact that the legal basis for the erosion of customary practices is founded on particular constitutional provisions, it is an urgent matter to revisit this document and make the necessary amendments. It is suggested that the doctrine of customary use be used as a starting point in this review. Of particular relevance here is Chapter IX of the Constitution dealing with trust land as well as Section 75 dealing with property. Amendments based on the doctrine of customary use can lead to adjustments in other relevant Acts of Parliament, as discussed above.

Notes

1. Walsh, 1993.
2. Biotechnology-based pharmaceuticals are defined as recombinant protein drugs, recombinant vaccines and monoclonal antibodies (including therapeutic MAbs and imaging agents). For details, see Bienz-Tadmor, 1993.
3. Spalding, 1993, p. 768.
4. Principle, 1989a, pp. 1–17.
5. Medicinal plants contribute to the pharmaceutical industry in at least three ways: through constituents isolated and used directly; by providing the base materials for the synthesis of drugs; and by providing natural products which serve as models for the synthesis of pharmacologically active compounds.
6. More than 50 drugs which exhibit anti-cancer properties are not marketed because of adverse effects but continue to be widely used in research.
7. Gupta, 1993, p. 29.
8. Lemma, 1991.
9. Aliro, O.K. 1993, pp. 5–6. Further research has shown that *endod* also controls the zebra mussel (*Dreisena polymorpha*) which causes damage to water utilities in the US and Canada.
10. It takes about 53 tonnes of dry leaves to make 100 grammes of vincristine which is worth about US$220,000 per kilogramme.
11. The estimated value of human life is an underestimate because people tend to place a higher value on reducing risks that are deemed involuntary.
12. Principle, 1991, p. 108. For more details on this aspect of risk analysis, see Violetta and Chestnut, 1986.
13. See, for example, Elisabetsky and Nunes, 1990. Some 120 plant-derived prescription drugs used worldwide come from just 95 species. It is estimated that only about 5,000 of the 250,000 species of flowering plants have had their medicinal potential tested in laboratories. For further details, see Lewington, 1990.
14. Reid (1994) defines biodiversity prospecting as "the exploration of biodiversity for commercially valuable genetic and biochemical resources" (p. 241). For details see Reid, 1994.
15. DiMasi, *et al.* 1991.
16. Alper, 1993, p. 150.
17. Sears, 1992.
18. Principle, 1991, p. 92.
19. McKenna, 1993.
20. This figure assumes one "lead" in 10,000 chemicals and a discount rate of 5%.
21. Davis, *et al.*, 1993.
22. Sasson, 1992, p. 35.
23. Emmett, 1992.
24. See the definition by Friedmann, 1973.
25. See The Constitution of Kenya, Section 75 (see Appendix I).
26. Lawson, 1958, p. 87. See also Hollowell, 1973, p. 16.
27. For a discussion of these methods, see Paton and Derham 1972, pp. 532–52.
28. See McAuslan, 1975, Chapter 3.
29. Okoth-Owiro, 1990.
30. de Klemm, 1989.
31. de Klemm, 1989, p. 50.

32. The incidents of ownership include eleven subrights: "These are the right to possess; the right to use; the right to manage; the right to income; the right to capital; the right to security; the incident of transmissibility (the right to pass on property to one's successors); the incident of absence of term (the right to hold onto property forever, if one lived forever); the prohibition of harmful use; the liability to prosecution (property may be taken to cover debts); and residuary rights (full rights to property after other limited interests in it cease)." Shrader-Frechette, 1993, p. 227.
33. See Juma, 1989a, Chapter 5; Okoth-Owiro, 1990, 20–22.
34. Chapter 385, *Laws of Kenya*. For a detailed discussion of the legal regime on conservation of plants, see Okoth-Owiro, 1989b.
35. WHO, 1976, p. 1.
36. WHO, 1976, p. 4. See also Good and Kimani, 1980, p. 303.
37. IDRC, 1980, pp. 6–7.
38. Reported by Farnsworth, 1985.
39. Principle, 1989b; Balandrin, 1985.
40. Ayensu, 1983.
41. Ampofo and Johnson–Romauld, *op. cit.* p.3.
42. Okoth-Owiro, 1989b.
43. See Juma, 1989a, pp. 63–64; and Okoth-Owiro, 1989b.
44. There are powers for control of importation of seeds and plants in various plant statutes. But these powers are intended to control plant diseases and maximize agricultural production.
45. Juma, *et al.*, 1995. See also Sánchez and Juma, 1990.

PART IV

PRIVATE PROPERTY, ENVIRONMENT AND CONSTITUTIONAL CHANGE

Towards ecological jurisprudence

12

J.B. OJWANG WITH CALESTOUS JUMA

Introduction

The relationship between land tenure and sustainable development in Kenya suggests that the current laws relating to property embody certain principles which are in conflict with the need to promote sustainable development. This potential conflict raises concern because Kenya has committed itself to promoting sustainable development. It has done so internationally by signing and ratifying various international agreements, and nationally by reflecting these goals of sustainable development in its national plans. But the implementation of the goals is likely to be hampered by the prevalence of a property regime whose philosophical underpinnings do not reflect the importance of incorporating ecological principles into development activities.

This chapter starts from the premise that the legal doctrines that guide Kenya's property rights system do not adequately reflect ecological principles, and as such they are likely to undermine efforts to implement sustainable development objectives. As Ackerman says, "it will be impossible to resolve the legal issues without confronting, and resolving as best we can, our philosophical perplexities."[1] And so, this chapter starts with a brief review of the concept of "sustainable development" and follows it with an assessment of the meaning and social function of jurisprudence. The third section of the chapter presents the relationship between the private property paradigm and environmental management, underscoring the limitations of conventional legal doctrines in dealing with the sustainable management of scarce resources. The last section presents options for incorporating ecological principles into the property paradigm.

Sustainable development and law

The phrase "sustainable development" is becoming so overworked that it risks being a mere cliché. Development "involves a progressive transformation of economy and society."[2] But this transformation can be done at the expense of the environment and will likely have only short-term gains. The concept of sustainable development, as articulated in *Our Common Future*, the report of the World Commission on Environment and Development, has been developed to provide a framework for implementing development objectives in such a way as to meet the needs of current generations without undermining the ability of future ones to meet theirs. In more concrete terms, sustainable development is concerned with the condition of life of humankind, in the context of the environment. The global plan of work from the 1992 UN Conference on Environment and Development has elaborated many of the functional aspects of achieving this.

Goulet has followed recent attempts to come to terms with the essence of development, and he remarks that an adequate definition ought to incorporate five elements: (i) an economic component dealing with the creation of wealth and improved material conditions of life; (ii) a social ingredient, measured as well-being in health, education, housing and employment; (iii) a political dimension, embodying values such as human rights, political freedom, enfranchisement, and some form of democracy; (iv) a cultural dimension, in recognition of the fact that cultures confer identity and self-worth to people; and (v) the "full-life paradigm", which is concerned with the ultimate meanings of life and history, as expressed in symbols and beliefs.[3] These elements, however, have to be perceived in the context of a world with fragile ecological systems and limited means to avail natural resources and absorb the waste associated with economic transformation.

In order to enhance the economic component of development, a people must have recourse to environmental resources. If the demographic condition, or the tempo of economic activity outstrips these resources, the people will, in seeking an improvement to their material condition, overrun the resources and undermine their very existence. An already improved economic condition, such as that which has been realized by a high degree of industrialization, will facilitate the process and mode of recourse to the environmental resources, with the result that relatively high returns are realized. But at the same time, high degrees of sophistication in economic production will release into the environment harmful wastes and energies, which the natural ecosystem cannot absorb and these will impair the existing social and biological amenities.

A distortion of the relationship between population levels and the quantity and quality of natural resources, will reduce essential supplies for humankind and will thus undermine biological survival, as well as the various social aspects of life, including health, housing, education and others. The release of deleterious matter from the process of economic production will also impair the environment and compromise human health and other social conditions. Imbalances between population levels and available resources, or between economic production and the absorptive capacity of ecosystems will impair human health and disrupt other social situations, ultimately having political consequence. These may compromise human rights, political freedom and democracy.[4]

Any development activity which undermines natural resources may disrupt important cultural dimensions of social systems. The norms, symbols and beliefs of rural communities will be found to originate in times past, when life's meaning and its expressions largely derived from the interplay between the human being and the natural environment, as discussed in the preceding chapters. Hence depletion of natural resources is bound to reduce the material basis of local culture and hence of traditional knowledge.

The dominant development approaches in Africa in general, and in Kenya in particular, owe their origins to historical processes which emanated from the industrialized countries. The industrial revolution, which is the main source of the current patterns of development, started when there was relative abundance of natural resources in Europe and abroad. In those circumstances, the enhancement of economic and material conditions was advanced to a comparably sophisticated level, without parallel preoccupation with environmental management. The economic system then prevailing attracted protective philosophies, notably utilitarianism, which were associated with *positivist legal doctrines*. The jurisprudence of the utilitarian era was built on liberalism and individualism. Its doctrines, it is worthy of note, still provide the baseline of legal and judicial systems in the industrialized countries of the North. These same doctrines are also dominant in the "official sector" of the developing countries. In order to understand the relationship between property rights and sustainable development, it is important to re-examine the meaning and social function of jurisprudence.

Meaning and social function of jurisprudence

Theoretical foundations

Jurisprudence, in its essence, was defined by Salmond as "the name given to a certain type of investigation into law, an investigation of an abstract, general and theoretical nature which seeks to lay bare the essential principles of law and legal systems."[5] As jurisprudence "is without rules, [and] allows a far greater play to the writer's own personal approach [as compared to the typical legal subject such as contract or tort]"[6], it may be thought that its contribution to a practical situation, such as sustainable development, could not but be limited. But, as Salmond states: "In jurisprudence . . . we are concerned . . . to reflect on the nature of legal rules, on the underlying meaning of legal concepts and on the features of a legal system."[7] The most direct aspects of law consist in authoritative sources that govern behaviour, and bind or empower juridical institutions in one way or another. But, in what way does one determine the nature or characteristics of such authority? The question belongs to jurisprudence, which covers the authority of the operative law, and provides the intellectual explanation and justification of the doctrines that shape the operative juridical approaches.[8] As Salmond notes, "one of the tasks of jurisprudence is to construct and elucidate organizing concepts serving to render the complexities of law more manageable and more rational; and in this way theory can help to improve practice."[9] Cotterrell defines jurisprudence as "the term most often used to refer to the whole range of actual and possible inquiries concerned in one way or another, with the broader significance of law."[10]

All the definitions of jurisprudence leave little doubt that its preoccupation is with the prevailing juridical doctrines; and these doctrines need not always have rational cause, and may indeed be formed around deep-seated ideologies, dogmas or even taboos which have gained dominance in the cultural setting. This perception has been underscored by Kerruish in *Jurisprudence as Ideology*, in which she says that "the analysis and explanation of jurisprudence reveals a special phenomenon, which I call rights fetishism."[11]

She continues:

> Rights fetishism is constituted by legal practices which regulate and adjudicate particular enterprises and disputes by use of general rules. What seems to happen is that *these general rules somehow cast loose their moorings as deliberately formulated standards for human action and float off to constitute a realm of the sacred. From within this realm, the mundane activities of lawyers, judges, and legislators become invested with a meaning and significance which goes beyond any down-to-earth account of what they are doing.*[12]

The emphasis placed on Kerruish's language will serve later to stress the point that the more practical concerns of life such as environmental conservation, generally call for regulatory norms of a relatively flexible kind—not norms endowed with fixed, sacred legal principles dating back to stages of development long since passed. Such novelties cannot always be reconciled with the old-style rights. There is a vast scope for jurisprudential rethinking and reform.

Social function of jurisprudence

There may not have been any firm legal theory in the social-conflict situations occurring in the communal social settings of pre-colonial Africa. Numerous studies[13] have demonstrated that in the pragmatic institutional arrangements of these societies, and especially given the dominance of the oral tradition of retaining and using information in such societies, there would have been little occasion to be preoccupied with jurisprudence, in the sense of "the practical study of law [and] the theoretical inquiry into the nature and foundations of law itself."[14] The overriding concern of dispute settlement (and the specific detail of this varied from the more hierarchical to the less hierarchical societies[15]) was mutual accommodation of all parties, and the preservation of good neighbourliness. In the words of Hamnett: "The principal goal of the procedures is to restore the social peace, rather than to impose on a reluctant defendant a set of obligations (to compensate, to repay a debt, to fulfill an undertaking) derived from an abstract calculation of universal liabilities."[16]

The same informality and pragmatism marked also the subject of access to vital resources of life such as agricultural or pastoral land, water supply, trees and vegetation. Land has been and still is the primary resource in the struggle for a livelihood in Africa. On this account customary law traditions evolved which treated land as the entitlement of all people, so that each family's right was only a right of access. On this point Hamnett thus states with reference to the position in Lesotho: "The fundamental principle of both the administration and the tenure of land in Lesotho is that 'the land belongs to the nation' (*mobu ke oa sechaba*)."[17] And with such a pronouncement the concern over common property resources acquired particular significance.

The cardinal underpinnings of legal rules in such societies are essentially pragmatic and specific to the local mode of production, and clearly not on the same plane as the dispute resolution concepts which for centuries evolved in the Western world. Jurisprudential thought in regard to Western legal practices, and that in relation to the pre-industrial African society, thus must take different approaches. Unfortunately the universalization of Western political traditions has unavoidably brought a major conflict and cultural dilemma to the doors of African social, cultural, and legal institutions. The juxtaposition of the small-scale economy and its trappings, with ideas and phenomena of the international market has unsettled the traditional systems.

Thus in practically all African countries there is a plural legal system in which property concepts are in conflict, rules of access to natural resources are set in competition, and the moral principles which had shaped the norms of access to primary resources such as land, now stand to question and cannot always claim validity. All the manifestations of such clashes of doctrines are evident in vital matters such as those governed by family laws, inheritance laws and land use laws. But at bottom, the conflict is a cultural one; all the new ideas represent a new culture, which seeks to negate and displace the old cultures that had been born of a different economy and society. No clear and immediate choice can be made between the two sets of values, because the transitional interface coincides with large-scale day-to-day practices which cannot be dropped off abruptly. The situation is thus evolutionary.

It has often been argued that traditional laws and institutions have in the past had the merit, over and above modern ones, of living in harmony with nature; and thus they had more scope for stabilizing ecosystems. This is probably true, though for reasons that were inevitable—rather than on account of original virtuous design. Not endowed with large-scale technological advance, the traditional society derived its survival needs directly from the fauna, flora, land and its resources. It was therefore essential that the use of such resources be managed so as to ensure present and future utility. And with relatively low populations it was quite feasible to keep the bulk of human activities integrated with natural processes. Indeed, the retention of this relationship became so central to the communities that often they had cultural and legal practices and doctrines incorporating tenets of conservation.[18]

Modern society came through fundamental changes and revolutions, which in the course of time, altered the equation of parity between humankind and natural resources. In this regard one may cite the industrial revolution in Europe, with its attendant technological changes and global command of natural resources, as the most critical factor in the introduction of a new world, with new kinds of social conflicts. In the train of the changed economic system—which put in place a world market, colonial empires, new approaches to the conduct of international relations, and a new body of international law built on the foundations of the domestic laws of the industrialized nations—many achievements came about that changed the relationship between human beings and their environment.

Modern social conflict, as it is known in the industrialized countries, has been reduced to the political and legal framework of solutions. The political framework establishes a basis of interest representation, through lobbies and political parties right up to the supreme law-making body. The laws of parliament then fall to the judicial systems, which are guided by structured procedures of fact assessment, by established legal principles, and by refined, justificatory legal doctrines shaped within the field of jurisprudence. The industrial revolution brought about a new society; and as Unger says: "Each society reveals through its law the innermost secrets of the manner in which it holds men together."[19]

The industrial revolution accentuated the atomization of people as collective groups. Employment in industry and industrial services, and in work attendant on industrial life, broke communities apart; and people came to live in places of work, and to regulate their relationships with employers and others on the basis of contract, tort, criminal sanctions and other legal practices. Urban life, by its targeted pattern of allocation of resources, brought substantial independence to individuals and families. This pattern of individualization was in line with social and intellectual trends which had been evolving for many years. Law became the basis of dispute settlement; and the operationalization of law rested with the judicial authorities, which were guided by legal doctrines developed by scholars of jurisprudence.

In the industrialized society's atomized social conditions, relationships involving persons are processed under specific legal concepts, which ultimately rest on the cardinal principles of right and duty. The broad concepts of "agreement" or "consensus" break down into agreements which create, transfer or extinguish rights.[20] Those which create rights are either contracts or grants. A contract creates a right or obligation only between those party to it. Torts constitute another major basis of obligation at common law. These are civil wrongs whose remedy is an action for damages. A tort arises by the general operation of law, rather than from a source based on some agreement.[21]

Contracts, torts and other juridical bases of right and obligation, are the subject of an elaborate body of common law principles, the main yardsticks of which are traceable to *property law*. So complex are the technicalities of these aspects of law, that they are the basis of a large body of jurisprudential doctrine. This jurisprudence, which today forms part of the received body of law in many countries, has its home and its ideology in Anglo-American territory. To quote Kerruish: "A condition of production of any text in philosophical jurisprudence is the jurisprudence of a developed system of legal doctrine. Doctrine is learned within the context of national legal system. English, United States, and Australian law are relevant in this way . . . . They are all called common law systems."[22]

Such is the scenario which represents a continuum, from the small-scale traditional society in Africa, with its informal procedures of conflict settlement, to the relatively impersonal industrial society with its right-duty basis of conflict settlement, and back mid-way to attempted mixes of the two sys-

315

tems in colonial and post-colonial Africa. Such a scenario will have major implications for the relationship between humankind and natural resources. The gains of the industrial revolution brought certain major improvements to human life, and the agricultural societies of Africa which have benefited from these, have substantially increased in population; but it has had the effect of changing the relationship between people and natural resources. The very same technical improvements of the industrialized countries have brought about a world market that rests largely on economic motivations, at the expense of the environment.

The examples set by the industrialized countries have introduced a market factor in public policy in Africa which detracts from the principle of maintaining ecological well-being. The resulting jurisprudential mixes have taken away the doctrinal basis of ecological well-being which may have existed in Africa in the pre-colonial period. Legal doctrines founded on the sanctity of property rights, which now form an important element in the governing public laws in Africa, are inherently inconsistent with new, ecological thought. Hence the need to re-examine jurisprudence in the light of the growing recognition that sustainable development is dependent on ecological well-being, even more than it would benefit from market incentives.

The property paradigm and environment

Africa's received legal tradition reflects the Euro-American intellectual and cultural heritage, and economic system and its values. But this legal tradition has its own theoretical characteristics. Its operative jurisprudence is built around *right* and *duty*—concepts which, in their turn, rest firmly on the property paradigm. Property values, in this respect, are seen as the most concrete expression of the market economy which is cherished as the ideal plan of national and international purpose.

This point is poignantly addressed by Neumann:

A competitive society requires general laws as the highest form of purposive rationality, for such a society is composed of a large number of entrepreneurs of about equal economic power. Freedom of the commodity market, freedom of the labour market, free entrance into the entrepreneurial class, freedom of contract, and rationality of judicial responses in disputed issues—these are the essential characteristics of an economic system which requires and desires the production of profit, and ever renewed profit, in a continuous, rational, capitalistic enterprise.[23]

The principle thus stated contains the guiding philosophy which common law jurisprudence has tapped to formulate more precise rules for the resolution of social disputes. The property interest is a calculation derived from the traditional liberal philosophy; and "[the] classical liberal conception of property embraces a number of broad aspects of indicia, often condensed to three: the exclusive rights to possession, use and disposition."[24] The courts, the most critical institution in the resolution of disputes, will give a hearing only on the basis of a right-to-be-heard that is founded on property interest:

> Property is an essential foundation of all legal systems. The relationships between man and things, the rights in relation to property, vary in different juridical contexts, such as inheritance, possession, finding, tort. *It is these rights that are the traditional subject matter of litigation and are the defined and precise tools most easily used by the judiciary.* Consequently, in establishing an interest in *locus standi* issues, rights arising from property often serve as the measurement of such an interest.[25]

The contours of legal doctrine in Anglo-American jurisprudence have been built on the rigid foundation of property; and property itself inheres in an overriding and long-standing economic philosophy of capitalism and a belief in the forces of profit and the free market. It is held that property rights, especially where they are freely traded, would create the incentives needed to facilitate the efficient utilization of natural resources. Property rights are the basis of stable legal criteria, and of professional work in the Western juridical domain. It is these fixed landmarks that one must address if one is to relate the current tradition of jurisprudence to the relatively new subject of environmental management. Whether or not environmental interests can be made part of the day-to-day social and economic transactions must depend on the doctrinal setting of the operative legal order, and on whether or not it will accommodate the concerns of environmental protection. Indeed, the fixed points of traditional Western jurisprudence do pose the greatest challenge to the now generally-accepted principles of environmental management.

The position of indigenous societies, with regard to the value attaching to environmental resources, is a pragmatic and organic one in a social sense; it does not, unlike under modern deep ecology, emanate from any romantic, or new intellectual perspectives. In the pre-industrial era there was hardly any alternative to total dependence on natural resources; and hence the emergence of cultural orientations that placed environmental values at the very centre of social activity.

Indigenous society's position on environmental values led to a distinct approach to the law relating to land and other natural resources. It is an approach resting on the principle of "the commons", and which, therefore, is entirely antithetical to the fundamental doctrines of Western property law. The approach may be thus summarized: Land cannot be appropriated and owned by any particular person; it can be attributed to a group, such as a clan or tribe, but ultimately the governing principle is *access* to that land. A person, a family or other collective group can have only limited interests in, or usufructuary rights over the land but no more as a general rule.

In a significant sense, the relationship that had existed between people and nature, in the distant past, is either no longer true, or is rapidly becoming anachronistic. The forces of the market have severely undermined the old relationships between people and natural resources. The death of custom, with its ecological underpinnings, and its replacement by a new set-up built on positive law, is well depicted by Jenkins: "As human groups become sufficiently large, complex and diversified, they suffer an erosion of the cohesion and stability that they formerly had. Men find themselves in novel situations and relationships that are not covered by common usage. Private interests diverge and conflict. In short, to borrow from Bagehot's phrase, the cake of custom crumbles. *As this occurs, the apparatus of positive law is created . . .* "[26]

The positive law that has been put in place since the advent of colonialism in Kenya, however, has had a less organic genesis than that described by Jenkins. It has constantly entailed two basic problems for environmental resources. Firstly, the many statutes which have been passed in relation to environmental resources either rest on basic principles of English common law, or merely reproduce English legislation, with only nominal modifications. As a result, such laws are built upon traditional common law jurisprudence, with its foundations on right, duty, privilege, no-right—concepts which have evolved under conditions of deep-seated individualism. The liberal origins of such legislation are distinctly inconsistent with the communal framework of environmental management in the pre-colonial period. And as there is bound to be a rather long time-lapse before the liberal social order can have full application in Africa, it follows that the mere adoption of received laws cannot at once provide a reliable scheme for the protection of environmental resources.

The second problem with the positive law being enacted in Kenya is that much of it deals with the environment as incidental to the pursuit of goals of economic production. Besides, such laws have a sectoral character, and each addresses itself to a separate environmental component, such as agriculture, health, forests and water. But there is no integral management system. Kenyan scholars have been making a case for a better scheme of legislation, which comprises a streamlined body of sectoral laws, operating in the context of a central framework law, that establishes an institution with ultimate authority for standard-setting and guidance in matters of environmental management. But as things stand, there is scope for a multiplicity of environmental jurisdictions which do not work to any common purpose. This lack of a definite management tool for natural resources has taken it out of the power of the public authorities to implement a consistent programme of environmental protection. Vital legislative procedures, such as those relating to environmental impact assessment, are missing, and so any successful measure of environmental protection will be of a purely anecdotal character and will hardly ever be part of the organized initiatives of the state.

The received common law, and its supporting legislative measures, have introduced the very notions of private property that are part of the Western tradition. When such principles are applied to land and its resources, the state's scope for taking appropriate measures of environmental management is considerably qualified. The Constitution incorporates the Western legal doctrine on property rights. Section 75 states: "No property of any description shall be compulsorily taken possession of, and no interest in or right over property of any description shall be compulsorily acquired . . .", subject to narrow and closely defined exceptions. To be sure, some of these exceptions could plausibly justify acquisition in the cause of environmental management. The most relevant exceptions here are, firstly, that of section 75(1)(a) of the Constitution, which states that a "taking of possession" will be within the law where it "is necessary in the interest of . . . public health, town and country planning or the development or utilization of property so as to promote the public benefit."

Secondly, any taking of possession or acquisition, effected within the limiting conditions prescribed, shall not be regarded as being inconsistent with the guaranteed property rights, where "it is reasonably necessary . . . because the property in question is in a dangerous state injurious to the health of human beings, animals or plants."[27] And thirdly, such acquisition, so long as it complies with the limiting conditions, is not to be treated as being inconsistent with the guaranteed rights where (and for so long only as may be necessary) it is effected "for the purpose of the carrying out thereon of work of soil conservation or the conservation of other natural resources or work relating to agricultural development or improvement (being work relating to the development or improvement that the owner or occupier of the land has been required, and has without reasonable excuse refused or failed, to carry out) . . ."[28]

However, it will be noted that the first of the "enabling" bases for environmental management set out above is cast in broad and laconic terms, and in this form, it is unlikely to be seen by the courts as establishing the legal criteria that can, in practice, override the deep-seated property rights entrenched in legal doctrine. The other "enabling" bases both have a highly qualified and dependent scope which cannot justify large-scale initiatives of environmental management. The taking of property because it is "in a dangerous state" is only a remedial measure, and would not confer upon the state a sufficiently broad and clear mandate to take major environmental decisions. In the same way the state can only take possession of private property for conservation reasons, for a limited period and only where the property holder had previously been required to take such conservation actions but he or she had refused.

These three means by which the state may take possession of property or rights over property is a strictly limited discretion that is considerably qualified by the doctrines of eminent domain and police power. The Constitution, moreover, even qualifies the essential principles recognized under police power, for it creates open areas of dispute by stipulating that even such taking as may be based on a claimed public interest, is only legal where "the necessity therefor is such as to afford reasonable justification for the causing of hardship that may result to any person having an interest in or right over the property."[29]

Furthermore, the taking can only be valid if it is done by virtue of a law that provides for "the prompt payment of full compensation."[30] Any taking thus runs through such a dense thicket of obstacles built on juridical doctrine, that in practice the legal machinery in place is not fully available as a mechanism of environmental management. Moreover, the judiciary's operational rules and the general administration of justice are based on doctrines that uphold the sanctity of property; any major departure from that orientation can only be seen as revolutionary and thus unacceptable.

There is thus no question that the received law and its accompanying doctrines, which are in substance reaffirmed in the Constitution, as well as the established methods of juridical work, have placed firm fetters on the governmental scope for regulation of private property interests. It is equally plain however, that official practices have hardly ever sought nor achieved ecologically-oriented controls on such rights. Indeed, governmental operations have even further enhanced the dominance of private-property values, by randomly taking away property interests from ecologically sensitive public lands, and vesting these in private owners, who then have proceeded to claim the protections of Section 75 of the Constitution, as well as benefiting from the well-worn common law doctrines. Excisions of forested areas, and even animal reserve sanctuaries have taken place on the fringes of national parks gazetted forests and these have been turned into private property.

It is ironic that the sanctity of property rights enshrined in the constitution is not accompanied by equally firm provisions regarding the ceding of ground in the public environmental domain, to private rights. Wildlife sanctuaries and forest areas, though protected by legislation, are easily converted to private property and passed on to individuals—a problem not within the concerns of traditional jurisprudence. Traditional legal doctrine sanctifies the property rights of the individual against the state, but perceives hardly any objection to the individuals appropriating more and more property rights at the expense of the public's larger interest in environmental resources as the common property of all. A clear recognition of the public's interest and of its rights of participation in the management of environmental resources would dictate the formulation of safeguards for the public domain *against the private domain*.

Such safeguards will be essential for protecting, in the public interest, ecological features such as watersheds which are critical to the survival of certain communities. As things now stand such areas can legally be turned into private property by mere ministerial discretion, which is not subject to justifiable or indeed any control procedure. In most cases such discretionary measures are taken without any impact survey, without due consideration of ecological issues, and often they are taken primarily on the basis of political criteria. Just as there is an urgent need to review the governing principles and the rules of property rights, so there is a pressing case to re-examine the manner in which ministerial discretion is exercised in relation to the allocation of public land.

If unyielding notions of the sanctity of property rights settle in Kenya as part of the recognized legal doctrine, state competence in environmental conservation retained in fulfillment of public trust will have been considerably compromised. This will be particularly so in those situations where the private property rights domain tends to expand at the expense of the public domain. But it is arguable that, given the state of knowledge of ecological processes, and the current concerns about the environment, a valid basis today exists for major policy changes that would modify the scheme of private rights and enlarge the basis of environmental regulation. Changes of this kind would tend to set a new balance between private and public rights and limit the expansion of the private domain at the expense of the public interest. They could lead to the development of new jurisprudential approaches based on the special characteristics of environmentally-inspired public interests.

Such a proposition must be expected to lead to serious objections. The main objection, perhaps, will be that the state authorities entrusted with such regulatory powers are apt to overstretch their mandate, and to undermine the vital inner core of private rights that sustain the normal functioning of civil society. This objection is likely to lead to concerns about current assumptions underlying the political order. To accommodate such practical matters, it will be necessary to establish safeguards for the private interest, as the state takes measures to safeguard the public interest. Such a safeguard can, at the administrative level, take the form of a public inquiry, or a tribunal hearing. Where a tribunal is used to determine any claims in conflict, provision should be made for an appeal to the high court.

In the present circumstances, legal doctrines that for centuries crystallized around private interests, have continued to serve as the organizing framework for juridical institutions, processes and thought. The consequence has been that the increasingly critical demands of the public domain cannot be adequately accommodated within the mechanisms of the legal order. This historical condition constitutes, perhaps, the main dilemma confronting current national and international endeavours to realize the goals of sustainable development. The way forward will require that ecological principles are integrated into jurisprudence, to create a new balance between property rights, on the one hand, and the public trust on the other.

Towards ecological jurisprudence

Law and jurisprudence

Law, which is the most sacrosanct category of social-regulatory norms, is established through a repeated course of human activity. Recurrence in such activity proves the functional utility of the usage, elicits the popular acquiescence, confers an aura of reverence, and consecrates the usage into law. But this is true only of evolved, or custom-based law. In the alternative, top-down institutional methods may be used to stamp particular norms with the impress of law. Most laws in this category are dictated by policy issues that reflect the dominant economic, social and political interests in the society.

Although the originating factors in law-making thus remain *social*, the law—especially where it has evolved over long durations and has come to guide the work of formal institutions, and also where it is created by hierarchical institutional processes—often evolves sharp doctrinal characteristics that tend to isolate it from the pattern of everyday values and priorities. One would, in such cases, get the impression that the law has acquired a certain independence from ordinary social values. This is the mark of Western law, which has been explicated by jurisprudents as if it was entirely autonomous from the ordinary social system.[31] The establishment of this approach was directed mainly by the fundamental notions of the liberal philosophy, which rested primarily on property values.[32]

Unlike the traditional African system of law, whose more flexible structure readily accommodated environmental values, the received European legal systems, and their attendant theories, have been preoccupied with private law rights rather than broader public interests such as the environment. Thus Denman maintains: "Property rights in land or rights analogous to them are, in the last analysis, the only power by which men can execute positive plans for the use of land and natural resources."[33] The effect is to subject all possible legal bases of natural resource protection to the doctrinal framework of private law rights—in particular private property rights. And Denman cautions us that there is no room for a jurisprudence of public interests, such as environmental interests! To move from this position towards ecological jurisprudence, it is important to understand some of the principles of ecological systems and how they relate to law.

Ecological principles

One of the problems of the dominant jurisprudence is that it was formulated at a time when ecological concerns were unknown and resources were abundant. One of the main issues at the time was how to create incentives that would facilitate the efficient allocation and utilization of natural resources. This utilitarian approach, of course, treated all ecological concerns as being external to the process of economic transformation, and natural resources were seen as infinite. Modern thinking, however, recognizes the importance of internalizing the ecological impacts of economic activities.

Furthermore, ecological systems are no longer seen as mere sources of natural material for economic utility, but they provide services which cannot be assessed in monetary or quantitative terms. These ecological services include improvement of air and water quality, hydrological circulation, soil generation, nutrient recycling, waste assimilation, crop pollination and pest control. Since these services are an essential aspect of the public interest, land and other resources cannot be viewed strictly in terms of their value as private property.

These services are not rendered through the independent operation of isolated parts of the ecosystem. They are a product of the complex interactions between its various parts. The manner in which these parts interact is little known to humankind. The ignorance about the interactions in ecosystems has resulted in the recognition of the *precautionary principle*. The ignorance is compounded by the fact that ecological processes are time-dependent and unpredictable. Disruptions in the ecology could take a long time before showing any serious damage. And when the effects are realized, they may be in places far removed from the original source of the disruption.

Another critical aspect of ecological processes is that they are not linear. Small changes in the ecological system could result in major disruptions with extensive impacts. In this regard, what may be seen as a minor nuisance may be the making of a major ecological disaster. In addition, these impacts are often irreversible and irreducible. When new organisms enter the environment, they create new processes that cannot be reversed and such impacts cannot be reduced to monetary value. The loss of biological diversity, for example, is both irreversible and irreducible. The dominant legal doctrines assume that ecological processes can be easily reversed through technological intervention or restoration practices and can be converted to monetary units.

The fact that natural resources are finite creates constraints that lie outside the domain of law. Even where natural resources are thought to be abundant, there is still the problem of finding sinks for the waste originating from their processing. In other cases, the limits may be in the form of sensitive natural features such as the ozone layer whose depletion has serious consequences for life on earth. Although environmental awareness is likely to create new political values which will in turn influence the direction of legislation, ecological imperatives require urgent attention, and the law cannot wait until politics charts the new path. The judicial system must be proactive.

Private property and ecological stewardship

There is a dominant belief, often influenced by economic theories, that the property paradigm can provide an effective basis upon which to equitably and efficiently allocate natural resources. This view is losing standing for a number of reasons. First, there is growing skepticism over the ability of property, contract and the free market to allocate resources efficiently and equitably. Various instruments—such as tradeable permits—designed to facilitate such allocation have run into operational and ethical difficulties. There is the view that the application of the property paradigm to natural resources has resulted in inequity and environmental pollution.

There is growing interest and support for the view that humankind must take responsibility for ecological stewardship. This is reinforced by a number of relevant factors. First, the complex interdependencies within and between ecosystems are becoming more appreciated, and as a result political and legal decisions can incorporate these factors. Absolutist "private property rules that attempt to treat natural resources as temporally and spatially bounded commodities make little sense."[34] Second, technological factors greatly enhance the ability of individuals to exploit natural resources, which increases the externalities associated with the process. Technological disparities have not only created disparities in the use of natural resources, but they have also generated inequalities in the distribution of the effects of industrial operations. This is illustrated, for example, by the dumping of industrial waste in poor neighbourhoods or countries. Market forces have not been very effective in dealing with inequities, and there is growing interest in the use of state intervention to correct the imbalances.

The growth in environmental awareness has resulted in the recognition that some natural resources are more critical to human welfare and ecological well-being than others. This is indeed, the first step in accepting the fact that natural resources are part of a larger ecological system that is essential for the survival of humankind. This view is starting to influence legal thought and resulting in efforts to incorporate ecological principles into decisions regarding private property.

An example from the United States, where the institution of property is an entrenched aspect of the juridical landscape, illustrates this evolution of property rights systems to take into account environmental consideration. The case in point, *Just* v. *Marinette County* involved wetlands on the property of Ronald and Kathryn Just in Wisconsin.[35] In 1965 the Wisconsin legislature passed a Water Quality Act that introduced shoreland regulation. In 1967 Marinette County adopted Shoreland Zoning Ordinance No. 24 which divided the shoreland into three categories: general purpose, general recreation, and conservancy districts. Certain uses of shorelands—wild crop harvesting, sustained yield forestry, transmission lines, hunting and fishing, preservation, hiking or riding rails, and wildlife raising—were expressly permitted. The ordinance also required permits for certain conditional uses which included farming, damming or relocation of water flow, filling, wetland drainage or dredging, removal of soil, cranberry bog operation, and building of piers, docks, or boathouses.

In 1961, the Justs had bought 36 acres of land near Lake Noquebay in the County, with over 2000 feet of lakefront. By 1967 they had subdivided and sold five parcels, retaining one, which fell under the "wetlands" category in the conservancy district. The use of this land for economic activity required a "Conditional Use Permit". The Justs began filling this land for use without a permit and were sued by the County for violating the ordinance. The Justs counter-sued on the basis that the law was unconstitutional. The trial court found them guilty and fined them US$100 but they took the matter to Wisconsin Supreme Court. It was the view of the court that the case represented a "conflict between the public interest in stopping the despoliation of natural resources, which . . . citizens until recently have taken as inevitable and for granted, and an owner's asserted right to use the property as he wishes."[36]

The court reviewed the matter and ruled in a manner that demonstrated the recognition of the importance of wetlands in general and of the ecology in particular:

What makes this case different from most condemnation or police power zoning cases is the interrelationship of the wetlands, the swamps and the natural environment of shorelands to the purity of the water and to such natural resources as navigation, fishing, and scenic beauty. Swamps and wetlands were once considered wasteland, undesirable, and not picturesque. But as the people become more sophisticated, an appreciation was acquired that swamps and wetlands serve a vital role in nature, as part of the balance of nature and are essential to the purity of the water in our lakes and streams. Swamps and wetlands are a necessary part of the ecological creation and now, even to the uninitiated, possess their own beauty of nature.[37]

The court specifically dealt with the issue of the supremacy of property rights over ecological functions when it asked: "Is the owner of a parcel of land so absolute [that he] can change its nature to suit any of his purposes?"[38] To this fundamental question, the court answered:

An owner of land has no absolute and unlimited right to change the essential natural character of his land so as to use it for a purpose for which it was unsuited in its natural state and which injures the rights of others. The exercise of the police power in zoning must be reasonable and we think it is not an unreasonable exercise for that power to prevent harm to public rights by limiting the use of private property to its natural uses.[39]

In this 1972 ruling, the court put emphasis on the natural use of the land, especially in relation to ecosystem services. These services, which are of interest to the public, could not be destroyed by virtue of private property rights. *Just* was a landmark decision that was followed by courts in Florida, South Carolina, New Hampshire and North Carolina. In a 1975 case, *Sibson* v. *New Hampshire*, the court argued that the denial for a permit to fill a marsh on private property was "not an appropriation of the property to a public use, but the restraint of an injurious private use . . ."[40] In *Sibson*, the court recognized that other uses of the marshland such as "wildlife observation, hunting, haying of marshgrass, clam and shellfish harvesting, and aesthetic purposes" had not been denied.[41] What was objected to, however, was the introduction of major changes in the marsh to enable the owner to "seek to make for speculative profit."[42]

But critics of this position have argued that the "normal bundle of property rights contains no priority for land in its natural condition; it regards use, including development, as one of the standard incidents of ownership."[43] And the courts "should view themselves less as the partner of co-equal branches of government, and more as the guardian of individual rights, property rights as well as civil rights."[44] The point, however, is that ecological concerns are creating situations where priorities on the use of land have to be established, calling for more environmental sensitivity when considering the various uses of land and the role of the police power.

Another significant case regarding ecological stewardship took place in 1983, *National Audubon Society* v. *Superior Court*, regarding Mono Lake), in California.[45] It held that established appropriative rights over water were still subject "to a duty of continuing supervision on the part of the state in order to protect the public trust in the state's waters."[46] The court prevented the city of Los Angeles from diverting water from streams that fed Mono Lake, on the ground that this was likely to diminish the value of the lake as a natural habitat. The significance of the case was that it established that natural resources could be used for multiple purposes to accommodate both economic and ecosystem values. It removed the simplistic approach to natural resource management which casts the issues in the form of a dichotomy, as in the case of "jobs *vs.* environment" or "people *vs.* wildlife".

The property paradigm has undergone significant evolution over the years to incorporate other concerns, and it is important that ecological considerations are give equal importance.[47] This accommodation is important because property regimes tend to become more relevant under conditions of scarcity, which is also the moment that conservation becomes more urgent. Under such circumstances, conflicts between property rights and sustainable use or conservation are likely to increase. The solution is to ensure that environmental considerations are reflected in revisions in property regimes.

The decisions considered above demonstrate that even in the United States, a country where private property rights are long settled, where indeed these rights have been perceived as "the guardian of every other right,"[48] the state machinery and the legal system can now treat it as perfectly reasonable that such rights be qualified by claims of the public interest. Although US court decisions on such matters are by no means unanimous,[49] and just as many cases have spoken unequivocally in support of private property rights, it is clear that the state institutions have come to recognize the unqualified importance of certain public interests which will sometimes be accorded primacy over private rights.

What, however, remains is for scholars to begin constructing new principles of law founded on *public law* foundations. This is a major challenge as it requires certain complex steps or processes: firstly, a recognition of the social limitations of private-law-based jurisprudence; secondly, the generation of new ideas built upon the dictates of the public interest; thirdly, the moderation of deep-seated socio-cultural ideologies; and fourthly the reconstruction of legal thought so as to accommodate past, present and future circumstances. Legal scholars need to hold themselves open to such new lines of inquiry; for in this way they may come up with improved legal frameworks for the pursuit of critical social goals.

It is paradoxical that the Kenyan juridical experience has had perhaps an even closer attachment to ancient Western doctrines, than that of the United States. The courts of Kenya, in the very limited number of environmental cases coming before them, are strictly guided by notions of the sacredness of property rights. In the main environmental case to have been decided by the Kenyan courts, *Wangari Maathai* v. *Kenya Times Media Trust*,[50] a public-spirited individual attempted to stop what she saw as a blatant violation of the public interest in the integrity and aesthetics of an urban recreation park. The defendant had set about constructing what was conceived as a 60-storey building, in the park. At common law, this kind of civil action is pursued by showing some irreparable damage or harm which is likely to arise, to the plaintiff's detriment. Maathai's case fell on the test of *locus standi*. It was held that for an individual to bring a suit against the proposed construction, he or she had to establish an injury to himself or herself, over and above the injury that would be occasioned to the general public; and consequently the only person with the competence to institute such proceedings is the attorney-general.

Although the decision was not explicit on the question whether a private citizen, though having no special interest in a matter of public interest, can institute proceedings on an environmental question, one may doubt, in the light of recent judicial approaches,[51] whether a plaintiff can easily get over the *locus standi* impediment.

It has to be recognized, of course, that a jurisprudence built around the terms and requirements of civil litigation cannot provide an ideal framework for environmental norms in a country such as Kenya, on account especially of the fact that litigation here lacks the spontaneity and frequency it has in the West. The prevailing state of poverty and lack of awareness, makes it difficult for the general public to use civil litigation as a device of environmental protection. Partly for this reason, Okidi proposes the establishment of an environmental ombudsman, as well as a special environmental tribunal. He observes:

> [O]ne of the critical considerations is that the machinery should be available to members of the public at no expense. The machinery should be equally available to the project proponents. Courts of law have the disadvantage of costs which will invariably deter members of the public from pressing for environmental action. Besides, the requirements of court procedures and processes are likely to be used by lawyers to frustrate actions on environmental matters.[52]

In the North as in the South, new lines of juristic thought must be cultivated, which duly recognize the primacy of the public interest, and especially the environmental interests. The task is still more arduous in the context of Southern countries, such as Kenya, which must also take into account the greater state of ferment in their social and cultural infrastructures.

Conclusion

This chapter has argued for the need to incorporate ecological principles into jurisprudence, in general, and into the property paradigm in particular. But this argument has a practical aspect to it. This incorporation can be given effect through constitutional provisions that emphasize the role of the government as the public trustee whose mandate clearly includes environmental management. The case for such a constitutional provision is to be seen in light of the pressure to promote the sustainable use of diminishing natural resources will require that a reasonable balance be maintained between the sanctity of property rights and the public interest. Access to natural resources, especially land, will continue to generate more conflicts, and it is important that the Constitution provides an innovative basis for preventing and resolving such conflicts.

Notes

1. Ackerman, 1977, p. 4.
2. WCED, 1987, p. 43.
3. Goulet, 1990, p. 38.
4. "Freedoms of conscience, expression, assembly, association and movement are meaningfully exercisable only by those who have health and life, in terms of [the] hierarchy of all vital freedoms," Okidi, 1994, p. 148.
5. Salmond, 1966, p. 1.
6. Salmond, 1966, p. 1.
7. Salmond, 1966, p. 1.
8. Salmond, 1966, p. 4.
9. Salmond, 1966, p. 4. See also Campbell, 1942, pp. 334–339.
10. Cotterrell, 1989, p. 2.
11. Kerruish, 1991.
12. Kerruish, 1991, p. 3 (emphases added).
13. See, for example, Gulliver, 1963; Gluckman, 1955; Fallers, 1969.
14. Campbell, 1942, p. 338.
15. Hamnett, 1975, pp. 9–23.
16. Hamnett, 1975.
17. Hamnett, 1975.
18 Mbiti, 1969, pp. 105–110.
19. Unger, 1977, p. 47.
20. Salmond, 1966, pp. 338–339.
21. Salmond, 1966, p. 453.
22. Kerruish, 1991, p. 81.
23. Neumann, 1953, p. 909.

24   Radin, 1988, p. 1667.
25.   Stein, 1979, p. 9 (emphasis added).
26.   Jenkins, 1980, p. 337 (emphasis added).
27.   S. 75(6)(v).
28.   S. 75(6)(vii).
29.   Constitution of Kenya, S. 75(1)(b)
30.   S. 75 (1) (c).
31.   Barrett and Yach, 1986, pp. 151–171; Hunt, 1988, pp. 146–164.
32.   Coval, Smith and Coval, 1986, pp. 457–475; Tawney, 1922.
33.   Denmann, 1969. In a similar vein, Coval, Smith and Coval say: "We argue that no charter could justifiably include the usual explicit rights and freedoms and not include the right of the individual to property since the latter is no less a condition of free action than are the former" (1986, p. 457).
34.   Lazarus, 1993, p. 199.
35.   [1972] 56 Wis. 2d NW 2d.
36.   Quoted in Hunter, 1988, p. 351.
37.   Hunter, 1988, p. 351.
38.   Hunter, 1988 p. 351–52.
39.   Hunter, 1988, p. 352.
40.   Hunter, 1988, p. 355.
41.   Hunter, 1988, p. 355.
42.   Hunter, 1988, p. 355.
43.   Epstein, 1985, p. 123.
44.   Paul, 1987, p. 266.
45.   [1983] 658 P.2d (Cal.).
46.   Sax, 1993, p. 147.
47.   Rose, 1990, pp. 577–594.
48.   Lee, 1775, quoted in Ely, p. 158.
49.   Ely, 1992; Paul and Dickman, 1989; Schultz, 1993, pp. 464–495; Bosselman, Callies and Bante, 1973.
50.   *Wangari Maathai* v. *Kenya Times Media Trust*, Nairobi High Ct. Civ. Cas. No. 5403 of 1989 (unrep.).
51.   *Kamanda v. Nairobi City Council*, Nairobi High Ct. Civ. Cas. No. 6153 of 1992 (unrep.).
52.   Okidi, 1994, p. 177.

Constitutional arrangements for environment and development

13

KENNETH K. ORIE

Introduction[1]

Over the past decade the goal of sustainable development has gained general acceptance,[2] yet how to achieve this objective is still subject to great debate. Measures designed to manage the environment which reflect its natural characteristics will undeniably be needed. Agenda 21, the programme of work adopted at the 1992 United Nations Conference on Environment and Development, states that:

> Laws and regulations suited to country-specific conditions are among the most important instruments for transforming environment and development policies into action . . . yet, although the volume of legal texts in this field is steadily increasing, much of the law-making in many countries seems to be ad hoc and piecemeal, or has not been endowed with the necessary institutional machinery and authority for enforcement and timely adjustment.[3]

On the legal front then, the challenge is that: "National and international law has traditionally lagged behind events. Today, legal regimes are rapidly outdistanced by the accelerating pace and expanding scale of impacts on the environmental base of development. Human laws must be reformulated to keep human activities in harmony with the unchanging and universal laws of nature."[4]

The case has been made in the previous chapters that constitutional arrangements for environmental management are crucial. The test here is whether such arrangements allow for environmental management in line with or in response to the natural continuum of the environment. The natural occurrence of water, air, land, ecosystems, vegetation and other natural resources does not correspond, in time and space, with political boundaries, whether internationally or intra-nationally. In other words, the environment of a given geo-political unit does not exist separately as well as independently of that of neighbouring geo-political units.

Furthermore, various components of the natural environment are constituted into a single whole in the sense of their interconnectedness. For example, air borne pollution would, over time, engage with precipitation to pollute water. Contaminated water pollutes animals and vegetation through the process of absorption. Rain on contaminated land could pollute surface water by runoff and groundwater by percolation. In addition, the dangers posed by deforestation, the greenhouse effect and the depletion of the ozone layer illustrate the indivisibility of the natural environment.

This chapter first reviews constitutional arrangements from the point of view of environmental concern. It then considers the case of the Canadian constitution and the implications for environmental management of its federalist provisions. This case is then juxtaposed with that of the Kenyan constitution and conclusions drawn regarding options for constitutional reform in Kenya.

This chapter recognizes the on-going federalism debate in Kenya. Views differ as to the fate of issues such as education, development, peace, unity and democracy under a federal system. But whether or not federalism would have a positive impact on the issues of concern to Kenyans depends on the form of federalism adopted. This would in turn depend on the nature of Kenyan politics and the forces of interests that shape the nation. Against this background, the chapter proposes, by drawing valuable lessons from the Canadian experience, the form of constitutional federalism that would best serve sustainable environmental management.

Constitutional arrangements

The constitution is the supreme law from which other laws derive their validity. The nature, strength and scope of regulations directed at environmental management are determined by the constitutional mandate of legislative authority which, in turn, is largely determined by the kind of constitution in place. While there are debates on the theoretical basis of classification and what classifications there are, we would rather focus on settled constitutional classifications and examine briefly how each readily permits the enactment of sound environmental management legislation.

Ojwang and Kanyeihamba have articulated the following classifications.[5] First, written and unwritten constitutions: the former is a formal legally binding document which establishes a system of government, the organs of the government and prescribes the powers, duties and rights of the government and its organs as well as those of the individuals who constitute the nation state. It is not, strictly, literally written as it could encompass certain unwritten cherished values of the people. Most countries' constitutions fall under this classification. An unwritten constitution is not contained in a single legal document. It is rather found in scattered pieces of legal documents as well as in a body of crystallized normative practices. Examples of such are the constitutions of Britain, New Zealand and Israel.

Second, flexible and rigid constitutions: a flexible constitution can be amended following the same procedure as for amending ordinary laws. But a rigid constitution is amended by following a special and often rigorous procedure. Observers however, say that frequency of constitutional amendment whether flexible or rigid, is largely determined by practical exigencies such as goals, priorities and preoccupation of the people of a given geo-political unit than by procedural requirements.[6]

Third, supreme and subordinate constitutions: the former's amendment is not exclusively the right of the parliament. Non-parliamentarians are involved one way or another. In other words, parliament cannot amend it without the approval of non-parliamentary bodies specified in the constitution. The latter, on the other hand, can be amended solely by parliament as in Kenya, for example.

Fourth, presidential and parliamentary constitutions: the presidential constitution is based on the principle of separation of powers. The constitution usually creates a presidential executive and mandates the executive, legislative and judicial arms of government to function independently of one another. The parliamentary constitution, on the other hand, is not influenced by the principle of separation of powers. The executive is merged with parliament in that executive members are generally required to be parliamentarians. Both arms are therefore rarely independent of each other. But special powers may be given to the president or prime minister to appoint some cabinet members from outside the parliament and to act with some degree of autonomy.

Fifth, republican and monarchical constitutions: the former establishes the office of the president or prime minister with political powers to run the affairs of the state. It requires the incumbent of such an office to be elected. It contrast, the monarchical constitution creates a royal office and gives the incumbent political powers over the affairs of the state. It is rarely democratic. Monarchical governments have been on the decline and revolutionary changes in the constitutions leave monarchs largely symbolic.

Six, general and detailed constitutions: the former prescribes the main principles of the fundamental laws without detailing them. Operationally, it is flexible as its interpretation could easily be liberal though could be prone to many controversies. The latter endeavours to encapsulate every aspect of the fundamental laws in a detailed fashion. It is likely to be more rigid but with fewer problems of interpretation since the detail helps to clarify most issues.[7]

Seventh, federal, confederal and unitary constitutions: a federal constitution provides for a central and component governments with each having a legislative power. Each entity's power is limited to specific subject matters and residuary power is specifically vested in either level of government. But a confederal constitution gives more power to the component governments and thus creates a weak central government. In contrast, a unitary constitution concentrates executive, legislative and judicial powers and functions in the central government exclusively, rendering it superior to any component government that may exist.

Most written constitutions are neither too general nor too detailed. Federal constitutions are normally more detailed as they are intended to cover aspects of the federation which are likely to be misunderstood or misinterpreted by the constituent governments. In contrast, it is generally sufficient for unitary constitutions to provide basic principles and leave the details to be dealt with by the general law of the state. However, not all unitary constitutions are general.

A constitution can fall into more than one of these classifications. The classifications give varying degrees of allowance for sound environmental legislation. A written constitution has the advantage of allowing articulation in a single document the environmental objectives and goals of a country on the basis of which appropriate legislation could be enacted to realize them. An unwritten constitution would provide for the environment in scattered legal documents; this will pose problems in terms of articulation and focus. It is analogous to releasing a dozen birds from a cage and having them fly in different directions. Hardly would any meaningful and practical environmental legislation be enacted unless the environmental provisions in the several scattered documents which constitute the unwritten constitution are first articulated into a single whole to give direction and focus to environmental management legislation. This is particularly so because sustainable management of the natural environment runs contrary to compartmentalized, separated as well as independent approaches.

While the environment is a coherent natural continuum, it is also a collection of dynamic natural processes. This would, *prima facie*, be suited to a flexible constitutional management approach. Under such a framework constitutional provisions can easily be amended in response to the dynamic character of the natural environment and consequently yield appropriate legislation. A rigid constitution would not have such an advantage. Rigidity may however, be employed within the framework of a flexible constitution for purposes of protecting fundamental environmental values such as the right to a clean and healthy environment and the duty to ensure such an environment. Alteration of such provisions under a rigid constitution would take a special procedure. Although a rigid constitution could easily be amended where practical exigencies such as perceived goals, priorities and preoccupation of the people dictate, it nevertheless, given the same circumstances, falls behind a flexible constitution in this regard.

To secure environment provisions in a constitution, the constitution must be supreme and not subordinate to the legislature (parliament). The amendment of such provisions should require the action of both parliament and non-parliamentarians. This is a crucial check on parliamentary whims and caprices which could influence legislators, under whatever political pressure or interest, to act irresponsibly. Arguably the involvement of non-parliamentarians in a constitutional amendment may connote the notion of a special procedure and thus suggest rigidity. But that would not necessarily amount to a rigorous process as would be the case under a typical rigid constitution. If environmental interest is secured in a supreme as opposed to a subordinate constitution, the environmental legislation enacted pursuant to it would enjoy a corresponding degree of security which it would not have otherwise.

Natural resources are a part of the environment but even if separated, the linkage between the two is very strong. The Brundtland Report, in recognition of the fact that natural resources cannot be managed independent of the environment hosting them, suggested that those who manage natural resources should also manage the environment associated with them. In a sense, this makes a parliamentary constitution appropriate for environmental management. Here the divide between the legislature and the executive is tenuous. Members of the latter are parliamentarians. Since the parliament makes law and the executive, whose members are parliamentarians, enforce it, this arrangement would easily allow concerted efforts towards the environment. In another sense, this constitutional arrangement may work against the environment if the legislature is misguided in enacting an environment legislation as the executive would likely enforce such being a part of the same body. The needed check could however, be provided by the judiciary through interpretation of the constitutional provisions. But this point assumes that the judiciary is independent of the other arms of government. It is a presidential executive constitution that guarantees the independence of the three arms of government.

A monarchical constitution runs the risk of not reflecting the aspirations of the people because it gives primacy to the royal institution; this is particularly so where it is not democratic. As participation of the public, as the resource users, is necessary for sustainable environmental management, the imposition of environmental goals and management approaches by a royal institution and which can only be changed or amended by that institution, can hardly be in the spirit of sustainability. To this extent, this kind of constitution is inappropriate for enacting sound environmental legislation. On the other hand, a democratic republican constitution either in parliamentary or presidential, federal or unitary form would provide an opposite and more desirable result.

A general constitution could facilitate sound environmental legislation because it would only provide or highlight fundamental environmental management principles and therefore provide flexibility for the formulation of appropriate legislation detailing management approaches for realizing the goal of the constitution. But such a constitution runs the risk of being vague and this might lead to problems of interpretation. A strong and well-informed judiciary would be needed to capture the mind of the legislature through interpretation of the constitution. As discussed elsewhere, US courts have generally interpreted the constitution liberally to accommodate environmental interest within the power of the federal government though the "environment" is not specifically mentioned in the constitution. The result has been desirable. Detailed constitutions could serve environmental management well if a general provision, for example, residual power, could be made to accommodate issues which could not be detailed for whatever reason. The advantage of a detailed constitution is that it minimizes interpretation difficulties, protects fundamental environmental rights and imposes fundamental environmental duties instead of leaving them to speculation and controversies.

The constitutions considered above are also institutional in the sense that they entrench a system of government, organs or arms of government such as executive, legislature and judiciary and their functions. We have seen how responsive environmental legislation could be to institutional constitutions. An institutional constitution could have a programmatic dimension. This means that in addition to establishing arms of government, it sets out the policies, objectives and goals of the government. It could for example, provide for the goal of a clean and healthy environment or conservation and protection of the environment to achieve sustainability. It may also give direction as to how to realize such goals. Typical examples of such a constitution are the 1979 Constitution of Portugal revised in 1982 (Article 66) and the Constitution of the Federal Republic of Brazil, 1988 (Section 225).[8] The environment will be served well under these arrangements because desirable environmental goals have been legally entrenched and guaranteed. The government is automatically under a duty to enact appropriate legislation and mobilize technical and financial resources to achieve such goals. The Kenyan constitution is somewhat programmatic to the extent that it creates trust land, vests it in county councils and mandates the councils to manage it in the interest of residents within its jurisdiction. County councils could then make bylaws to carry out this duty. Unfortunately, this programmatic provision is couched in a way that negates or extinguishes customary law, aspects of which are environment friendly.[9] Therefore, depending on how a programmatic constitution is designed it could promote or constrain environmental interest.

Responsiveness of environmental management legislation under federal and unitary constitutions as represented by Canada and Kenya, respectively, is the main focus of this chapter and need not be preempted here.

The case of Canada

Canadian politics and the Constitution

Canadian society and politics evolved along differences in culture and ethnicity, history, geography and economy. Geographically, physical barriers divide Canada into at least five major territories which are united by waterways. Historically, the pattern of settlement by people from different ethnic groups and culture was disjointed in both time and space. According to the Task Force on Canadian Unity:

> . . . the various regions of what is now one country (Canada) were settled and developed by Europeans rather as 'islands' unto themselves, largely unrelated to their neighbours, but linked by sea to the mother countries and to other parts of the world. Before confederation, the regions of present day Canada were rather like a bunch of balloons, unattached to each other but held by separate strings in one hand.[10]

The presence of different ethnic groups meant different social, cultural, religious, economic and political interests which contribute to the political differences in the country. Furthermore, there are differences in the economic base of the regions stemming from the endowment of natural resources and consequently uneven industrialization and population, and unequal access to both domestic and foreign markets resulting from poor geographic locations of some regions. The unequal distribution of economic well-being has not helped Canadian unity.

While all the regions in Canada share the differences discussed above, the most prominent cleavage in Canada is the cultural differences between the province of Quebec and the rest of the country. The former is French and the latter is English. Both powers scrambled for the occupation of what is now Canada. These historical circumstances have remained a source of bitterness between the two and have often triggered the quest for separation by Quebec.

The foregoing factors have made Canadian politics highly volatile. This political orientation makes it difficult to muster co-operation among the different political units, except on some extremely important issues of common good. There are, however, increasing indications that some provinces are willing to engage in common endeavours for common good. Experience has shown that financial and technical incentives from the federal government help to achieve such co-operation. Perhaps the most concrete expression of the nature of Canadian politics is its kind of loose federation or confederation. This arrangement recognizes and endorses the country's cultural diversity[11] and the pervading traditional trend of strong regional loyalty by Canadians. This political sensitiveness has been reflected in constitutional debates over the years, with each province overly protective of its interests. It is obvious that Canadian politics revolve around the assertion of the rights of each confederate.

This nature of Canadian politics has been given expression in the Canadian Constitution. The Constitution, in turn, has been interpreted in ways that support the perpetuation of this kind of politics and consequently, the laws of the different confederates run according to their different interests. Purely on a legal score, as discussed below, this does not serve environmental interests adequately.

The Canadian Constitution and environment

Canada is a federation. A central government (federal) and component governments (provincial) share legislative and administrative powers provided for in the Constitution. Federalism may be co-ordinate, co-operative or organic. There is no practical distinction between co-ordinate and co-operative federalism; both imply that the component governments which make up a federal state enjoy some degree of autonomy.[12] In a system of co-ordinate federalism, there are both the capacity for autonomous activity as well as the absence of a combined action by the governments, necessitating co-operation between the governments. None of them, not even the central government, plays a dominant role because each government is autonomous and can decline co-operation if it is pushed too far. This is different in a system of organic federalism. Here, the central government plays a dominant role in policy formulation and spending choices and in supervising the component governments which are assigned mere administrative role over the issues determined by the central government.

Organic federalism will promote a unified approach to managing the environment because the dominant role of the central government can be used to enhance co-ordination and compliance. Co-ordinate and co-operative federalism on the other hand, are fraught with the risk of a component government declining co-ordination or co-operation in environmental matters since it has autonomous power. It will be demonstrated that Canadian federalism is co-operative not organic and thus poorly encourages a unified approach to environmental management. The purpose of the Constitution of Canada, otherwise known as the British North American Act 1867, "was not to weld the provinces into one, nor to subordinate provincial governments to a central authority, but to create a federal government in which they should all be represented, entrusted with the exclusive administration of affairs in which they had a common interest, each province retaining its independence and autonomy."[13]

It is, therefore, not difficult to see why the legal approach to environmental management is fragmented along constitutional division of powers between the federal government and the individual provinces (hence institutional or jurisdictional fragmentation). Each level of government has plenary legislative powers under the Constitution of Canada. Section 91 of the Constitution enumerates the heads of legislative powers of the federal parliament while section 92 enumerates those of the provincial legislative assemblies. No level of government is allowed to arrogate to itself matters which belong to the other level. The scope of each head of power has been the subject of a number of judicial decisions and scholarly debates.

The word "environment" is not mentioned in the Constitution. Therefore, as between the federal and provincial governments, jurisdiction over the environment has to be deduced from the enumerated heads of powers. Section 91 of the Constitution empowers the federal government to make laws for the peace, order and good government of Canada (hereinafter the POGG power) in respect of all matters not exclusively assigned to the provinces. This power and the federal spending power are discussed as they seem to be the most appropriate grounds upon which a unified approach to environmental management, if constitutionally possible, may be allowed. The possibilities for political co-operation and inter-provincial management institutions are then examined.

The POGG power. The courts have consistently applied tests which preserve the federal-provincial power balance upon which rests Canadian federalism. For example, in *A.G. Ontario* v. *Canada Temperance Federation*[14] Lord Viscount Simon stated that matters which by their nature transcend provincial concern can be legislated upon by the federal parliament in the exercise of the POGG power, notwithstanding that such an exercise may incidentally touch on matters wholly under provincial legislative jurisdiction. This national concern test was followed in *Interprovincial Cooperatives* v. *Manitoba*[15] in which the effect of sections 92(5) and 109 of the Constitution were considered. Section 92(5) provides: "In each province the legislature may exclusively make laws in relation to matters coming within the classes of subjects next hereinafter enumerated, that is to say, the management and sale of the public lands belonging to the province and of the timber and wood thereon." Section 109 provides:

> All lands, mines, minerals and royalties belonging to the several provinces of Canada, Nova Scotia, and New Brunswick at the Union, and all sums then due or payable for such lands, mines, minerals, or royalties, shall belong to the several provinces of Ontario, Quebec, Nova Scotia and New Brunswick in which the same are situate or arise, subject to any trusts existing in respect thereof, and to any interest other than that of the province in the same.

Pigeon holds, for the majority of the Supreme Court of Canada, that while the provinces can regulate rivers within their boundaries pursuant to sections 92(5) and 109 of the Constitution, interprovincial waters and their pollution are matters of national concern. According to the judge, "the basic rule is that general legislative authority in respect of all that is not within the provincial field is federal."[16] It has, however, been argued that this case is of little "presidential authority" because of the different grounds upon which the majority based their decisions.[17] Nevertheless, it seems clear from the case that interprovincial environmental matters fall under federal jurisdiction.

It is clear that the environment is a unity; the problem is to find a constitutional basis upon which laws could be designed to respond to that unity. One way of finding such a basis is to concentrate legislative power over the environment on a single legislative authority, that is, the Parliament of Canada.[18] This was attempted in *The Queen* v. *Crown Zellerbach Canada Ltd. et al.*[19] where Le Dain, for the majority of the Supreme Court of

Canada, outlines circumstances that amount to a matter of national concern warranting the enactment of a federal law applicable across Canada. According to the judge,

3) For a matter to qualify as a matter of national concern in either sense it must have a singleness, distinctiveness and indivisibility that distinguishes it from matters of provincial concern and a scale of impact on provincial jurisdiction that is reconcilable with the fundamental distribution of legislative power under the Constitution;

4) In determining whether a matter has attained the required degree of singleness, distinctiveness and indivisibility that clearly distinguishes it from matters of provincial concern it is relevant to consider what would be the effect on extra provincial interests of a provincial failure to deal effectively with the control or regulation of the intra-provincial aspects of the matter (i.e. provincial inability test).[20]

According to the court, the provincial inability test is one of the indices for determining "whether a matter has that character of singleness or indivisibility required to bring it within the national concern doctrine."[21] But this, in the view of the court, does not mean that any one level of government has the plenary jurisdiction to deal with such matters. Rather, it means that the interrelationship of intra-provincial and extra-provincial aspects of the matter might better be dealt with under a single legislative approach.

The learned judge found that marine pollution met the criteria of singleness, distinctiveness and indivisibility and was therefore a matter of national concern. Although the provincial inability test could, in a proper case, deny federal jurisdiction where a province has the ability to deal with a matter, the overriding consideration in Le Dain's judgement seems to be the unity of the marine environment, necessitating a single legislative approach.[22] Because of this unity the failure of a province to deal with environmental problems in its marine waters would inevitably spread such problems to the rest of the marine environment.

Le Dain's judgement which suggests a single legislative approach, is arguably limited to the marine environment. Apparently it does not extend to the environment as a whole. In *The Queen in Right of Alberta et al.* v. *Friends of the Oldman River Society,*[23] LaForest, for the Supreme Court of Canada, seems to deny that the environment is a subject which requires unity of legal efforts to deal with. According to the judge, ". . . environmental control, as a subject matter, does not have the requisite distinctiveness to meet the test under the 'national concern' doctrine. . . "[24]

Therefore, the environment fails the distinctiveness test of the national concern doctrine.[25] LaForest's decision supports a fragmented approach to managing the environment in line with the constitutional division of powers. The judge emphasizes that federal legislation is valid only if the "pith and substance" relates to matters assigned to the federal government under the Constitution. He maintains that the environment is a diffuse subject which comes under the different federal and provincial heads of powers under the Constitution in different degrees depending on the nature of each head of power. Diffuse, not in the sense that the environment is compartmentalized but in the sense that the exercise of each of the different traditional heads of powers under the Constitution may touch on the environment. The difficulty with this decision is that it acknowledges the unity of the natural environment but insists that the federal and provincial governments must follow the constitutional division of powers which supports a fragmented approach in dealing with it.

One means of recognizing the unity of the environment in management is for those who manage natural resources to also manage the associated environmental problems. This is in the spirit of avoiding institutional or jurisdictional polarization of inter-related or even integrated issues like the environment. In Canada, natural resources are owned and managed by the provinces by virtue of Section 109 of the Constitution and the associated environmental problems fall under provincial jurisdiction. To hold otherwise would deny the provinces jurisdiction over their natural resources.[26] Therefore, the provinces should manage their resources as well as the associated environmental problems. It is also possible that, if the federal government manages the environment as a unity without managing the provincial natural resources associated with it, such management will not be efficient. On the other hand, the environmental problems may not always be confined to the spatial unit within which a particular resource manager, for example, a province, has jurisdiction. Provinces may also ignore the natural unity of the environment and risk being inefficient.

It is therefore clear that within the Canadian constitutional context, two important ideals of sustainable development—the institutional and jurisdictional principle which requires those who manage natural resources to also manage the associated environmental problems on the one hand, and a unified management approach based on the unity of the environment on the other hand—run in different directions.[27] While the former principle is pursued at the provincial level, the latter can only be realized at the federal level and there is no legal impetus to effect it.

Therefore, other than the clear-cut cases of interprovincial environmental matters, the POGG power cannot provide a basis for a unified action to deal with environmental issues in a broader scope such as having a federal umbrella legal framework to which the provinces must subscribe. And the fact remains that a province will not always have the ability to deal with a matter such as the environment which does not respect political boundaries. Consequently, environmental laws are generally weak and fragmented along provincial and federal lines. Federal environmental legislation in particular seems not decisive and forceful enough to achieve desired environmental goals. For example, Part I of the Canada Water Act contemplates a comprehensive water management role for the federal government and emphasizes federal–provincial co-operation. Yet, as Saunders submits, "despite its description as comprising 'comprehensive water management', there is very little that is comprehensive about Part I of the Act, in the sense of asserting *a wider federal role.*"[28]

Powers under Section 11 and Section 13 of the Act which include unilateral establishment and implementation of a water quality management programme by the federal government where necessary, have not been exercised. Despite the existence of situations warranting such an action, it is feared that such an exercise of power would provoke a constitutional challenge in court. The Act illustrates the constitutional impossibility to act organically towards the management of water resources and the environment.

The constitutionally-precipitated weakness of the federal government in aggressively pursuing environmental goals is also manifested in the way the Canadian Environmental Protection Act (CEPA) which regulates "toxic substances that may endanger life and health . . ." is cast. Although legitimately enacted and somewhat comprehensive, the provisions of the Act are too general and loose to be effective. For example, the Act deals with international air pollution but avoids direct control of domestic air pollution in order not to encroach upon provincial jurisdiction over property and commercial activities.[29] Neither CEPA nor any other federal legislation regulates environmental issues in the provinces directly.[30]

Not surprisingly, in terms of legal approach, each level of government as well as each individual province, appears to be concerned only with the portion of the environment within its boundaries with little regard for their interconnectedness. The efforts of the federal and provincial governments and the combined efforts of the individual provinces are not sufficiently unified to deal with the problem. This approach undermines the natural unity of the environment and is, therefore, ineffective. Harmonizing or unifying these efforts in a practical way is a major challenge facing environmental managers.[31] Hence, the status quo conflicts with the need for a strong federal role, at least, to set a binding standard umbrella criteria to which the provinces must subscribe.

Federal spending power. There is no explicit enumeration of federal spending power under Section 91 of the Constitution. Commentators, however, agree that this power is inherent in public debt and property power under Section 91(1A) and taxation power under Section 91(3).[32] Also, the common law doctrine of royal prerogative which is said to be inherent in the Constitution enables the federal government to spend its money or dispose of its property in whatever manner it wishes.[33] The federal government can, therefore, use its spending power to influence and determine environmental management programme at the provincial level by linking aid and grants to the conditions that such programmes be pursued. However, the extent of this power, that is, whether or not it is limited by the "pith and substance" test is unsettled. The power has not been used with any significant force. Given this constitutional uncertainty, it is safer to exercise this power in a non-binding co-operative setting.

Political co-operation and management institutions. We will first examine federal and provincial co-operation. The 1982 amendment of the Canadian constitution avoided altering the existing federal-provincial power balance because of the sensitivity of the issue. Needed federal-provincial co-operation in environmental and natural resources matters remains on the terrain of political will of both levels of government

A former prime minister of Canada has said that Canada is the most decentralized form of federalism in the world as the provinces wield power in a proportion that makes a federal union almost practically impossible.[34] Political co-operation to maintain the federal union revolves around issues of common good. Component governments must be persuaded to see how they can benefit from the goals or purposes of, for example, environmental projects or programmes. They would also need to recognize their stake in such projects or programmes and how the absence of co-operation could threaten or jeopardize their interests. Diplomacy based on reciprocity can promote tolerance and the accommodation of different interests in a society such as Canada. This, according to one scholar, is "co-operative federalism".[35] While co-operative federalism is to be extra-constitutional, it would be valid only if it does not fundamentally offset the constitutional balance of power. Given the Canadian constitutional context, co-operative federalism is the most appropriate form of federalism because the provinces have autonomous powers over the subject matters assigned to them and they cannot be stripped of these powers. Clearly, organic federalism is not possible in Canada as it purports to take away legislative powers of the provinces and leaves them with only administrative roles. This would be unconstitutional.

Where an important issue is constitutionally-adjudicated against what a province considers to be one of its pivotal interests, it may nevertheless refuse compliance.[36] Securing political co-operation in such a case will become very crucial. But in the environmental context, situations where a court decision will so radically affect the interest of a province in favour of the federal government as to trigger non-compliance, are not very likely. As reviewed earlier, the key Supreme Court of Canada's decisions seem to maintain environmental management along the traditional division of powers between both levels of government under the Constitution. So, here, political reciprocity should always be the only necessary approach.

The spirit of co-operation is evident, for example, in existing federal–provincial agreements on water resources and environmental matters. The Water Advisory Committee of the Canadian Council of Ministers of the Environment (CCME) is drafting general principles for water management which will contribute to a more co-ordinated water management approach. The CCME has also instituted a clean-up programme for contaminated sites known as the National Contaminated Sites Remediation Program. Under this programme the federal government has signed six separate bilateral agreements with six provinces providing funding for the implementation of the programme where the provinces agree to follow federal guidelines. Thus for these provinces, the federal clean-up programme is also essentially theirs.

Although some measure of success has been achieved,[37] co-operative efforts are not guaranteed as "negotiated solutions will not always be found."[38] Furthermore, the conclusion of such agreements consumes time and resources and usually "the parties are interested less in the value of the overall project than they are in getting the largest share of benefits for themselves."[39] Again, such agreements may be challenged in court by citizens where they are reached at the expense of the legislative powers of either level of government.

Generally, there is an inherent constitutional duty placed upon citizens of a country to uphold the principles enshrined in its Constitution. In Canada, private actions have been successfully pursued to protect and uphold the provisions of the Constitution.[40] A private action would also be sustained where the issue hinges on the constitutional basis of an environmental management measure as was the case in the *Oldman River* case[41] or where environmental measures are being taken at the expense of the constitutional balance of power. It is, however, for the court to decide whether or not that balance has been offset in a particular case. But by emphasizing the "pith and substance" test in the *Oldman River* case, it is unlikely that the court would give a liberal interpretation to the question of balance of power as the

Constitution is not intended to erode provincial powers in favour of the federal government.

A right to environmental protection can also be the subject of a constitutional or charter provision. Article 66 of the Portuguese Constitution provides, for example, that: "Everyone shall have the right to a healthy and ecologically balanced human environment and the duty to defend it."[42] Another dimension to this right is seen in the German *Mulheim-Karlich case*, where the Federal Constitution Court held that Article 2(2) of the Basic Law which protects life and physical integrity enables the individual to assert his or her right to life and physical integrity against potentially toxic emissions from a state-licensed or state-owned nuclear plant. Thus, "protection of 'life and physical integrity' encompasses not only the literal aspects of the phrase, but also a guarantee of surroundings worthy of human beings."[43] This German example is likely to open a flood-gate of frivolous and vexatious litigation unless the court establishes guidelines to check such actions. Apparently, for this reason, neither the Canadian Constitution nor the Charter of Rights and Freedom has been interpreted as liberally as those of Germany.

In the context of environmental issues which are totally divorced from constitutional questions, a private action can be maintained as a private nuisance. But traditionally a private action seeking to redress a public wrong is subject to the Public Nuisance Rule except where statutes provide otherwise.[44] Under this rule, in matters of public interest such as the environment, only the attorney-general is allowed to redress public wrongs on behalf of the state. Private persons can only maintain an action as individuals with the consent of the attorney-general (i.e., a relator action) or where they can demonstrate that they have suffered harm, or that they possess an interest that distinguishes them from the general public.[45] But in Kenya, establishing "real interest" in a matter may be a basis for a private person's *locus standi* in public interest litigation.[46]

Evidently a successful private action against federal–provincial co-operation for enhanced environmental management in Canada would have negative consequences since co-operation is needed for efficient environmental management. The possibility of such a private action has contributed to the weakness of existing federal–provincial agreements. Given the gaps in, and weaknesses of such agreements, they cannot be a substitute for a clear constitutional mandate given to the federal government to both unify and co-ordinate environmental management efforts. Yet a non-binding co-operative approach is better than the present constitutionally-backed approach which is largely fragmented.

We now turn to intra-provincial management institutions. At the provincial level, the polarization of environmental and resource management institutions is of a kind that is somewhat regressive. In the province of Ontario, for example, the management of water quality is handled by several institutions and this is "typical of many (Canadian) jurisdictions."[47] Several complaints about inefficiency led the province of Saskatchewan to streamline institutional management of water quantity.[48] Yet a recent report on water management in some provinces including Saskatchewan shows, for example, that in each province several agencies are involved in groundwater management leading to contradictions in planning, policy formulation and implementation. Streamlining of these institutions should be more thorough with a view to increasing efficiency and effectiveness. In summary, on the whole, Canada has been using political co-operation and, to a limited extent, federal spending power to get around the limitations of the Constitution in dealing with environmental issues.

The case of Kenya

Kenyan politics and the constitutional order

Indigenous ethnic groups in pre-colonial Kenya enjoyed different degrees of social and economic interactions. Some migrated from one region to another. Others were assimilated by larger and more dominant tribes. Arabs in search of slaves settled in Mombasa and along the Indian Ocean coast. European missionary activities in Kenya prepared the way for the imperialist British power who colonized the region for economic and political gain. According to one writer, ". . . all people [of Kenya] come, in history's long run, out of a variety of ethnic backgrounds intermingled."[49]

Each ethnic group had its own system of governance. There was no central chieftaincy or political authority presiding over the area The colonialists recognized this *status quo* and tried to maintain it through a divide-and-rule policy reinforced through the establishment of tribal reserves which became the focal unit of administration. African nationalists were, at first, allowed to form political associations at the regional level, a deliberate policy to weaken African solidarity towards independence. A nation-wide political body was resisted by the colonial government.[50] This led to the formation of several political bodies which were essentially along tribal lines. But the conviction of the nationalists that independence could be achieved faster with a united political body persisted. Finally, after much confrontation, the colonial government reluctantly allowed the nationalists to form the Kenya African National Union (KANU) in March 1960.[51] But some critics fearing the domination of the Kikuyu and Luo ethnic groups in KANU, formed a second political party, the Kenya African Democratic Union (KADU), constituted mainly by Kalenjin, Maasai, Mijikenda and Abaluhya. Following a disagreement within KANU, a Kamba-based, African Peoples Party (APP) was formed. Thus at independence on December 12, 1963, there existed three political parties.

Most nationalists had learned from the experience of regional political associations under colonialism that common goals could not be achieved under that kind of arrangement. Thus the post-colonial existence of more that one political party was seen as a barrier to unity and the enterprise of nation-building, the political philosophy and goal of KANU. This was particularly resented by Jomo Kenyatta, the leader of KANU and the first prime minister and later president of independent Kenya who viewed disunity as a colonial legacy which must be destroyed.

In his post-election speech, Kenyatta emphasized the need for the country to work together. According to him the supreme task of his government was the unity of Kenya. He stressed that whatever differences that existed would be subordinated to this goal.[52] With this, the process of winning over the opposition began. Both diplomacy and force were used. Subsequently, KADU merged with KANU and APP was swept away by the wave of political unity. On the occasion of the merger, Kenyatta declared that "the wrangling, the opposition for opposition's sake, have now died forever and ever, Amen. . . . We shall work as one team, working for the sake of Kenya alone, and I think that now with one party leading the country, the fruit of our victory will be seen very soon."[53]

In Kenyatta's view, a one-party system was the "most prudent method for attaining those aims and objects which our people hold dear" namely, Africanism which seeks to "fulfil what our people want to be, to do, [and] to have"[54] He maintained that unity and solidarity was:

We reject a blue print of the Western model of a two-party system of government because we do not subscribe to the notion of the government and the governed in opposition to one another. One clamouring for duties and the other crying for rights . . . all two-party states are not necessarily democratic and all one party states are not necessarily authoritarian. . . . Through the historical process which has taken place within the last century we find ourselves with myriad relevant grounds and conditions for a one party state. It is inevitable. In our particular situation, practice will have to precede theory. Should relevant ground for a multi-party state evolve in the future, it is not the intention of my government to block such a trend through prohibitive legislation.[55]

On December 12, 1964, Kenya became a republic. The federal (*majimbo*) constitution inherited from the colonial government was abolished and a unitary constitution and government were introduced. The office of the prime minister was replaced by that of the president. The bicameral legislature was abolished and replaced with a unicameral one in 1966. With these changes KANU assumed a strong central government.

Opposition, if any, was marginalized and confined to the one-party system. Oginga Odinga, briefly Kenya's first vice-president, and his supporters thought that Kenyatta's government was pursuing neo-colonial ideology, and their Kenya Peoples Union (KPU) was systematically eliminated. First, a law was passed requiring them to seek re-election into parliament since they had left KANU on whose platform they were initially elected. The by-election left the KPU with drastically fewer seats than they had originally. Finally, the party was banned in 1969 following some political disturbances at Kisumu, Odinga's home base, during which Kenyatta was stoned. Following Kenyatta's lead, President Moi continued the campaign of unity among Kenyan tribes as a *sine qua non* for nation-building. He outlawed tribal associations which were prone to divide rather than unite the nation. The constitution was amended in 1992 when repeal of Section 2A of the constitution once again allowed multi-party politics. But purely on a constitutional score, the country remains a unitary system of government.

Such was the political orientation and perhaps indoctrination which shaped Kenya's post-colonial politics. Opposition was seen as an enemy to the task of unity and nation-building. Federalism which encourages opposition, usually in a multi-party system has always been associated with disunity which many believe is not the choice of Kenyans. The marginalization of opposition could be a reason for the absence of any legal challenge to the constitutionality of laws passed by parliament. Since 1965, when the government stated its central policy position on the environment in Sessional Paper No.10 on *African Socialism and its Application to Planning in Kenya*, there has been no such legal challenge. The legitimization of opposition as under a federal system of government would probably have created the necessary conditions for such a challenge as is the case in Canada.

The political setting in Kenya is, therefore, in sharp contrast with that in Canada. Kenya is not a federation. Although there are three levels of government, the central, the provincial and the district, only the central government wields legislative powers under Section 30 of the Constitution. For this reason, the country runs a unitary or a central government system. Ideally, this kind of political system puts the government in a position to act organically towards the management of the environment. Whether or not the government is acting in this way is examined below.

Legislative authority and environment

Unlike Canada, there is no question as to the power of the central government to enact environmental laws. Although the word "environment" is not mentioned in the Constitution, legislative powers and limits over the subject are embedded in the constitutional mandate of the central government to provide for the welfare of its people. Even assuming that there is no such derivation of power over the environment, the fact that the Parliament of Kenya is the only constitutionally-recognized legislative authority gives it such a power because residuary legislative power does not vest in any other body. Therefore, there is no constitutional basis for the polarization of legislative jurisdiction upon which the other two levels of government can proceed to make laws. This reduces the risk of fragmenting legal response to environmental management.

The authority of parliament to legislate on environmental matters is limited by Section 75 of the Constitution which deals with the sanctity of private property. Nevertheless the private property right is not inviolable. In public interest matters such as the environment, property could, under the same section, be expropriated with compensation where it would otherwise jeopardize the public interest. Where a state assumes ownership of property by expropriation or otherwise, it is under a duty to use it for the public benefit. The public trust doctrine which unfortunately is not well developed in Kenya, should ensure that this is done. The doctrine is intended to serve as a check on state ownership of property to avoid abuse. Under this doctrine, property owned by the state is held in trust for the benefit of the public and should take into account issues such as gender equality. The doctrine imposes a duty on the state to manage the property in the interest of the public. Where the state fails, members of the public can employ legal means to compel it to act in the public interest, provided they have *locus standi*.[56]

The doctrine of public trust as originally developed applied to navigable or tidal waters. It ensured that state's management of the exploitation and use of economic resources (commodity uses) were in the public interest. In the American case of *National Audubon Society* v. *Superior Court*[57] it was held that existing appropriative water right of an individual "remained subject to a duty of continuing supervision on the part of the state in order to protect the public trust in the state's waters".[58] Furthermore, the court held that water diversion pursuant to existing water rights which would have a long-term negative impact on a natural system could be enjoined. This decision has added maintenance of ecological integrity to the traditional list of commodity uses in respect of which the public trust doctrine checks abuses by a state or an individual. This decision puts commodity uses and the maintenance of ecological (natural) systems on the balancing scale of the public trust doctrine. The state's power to carry out activities is therefore fettered by the environmental threshhold imposed by the public trust doctrine.

Hence, Kenya runs a centralized style of environmental management following the various policy papers and national development plans formulated since independence. This has been attributed to the hitherto one-party system which epitomized unity of political will and purpose and consequently the circumvention of constitutional problems. It is, however, feared that the *status quo* will alter with the recent emergence of a multi-party system. The *status quo*, in the sense of a single legislative authority which makes centralization possible, is consistent with environmental management objectives to the extent that those objectives seek to approach the environment organically because of its unity. A decentralized approach would hardly be holistic and therefore efficient unless a strong co-ordination machinery is in place. This might amount to a euphemism for centralization.

Multi-party politics, federalism and environment

A multi-party system will certainly engender politically-motivated judicial challenge of the constitutionality of some environmental legislation. But as long as Kenya remains a unitary as opposed to a federal system of government, party pluralism cannot scuttle the centrality of environmental management. The officials of the provincial and district governments appointed by the president will, no doubt, implement environmental objectives or laws handed down by higher authorities. Even if they are to be elected and a different political party forms the government in a province or district, still the *status quo* cannot be off-set as legislative powers would not as yet be shared by these levels of government. The kind of legislative jurisdictional barriers to a unified environmental management found in Canada will still be improbable in Kenya under the current system.

There is an on-going debate on the adoption of federalism (known as *majimbo*) in Kenya. On the one hand, proponents of federalism argue that the system would promote regional development and democratic principles and would relieve minor ethnic groups from the oppression and exploitation of the major ones.[59] This line of thinking is almost tantamount to self-determination of each regional government. It would mean co-operative federalism with a crucial balance of power between the central and regional governments. On the other hand, opponents of the system argue that it is prone to fragmenting the country along ethnic lines. They recall that this was the experience immediately after independence which led to a unitary system of government in an attempt to weld trans-tribal unity across the country. Some educators fear that federalism would cripple the education system as the few tertiary institutions would be owned by and educate exclusively the people from the region where they are located. Even some clergymen have rejected the system as "demonic and evil" because, according to them, it is divisive, tribal and will lead to the demise of the country. This fear became more apparent when the new parties were formed largely along ethnic cleavages which made voting in the 1992 multi-party elections follow ethnic lines.

Evidently, there have been mix feelings about federalism. But federalism does not necessarily mean the regionalization of everything. Of course, this depends on whether organic or co-operative federalism is adopted. Given the dominance of the view of the opponents of federalism, it is likely that even if the system were to be introduced, it would likely be organic federalism which seems to be less vulnerable to ethnic divisiveness. Some educators have suggested that should federalism be adopted, education should remain the responsibility of the central government. The same argument can be made for the environment based on the Canadian experience. Paramount power over environmental matters should reside with the central government. Regional governments should have only subordinate powers over the environment. Since environmental issues are generic and common by nature, such an arrangement will make it easier for the government to adopt common approaches to environmental management. But the debate is not over and the winner of it remains to be seen.

The actualization of federalism would be a paradigm shift with far-reaching implications for the management of the environment depending, of course, on the type of federalism. For example, should Kenya decide to adopt co-operative or co-ordinate federalism as in Canada, it must then contend with the difficulty of unifying environmental efforts should the component governments belong to parties different from the central government or for other reasons be bent on exercising their legislative powers differently. There would, however, be a different scenario if the country were to adopt organic federalism. Or it might, as in the United States,[60] evolve constitutional principles through judicial interpretations. These give the federal government dominant power over environmental issues and give subsidiary powers to the component governments. For this reason, the US congress has little restraint in exercising its legislative powers.[61] As some scholars have rightly observed: "In the American Constitutional system, the federal role is pre-eminent but not exclusive. The Congress has constitutional power to regulate pollution, land use, and resource exploitation as it sees fit . . . *states have an important . . . role under the terms of the federal legislation..*"[62]

Although there is political will and purpose translated into centrality of environmental management in Kenya, there is still some degree of fragmentation of legal and institutional approaches to environmental management. This does not stem from the polarization of legislative authority as in Canada. Rather, it is a result of the inability of the central government to articulate sound environmental management strategies especially with regard to institutional framework.

Legal framework and institutional arrangements

The polarization of environmental management institutions responsible for the environment in Kenya is, for the most part, rooted in the fragmented legal framework handed down by the central government. This framework reflects the compartmentalized and production-oriented system established by the British based on Western legal and institutional traditions. As a result, provisions relating to environmental management are somewhat obscure and scattered in a patchwork of legislation. Most of this legislation is sectoral, focusing for example, on water, agriculture and forestry. Its primary concern is resource allocation and exploitation. It responds to environmental degradation only in very serious cases and in a piecemeal fashion. Furthermore, sectoral legislation has been generally rule-oriented, using an iron fist to secure compliance rather than management oriented, which could yield public input for rational environmental management. It is not designed for a comprehensive environmental management approach.

This legislation generally predates the emerging concepts of environmental sustainability—which is reflected in the country's national policy—and so do not reflect this paradigm.[63] Sound environmental management under this dispensation is elusive because the legislation treats the environment sectorally and undermines its unity. While it is proper to maintain specialization, the various linkages in the sphere of the environment and natural resources must be carefully articulated and respected in planning, policy making and implementation. Such linkages call for a comprehensive or umbrella legal framework for sound environmental management. Interestingly, the development and drafting of such a legislation has been attempted on a number of occasions and there is a continuing effort to achieve this objective, including a National Environmental Action Plan.

Let us now turn to the institutional and jurisdictional framework. In most developing countries, environmental management is "organizationally fragmented, piecemeal and uncoordinated."[64] It must be understood that the drive for a comprehensive legal framework for environmental management should automatically trigger the streamlining of environmental management institutions. Otherwise what is gained by such legislation will be lost in institutional operations. The present dispensation in Kenya is fraught with overwhelming institutional polarity. For example, under Section 4 of the Forests Act, the forest department of the central government has management powers over gazetted "forest areas" only. But non-gazetted forests and woodlands found usually in private and trust lands are managed by county councils and local authorities under the Local Government Act and sections of the Trust Land Act.[65]

Although the forestry department liaises with the ministry of agriculture and provincial administration to control deforestation outside forest areas, there is a persistent need to extend the mandate of the department to cover such areas and to harmonize and maintain consistent policies among the different relevant authorities.[66] The power of the forest department under the Forests Act to strip an area of its "forest area" status and thus open it up for agricultural activities threatens to cancel declared "protected water catchment areas" under the Water Act which fall within such forest areas.[67]

The need to co-ordinate the activities of sectoral environmental and resource management institutions to ensure consistency triggered the establishment of the National Environmental Secretariat (NES) in 1974 under the office of the president where it remained until 1981. The NES has no statutory powers to co-ordinate sectoral institutions which do enjoy statutory powers. Since 1981, NES has lost its presidential prestige and command having been degraded to a department under the ministry of environment and natural resources. The threat of soil degradation led to the establishment of the permanent presidential commission for soil conservation and afforestation in 1981 to co-ordinate initiatives and to take measures to arrest imminent or present injuries to the environment. The commission, however, has no statutory powers and risks being inefficient. This is also true of the district environment committees (DECs) which co-ordinate environmental activities at the district level. The DECs, however, rely on the co-operation of local chiefs who exercise their powers under the Chiefs' Authority Act to enforce environmental regulations. A close collaboration between the DECs on the one hand and the NES and the commission on the other hand is needed to ensure that national environmental policies and planning are implemented at the local level with appropriate adaptation warranted by ecological differences. Statutory powers for these institutions are important. In fact, in place of the commission, the ministry of agriculture which has statutory powers under the Agriculture Act should have been compelled by the government to execute the duties of the commission and strengthened to do so.[68]

Reviewing the effectiveness of environmental impact assessment (EIA) and mechanisms to control four major dams in Kenya, two scholars noted that the Tana and Athi Rivers Development Authority (TARDA) consistently ignored the procedural requirements for EIA which were part of the 1979–1983 Development Plan imposed by NES. Instead, the authority responded to instrumental control imposed by foreign financiers of the projects. TARDA was not penalized because the NES lacked both the legal and political leverage to enforce the requirements.[69] Such unrestrained aberration of the national environmental objectives by a recalcitrant government agency underscores the inability of the government to galvanize or co-ordinate institutional efforts to ensure sound environmental management.

Furthermore, with regard to the weakness of the present land-use system in combating desertification, the Inter-governmental Authority on Drought and Development (IGADD) has decried the absence of systematic land use practices and approaches in the IGADD countries including Kenya.[70] While recognizing the centrality of land use planning in Kenya, IGADD regrets that "at the moment . . . no area plans have been formulated of the various ecological regions of the country. Land use and development are therefore haphazard and land use decision-making largely ad hoc."[71] This *laissez faire* approach to environmental management stems from the existence of several administrative bodies under the different environment-related statutes in Kenya which make and implement land-use decisions. Thus while there is centrality of land-use planning, land-use decision-making is fragmented with the risk of potential or actual conflicting decisions and disrespect for the unity of the environment.

A solution to the problem of legal and institutional fragmentation of environmental management can be seen in comprehensive environmental management legislation and apex management institutions. Comprehensive environmental management legislation does not suggest a negation of sectoral interests. Rather, it is a recognition of cross-sectoral and multi-sectoral interests which must be addressed simultaneously in order to achieve efficiency and effectiveness and thus attain sustainability. An environmental body should be established by such legislation to articulate such confluence of interests in the stages of sustainable development planning, policy formulation and implementation. Compliance and enforcement may be properly handled by an environmental board with quasi-judicial powers. Such a board can intervene where a sectoral authority is not complying with the reciprocity required in environmental management. Unlike Canada, Kenya's constitutional setting permits the devolution of legal powers to such institutions which are necessary for them to make binding decisions and to take binding actions.

Comparative analysis and conclusion

It is clear that the politics of Canada and Kenya evolved differently with different results reflected in their national constitutions. While the nature of Canadian politics dictated a co-operative constitutional federalism, permitting two levels of legislative authority with none being subordinated to the other, Kenyan politics engaged a unitary constitution with a unicameral legislature. The Canadian arrangement encourages opposition and this is evident from the court challenges of environment related matters. The continuing debate over the status of Quebec Province further illustrates this point. The Kenyan arrangement, on the other hand, marginalized and confined opposition and maintained a one-party system of government until the early 1990s.

A unity of management efforts corresponds to the unity of the environment and will ideally lead to sustainable development. Kenya, unlike Canada, has not had strong constitutional barriers to formulating environmental laws and policies which take into account the unity of the environment. It is suggested here that the legal direction takes the form of comprehensive environmental management legislation. Such legislation must be non-sectoral and must articulate cross sectoral and multi-sectoral environmental interests. It should define and provide the specific actions each concerned sector should take and when. Such actions could, for example, be in the context of planning, policy formulation and implementation with the ultimate and supreme goal of attaining sustainable development.

While a comprehensive or framework legislation should not negate the existing sectoral laws, the latter should be revised to incorporate environmental management elements such as environmental impact assessment, environmental monitoring and auditing and other precautionary measures at all levels of resource planning, development and utilization. The challenge is for national and international laws to be brought up to date to cope with present developmental and environmental realities. Revising these laws along the lines suggested, will bring them into conformity with the principle of sustainable development, a concept which they were not originally designed to address. In addition, each sectoral law should, as a follow-up to the provisions of the comprehensive environmental management legislation, highlight the different areas where it has joint environmental interests with the other sectors. This will enable the different sectoral authorities to focus managerial actions more appropriately. Both the comprehensive and sectoral legislation should provide specifically for the exchange of information among the different sectors to promote teamwork and avoid duplication, conflict or neglect.

Canada already has the CEPA which is somewhat comprehensive. CEPA does not specifically articulate areas of confluence of interests of the two levels of government or among their various sectors. Rather it has the "equivalency provision" (Section 34) under which the federal government declines to take measures where a province has taken measures considered to be equivalent to what would have been federal measures. This is only on issues where Section 95 of the Constitution gives concurrent power to both levels of government, such as agriculture. It has been pointed out that the loose nature of this legislation stems from the constitutional division of legislative powers. Thus the kind of comprehensive environmental management legislation often suggested for Kenya is not possible for Canada.

With regard to institutional arrangements for Kenya, it is suggested that two supreme environmental bodies with different functions, administrative and judicial, be established. The administrative body will, in accordance with the comprehensive legislation, ensure that the articulated confluence of cross sectoral and multi-sectoral interests are integrated into all stages of development (planning, policy formulation and implementation). It would serve as an umbrella body overseeing environmental activities at the sectoral level as well. The judicial body would have the responsibility for compliance and enforcement of environmental imperatives.

Canada already has the CCME and other bodies constituted by federal and provincial representatives. But they have no legal power to, for example, demand the compliance of an unco-operative province or agency. Their success depends only upon the political will of those concerned—a ground too slippery to address environmental problems adequately. The fact that Kenya's NES, for example, does not have legal powers is purely the choice of the executive arm of the government. Unlike the Canadian government, the Kenya government has no constraints to give such powers to the institution within political and constitutional limits. It is in light of this possibility that the two supreme environmental bodies with legal powers have been suggested above.

Should Kenya decide to become a federation it should be careful to ensure that constitutional changes do not polarize legislative authority with regard to the environment. It should avoid the Canadian scenario in this regard. This would help to promote the unity of legal and institutional efforts directed at the environment. Should it become necessary for component governments to own certain natural resources, provisions should be made for the federal government to share or even take a leading role in the management of environmental problems associated with those resources. A sharing arrangement rather than an exclusive control by the federal government would, arguably, not scuttle the sustainable development principle of those who manage natural resources to also manage the associated environmental problems. In this way, a federal Kenya would have the legal clout to wield the co-operation of component governments and yet not be encumbered with the risk of securing co-operation on a mere political basis as in Canada.

Kenya is contending with internal contradictions within a single legislative authority which manifest in fragmented and sometimes contradictory laws and institutions. But the implementation of the suggestions made above would help Kenya to improve environmental management. Canada is saddled with both the kind of contradictions found in Kenya, that is, within each individual legislative authority and the inter-governmental contradictions emanating from the constitutional division of legislative powers between the federal and provincial governments. It is this latter conflict that has engendered several politically-motivated co-operative agreements between the federal and component governments. Such agreements cannot, however, take the place of a legally-secured co-operation. In the case of Kenya, such legal security could be embedded in the Constitution through relevant amendments.

Notes

1. An earlier version of this chapter was published in *Environmental Policy and Law*, Vol. 25, No. 1/2 of 1995.
2. See WCED, 1987; United Nations, 1993.
3. Agenda 21, Chapter 8.13 (United Nations, 1993).
4. WCED, 1987, p. 330.
5. Ojwang, 1990, pp. 221–227; Kanyeihamba, 1975, p. 133.
6. Ojwang, 1990b, p. 223.
7. Kanyeihamba, 1975, p. 131.
8. Brandl and Bungert, 1992, pp. 65–66.
9. The Constitution of Kenya, 1992 rev. Sections 115, 116, 117.
10. Task Force on Canadian Unity, 1987, p. 97.
11. But Smiley notes that the original intention of the fathers of confederation was not to use confederation to promote cultural conflicts especially between English and French Canada, but to establish, *inter alia*, economic union for the provinces (1987, pp. 64–65).
12. The expression "co-operative" implies that the system, to a considerable degree, has the quality of co-ordination.
13. See Wheeler, 1896 for an account of the history of the Canadian Constitution.
14. (1946) A.C. 193.
15. (1976) 1 S.C.R. 477, 53 D.L.R. (3d) 321.
16. (1976) 1 S.C.R.477, 53 D.L.R. (3d) 321, p. 357.
17. Hertz, 1976, p. 84.
18. The rationale being that it is easier for a single legislative authority to have considerable scale of consistency and harmony in making laws which take a comprehensive or holistic view of the subject matter of the legislation than to

have several legislative authorities which may have different priorities and competing interests to this.

19. (1988) 1 S.C.R. 400, pp. 415-417.
20. (1988) 1 S.C.R. 400, pp. 431–432.
21. (1988) 1 S.C.R. 400, p. 434.
22. (1988) 1 S.C.R. 400, pp. 447–448, 457, 459: LaForest declined arguing that the majority decision has the potential of eroding provincial powers in respect of matters over which the provinces have jurisdiction. According to him, his decision maintains the federal–provincial power balance.
23. (1992)1 S.C.R. 3.
24. (1992) 1 S.C.R. 3, p. 64.
25. Contrast with Hogg who submits that where a matter requires the uniformity of actions in such a way that the failure of a province to co-operate would affect other provinces then it is a national concern requiring the exercise of POGG power. (1985, pp. 372–373, 379–380).
26. Arguably, there will not be such a result in the case of the marine environment which is part of the ocean over which the federal government has jurisdiction, thus a justification for the decision of Le Dain on this score.
27. The more POGG power is exercised in favour of the environment as a unity, the more the provinces are denied powers to manage environmental problems associated with management of their resources. Walters, 1991, p. 446.
28. Saunders, 1988, p. 28.
29. Lucas, 1987, p. 39.
30. The exception is Section 2(1) of the Canada Water Act, which defines "interjurisdictional waters" as including water situated wholly in a province the management of which has extra-jurisdictional effect. As stated earlier, this provision has never been unilaterally exercised by the federal government for fear of provoking political tension with the provinces.
31. Harmonization or unification of efforts here does not necessarily mean having a strict uniform law across Canada. Rather, it means that every jurisdiction should, while respecting local circumstances, have in its law standard guidelines which respect the unity of the environment.
32. Hanssen, 1986, pp. 1–2; Franson, and Lucas, 1978, pp. 260–261, 263; Andrews, 1987, p. 22.
33. Scott argues that the "Crown is a person capable of making gifts or contracts like any other person, to whomsoever it chooses to benefit," (1955, p. 6).
34. Trudeau, 1980, p. 95.
35. Lederman, 1975, p. 615.
36. Orban, (1991, pp. 89-93) discusses *inter alia*, the effect of the decisions of the Supreme Court of Canada on Quebec interests and how the latter has reacted to them. See also, Milne, (1986, p. 99) on the decision of the Supreme Court of Canada against the province of Newfoundland in favour of the federal government on exclusive right to the exploitation and development of the offshore. But in a compromise effort, the federal government decided to share that right with the province.
37. Barton, 1986, p. 248.
38. Barton, 1986, p. 248.
39. Mackenzie, 1961, p. 509.
40. *Thornson* v. *A.G. of Canada* (1975) 1 S.C.R. 138; *Nova Scotia Board of*

Censors v. *McNeil* (1976) 2 S.C.R. 265; *Minister of Justice of Canada* v. *Borowski* (1981) 2 S.C.R. 575. In these cases, private persons successfully challenged certain legislation as being unconstitutional. The Supreme Court of Canada refused to apply the public nuisance rule to prevent the private actions. According to the court, since the attorney-general did not redress the wrong, preventing a private action would mean to allow a constitutional wrong to go unredressed.

41. Supra, pp. 17–18: one of the issues was the constitutionality of the federally enacted *Environmental Assessment and Review Process Guidelines Order* (herein Guidelines Order) which the responsible federal minister did not follow when he gave the Province of Alberta permission to go ahead with the Oldman River dam project. The province argued that the federal government had no power under the Constitution to enact the Guidelines Order and so did not need to abide by it in giving or refusing permission for the project. The private person successfully argued that the federal government has a constitutional basis for enacting the Guidelines Order. *A fortiori*, a private person can also challenge a federal–provincial environmental action which offsets the constitutionally entrenched balance of power between the two levels of government.

42. Cited in Brandl, and Bungert, 1992, pp. 65–66. A similar right exists under Section 225 of the 1988 Constitution of the Federal Republic of Brazil.

43. Brandl and Bungert, 1992, p. 34.

44. The Fisheries Act (Canada) gives licensed commercial fishermen the right to recover damages for loss of income arising from unauthorized dumping of harmful substances in water.

45. Ontario Law Reform Commission, 1989, p. 1.

46. See the Kenyan case of *Maina Kamanda & Another* v. *Nairobi City Council & Another* where the court dismissed the objection of *locus standi* against two ratepayers who brought an action to restrain the Nairobi City Council from permitting a former chairman of the Council to enjoy the facilities of the Council after the latter was dissolved. Contrast with *Wangari Maathai* v. *Kenya Times Media Trust*. See also *Alfred Njau* v. *City Council of Nairobi* on the issue of "real interest" of the applicants to enable them to come to court.

47. de Loe, 1991, pp. 28, 33, 40–41.

48. MacLean, R.A. 1986, p. 63.

49. Ogot, 1976, pp. 17–18.

50. Gertzel *et al.*, 1969, pp. 104–106.

51. Ochieng, 1985, p. 141.

52. Kenyatta maintained that "there will be no privileges for any minority. Equally, we shall see that no member of any group undergoes discrimination or oppression at the hands of the majority." (Gertzel *et al.*, 1969, p. 21).

53. Gertzel *et al.*, 1969, p. 111.

54. *Daily Nation* of 14 August, 1964 reproduced in Gertzel, *et al.*, 1969, pp. 111–112.

55. KANU was also seen as a mass movement with a commitment to break down "tribal, linguistic and racial and cultural barriers" necessary for achieving African socialism (Gertzel *et al.*, 1969, pp. 112–113, 115).

56. Robinson, 1993, pp. 301–302.

57. (1983) 658 p. 2d. 709 cited in Sax, 1993, p. 149.
58. Sax, 1993, p. 149.
59. *Standard on Sunday* December 5, 1993, pp. 1, 2.
60. *Constitution of the United States of America* with Amendments, Art. I, Sec. 8, clauses 1, 18; Art. IV, Sec. 3(2) provide for the general welfare power, the spending power and the necessary and proper power. See Tribe, 1988, pp. xxxi–xivii.
61. "The practical dependence upon federal funding has put Congress in the position of being able to influence, and often practically control the policies of recipient States and local governments and institutions, as well as private recipients of federal funds, with respect to all activities extraneous to legitimate federal concerns; for having absolute discretion over the expenditure of federal monies, Congress may extend its largesse however, it chooses, to whomsoever and under whatsoever conditions it might wish . . . unless there is offense to some other constitutional limitation (such as the Bill of Rights-type limitations) . . . there is no constitutional restraint." (Engdahl, 1987, pp. 60, 174–176).
62. Huffman and Coggins, 1986, pp. 58–59.
63. Ogolla, 1992, p. 166.
64. UNEP, 1991a, pp. 6.
65. Sections 147(d), 154(d) and 155(f) of the Local Government Act, and sections 2,37(b) and 65(1) of the Trust Land Act.
66. Ogolla, 1992, p. 168.
67. Section 4(c) of the Forests Act, and sections 14 and 150 of the Water Act.
68. Okidi, 1993, pp. 68–69.
69. Hirji, and Ortolano also noted that even when TARDA knew that the Munyu Dam project would cause water quality problems, it went ahead with the project without seriously considering alternative dam sites just to keep its earlier commitment to execute the project. Thus the results of the EIA were ignored. (1991, p. 166).
70. IGADD, 1993, p. 20.
71. IGADD, 1993, p. 20.

Private property, environment and constitutional change

14

CALESTOUS JUMA

Introduction

The future of Africa's economies and political systems will depend on how well those countries manage their natural resources such as soils, water, forests and wildlife. But in many African countries efforts to manage these resources are being compromised by limitations in the constitutional provisions and laws that relate to property rights in land. In the case of Kenya, the 1994–96 development plan admits that there "has been overemphasis on the protection of property rights and inadequate provision for the regulation of the said rights in the interest of soil conservation." Indeed, "creating severable property interests in interrelated natural systems like surface and groundwater, or dividing single surface systems into discrete ownership units . . . without considering the impact on the larger ecosystem, is inconsistent with the laws of nature."[1]

The aim of this chapter is to provide options for incorporating environmental provisions into national constitutions. The first section provides the conceptual basis and doctrinal foundations upon which new constitutional provisions can be based. The section proposes the use of *public trust* and *customary use* doctrines as well as the *rights of living forms* as bases for the new provisions. The second section summarizes the main arguments for entrenching environmental provisions in constitutions. It provides examples of how this has been done in other countries. In reviewing experiences in other countries, the section shows that in earlier years constitutional provisions were concerned mainly with fundamental environmental rights and particularly those related to the protection of human beings against pollution. But as important principles continue to be derived from national and international practices, statements of public policy have started to accompany the fundamental environmental rights. More recently, especially in light of the recognition of the importance of balancing developmental with environmental goals, countries are starting to build environmental provisions into their constitutions. Section three presents the various options by which countries can entrench environmental provisions into their Constitutions. It suggests that this be done through provisions covering both human-centred environmental rights and the rights of nature. These rights could be reflected in three ways: as goals and guiding principles for public policy, as fundamental rights, and as statements of public policy. The final section examines the judicial enforceability of the suggested constitutional provisions and proposes a number of measures, some which will require fundamental reforms in the way judicial systems function.

The basis for constitutional reform

Environment, sustainable development and law

In seeking to introduce amendments in constitutions to accommodate environmental concerns, it is important to build on established principles in common law as well as in international law. The goal is to arrive at a legal system that ensure that private property interests are in line with laws of nature. It is through an effective alignment of property rights interests with the laws of nature that sustainable development can be guaranteed. Common law provides two important doctrines dealing with public trust and customary use which are an appropriate foundation upon which to introduce environmental provisions in constitutions. In addition, recent developments in international law have provided important principles related to the rights of nature which could be incorporated into constitutions.

The concept of "sustainable development" has been defined by *Our Common Future*, the report of the World Commission on Environment and Development, as the ability to meet the needs of current generations while at the same time not undermining the ability of future ones to meet theirs.[2] This concept embodies a number of principles such as equity, integrative responsibility, precaution, obligations to future generations and sustainability. At the heart of the concept of sustainable development lies fundamental principles of environmental management.

One of the key principles underlying environmental thought is the interaction between the various parts of any natural environment. Over the centuries different societies have formulated rules of social interaction which take into account the laws of nature. However, Western approaches to property rights—and their underlying philosophy of law—have been developed and are being implemented without considering the need to maintain the integrity of the environment. As Feyfogle states, the "boundaries that we draw between farm A and ranch B, carry no meaning in nature's terms. No [wild animals] read our deeds; no percolating groundwater stops to ask permission to enter."[3] He concludes that it is "an error to suggest, as the law largely does, that how an owner treats a part of nature is his business alone. How a person deals with the land, given the linkages in nature, is public business, the concern of all Creation."[4]

The concept of equity is essential to any environmentally-sensitive land use policy. The concept can be elaborated in space and in time. Intra-generational equity may involve the distribution of rights on the basis of gender, geography or ethic identity. The gender issue is critical because women are the main managers of natural resources as they work on the land, gather wood, collect water and act as the repositories of indigenous knowledge.[5] They are also the loci from which cultural practices are propagated in society. Hence granting them equality is not only important on moral and socio-economic grounds, but it is essential for ecological reasons. The issue of gender equality has been a subject of much debate in Africa and there is additional environmental justification for it.

The issue of ethnic equity is one of the most troublesome features of African politics in general. It can be argued that since traditional approaches to natural resource management have an ethnic basis, a constitutional system that does not recognize these entities may not achieve any of its objectives that rely on community participation and the application of indigenous knowledge. The issue here is not to promote any form of ethnic aggrandizement, but to recognize the fact that centuries of ethnic evolution have resulted in numerous solutions to local problems. Every ethnic group represents an innovation in cultural evolution and deserves constitutional protection. And with such protection may come the promotion of ecologically-sound cultural practices. A political system that does not recognize ethnic diversity is not likely to offer the best chances for socio-cultural evolution which is essential for national development.[6]

Also of critical importance is the issue of distributive justice.[7] The argument for distributive justice has often been made on economic and political grounds. But recent evidence shows that the less advantaged members of society are often driven into the unsustainable use of natural resources.

The poor, who are often blamed for much of the environmental degradation in the developing countries, have limited opportunities to improve their lot and cannot reduce the pressure they place on natural resources. It is notable that those countries that have undertaken major land redistribution programmes are also among those that have experienced rapid economic transformation in the last four decades and show great promise in using the latest technologies and economic incentives in managing the environment.[8] The practice of settling the landless already recognizes the importance of distributive justice.

Rationale for constitutional entrenchment

The main aim of environmental law is to provide a legal basis for protecting the environment. However, the objective of protecting the environment is now part of a larger goal of promoting sustainable development. Principle 4 of the Rio Declaration on Environment and Development adopted at the 1992 United Nations Conference on Environment and Development (UNCED) states that in order "to achieve sustainable development, environmental protection shall constitute an integral part of the development process and cannot be considered in isolation from it." Environmental law is the legal means for achieving sustainable development. Indeed, this point is emphasized in Chapter 8 of Agenda 21, the programme of work adopted at UNCED which says that laws and regulations "are among the most important instruments for transforming environment and development policies into action, not only through 'command and control' methods, but also as a normative framework for economic planning and market instruments." The chapter recognizes the need to "develop and implement integrated, enforceable and effective laws and regulations that are based upon sound social, ecological, economic and scientific principles."[9]

The scope of such laws and regulations and their cross-sectoral character requires that their underlying principles be given a constitutional basis. There are several reasons for this. First, the constitution, as the country's supreme scheme of governance would directly affect the degree to which a country is able to implement sustainable development objectives. In turn, the implementation of some of the sustainable development objectives may impinge on constitutional provisions, requiring changes in the constitution. This point is particularly important in light of the fact that Africa's economies are dependent on natural resources for their growth.

Second, the integration of sustainable development goals into the constitution would bring environmental law at par with other legal norms and would allow environmental considerations to be integrated into laws, regulations and court decisions. For example, the right to a clean and healthy environment would be at par with other fundamental rights such as freedom of association and expression.

Third, environmental considerations would cease to be a concern of special groups and narrow political interests and would be lodged into the legal order through specific constitutional provisions. This would allow environmental matters to be dealt with at the highest level of the legal order and would show the seriousness a country attaches to sustainable development.

Fourth, as the supreme scheme of governance for a country, the constitution would guide and influence public behaviour and discourse on environmental matters. This is critical in the early stages of the development of a new field of public interest. Many African countries are in the process of reforming their constitutions and new editions will become a subject of much public interest. Indeed, the process of constitution-making itself generates considerable awareness over the issues being considered.

Finally, international environmental law is codifying a number of important principles which should be reflected in national constitutions. It would make it easier for countries to implement many of the emerging environmental conventions if national constitutions provide for commitment to environmental management. A constitutional requirement that such conventions be discussed in the legislature and integrated into domestic law would bring environmental practices in line with the countries' commitments to environmental treaties. On the whole, there is adequate environmental awareness in many African countries to support an informed debate on how to incorporate environmental provisions into the constitution.

The nature of constitutions

National constitutions fall into two broad categories: institutional and programmatic.[10] These categories reveal what emphasis a constitution places on issues related to the structure of government and the national programme for long-term change. All constitutions generally contain articles on institutional arrangements for governance, national policy, a bill of rights and ways by which the constitution can be amended. A constitution is meant to foster good governance and provide stability, predictability, transparency and accountability in overall political life. It guides the process of change but at the same time responds to change. A constitution that can be arbitrarily amended may be as detrimental to overall national welfare as a rigid one.[11]

Institutional constitutions assume that most of the principles needed to govern a country have already been identified and what is important is to reflect them in a set of institutional arrangements and social behaviour. Institutional constitutions tend to put emphasis on the organs and structure of government as well as "universal" principles such as fundamental rights and freedoms. Such constitutions are normally brief and expect that the necessary laws and institutional arrangements will be created by the legislature and the executive branch. Considerable attention is also given to balancing between the various arms of government and creating the necessary separation of powers.

Programmatic constitutions, on the other hand, tend to give more attention to anticipating future developments and providing specific programmes for the state to implement. Programmatic constitutions reflect a view that the world is rapidly changing and the supreme scheme of national governance needs to reflect this perspective. In other words, such constitutions are programmes for the future which are gradually translated into reality. They are often flexible and can be amended with relative ease in light of major changes in the social, political and economic milieu. They tend to avoid the view that most of the answers to social problems are embodied in past practices and institutional arrangements. Emerging issues such as sustainable development can be more easily incorporated in constitutions which allow for programmatic provisions.

While it is important to reflect some major programmatic issues in the constitution, there is also the danger that developing countries may wish to include almost every aspect of social life in this document. The constitution cannot be used as a substitute for specific laws and policy pronouncements but it must at the same time take into account the most critical issues that require entrenchment at the highest level of the legal order. It is not a surprise, for example, that the issue of trust lands is incorporated into the Kenyan constitution as a programmatic theme. The essence of the constitutional provisions on trust lands is the introduction of "modern" development practices. These practices had the effect of eroding customary rights and interests. Indeed, the main focus of the colonial economic was to replace traditional land and agricultural practices with settler ones.[12]

The point, however, is that there is already a precedent for including both institutional and programmatic issues in the Constitution of Kenya. The challenge is how to determine which programmatic issues need to be incorporated while maintaining a balance between such issues and institutional provisions relating to the structure and organs of government as well as fundamental rights and freedoms.

By balancing between institutional and programmatic provisions, it is possible for the Constitution to incorporate both fundamental environmental rights and statements of public policy. It can be argued that poorer nations may be less interested in entrenching environmental provisions in their constitutions because they have pressing problems such as poverty and unemployment. However, it is also through adopting sustainable development programmes that these countries can solve these problems. In fact, relatively poor or developing countries such as Portugal, Mozambique, Uganda, South Africa, Turkey, Mexico, India and Brazil have found it compelling to include environmental provisions in their constitutions.

Countries which already have a long tradition of environmental management and awareness may not need to incorporate such provisions. This is because these issues may have already become part of the political and legal tradition. "It is precisely in those countries in which the general public neglects environmental concerns that constitutional provisions are needed, both to educate the people and to guide the decision-making process of the government."[13] Environmental provisions in federal constitutions may also provide a basis for reflecting such concerns in state or regional constitutions, as discussed in the preceding chapter. State or regional governments have a more direct interest in local natural resources, especially where they are linked to cultural practices and specific economic interests. Issues such as cultural identity play a major role in state or regional politics and are often reflected in the interest to protect certain ecological features such as landscapes, forests, species and other utilitarian features that form part of a culture.

A federal system which does not have adequate environmental safeguards may undermine the environment. This is mainly because reductions in financial support from central government could lead to intensification in the exploitation of localized natural resources which could have negative impacts. The need to generate revenue for local development may lead authorities to overlook the need for environmental protection. Already, there are indications in a number of African countries that reductions in public expenditure due to macro-economic reform policies are affecting the ability of local authorities to manage natural resources. Such a trend could be worsened by the creation of state governments with inadequate provisions for environmental management.

One of the key aspects of constitutions is the emphasis placed on private property. Section 75(1) of the Kenyan constitution, for example, says that "no property of any description shall be compulsorily taken possession of, and no interest in or right over property of any description shall be compulsorily acquired." Property can only be compulsorily acquired where it "is necessary in the interest of . . . public health, town and country planning or the development or utilization of property so as to promote the public benefit." The acquisition can only take place if "the necessity thereof is such as to afford reasonable justification for the causing of any hardship that may result to any person having an interest in or right over the property." Other requirements for compulsory acquisition are proof that the action will promote the public interest and that there will be prompt payment of compensation.[14]

The outcome of these provisions has been a strong institution of private property related to land ownership articulated through a number of laws. This institution allows individuals to acquire and dispose of land as they wish (under the principle of "willing-buyer-willing-seller"). The state, however, can acquire land in the public interest under the provisions of the Land Acquisition Act. The provisions for regulating land use are deposited in statutes such as the Agriculture Act, the Public Health Act, the Chiefs' Authority Act, the Local Government Act, the Town Planning Act, the Land Planning Act and the Water Act. Under the Agriculture Act, for example, the director of agriculture is authorized to issue land preservation orders to land owners prohibiting them to undertake certain activities or requiring them to take certain land management measures.

The Kenyan legal system links the ability of individuals or groups to file suits in the courts to their private property interests. The issue of *locus standi* (or standing in law) is often related to whether one has a property interest in the matter being considered. In the 1989 *Wangari Maathai* v. *Kenya Times Media Trust* case, an individual attempted to stop what was seen as a violation of the public interest in the integrity and aesthetics of an urban public recreation park. The defendant was to build a 60-storey building in Nairobi's Uhuru Park. The case fell on the test of *locus standi*. It was held that for an individual to bring a suit against the proposed construction, she or he had to establish an injury to herself or himself over and above the injury that would be caused to the general public. The only person with the competence to institute such proceedings is the attorney-general.

Another problem with the current constitutional provisions is that they restrict opportunities for creating multiple land uses based on simultaneous production of renewable resources which are necessary for the conservation of wildlife.[15] For purposes of soil conservation or the conservation of other natural resources, the state can expropriate land provided that the owner has been required to carry out certain measures and has failed to do so. Other environmental needs such as corridors for wildlife migration on private land cannot be easily accommodated under such provisions.

While it is necessary to include in the constitution the right of individuals to a healthy environment, it is also critical to review the provisions relating to private property (especially land tenure) and bring them in line with the requirements of sustainable development in general and natural resource management in particular. The specific nature of the provisions need to be carefully studied in light of the current debate on constitutional change and land issues in African countries. While there are general provisions that relate to the right to a healthy environment, specific issues such as legal standing and elimination of discrimination on the basis of gender, use of instruments such as environmental impact assessments (EIA) and the right of access to environmental information may need to be reflected in the constitution. The last item is particularly relevant because of the public cannot play a vital role in environmental management unless it has access to scientific and technical information. Such a constitutional provision would also legitimize activities such as environmental monitoring.

Doctrinal foundations

The public trust doctrine

The government as a trustee has the fundamental duty of "to preserve and enhance the value of assets, ranging from cultural products of the past to the resources and an environment that will guarantee our future and that of our descendants."[16] One of the main problems with the Kenyan constitution is that it articulates the notion of public trust in such a way that it works against local communities. The constitutional provisions and laws pertaining to trust lands, for example, have worked expressly against the interest of the trust lands' inhabitants. The provisions which allow for the abolition of those customary practices that are repugnant to written law are becoming a hindrance to sustainable development in general and community participation in particular. The conservation of resources such as water, forests and wildlife could be promoted through a system of public trusteeship rather than state ownership. But this will require that the concept of public trust be defined in a positive way that will allow the state to act as a genuine custodian of the long-term interests of the people.

Under the public trust doctrine certain resources can be held in trust for the citizens of various parts of the country. The doctrine requires that such resources are used solely in the interest of the public. In the 1983 *National Audubon Society* v. *Supreme Court* case, the California Supreme Court ruled that public trust is "an affirmation of the duty of the state to protect the people's common heritage of streams, lakes, marshlands and tidelands, surrendering the right of protection only in rare cases when the abandonment of that right is consistent with the purposes of the trust . . ."[17] The public trust doctrine can thus be used to protect the interests current and future generations. The doctrine restrains the state from converting publicly-held resources to private interests, which is one of the main criticism of government dealings in land in African countries. It also gives the state the authority to conserve natural resources on private land.

The doctrine of public trust is not alien in African society and is not a peculiarity of "modern" law. In fact, this doctrine is central to traditional juridical systems and has governed the management of natural resources, especially land, for generations. In many African societies, land used to be owned by the overall ethnic unit which held it in trust for the members of the community. At a more localized level of social organization, other forms of property rights prevailed. The application of the public trust doctrine included the assertion of sovereignty and the military defence of the territory. There is already a sense of familiarity with the doctrine among many African societies, provided it is presented in a way that distinguishes it from many current forms of state ownership which do not necessarily satisfy the requirements of genuine public trusteeship.

The customary use doctrine

In evolutionary legal system the customs of a country form the basis of its common law. Indeed, custom is defined as long-established practice considered as unwritten law. This is the certainly the case in Britain where customary law has over the centuries become English common law which has been then exported to other countries. In Britain custom is now recognized as local common law (*lex loci*) which allows residents of a certain area to use their common natural resources. It often includes rights to collect wood, graze animals, collect water, cut grass and engage in recreational activities. These rights are akin to those practices on a larger scale in Africa and form the basis of traditional customs.

To qualify as *lex loci* and recognized as a customary right, the practice must be reasonable and have existed undisputed beyond living memory. Furthermore, the customary rights are required to be certain, peaceful and obligatory. In addition, they should not be repugnant to other laws or accepted customs. The repugnancy test is of vital importance here because it entails a cultural judgement. Repugnancy must be defined in the context of the prevailing traditional values to a avoid a situation where it is used to suppress customary practices and to promote rights based on imported legal principles.

Customary rights have found expression on regional constitutions. For example, Article 141(3) of the Bavarian Constitution (in Germany) links environment and culture: "Every one is permitted to enjoy the wilderness and to seek recreation in open country, particularly to enter forest and alpine pasture, to travel over the waters and to appropriate wild growing fruits of the forest to the extent which is customary. In doing this, everyone is obliged to take good care of nature and countryside."

Unfortunately, some African countries, such as Kenya provide the basis for the erosion of customary rights in their constitutions. Section 115(2) of the Kenyan constitution articulates the modernization programme by stating that county councils can hold trust land for the benefit of local communities and shall give "effect to such rights, interests and other benefits in respect of the land as may, under the African customary law . . . be vested in any tribe . . ." provided that such rights, interests and benefits are not repugnant to any written law. The underlying philosophy here is that such customary traditions should gradually give way to new development practices backed by written law. There are several other provisions in the Constitution as well as statutes which give effect to the transformation programme. It is argued elsewhere in this book that this transformation programme was misconceived and needs to be reviewed, especially in light of the importance of community-based management of natural resources.

Customary rights, if recognized in constitutions and given the appropriate life in legislation, can serve important conservation functions. For example, customary rights can be extended to forests, wildlife, water and other resources without affecting the property rights in the land on which they occur. The custom doctrine can also be used to justify and extend the use of easement as an instrument for conservation without effecting compulsory acquisition of land. The current widespread use of customary rights and practices makes it possible to promote this doctrine in Africa, especially in pastoral lands. The fact that local communities have a detailed understanding of their environment makes it easier for them to contribute effectively to conservation and development programmes. In addition, customary practices can form the foundation upon which to craft new institutions such as community land trusts.

The rights of living forms

The human-centred approach to environmental conservation has been undergoing modification in the last few decades to reflect the needs of future generations. The 1972 Stockholm Declaration of the United Nations Conference on the Human Environment says that humanity "bears a solemn responsibility to protect and improve the environment for present and future generations." Intergenerational responsibilities have become a central part of the concept of sustainable development. Indeed, Principle 1 of the Rio Declaration states that "human beings are at the centre of concerns for sustainable development. They are entitled to a healthy and productive life in harmony with nature." This statement reflects the human-centred basis for sustainable development but also reflects the need to create a balance between human needs and nature.

The fact that nature has intrinsic value that is independent of its direct human utility is starting to be recognized in international law.[18] One of the first substantive articulations of this view is in the 1982 World Charter for Nature which states that "every form of life is unique, warranting respect regardless of its worth to man." The 1992 Convention on Biological Diversity recognized the "intrinsic value of biological diversity and the ecological, genetic, social, economic, educational, cultural, recreational and aesthetic values of biological diversity and its components." In addition, the signatories to the Convention are also conscious "of the importance of biological diversity for evolution and for maintaining life sustaining systems in the biosphere." The Convention clearly distinguishes between intrinsic and utilitarian values of biological diversity. Such language provides a basis upon which nations can articulate nature's rights to reinforce the human-centred provisions which are already being reflected in an increasing number of constitutions and laws.

There are a number of contending views on the extent to which rights can be extended beyond those beings that do not feel pain or pleasure. Already, many African countries have introduced laws that provide for the prevention of cruelty against certain animals and its extension is consistent with modern thinking. There are other arguments relating to whether living forms need to be protected because of their utility to humankind or because of the moral view that they have interests that are independent of human needs and perceptions. The application of the utilitarian argument is sufficient to argue a case for granting rights to living forms. Since the protection of endangered species is already an accepted practice, it is possible to argue the case for precautionary measures for the protection of living forms in ways that are consistent with ecological dynamics. The conservation of certain ecosystems, for example, could be a matter of constitutional concern. An ecosystem approach, provided it does not diminish the importance of species, can be used to cover the related non-living forms. The time may not have come to grant rights to non-living forms.[19]

It should also be noted that idea of granting rights to living forms or ecosystems would not be inconsistent with African culture. To the contrary, most traditional societies have maintained sophisticated belief systems which contribute to the conservation of certain species or habitats, through, for example, the use of totems and shrines. The reverence for nature, which is so central in African spirituality ensured that "forests, certain kinds of trees, animals, and sources of water were preserved in the name of religion."[20] Freedom of worship as provided in constitutions could be expanded to accommodate traditional worship systems, which would also provide for the protection of natural resources.

It seems easy to dismiss the ecological wisdom embodied in traditional practices on the assumption that social advancement has moved us a step away from animism. But it is also notable that it is precisely in the more industrialized countries that search for ecological roots of humankind is most intense. What seemed like technological liberation from the vagaries of mother nature has turned out to be an ecological alienation. Both in modern ecological thought and in African cultural values there is a strong basis upon which to formulate constitutional provisions that would protect species and ecosystems for utilitarian and ethical reasons.

Experiences with environmental provisions

Environmental provisions are increasingly being incorporated into the constitutions of nations and their constituent states.[21] Some constitutions have placed environmental considerations in the framework of human development. For example, Article 45(1) of the 1978 Spanish constitution states that "everyone has the right to enjoy an environment suitable for the development of the person as well as the duty to preserve it." In its attempts to entrench environmental provisions into the constitution, an expert commission sought in 1981 to modify Article 20(1) of the German Basic Law to read as follows: "The Federal Republic of Germany shall be a democratic and social federal state. *It shall protect and preserve the culture and the natural fundamentals of human life.*"[22] It is understood that the "natural fundamentals of human life" include the natural resource base upon which economic activities are founded.

The Federal Republic of Austria, in Section 1 of its 1984 Constitution, declared that the country "subscribes to universal protection of the environment." This means "the preservation of the natural environment, being the basis for human existence, from harmful influences. Universal environmental protection in particular consists of measures to keep clear air, water and soil, as well as avoidance of nuisances caused by noise."

Such constitutional provisions are not limited to highly industrialized countries. Article 225(1) of the 1988 Constitution of the Federal Republic of Brazil provides that: "Everyone is entitled to an ecologically balanced environment, which is an asset of everyday use to the common man and essential to a healthy quality of life; this imposes a duty on the government and the community to protect and preserve it for the present and future generations."[23] Paragraph I of Article 225(1) calls upon the government to "preserve and restore essential ecological processes and arrange for the ecological management of species and ecosystems."

Brazil's elaborate constitutional provisions on environment cover the conservation of biological diversity and genetic resources, creation of protected areas, application of environmental impact assessments, biological and chemical risk management, environmental education, protection of flora and fauna and prevention of cruelty to animals, and prevention of species extinction. Other issues covered by the Constitution include land restoration in mining areas, location of nuclear power plants, and specially protected areas (including the Amazonian forest, the Atlantic jungle, the Serra do Mar mountain range, the Mato Grosso swamp, and the Coastal zone).

The 1990 Mozambican Constitution has been formulated along the lines of the Portuguese and Brazilian constitutions, and provides that "all citizens shall have the right to live in a balanced environment and the duty to defend it."

The Namibian Constitution covers environmental issues in the form of a statement of public policy. In Article 95(l), the Constitution says that the state shall promote the welfare of the people through "maintenance of ecosystems, essential ecological processes and biological diversity of Namibia and utilization of living natural resources on a sustainable basis for the benefit of all Namibians, both present and future; in particular the Government shall provide measures against the dumping or recycling of foreign nuclear and toxic waste on Namibian territory."

South Africa has included environmental rights in its 1994 Interim Constitution in the following formulation: "Every person shall have the right to an environment which is not detrimental to his or her health or well-being." This negative formulation is not ideal as it does not impose a duty on the part of the state to protect or improve the environment.[24] In addition, it may create a hierarchy of rights where positively-formulated rights may be considered to have priority over environmental rights. The provision, however, is accompanied by other constitutional provisions which deal with the right to information and administrative justice.[25]

The 1992 draft Constitution of Uganda has identified environmental protection as a national objective at par with political, economic, social and cultural and foreign policy objectives. Article 36(1) states that "it shall be the duty of the State to ensure that all persons enjoy a clean and healthy environment." In Article 36(2) the draft Constitution establishes the link between environmental protection and sustainable development by stating that "in order to attain sustainable development, environmental protection and improvement shall form an integral part of the development process."

In this regard, environmental protection is seen as part of the broader social and development goals of society. It is notable that other natural resource issues are reflected in Article 29(2a) under a section of social objectives which calls upon the State to "prevent or minimize damage and destruction to water resources resulting from pollution or other causes." Article 29(2c) invokes sustainable development principles by calling upon the state to "promote public awareness of the need to manage water resources in a balanced and sustainable manner, for present and future generations."

In Article 66(1) the draft Constitution states that "every Ugandan shall have the right to a clean and healthy environment." In a public policy statement deposited in Article 66(2) the draft Constitution calls upon Parliament to "enact laws for taking of necessary measures against pollution and destruction of the environment, and generally for the protection of the environment." More extended environmental provisions are lodged in Article 278 which calls upon Parliament to formulate laws which provide for "measures intended to protect and preserve the environment from abuse and degradation and to manage the environment for sustainable development . . ." The Article deals more specifically with protected areas, soil erosion, biological risks, chemical pollution, toxic and nuclear waste, urban waste, physical planning, air and water pollution, biophysical state and ecological balance, and environmental awareness. Hence, the draft Constitution deals with environment as issues of state objectives, fundamental rights, and public policy statements.

What is notable in these constitutions is that there is no indication that other fundamental rights may affect the degree to which environmental rights can be enforced. There are no provisions that explicitly modify the way private property rights can be enforced. The 1917 Constitution of Mexico, however, imposes public interest restrictions on the use of private property.[26] Article 27 says: "The Nation shall at all times have the right to impose on private property such limitations as the public interest may demand, as well as the right to regulate the utilization of natural resources which are susceptible of appropriation, in order to conserve them to ensure a more equitable distribution of public wealth, to attain a well-balanced development of the country and improvement of the living conditions of the rural and urban population."

Options for constitutional reform

Environment and national identity

The language and emphasis on constitutional environmental provisions tends to reflect and enhance the identity of a country. Certain countries are associated with certain environmental features which give them their identity and have over the decades or centuries influenced their outlook. The Netherlands Constitution, for example, makes specific reference to the improvement of the environment which is an attribute of the culture. The Netherlands exists in its present form because of human investment in reclaiming land from the sea. The Brazilian constitution, on the other hand, recognizes that forests and other living forms are part of its identity and pays particular attention to the conservation of biological diversity. The constitution makes specific reference to the Amazonian forest. Other countries that place emphasis on their cultural heritage have sought to link environmental conservation with cultural preservation.

Kenya, like many of these countries, could give consideration to its identity and reflect it in the formulation of environmental constitutional provisions. Issues that could be considered include the link between cultural diversity and biological diversity. The conservation of biological diversity is closely tied to the maintenance of the country's cultural identities. It would be inadequate to call for the maintenance of these identities without at the same time taking into account the conservation of the material basis (particularly plants, animals and landscapes) on which they are founded. It is the diversity of landscapes and their constituent plants and animals that has given African countries their cultural wealth. In this regard, plants and animals have more than just a utilitarian function; their existence value is critical for the maintenance of cultural identities.

Another area of importance is the conservation of wildlife and the related plants and landscapes. Although this aspect has a strong utilitarian function, it is equally important to recognize that nature's rights are becoming a strong case for conserving wildlife. The case for preserving certain species for their existence value is gaining in momentum. This is already reflected in the Convention on Biological Diversity which many African countries have ratified.

In seeking an environmental identity, it is important to take into account the relationship between culture, the existence of species and the preservation of landscapes. These relationships will require that a balance be created between human-centred environmental rights on the one hand and nature's rights on the other. The recognition of the latter does not necessarily mean that they will stand in the way of development. To the contrary, they will enhance many of the country's development objectives but also give higher moral standing to conservation efforts. This argument can be extended further to argue for greater reflection of environmental matters in foreign policy, such as management of trans-boundary natural resources.

Human-centred environmental provisions

Most of the recent national and state constitutions contain sections dealing with national objectives and guiding principles for public policy. A section on objectives and principles helps to guide the various branches of government as well as the general public on how to implement or interpret the various sections of the constitution. The objectives and principles reveal the underpinnings of the constitutional provisions and can help in the interpretation of the laws created to implement the constitution. Objectives and principles can also serve as preambular statements which provide the background against which the provisions of the constitution are formulated. They therefore reflect the overall goals of the constitution. Objectives and principles tend to appear in constitutions that seek to be programmatic. They reflect a sense of purpose to change the *status quo* and are therefore dynamic in character. In some constitutions such provisions may require the head of state to report to parliament on progress on the implementation of the constitutional programme.

Where fundamental environmental rights are provided, they must be clear and self-executing (which means they should not require additional enabling legislation). They should provide individuals with the fundamental right of freedom from negative environmental effects (e.g pollution) while at the same time granting them a right to a clean and healthy environment. In addition to granting rights, they should also impose duties on the citizens and government agencies to protect the environment. In order for them to be truly self-executing, judicial mechanisms such as courts that can deal with constitutional matters must be created. It may not be sufficient to simply state that citizens shall have a right to a clean, healthy and balanced environment. There must be other constitutional provisions that enable the people to have access to the information needed to enforce their rights.

In addition, other fundamental rights related to property, especially those of women and children, must be strengthened and clearly articulated in a constitution. Section 70 of the Kenyan constitution provides for the fundamental rights and freedoms of the individual "whatever his race, tribe, place of origin or residence or other local connexion, political opinions, colour, creed or sex. . ." However, the provision which provides for execution of these rights and freedoms, Section 82, specifically omits "sex" from those attributes which should be protected from discriminatory law-making. This sends a signal to the judiciary that the mention of gender is merely a declaration and need not be accorded the full support of the law. Women's critical role in environmental management makes reform of this provision even more urgent.

Statements of public policy are aimed at encouraging governmental action on particular issues. They are dynamic and anticipate solutions to future problems. Public policy statements fall in two categories: those that call upon the legislature to regulate specific areas; and those that provide guidelines for the state as a whole (covering all branches of government and other constitutional entities). They provide considerable scope for the government to enact laws, create enabling institutions and formulate specific programmes for implementation.

Nature's rights

Provisions relating to nature's rights—a term used here to cover species and ecosystems—should be closely related to those dealing with human-centred environmental rights to avoid potential conflicts of misinterpretation.[27] If possible such rights should be liked to the human-based environmental rights, especially where such rights are tied to national identity. Implementing nature's rights will require changes in other judicial areas. For example, it will require the extension of *locus standi* to a wider range of interested parties. Such changes in the judicial process could be linked to the legitimization of the role of citizens or custodians of certain resources in implementing environmental constitutional provisions.

Recognizing nature's rights would not mean that non-living things would automatically get priority over human needs. It simply means that defined areas of nature's rights, for example, plants and animals, would be given legal standing in their own right as part of a larger effort to protect the environment. Acknowledging nature's rights would have a number of practical implications. The first area requiring clarification would be to define the nature of the rights and how they could be reflected in the constitution and in the relevant laws. The second issue is how such rights could be asserted. The character of rights pertaining to natural entities and animals could be based on a shared right of survival and avoidance of suffering. The existence of laws that prohibit cruelty against animals and the recognition of the intellectual and social capabilities of animals such as whales and elephants provides a basis for broadening the scope of nature's rights.[28] Some countries have incorporated a compassion clause in their constitutions. Article 51A(g) of the Indian constitution, for example, imposes a duty on "every citizen to protect and improve the natural environment . . . and to have compassion for living creatures."

One of the first countries to recognize nature's rights and to embody them in its constitution is Brazil. Paragraph VIII of Article 225(I) calls upon the state to "protect the flora and fauna; practices that place their ecological function at risk, lead to the extinction of species, or submit animals to cruel treatment are hereby prohibited." This provision not only recognizes the right of flora and fauna to exist, but it also take into account the fact that animals are capable of feeling and should not be subjected to cruelty.

Recognizing nature as a holder of rights like other juristic persons is less complicated than defining the character of the rights. Indeed, inanimate objects such as ships can be parties in litigation. Corporations, for example, are juristic persons and obtain legal representation through their boards of directors or trustees. Like such boards, it is possible and feasible to give legal standing to conservation groups to represent nature. On the whole, legislation providing for nature's rights would require a great deal of innovative thinking to ensure that there is a balance between nature's rights and the rights of individuals, corporations, estates and other legal entities.

Judicial enforcement

The effective implementation of environmental provisions in constitutions will depend largely on the enforcement system. The existence of constitutional provisions that cannot be enforced can over time undermining the standing of the constitution itself. For example, Article 15(2) of the constitution of the former German Democratic Republic (GDR) provided that: "In the interests of the welfare of citizens, the state and society shall protect nature. The competent bodies shall ensure the purity of the water and the air, and protection for flora and fauna and the natural beauties of the homeland; in addition this is the affair of every citizen." However, recent evidence from the GDR has revealed extensive environmental degradation and cast doubts about the efficacy of other provisions in the constitution. In many countries constitutional issues are handled by special constitutional courts or the highest national court. Courts may not enforce provisions that are merely declarations and require additional legislation to be enforced. In other words, critical constitutional provisions must be self-executing.

Self-execution

The effectiveness of certain constitutional provisions on environment will depend on whether they are self-executing. In other words whether they can be implemented without requiring additional legislation to put them into effect.[29] Many constitutional statements are non-mandatory and therefore are not self-executing. Such provisions are expressions of public sentiment or statements of public policy. Many of the self-executing provisions are mandatory in character. They order a particular outcome, grant a right, or impose a limitation or duty. They are only self-executing insofar as they can be judicially enforced. Mandatory provisions imposing prohibitions or limits of legislative agencies are often self-executing. For example, Article 82(1) of the Kenyan Constitution says that "no law shall make any provision that is discriminatory either of itself or in its effect." Such mandatory-prohibitory provisions can be enforced by declaring that laws that contain the offending provisions are unconstitutional.

Constitutional provisions can also be framed in a mandatory non-prohibitory manner. The provisions can oblige the legislature to grant a right, for example: "Parliament shall enact laws which set up agencies to formulate regulations to protect the environment." Other statements may contain public policy declarations, for example: "The laws of the country shall ensure a healthy environment for present and future generations." Article XI(2) of the constitution of the State of Illinois (USA) provides that "each person has the right to a healthful environment. Each person may enforce this right against any party, government or private, through appropriate legal proceedings subject to reasonable limitation and regulation as the General Assembly may provide by law."

Similarly, Article XLIX of the Massachusetts constitution (USA) states that the "people shall have the right to clean air and water, freedom from excessive and unnecessary noise, and the natural, scenic, historic and aesthetic qualities of their environment; and the protection of the people in their right to conservation, development and utilization of the agricultural, mineral, forest, water, air and other natural resources is hereby declared to be a public purpose. The general court shall have the power to enact legislation necessary or expedient to protect such rights."

Legal standing and environmental representation

The issue of *locus standi* or legal standing regarding environmental matters is of prime importance when dealing with judicial enforceability of constitutional provisions. It is tempting for governments to limit the categories of persons who can enforce environmental constitutional provisions to government agencies. Provisions that allow private enforcement, under defined circumstances, would given such provisions more life and would enhance their enforceability. The constitution or derivative legislation can define those who have *locus standi* to include individuals, interest groups, environmental trustees or guardians. In light of the importance of implementing sustainable development objectives, such standing could also be formulated in such a way as to cover the interests of future generations or of nature.

The area of popular action is an important source of judicial enforcement of environmental constitutional provisions. Since environmental matters are deemed to affect the public in general, members of the public as individuals should have the right to bring legal action to enforce the relevant constitutional provisions. One of the main problems in such suits is the payment of costs in case private citizens lose a case in which they are acting in the interest of the public. The Brazilian Constitution "exempts losing plaintiffs from the payment of costs and the opposing party's attorney's fees unless they sue in bad faith."[30] To avoid creating an unduly litigious society, the constitution may provide guidelines on how social action can be invoked, possible through a system under which environmental interests are articulated through *bona fide* representatives. Such a system should also ensure that access to the courts is not limited by legal fees.

The ability of private citizens to enforce a public duty is central to the implementation of environmental provisions. Indeed, "a test based on private rights is insufficient for effective enforcement of public duties by individuals."[31] A solution to this problem would be the liberalization of the standing requirement. As argued by Harding, "the important task is to rid the law once and for all of the illogical and possibly dangerous notion that public duties can only be enforced by the Attorney-General."[32] With the growing liberalization of the political and economic systems, it is equally important to extend standing beyond government agencies and individuals who have private rights to protect.

An example is provided by the 1976 Constitution of Portugal (as revised in 1982) which contains both fundamental rights and duties of the citizens in Article 66(1): "Everyone shall have the right to a healthy and ecologically-balanced human environment and the duty to defend it." Article 66(3) enables private citizens to sue in the interest of the environment. It says that everyone "shall have the right, in accordance with the law, to promote the prevention or cessation of factors leading to the deterioration of the environment and, in the case of direct losses, to a corresponding compensation." The state also has a role to play. According to Article 9(e), the basic task of the state shall be to "protect and enhance the cultural heritage of the Portuguese people, defend nature and the environment and scarce natural resources."

The 1983 Constitution of Turkey provides in Article 56(1) that "everyone has the right to live in a healthy, balanced environment." This fundamental right is followed in Article 56(2) with a statement of public policy declaring that "it is the duty of the State and the citizens to improve the natural environment, and to prevent environmental pollution." The implementation of this provision, however, is circumscribed by Article 65 which says that "the state shall fulfill its duties as laid out in the Constitution in the social and economic fields, within the limits of its financial resources, taking into consideration the maintenance of economic stability."

To avoid a situation where statements of public policy go unimplemented because they are not self-executing, the constitution can provide for a mechanism to effect the implementation of those provisions that give standing to certain legal or juristic persons. In the case of Brazil, for example, the supreme federal tribunal can call upon the relevant sections of the government to implement a particular constitutional provision within 30 days. But an action alleging unconstitutionality by omission can only be brought about by the president, the presiding officers of the senate, the chamber of deputies, the legislative assembly, a state governor, the attorney-general, the federal council of the brazilian bar association, a political party of the national congress or a labour union.[33]

The concept of juristic persons (such as corporations, firms, associations, trusts, foundations, community groups, clubs, traditional institutions, non-governmental organizations (NGOs) and other civil institutions) has been recognized in the Interim Constitution of South Africa which has significantly liberalized *locus standi*. Environmental organizations or other parties—including state agencies—could, as defined by specific pieces of legislation, act as guardians of nature and be given the legal standing to act or sue on behalf of nature. But in order to strengthen the role of juristic persons, it is equally important to ensure that their lives are given adequate constitutional protection.

Under conditions of rapid political change there is often a tendency for governments to seek to restrict the freedom association. Such efforts often affect the operation of certain juristic persons, especially where they are deemed to have political implications. The liberalization of standing will necessarily go hand in hand with the provision of safeguards against the taking away of the lives of juristic persons without fair and reasonable due process of the law. There is already a hierarchy in the respect of the lives of juristic persons with government corporations and private firms at the top and institutions of civil society such as NGOs at the bottom. All juristic persons should have equal constitutional protection. It may be appropriate to consider an extension of the current provisions regarding freedom of association to cover such juristic persons or to propose a new provision altogether.

India offers an advanced example of "representative standing" with highly simplified procedures for effecting social action litigation. Any concerned citizen or group can exercise representative standing by simply sending an ordinary letter to the high court or supreme court stating where fundamental rights of any group are being violated. Such a letter or postcard is then treated by the courts as a writ. This is followed by investigation, provision of legal aid and a court hearing.

Information, participation and conflict management

The enforcement of environmental rights is dependant on the ability of the general public to have access to information and to be able to participate effectively in making environment-related decisions. The right-to-know and the right-to-know-more are important requirements for effective decision-making. Most African countries put considerable emphasis on official secrecy while managing public affairs. But this is starting to change. For example, Section 23 of the Interim Constitution of South Africa states: "Every person shall have the right of access to all information held by the state or any of its organs at any level of government in so far as such information is required for the exercise or protection of any of his or her rights."

Such a provision, especially when coupled with the right to environmental education, is a powerful tool for the enforcement of environmental rights.[34] Its limitation, however, lies in the emphasis on government organs. Much of the information needed to enforce environmental rights is held by private firms, independent institutions and private individuals. With the growing privatization of economic activities, even more of the information needed for making decisions on environmental management will lie in the private sector. Constitutional provisions could extend their coverage to such sources of information.

In the absence of an explicit constitutional provision on the right to information, much can be achieved through an extended interpretation of the provisions regarding freedom of expression. Section 79(1) of the Kenyan constitution, for example, takes freedom of expression to include "freedom to hold opinions . . . freedom to receive ideas and information . . . freedom to communicate ideas and information . . . and freedom from interference with his correspondence."

The right to participate in environmental decision-making should be made a cornerstone of administrative justice. This would include principles such as fairness, democratic representation, reasonableness, transparency and accountability. Article 18 of the Namibian constitution, for example, sets out a clear administrative justice provision: "Administrative bodies and administrative officials shall act fairly and reasonably and comply with the requirements imposed on such bodies and officials by common law and any relevant legislation and persons aggrieved by the exercise of such acts and decisions shall have the right to seek redress before a competent court or tribunal."

The holistic nature of ecological processes also creates overlapping interests and the potential for conflicts. Creating a balance between private ownership and public interest is not an act that can be achieved in one moment and frozen in time; it is an evolutionary process requiring continuous generation of information and knowledge. The interconnectedness of ecological features necessarily creates conditions of intertwined interests. Many of the conflicts arising from such interlinkages can be dealt with more effectively through approaches that are based on mediation rather than litigation. This has indeed been the method in many traditional societies and modern thought is already lending support to mediation on the account that it entails lower transaction costs.[35] Mediation and the related conflict settlement methods also take into account the pervasive ignorance over ecological processes.

Institutional Implications

The effective implementation of environmental provisions in the constitution in general, and environmental law and policies in particular, will entail significant reforms in the overall system of government. It will require changes in the existing structure of the judicial system that may involve the creation of new constitutional offices. It may, for example, require the creation of special courts to deal with a wide range of issues including environmental questions. Already, special courts to deal with land matters have been suggested.[36] Such courts would inevitably deal with issues related to natural resource management.

An ombudsman or its equivalent could also be created as a constitutional office, with full autonomy and independence to handle environmental complaints. Such a provision already exists in Article 91(c) of the Constitution of Namibia. The function of the environmental ombudsman is to: "Investigate complaints concerning the over-utilization of living natural resources, the degradation and destruction of ecosystems and the failure to protect the beauty and character of Namibia." But there is little evidence that the ombudsman alone can deal with the complex issues related to environmental rights.

More thought will need to be given to the scope of institutional reforms needed to bring environmental considerations effectively into the purview of the constitutional order. For example, customary land rights overlap in time and in space and their enforcement requires institutional arrangements that are flexible and can handle diverse conflicts. Litigation may not be the best way of dealing with conflicts arising from such complex social set-ups. It may be necessary to give legal standing to measures aimed at preventing conflicts. The delegation of responsibility for conflict management to the community level would reduce the transaction costs of enforcing property rights. This implies that customary institutions would be expected to carry out the administrative functions currently performed by the government.[37]

Other areas of institutional change include the creation of bodies that facilitate public access to the courts. The establishment of institutions that provide legal aid is important in ensuring that members of the public have access to the legal system. The formation of governmental and non-governmental legal aid schemes, especially those that serve rural populations, will improve the possibilities for enforcing environmental provisions in the constitution. So far, access to the courts is largely a facility for the rich and those who live in urban areas.

Penalties and sanctions against those who violate environmental provisions play a key role in the effectiveness of these provisions. Institutional capacity and will to monitor, investigate and act on infringements is required. The 1978 Spanish constitution, Article 45(2), states that the "public authorities shall concern themselves with the rational use of all natural resources for the purpose of protecting and improving the quality of life and protecting and restoring the environment . . ." Those who violate the provisions are liable to penal or administrative sanctions and shall be obliged to repair the damage caused.

Conclusion

Constitution-making is a long-term process. It is largely a reflection of how a society has internalized certain social innovations and made them part of the cultural routines. This book has suggested that the field of environmental management in particular, and sustainable development in general, is emerging as a compelling candidate for inclusion in national constitutions. But ultimately the successful inclusion of the provisions and their effective implementation will depend largely on the political mood prevailing in the country. For Kenya and other countries in similar situations there are different avenues for pursuing reform programmes. The first and easiest route would be to take advantage of opportunities when the constitution is under review for other reasons and to argue the case for the inclusion of environmental provisions.

It is unlikely that there will be adequate political or public pressure to compel parliament to introduce environmental provisions in the constitution. In the absence of such pressure it seems likely that many countries will go the route of countries such as the United States and India where the case for constitutional change has been made through judicial activism. In both countries the promotion of environmental rights has been largely a result of judicial innovations. In India, for example, the courts have expanded the constitutional provisions on fundamental rights to cover environmental issues, especially through arguments that link environmental welfare to human survival. A determined judiciary would easily find a link between adverse environmental change and Section 70(1) of the Kenyan constitution which says that no "person shall be deprived of his life intentionally . . ." Similarly, considerable progress on access to information can be made through a progressive interpretation of Section 79 of the constitution regarding freedom of expression.

Government projects which lead to changes in the availability of natural resources for local communities or undermine human well-being through pollution can be seen as violating the fundamental rights of those affected. Such cases will of course have to be argued. But as the Indian experience shows, there is considerable scope for using judicial activism to promote environmental goals. Social action litigation has been so successful because the courts adopted approaches that based environmental claims on fundamental rights. "Social action litigation brought a variety of environmental issues before the courts: deforestation by mining, pollution by mining, industrialization and its effluents, environmental aspects of dams and other large-scale development projects, gas leaks, issues regarding hazardous substances, pollution of rivers, over-use of groundwater, air pollution by vehicles, issues relating to urban planning, and protection of parks and sanctuaries."[38]

Indian courts have also introduced a number of innovations aimed at ensuring compliance with the law. The deep-pocket theory is an example of an approach that ensures that environmental penalties have a deterrent effect. Under this rule, the magnitude of compensation in case of environmental damage is correlated to the size and capacity of the enterprise or its ability to pay. The larger the enterprise, the greater the amount of payable compensation. Other judicial innovations such as injunctive relief in the form of interim remedies have also been applied to protect the interest of parties until the courts have reached a decision. In other situations, the courts have created their own investigative and administrative machineries. Oversight and monitoring institutions have also been created by the courts to ensure compliance with their orders. Court orders have also been extended to the provision of public awareness programmes through radio and television.

Given the rapid growth in environmental awareness in the general population and the appreciation of technical matters by the judiciary, phases of judicial activism seem to be a natural course in countries that are slow to recognize and enforce environmental rights through appropriate constitutional arrangements. But such activism does not necessarily lead to consistent action. Governments will be well-advised to avoid going through such phases of judicial activism by effecting constitutional reforms that seek to balance the private and public interests on the one hand, and environment and development on the other.

Notes

1. Babcock, 1995, p. 63.
2. WCED, 1990. p. 34.
3. Freyfogle, 1993, p. 1279.
4. Freyfogle, 1993, p. 1281.
5. See Khasiani (1992) and Sigot et al., (1995) for further discussion.
6. This position is not acceptable to all scholars. It has been argued that liberal constitutionalism cannot take root in a political culture dominated by ethnic diversity. For this view, see Franklin and Baun, 1995.
7. Beatley, 1994, p. 236.
8. O'Connor, 1994.
9. United Nations, 1993.
10. This categorization is based on Brandl, and Bungert, 1992.
11. For details, see Elster, 1995.
12. The Rev. Canon Leakey, a native representative in the Legislative Council, commented that the original 1926 bill that set out to establish native reserves (which later became trust lands) "seemed almost as if [it] was rather intended to regularize the methods by which land might be taken away from natives for the use and benefit of non-natives." Quoted in Okoth-Ogendo, 1991, p. 56. In his support for the bill, Conway Harvey said: ". . . if some land at present in native ownership is not required by natives for their use, it is only fair, just, reasonable and quite proper . . . that land should be leased to non-natives or others who are willing to work it entirely in the interests of the native owners themselves." Quoted in Okoth-Ogendo, 1991, p. 56.

13. Brandl and Bungert, 1992, p. 84.
14. See Berlin, (1993) for a review of the issue of just compensation.
15. Blumm, 1994, pp. 420–430.
16. Brown, 1994, p. 111.
17. Quoted in Babcock, 1995, pp. 37.
18. See Rolston III (1988), Johnson (1991) and Oruka, (1994), for detailed discussions of environmental ethics.
19. The granting of such rights is eloquently argued by Stone, (1974).
20. Omari, 1990, p. 169. "In the case of shrines and initiation rite centres, taboos developed around the destruction of trees, shrubs, and the sacred places themselves . . . . Perhaps people did not plan to practise such attitudes in the way a modern person would conserve the forests, but out of their religious beliefs and values and their reverence for sacred public places, an ecological and environmental concern was developed.
21. The account of international constitutional developments provided below draws heavily from Brandl and Bungert (1992).
22. Brandl and Bungert, 1992, p. 25. The change was not made, partly due to the difficulties associated with amending the German constitution.
23. The concept of an "ecologically balanced human environment" was earlier introduced in the Portuguese constitution and reflects a recognition of the interaction between human activities and ecological systems. However, the notion of ecological balance, which is drawn from equilibrium theory has recently come under criticism and has given way to the more realistic concept of "ecological integrity". For a detailed critique of equilibrium theories in ecology, see Caldwell and Shrader-Frechette, 1993, pp. 211–213.
24. Winstanley, T. 1995. pp. 93–95.
25. The following formulation, however, has been proposed: "Every person shall have the right to a sustainable environment which promotes health and well-being. All persons (including juristic bodies) and the state shall have the duty to uphold this right for present and future generations and, in so doing, shall ensure the wise use of land and all natural resources and the minimization of waste generation and pollution," Winstanley, T. 1995, p. 94.
26. The incidents of ownership include eleven sub-rights: "These are the right to possess; the right to use; the right to manage; the right to income; the right to capital; the right to security; the incident of transmissibility (the right to pass on property to one's successors); the incident of absence of term (the right to hold onto property for ever, if one lived forever); the prohibition of harmful use; the liability to prosecution (property may be taken to cover debts); and residuary rights (full rights to property after other limited interests in it ceases)," Shrader-Frechette, K. 1993, p. 227.
27. Rose (1994) has used the term "biological rights" to refer to nature's rights.
28. Emmenegger, and Tschentscher, 1994, pp. 584–588.
29. For details, see Fermandez, 1993.
30. Brandl, and Bungert. 1992, p. 80.
31. Harding, 1989, p. 222.
32. It has been noted that: "The office of Attorney-General does not have an illustrious history of enforcing public duties. Attorneys-General are unwilling to act against public bodies and the courts seem to be unwilling to review their reasons, however poor, for failing to act," Harding, 1989, p. 227.

33. Brandl, and Bungert, 1992, p. 79.
34. See, for example, Winstanley, 1995.
35. Swift, 1995, p. 159–160.
36. H.W.O. Okoth-Ogendo. 1994. *Personal Communication*. Nairobi.
37. Swift, J. 1995, p. 157.
38. Dias, A. 1994, p. 248.

APPENDICES

Appendices

Appendix I

The Constitution of Kenya: Excerpts

Chapter II

The Executive

Executive Powers

23. (1) The executive authority of the Government of Kenya shall vest in the President and, subject to this Constitution, may be exercised by him either directly or through officers subordinate to him.

(2) Nothing in this section shall prevent Parliament from conferring functions on persons or authorities other than the President.

24. Subject to this Constitution and any other law, the powers of constituting and abolishing offices for the Republic of Kenya, of making appointments to any such office and terminating any such appointment, shall vest in the President.

25. (1) Save in so far as may be otherwise provided by this Constitution or by any other law, every person who holds office in the service of the Republic of Kenya shall hold that office during the pleasure of the President:

Provided that this subsection shall not apply in the case of a person who enters into a contract of service in writing with the Government of Kenya by which he undertakes to serve the Government for a period which does not exceed three years.

(2) In this section "Office in the service of the Republic of Kenya" means office in or membership of the public service, the armed forces of the Republic,

the National Youth Service or any other force or service established for the Republic of Kenya.

26. (1) There shall be an Attorney-General whose office shall be an office in the public service.

(2) The Attorney-General shall be the principal legal adviser to the Government of Kenya.

(3) The Attorney-General shall have power in any case in which he considers it desirable so to do—

(a) to institute and undertake criminal proceedings against any person before any court (other than a court-martial) in respect of any offence alleged to have been committed by that person;

(b) to take over and continue any such criminal proceedings that have been instituted or undertaken by another person or authority; and

(c) to discontinue at any stage before judgment is delivered any such criminal proceedings instituted or undertaken by himself or another person or authority.

(4) The Attorney-General may require the Commissioner of Police to investigate any matter which, in the Attorney-General's opinion, relates to any offence or alleged offence or suspected offence, and the Commissioner shall comply with that requirement and shall report to the Attorney-General upon the investigation.

(5) The powers of the Attorney-General under subsections (3) and (4) may be exercised by him in person or by officers subordinate to him acting in accordance with his general or special instructions.

(6) The powers conferred on the Attorney-General by paragraphs *(b)* and *(c)* of subsection (3) shall be vested in him to the exclusion of any other person or authority:

Provided that where any other person or authority has instituted criminal proceedings, nothing in this subsection shall prevent the withdrawal of those proceedings by or at the instance of that person or authority and with the leave of the court.

(7) For the purposes of this section, an appeal from a judgment in criminal proceedings before any court, or a question of law reserved for the purpose of those proceedings to any other court, shall be deemed to be part of those proceedings:

Provided that the power conferred on the Attorney-General by subsection (3) *(c)* shall not be exercised in relation to an appeal by a person convicted in criminal proceedings or to a question of law reserved at the instance of such a person.

(8) In the exercise of the functions vested in him by sub sections (3) and (4) of this section and by sections 44 and 55, the Attorney-General shall not be subject to the direction or control of any other person or authority.

Chapter V

Fundamental Rights and Freedoms of the Individual

70. Whereas every person in Kenya is entitled to the fundamental rights and freedoms of the individual, that is to say, the right, whatever his race, tribe, place of origin or residence or other local connexion, political opinions, colour, creed or sex, but subject to respect for the rights and freedoms of others and for the public interest, to each and all of the following, namely—

(a) life, liberty, security of the person and the protection of the law;

(b) freedom of conscience, of expression and of assembly and association; and

(c) protection for the privacy of his home and other property and from deprivation of property without compensation,

the provisions of this Chapter shall have effect for the purpose of affording protection to those rights and freedoms subject to such limitations of that protection as are contained in those provisions, being limitations designed to ensure that the enjoyment of those rights and freedoms by any individual does not prejudice the rights and freedoms of others or the public interest.

71. (1) No person shall be deprived of his life intentionally save in execution of the sentence of a court in respect of a criminal offence under the law of Kenya of which he has been convicted.

(2) Without prejudice to any liability for a contravention of any other law with respect to the use of force in those cases hereinafter mentioned, a person shall not be regarded as having been deprived of his life in contravention of this section if he dies as the result of the use of force to an extent as is reasonably justifiable in the circumstances of the case—

(a) for the defence of any person from violence or for the defence of property;

(b) in order to effect a lawful arrest or to prevent the escape of a person lawfully detained;

(c) for the purpose of suppressing a riot, insurrection nor mutiny; or

(d) in order to prevent the commission by that person of a criminal offence, or if he dies as the result of a lawful act of war.

72. (1) No person shall be deprived of his personal liberty save as may be authorized by law in any of the following cases—

(a) in execution of the sentence or order of a court, whether established for Kenya or some other country, in respect of a criminal offence of which he has been convicted;

(b) in execution of the order of the High Court or the Court of Appeal punishing him for contempt of that court or of another court or tribunal;

(c) in execution of the order of a court made to secure the fulfilment of an obligation imposed on him by law;

(d) for the purpose of bringing him before a court in execution of the order of a court;

(e) upon reasonable suspicion of his having committed, or being about to commit, a criminal offence under the law of Kenya;

(f) in the case of a person who has not attained the age of eighteen years, for the purpose of his education or welfare;

(g) for the purpose of preventing the spread of an infectious or contagious disease;

(h) in the case of a person who is, or is reasonably suspected to be, of unsound mind, addicted to drugs or alcohol, or a vagrant, for the purpose of his care or treatment or the protection of the community;

(i) for the purpose of preventing the unlawful entry of that person into Kenya, or for the purpose of effecting the expulsion, extradition or other lawful removal of that person from Kenya or for the purpose of restricting that person while he is being conveyed through Kenya in the course of his extradiction or removal as a convicted prisoner from one country to another; or

(j) to such extent as may be necessary in the execution of a lawful order requiring that person to remain within a specified area within Kenya or prohibiting him from being within such an area, or to such extent as may be reasonably justifiable for the taking of proceedings against that person relating to the making of any such order, or to such extent as may be reasonably justifiable for restraining that person during a visit that he is permitted to make to a part of Kenya in which, in consequence of the order, his presence would otherwise be unlawful.

(2) A person who is arrested or detained shall be informed as soon as reasonably practicable, in a language that he understands, of the reasons for his arrest or detention.

(3) A person who is arrested or detained—

(a) for the purpose of bringing him before a court in execution of the order of a court; or

(b) upon reasonable suspicion of his having committed, or being about to commit, a criminal offence,

and who is not released, shall be brought before a court as soon as is reasonably practicable, and where he is not brought before a court within twenty-four hours of his arrest or from the commencement of his detention, or within fourteen days of his arrest or detention where he is arrested or detained upon reasonable suspicion of his having committed or about to commit an offence punishable by death, the burden of proving that the person arrested or detained has been brought before a court as soon as is reasonably practicable shall rest upon any person alleging that the provisions of this subsection have been complied with.

(4) Where a person is brought before a court in execution of the order of a court in any proceedings or upon suspicion of his having committed or being about to committee an offence, he shall not be thereafter further held in custody in connexion with those proceedings or that offence save upon the order of a court.

(5) If a person arrested or detained as mentioned in subsection (3) *(b)* is not tried within a reasonable time, then, without prejudice to any further proceedings that may be brought against him, he shall be released either unconditionally or upon reasonable conditions, including in particular such conditions as are reasonably necessary to ensure that he appears at a later date for trial or for proceedings preliminary to trial.

(6) A person who is unlawfully arrested or detained by another person shall be entitled to compensation therefor from that other person.

73. (1) No person shall be held in slavery or servitude.

(2) No person shall be required to perform forced labour.

(3) For the purposes of this section "forced labour" does not include—

(*a*) labour required in consequence of the sentence or order of a court;

(*b*) labour required of a person while he is lawfully detained that, though not required in consequence of the sentence or order of a court, is reasonably necessary in the interests of hygiene or for the maintenance of the place at which he is detained;

(*c*) labour required of a member of a disciplined force in pursuance of his duties as such or, in the case of a person who has conscientious objections to service as a member of an armed force, labour that that person is required by law to perform in place of such service;

(*d*) labour required during a period when Kenya is at war or an order under section 85 is in force or in the event of any other emergency or calamity that threatens the life or well-being of the community, to the extent that the requiring of the labour is reasonably justifiable, in the circumstances of a situation arising or existing during that period or as a result of that other emergency or calamity, for the purpose of dealing with that situation; or

(*e*) labour reasonably required as part of reasonable and normal communal or other civic obligations.

74. (1) No person shall be subject to torture or to inhuman or degrading punishment or other treatment.

(2) Nothing contained in or done under the authority of any law shall be held to be inconsistent with or in contravention of this section to the extent that the law in question authorizes the infliction of any description of punishment that was lawful in Kenya on 11th December, 1963.

75. (1) No property of any description shall be compulsorily taken possession of, and no interest in or right over property of any description shall be compulsorily acquired, except where the following conditions are satisfied—

(a) the taking of possession or acquisition is necessary in the interests of defence, public safety, public order, public morality, public health, town and country planning or the development or utilization of property so as to promote the public benefit; and

(b) the necessary therefor is such as to afford reasonable justification for the causing of hardship that may result to any person having an interest in or right over the property; and

(c) provision is made by a law applicable to that taking of possession or acquisition for the prompt payment of full compensation.

(2) Every person having an interest or right in or over property which is compulsorily taken possession of or whose interest in or right over any property is compulsorily acquired shall have a right of direct access to the High Court for—

(a) the determination of his interest or right, the legality of the taking of possession or acquisition of the property, interest or right, and the amount of any compensation to which he is entitled; and

(b) the purpose of obtaining prompt payment of that compensation:

Provided that if parliament so provides in relation to a matter referred to in paragraph *(a)* the right of access shall be by way of appeal (exercisable as of right at the instance of the person having the right or interest in the property) from a tribunal or authority, other than the High Court, having jurisdiction under any law to determine that matter.

(3) The Chief Justice may make rules with respect to the practice and procedure of the High Court or any other tribunal or authority in relation to the jurisdiction conferred on the High Court by subsection (2) or exercisable by the other tribunal or authority for the purposes of that subsection (including rules with respect to the time within which applications or appeals to the High Court or applications to the other tribunal or authority may be brought).

(6) Nothing contained in or done under the authority of any law shall be held to be inconsistent with or in contravention of subsection (1) or (2)—

(a) to the extent that the law in question makes provision for the taking of possession or acquisition of property—

(i) in satisfaction of any tax, duty, rate, cess or other impost;

(ii) by way of penalty for breach of the law, whether under civil process or after conviction of a criminal offence under the law of Kenya;

(iii) as an incident of a lease, tenancy, mortgage, charge, bill of sale, pledge or contract;

(iv) in the execution of judgments or orders of a court in proceedings for the determination of civil rights or obligations;

(v) in circumstances where it is reasonably necessary so to do because the property is in a dangerous state or injurious to the health of human beings, animals or plants;

(vi) in consequence of any law with respect to the limitation of actions; or

(vii) for so long only as may be necessary for the purposes of an examination, investigation, trial or inquiry or, in the case of land, for the purposes of the carrying out thereon of work of soil conservation or the conservation of other natural resources or work relating to agricultural development or improvement (being work relating to the development or improvement that the owner or occupier of the land has been required, and has without reasonable excuse refused or failed, to carry out),

and except so far as that provision or, as the case may be, the thing done under the authority thereof is shown not to be reasonably justifiable in a democratic society; or

(b) to the extent that the law in question makes provision for the taking of possession or acquisition of—

(i) enemy property;

(ii) property of a deceased person, a person of unsound mind or a person who has not attained the age of eighteen years, for the purpose of its administration for the benefit of the persons entitled to the beneficial interest therein;

(iii) property of a person adjudged bankrupt or a body corporate in liquidation, for the purpose of its administration for the benefit of the creditors of the bankrupt or body corporate and, subject thereto, for the benefit of other persons entitled to the beneficial interest in the property; or

(iv) property subject to a trust, for the purpose of vesting the property in persons appointed as trustees under the instrument creating the trust or by a court or, by order of a court, for the purpose of giving effect to the trust.

(7) Nothing contained in or done under the authority of an Act of Parliament shall be held to be inconsistent with or in contravention of this section to the extent that the Act in question makes provision for the compulsory taking possession of property or the compulsory acquisition of any interest in or right

over property where that property, interest or right is vested in a body corporate, established by law for public purposes, in which no moneys have been invested other than moneys provided by Parliament.

76. (1) Except with his own consent, no person shall be subjected to the search of his person or his property or the entry by others on his premises.

(2) Nothing contained in or done under the authority of any law shall be held to be inconsistent with or in contravention of this section to the extent that the law in question makes provision—

(*a*) that is reasonably required in the interests of defence, public safety, public order, public morality, public health, town and country planning, the development and utilization of mineral resources, or the development or utilization of any other property in such a manner as to promote the public benefit;

(*b*) that is reasonably required for the purpose of promoting the rights or freedoms of other persons;

(*c*) that authorizes an officer or agent of the Government of Kenya, or of a local government authority, or of a body corporate established by law for public purpose, to enter on the premises of a person in order to inspect those premises or anything thereon for the purpose of a tax, rate or due or in order to carry out work connected with property that is lawfully on those premises and that belongs to that Government, authority or body corporate, as the case may be; or

(*d*) that authorizes, for the purpose of enforcing the judgment or order of a court in civil proceedings, the entry upon premises by order of a court,
and except so far as that provision or, as the case may be, anything done under the authority thereof is shown not to be reasonably justifiable in a democratic society.

78. (1) Except with his own consent, no person shall be hindered in the enjoyment of his freedom of conscience, and for the purposes of this section that freedom includes freedom of thought and of religion, freedom to change his religion or belief, and freedom, either alone or in community with others, and both in public and in private, to manifest and propagate his religion or belief in worship, teaching, practice and observance.

(2) Every religious community shall be entitled, at its own expense, to establish and maintain places of education and to manage a place of education which it wholly maintains; and no such community shall be prevented from providing religious instruction for persons of that community in the course of any education provided at a place of education which it wholly maintains or in the course of any education which it otherwise provides.

(3) Except with his own consent (or, if he is a minor, the consent of his guardian), no person attending a place of education shall be required to receive

religious instruction or to take part in or attend a religious ceremony or observance if that instruction, ceremony or observance relates to a religion other than his own.

(4) No person shall be compelled to take an oath which is contrary to his religion or belief or to take an oath in a manner which is contrary to his religion or belief.

(5) Nothing contained in or done under the authority of any law shall be held to be inconsistent with or in contravention of this section to the extent that the law in question makes provision which is reasonably required—

(a) in the interests of defence, public safety, public order, public morality or public health; or

(b) for the purpose of protecting the rights and freedoms of other persons, including the right to observe and practise a religion without the unsolicited intervention of members of another religion, and except so far as that provision or, as the case may be, the thing done under the authority thereof is shown not to be reasonably justifiable in a democratic society.

(6) Reference in this section to a religion shall be construed as including references to a religious denomination, and cognate expressions shall be construed accordingly.

79. (1) Except with his own consent, no person shall be hindered in the enjoyment of his freedom of expression, that is to say, freedom to hold opinions without interference, freedom to receive ideas and information without interference, freedom to communicate ideas and information without interference (whether the communication be to the public generally or to any person or class of persons) and freedom from interference with his correspondence.

(2) Nothing contained in or done under the authority of any law shall be held to be inconsistent with or in contravention of this section to the extent that the law in question makes provision—

(a) that is reasonably required in the interests of defence, public safety, public order, public morality or public health;

(b) that is reasonably required for the purpose of protecting the reputations, rights and freedoms of other persons or the private lives of persons concerned in legal proceedings, preventing the disclosure of information received in confidence, maintaining the authority and independence of the courts or regulating the technical administration or the technical operation of telephony, telegraphy, posts, wireless broadcasting or television; or

(c) that imposes restrictions upon public officers or upon persons in the service of a local government authority, and except so far as that provision or, as the case may be, the thing done under the authority thereof is shown not to be reasonably justifiable in a democratic society.

80. (1) Except with his own consent, no person shall be hindered in the enjoyment of his freedom of assembly and association, that is to say, his right to assemble freely and associate with other persons and in particular to form or belong to trade unions or other associations for the protection of his interests.

(2) Nothing contained in or done under the authority of any law shall be held to be inconsistent with or in contravention of this section to the extent that the law in question makes provision—

(a) that is reasonably required in the interests of defence, public safety, public order, public morality or public health;

(b) that is reasonably required for the purpose of protecting the rights or freedoms of other persons;

(c) that imposes restrictions upon public officers, members of a disciplined force, or persons in the service of a local government authority; or

(d) for the registration of trade unions and associations of trade unions in a register established by or under any law, and for imposing reasonable conditions relating to the requirements for entry on such a register (including conditions as to the minimum number of persons necessary to constitute a trade union qualified for registration, or of members necessary to constitute an association of trade unions qualified for registration, and conditions whereby registration may be refused on the grounds that another trade union already registered or association of trade unions already registered, as the case may be, is sufficiently representative of the whole or of a substantial proportion of the interests in respect of which registration of a trade union or association of trade unions is sought).

and except so far as that provision or, as the case may be, the thing done under the authority thereof is shown not to be reasonably justifiable in a democratic society.

81. (1) No citizen of Kenya shall be deprived of his freedom of movement, that is to say, the right to move freely throughout Kenya, the right to reside in any part of Kenya, the right to enter Kenya, the right to leave Kenya and immunity from expulsion from Kenya.

(2) Any restriction on a person's freedom of movement that is involved in his lawful detention shall not be held to be inconsistent with or in contravention of this section.

(3) Nothing contained in or done under the authority of any law shall be held to be inconsistent with or in contravention of this section to the extent that the law in question makes provision—

(a) for the imposition of restrictions on the movement or residence within Kenya of any person or on any person's right to leave Kenya that are reasonably required in the interests of defence, public safety or public order;

(b) for the imposition of restrictions on the movement or residence within Kenya or on the right to leave Kenya of persons generally or any class of persons

that are reasonably required in the interests of defence, public safety, public order, public morality, public health or the protection or control of nomadic peoples and except so far as that provision or, as the case may be, the thing done under the authority thereof is shown not to be reasonably justifiable in a democratic society;

(c) for the imposition of restrictions, by order of a court, on the movement or residence within Kenya of any person or on any person's right to leave Kenya either in consequence of his having been found guilty of a criminal offence under the law of Kenya or for the purpose of ensuring that he appears before a court at a later date for trial of such a criminal offence or for proceedings preliminary to trial or for proceedings relating to his extradition or lawful removal from Kenya;

(d) for the imposition of restrictions on the acquisition or use by any person of land or other property in Kenya;

(e) for the imposition of restrictions upon the movement or residence within Kenya or on the right to leave Kenya of public officers or of members of a disciplined force;

(f) for the removal of a person from Kenya to be tried or punished in some other country for a criminal offence under the law of that other country or to undergo imprisonment in some other country in execution of the sentence of a court in respect of a criminal offence under the law of Kenya of which he has been convicted; or

(g) for the imposition of restrictions on the right of any person to leave Kenya that are reasonably required in order to secure the fulfilment of any obligations imposed on that person by law and except so far as that provision or, as the case may be, the thing done under the authority thereof, is shown not to be reasonably justifiable in a democratic society.

(4) If a person whose freedom of movement has been restricted by virtue of a provision referred to in subsection (3) *(a)* so requests at any time during the period of that restriction not earlier than three months after the order was made or three months after he last made the request, as the case may be, his case shall be reviewed by an independent and impartial tribunal presided over by a person appointed by the President from among persons qualified to be appointed as a judge of the High Court.

(5) On a review by a tribunal in pursuance of subsection (4) of the case of a person whose freedom of movement has been restricted, the tribunal may make recommendations concerning the necessity or expediency of continuing that restriction to the authority by whom it was ordered and, unless it is otherwise provided by law, that authority shall be obliged to act in accordance with any such recommendations.

(6) Until it is otherwise provided by Act of Parliament nothing in this section shall affect the operation of the Outlying Districts Act or the Special Districts (Administration) Act of any law amending or replacing either of those Acts:

Provided that no law amending or replacing either of those Acts shall impose, or authorize the imposition of, restrictions on those rights in force under that Act on 31st May, 1963, and no such restriction shall be imposed under either of those Acts, or by or under any such law, in or in respect of any area other than an area in or in respect of which a restriction was in force under that Act on 31st May, 1963.

82. (1) Subject to subsections (4), (5) and (8), no law shall make any provision that is discriminatory either of itself or in its effect.

(2) Subject to subsections (6), (8) and (9), no person shall be treated in a discriminatory manner by a person acting by virtue of any written law or in performance of the functions of a public office or a public authority.

(3) In this section the expression "discriminatory" means affording different treatment to different persons attributable wholly or mainly to their respective descriptions by race, tribe, place of origin or residence or their local connexion, political opinions, colour or creed whereby persons of one such description are subjected to disabilities or restrictions to which persons of another such description are not made subject or are accorded privileges or advantages which are not accorded to persons of another such description.

(4) Subsection (1) shall not apply to any law so far as that law makes provision—

(a) with respect to persons who are not citizens of Kenya;

(b) with respect to adoption, marriage, divorce, burial, devolution of property on death or other matters of personal law;

(c) for the application in the case of members of a particular race or tribe of customary law with respect to any matter to the exclusion of any law with respect to that matter which is applicable in the case of other persons; or

(d) whereby persons of a description mentioned in subsection (3) may be subjected to a disability or restriction or may be accorded a privilege or advantage which, having regard to its nature and to special circumstances pertaining to those persons or to persons of any other such description, is reasonably justifiable in a democratic society.

(5) Nothing contained in any law shall be held to be inconsistent with or in contravention of subsection (1) to the extent that it makes provision with respect to standards or qualifications (not being standards or qualifications specifically relating to race, tribe, place of origin or residence or other local connexion, political opinion, colour or creed) to be required of a person who is appointed to an office in the public service, in a disciplined force, in the service of a local government authority or in a body corporate established by any law for public purposes.

(6) Subsection (2) shall not apply to—

(a) anything which is expressly or by necessary implication authorized to be done by a provision of law referred to in subsection (4); or

(b) the giving or withholding of consent to a transaction in agricultural land by any body or authority established by or under any law for the purpose of controlling transactions in agricultural land.

(7) Subject to subsection (8), no person shall be treated in a discriminatory manner in respect of access to shops, hotels, lodging-houses, public restaurants, eating houses, beer halls or places of public entertainment or in respect of access to places of public resort maintained wholly or partly out of public funds or dedicated to the use of the general public.

(8) Nothing contained in or done under the authority of any law shall be held to be inconsistent with or in contravention of this section to the extent that the law in question make provision whereby persons of a description mentioned in subsection (3) may be subjected to a restriction on the rights and freedoms guaranteed by sections 76, 78, 79, 80 and 79 (2), 80 (2), or paragraph (a) or (b) of section 81 (3).

(9) Nothing in subsection (2) shall affect any discretion relating to the institution, conduct or discontinuance of civil or criminal proceedings in a court that is vested in a person by or under this Constitution or any other law.

Chapter IX

Trust Land

114. (1) Subject to this Chapter, the following descriptions of land are Trust land—

(a) land which is in the Special Areas (meaning the areas of land the boundaries of which were specified in the First Schedule to the Trust Land Act as in force on 31st May, 1963), and which was on 31st May, 1963 vested in the Trust land Board by virtue of any law or registered in the name of the Trust Land Board;

(b) the areas of land that were known before 1st June, 1963 as Special Reserves, Temporary Special Reserves, Special Leasehold Areas and Special Settlement Areas and the boundaries of which were described respectively in the Fourth, Fifth, Sixth and Seventh Schedules to the Crown Lands Ordinance as in force on 31st May, 1963, the areas of land that were on 31st May, 1963 communal reserves by virtue of a declaration under section 58 of that Ordinance, the areas of land referred to in section 59 of that Ordinance as in force on 31st May, 1963 and the areas of land in respect of which a permit to occupy was in force on 31st May, 1963 under section 62 of that Ordinance; and

(c) land situated outside the Nairobi Area (as it was on 12th December, 1964) the freehold title to which is registered in the name of a county council or the freehold title to which is vested in a county council by virtue of an escheat:

Provided that Trust land does not include any estates, interests or rights in or over land situated in the Nairobi Area (as it was on 12th December, 1964)) that on 31st May, 1963 were registered in the name of the Trust Land Board under the former Land Registration (Special Areas) Ordinance.

(2) In this Chapter, references to a county council shall, in relation to land within the areas of jurisdiction of the Taveta Area Council, the Pokot Area Council, the Masop Area Council, the Tinderet Area Council, the Elgeyo Area Council, the Marakwet Area Council, the Baringo Area Council, the Olenguruone Local Council, the Mukogodo Area Council, the Elgon Local Council, and the Kuria Local Council, be construed as references to those councils respectively.

115. (1) All Trust land shall vest in the county council within whose area of jurisdiction it is situated:

Provided that there shall not vest in any county council by virtue of this subsection—

(i) any body of water that immediately before 12th December, 1964 was vested in any person or authority in right of the Government of Kenya; or

(ii) any minerals or mineral oils.

(2) Each county council shall hold the Trust land vested in it for the benefit of the persons ordinarily resident on that land and shall give effect to such rights, interests or other benefits in respect of the land as may, under the African customary law for the time being in force and applicable thereto, be vested in any tribe, group, family or individual:

Provided that no right, interest or other benefit under African customary law shall have effect for the purposes of this subsection so far as it is repugnant to any written law.

(3) Notwithstanding subsection (2), provision may be made by or under an Act of Parliament enabling a person to be granted a right or interest to prospect for minerals or mineral oils on any area of Trust land, or to extract minerals or mineral oils from any such area, and the county council in which the land is vested shall give effect to that right or interest accordingly:

Provided that the total period during which minerals or mineral oils may be prospected for on, or extracted from, any particular area of land by virtue of any grant or grants while the land is not set apart shall not exceed two years.

(4) Subject to this Chapter, provision may be made by or under an Act of Parliament with respect to the administration of Trust land by a county council.

116. (1) A county council may, in such manner and subject to such conditions as may be prescribed by or under an Act of Parliament, request that any law to which this sub-section applies shall apply to an area of Trust land vested in that county council, and when the title to any parcel of land within that area is registered under any such law otherwise than in the name of the county council it shall cease to be Trust land.

(2) The laws to which subsection (1) applies are—

(a) the Land Consolidation Act and the Land Adjudication Act; and

(b) any other law permitting the registration of individual titles to estates, interests or rights in or over land that, immediately before registration, is Trust land (except so far as the law permits the registration of estates, interests or rights vested in persons or authorities for whose use and occupation the land has been set apart under this Chapter).

117. (1) subject to this section, an Act of Parliament may empower a county council to set apart an area of Trust land vested in that county council for use and occupation—

(a) by a public body or authority for public purposes; or

(b) for the purpose of the prospecting for or the extraction of minerals or mineral oils; or

(c) by any person or persons for a purpose which in the opinion of that county council is likely to benefit the persons ordinarily resident in that area or any other area of Trust land vested in that county council, either by reason of the use to which the area so set apart is to be put or by reason of the revenue to be derived from rent in respect thereof,

and the Act of Parliament may prescribe the manner in which and the conditions subject to which such setting apart shall be effected.

(2) Where a county council has set apart an area of land in pursuance of this section, any rights, interests or other benefits in respect of that land that were previously vested in a tribe, group, family or individual under African customary law shall be extinguished.

(3) Where a county council has set apart an area of land in pursuance of this section, it may, subject to any law, make grants or dispositions of any estate, interest or right in or over that land or any part of it to any person or authority for whose use and occupation it was set apart.

(4) No setting apart in pursuance of this section shall have effect unless provision is made by the law under which the setting apart takes place for the prompt payment of full compensation to any resident of the land set apart who—

(a) under the African customary law for the time being in force and applicable to the land, has a right to occupy any part of the land; or *(b)* is, otherwise than in common with all other residents of the land, in some other way prejudicially affected by the setting apart.

(5) No right, interest or other benefit under African customary law shall have effect for the purposes of subsection (4) so far as it is repugnant to any written law.

118. (1) Where the President is satisfied that the use and occupation of an area of Trust land is required for any of the purposes specified in subsection (2), he may, after consultation with the county council in which the land is vested, give written notice to that county council that the land is required to be set apart for use and occupation for those purposes; and the land shall then be set apart accordingly and there shall be vested in the Government of Kenya or in such other person or authority referred to in subsection (2) as may be specified in the written notice, such estates, interests or rights in or over that land or any part of it as may be specified in the written notice.

(2) The purposes for which Trust land may be set apart under this section are—

(a) the purposes of the Government of Kenya;
(b) the purposes of a body corporate established for public purposes by an Act of Parliament;
(c) the purposes of a company registered under the law relating to companies in which shares are held by or on behalf of the Government of Kenya;
(d) the purpose of the prospecting for or the extraction of minerals or mineral oils.

(3) This section shall apply to land that has already been set apart in pursuance of section 117 as it applies to other land, and in that case a setting apart under this section shall extinguish any estate, interest or right in or over the land or any part thereof that may be vested in any person or authority in consequence on the setting apart under that section, but section 75 shall apply in relation to the setting apart under this section as if it were a compulsory acquisition by the Government of Kenya under an Act of Parliament of the estate, interest or right so extinguished.

(4) Where land is set apart under this section—
(a) any rights, interests or other benefits in respect of that land that were previously vested in any tribe, group, family or individual under African customary law shall be extinguished; and

410

(b) the Government of Kenya shall make prompt payment of full compensation for the setting apart to such persons as under section 117(4) are entitled to compensation when land is set apart in pursuance of that section.

(5) Subject to this section, parliament may prescribe the manner in which and the conditions subject to which a setting apart under this section shall be effected.

119. Where the President is satisfied that any land that has been set apart under section 118 is no longer required for any of the purposes specified in that section, the President shall in writing so notify the county council in whose area of jurisdiction the land is situated, and thereupon the setting apart shall cease to have effect and any estate, interest or right vested in any person or authority in consequence of the setting apart shall be extinguished and (without prejudice to the subsequent making of a further setting apart under any provision of this Chapter) the land shall again be held by the county council in accordance with section 115:

Provided that, where an estate, interest or right that is vested in a person or authority other than the Government of Kenya is extinguished in pursuance of this section, section 75 (except paragraphs *(a)* and *(b)* of subsection (1) thereof) shall apply to that extinguishment as if it were a compulsory acquisition by the Government of Kenya under an Act of Parliament of the estate, interest or right so extinguished.

120. (1) Where a person in whom there is vested an estate, interest right in or over land to which this section applies dies intestate and without heirs, that estate, interest or right shall escheat to the county council in whose area of jurisdiction the land is situated.

(2) Where a company in which there is vested any estate, interest or right in or over land and to which this section applies is dissolved, then, except so far as provision is made by the law relating to companies for the vesting of that estate, interest or right in some other person or authority, it shall escheat as if it were vested in a person who dies intestate and without heirs.

(3) The land to which this section applies is the land, other than land that is situated in the Nairobi Area (as it was on 12th December, 1964), that is specified in paragraphs *(a)*, *(b)* and *(c)* of section 114 (1).

Appendix II
List of Statutes

List of Statutes

Kenyan Statutes

Agriculture Act (Cap. 318)
Agricultural Produce (Export) Act (Cap. 319)
Agricultural Produce Marketing Act (Cap. 320)
Animal Diseases Act (Cap. 364)
Antiques and Monuments Act (Cap. 215)
Canning Crops Act (Cap. 328)
Cattle Cleansing Act (Cap. 358)
Chattels Transfer Act (Cap. 28)
Chiefs' Authority Act (Cap. 128)
Civil Procedure Code (Cap. 21)
Coast Development Authority Act (Cap. 449)
Coconut Industry Act (Cap. 331)
Coconut Preservation Act (Cap. 332)
Coffee Act (Cap. 333)
Constitution of Kenya
Co-operative Societies Act (Cap. 490)
Cotton Act (Cap. 335)
Crop Production and Livestock Act (Cap. 321)

Dairy Industry Act (Cap. 336)
Dangerous Drugs Act (Cap. 245)
Electric Power Act (Cap. 314)
Equitable Mortgages Act (Cap. 291)
Ewaso Ngiro North River Basin Development Authority Act (Cap. 448)
Ewaso Ngiro South River Basin Development Authority Act (Cap. 447)
Export Processing Zones Act (Cap. 517)
Factories Act (Cap. 514)
Fertilizers and Animal Foodstuffs Act (Cap. 345)
Fisheries Act (Cap. 378)
Food, Drugs and Chemical Substances Act (Cap. 254)
Forests Act (Cap. 385)
Geothermal Resources Act (No. 12 of 1982)
Government Fisheries Protection Act (Cap. 379)
Government Lands Act (Cap. 280)

Grass Fires Act (Cap. 327)
Hide, Skin and Leather Trade Act (Cap. 359)
Housing Act (Cap. 117)
Industrial Property Act (Cap. 509)
Irrigation Act (Cap. 347)
Judicature Act (Cap. 8)
Kenya Meat Commission Act (Cap. 363)
Kenya Tourist Development Corporation Act (Cap. 382)
Kerio Valley Development Authority Act (Cap. 441)
Lake Basin Development Authority Act (Cap. 442)
Lakes and Rivers Act (Cap. 409)
Land Acquisition Act (Cap. 295)
Land Adjudication Act (Cap. 284)
Land Consolidation Act (Cap. 283)
Land Control Act (Cap. 302)
Land Disputes Tribunals Act (No. 18 of 1990)
Land (Group Representatives) Act (Cap. 287)
Land Planning Act (Cap. 303)
Land Titles Act (Cap. 282)
Local Government Act (Cap. 265)
Magistrates' Courts Act (Cap. 10)
Malaria Prevention Act (Cap. 246)
Maritime Zones Act (Cap. 371)
Meat Control Act (Cap. 356)
Merchant Shipping Act (Cap. 389)
Mining Act (Cap. 306)
National Museums Act (Cap. 216)
Non-Governmental Organisations Co-ordination Act (Act No. 19 of 1990)
Penal Code (Cap. 63)
Pest Control Products Act (Cap. 346)
Petroleum (Exploration and Production) Act (Cap. 308)
Pig Industry Act (Cap. 361)

Plant Protection Act (Cap. 324)
Preservation of Public Security Act (Cap. 507)
Prevention of Cruelty to Animals Act (Cap. 360)
Protected Areas Act (Cap. 204)
Public Health Act (Cap. 242)
Public Roads and Roads of Access Act (Cap. 399)
Public Trustee Act (Cap. 168)
Pyrethrum Act (Cap. 340)
Rabies Act (Cap. 365)
Radiation Protection Act (Cap. 243)
Registered Land Act (Cap. 300)
Registration of Documents Act (Cap. 285)
Registration of Titles Act (Cap. 281)
Science and Technology Act (Cap. 250)
Seeds and Plant Varieties Act (Cap. 326)
Sisal Industry Act (Cap. 341)
Standards Act (Cap. 496)
Suppression of Noxious Weeds Act (cap. 325)
Tana and Athi Rivers Development Authority Act (Cap. 443)
Tea Act (Cap. 343)
Timber Act (Cap. 386)
Town Planning Act (Cap 134)
Traffic Act (Cap. 403)
Trust Land Act (Cap. 288)
Use of Poisonous Substances Act (Cap. 248)
Valuation for Rating Act (Cap. 266)
Water Act (Cap. 372)
Wildlife (Conservation and Management) Act (Cap. 376)

Colonial Statutes

Crown Lands (Amendment) Ordinance (1938)

Crown Lands Ordinance (1902, 1915)
Indian Land Acquisition Act (1894)
National Parks Ordinance (1945)
Native Lands Trust Ordinance (1938)

Foreign Statutes

Beachfront Management Act (USA)
Constitution of Brazil, 1988

Constitution of Canada, 1867
Constitution of Portugal, 1982
Constitution of the United States, 1776
Draft Constitution of Uganda, 1992
Environmental Protection Act (Canada)
Fisheries Act (Canada)
Foreign Jurisdiction Act (UK)
Water Act (Canada)

Appendix III

List of cases

A.G. Ontario v. *Canada Temperance Federation* (1946) Appeal Cases p. 193.

Alan Kiama v. *Ndia Muthunya & Ors C.A.* No. 42/1978.

Alfred Njau v. *Council of Nairobi*, 1993 (Decisions of the Court of Appeal of Kenya).

Attorney General v. *Burridge, The Portsmouth Harbour Case* (1822) 10 Price 350, 147 E.R. 385.

B.P. Bhatt and Another v. *Habib Versi Rajani* [1958] E.A. 536.

Barkya Thakur v. *State of Bombay* AIR [1960] SC 1203.

Belinda Murai & Drs v. *Amos Wainaina* C.A. No. 46/1977.

Blackburn v. *Somers* (1879) 5.L.R. Ir. 1.

Bradford Corporation v. *Pickles* [1895] A.C. 587.

Chasemore v. *Richards* (1859)7 H.L.C37411 ER 140.

Citizens Action Committee v. *Civil Surgeon, Mayo (General) Hospital, Nagpur* A.I.R. 1986, BOM.

Clark v. *Nash* [1905] 190 US 361.

Destro v. *The Attorney-General* [1980] KLR 80.

Edward Limuli v. *Marko Sabayi* H.C.C.C. No. 22/1978.

Embry v. *Owen* [1851] 6 Ex. 353, 155 E.R. 579 at 585–586, per B. Parke.

Esiroyo v. *Esiroyo* (1973) EA 388.

Ewart v. *Belfast Guardians* (1882) 9 L.R Ir. 172.

Haridas Chhagan Lal v. *Kericho Urban District Council* [1965] E.A. 370.

Hodgekinson v. *Ennor (1963) 4 B&S 229, 122 E.R. 446.*

Illinois Central RR v. *Illinois, Natural Resources Journal* 32(3), 1992.

Institute of the Blessed Virgin Mary v. *The Commissioner of Lands* [1980] KLR 5.

Interprovincial Cooperatives v. *Manitoba* (1976) vol. 1 Supreme Court of Canada Report p. 477.

Jones v. *Llanrwrst Urban District Council* (1911) 1 Ch.D.

Liggins v. *Inge* [1831] 7 Bing. 682, 131E.R. 263 at 268 per C.J. Tindall.

Lucas v. *South Carolina Coastal Council* (1992) 112 S. Ct., 22 ELR.

Lyon v Fishmongers Co. [1876] 1 App. Cas. 662.

Maina Kamanda & Another v. *Nairobi City Council & Another* [1991] Nairobi HCCC No. 6153 unreported.

Mulheim-Karlich Case *cited* in Brandl and Bungert, 1992.

Municipal Council Ratlam v. *Uarthichand* A.I.R. 1980 S.C. 1622.

Mwangi Muguthu v. *Maina Muguthu* H.C.C.C. No. 377/1968.

National Audubon Society v. *Superior Court* [1983] 658 p.2d709.

New Munyu Sisal Estate Ltd. v. *The Attorney-General* [1972] EA 77.

Ormerod v. *Todmorden Mill Co.* (1883) 11 Q.B.D.

Pennsylavania Coal Co. v. *Mahon* (1922) 260 US 393.

Puran Chand Manay v. *The Collector* (1957) EA 125.

R.L. Arora v. *State of Utar Pradesh* AIR [1962] SC 764.

Race v. *Ward* 4 E.&B. 702, 119 E.R. 259.

Rylands v. *Fletcher* [1866] L.R. 1 Ex. 265.

Samuel Thata Misheck & Drs v. *Priscilla Wambui & Anor* H.C.C.C. No. 1400/1973.

Selah Obiero v. *Orego Opiyo* (1972) EA 227

Somaranti v. *State of Punjab* AIR [1963] SC 151.

State of Bihar v. *Kemeshwar Singh* AIR, [1952] SC 275.

Tenant v. *Goodwin* 2 Ld. Raym 1098, Slak. 21

The Queen in Right of Alberta et al. v. *Friends of the Oldman River Society* (1992) vol. 1 Supreme Court of Canada Report, p. 3.

The Queen v. *Crown Zellerbach Canada Ltd. et al.* (1988) Vol. 1 Supreme Court of Canada Report, p. 400.

Wangari Maathai v. *Kenya Times Media Trust* (1989) Nairobi H.C.C.C. No. 5403 unreported.

Glossary[1]

JOHN W. BRUCE

access:	The ability to use land or another resource
agrarian reform:	Our broadest term for the attempt to change agrarian structure, which may include land reform land tenure reform, and other supportive reforms as well, such as reform of the credit system
agrarian structure:	The pattern of land distribution among land owners
bimodal agrarian structure:	A distribution pattern for land in which most land is owned by the largest landholders and the smallest landholders
bundle of rights:	The several rights which constitute a tenure; alternatively, all the rights belonging to various persons or groups in a piece of property
chattels:	Moveable property not attached to land
co-ownership:	Joint ownership by more than one legal person
common property institution:	An organization which manages common property; or the common property tenure arrangement itself
common property management:	Management of a resource as common property
common property resource:	A resource managed under a common property regime

common property:	A commons from which a community can exclude non-members and over which the community controls use
common, right of:	A right to take something off the land of another
commons:	Land or another natural resource used simultaneously or serially by the members of a community
communal land tenure:	Tenure involving substantial community control of land access and use, which will typically include household and individual rights short of full ownership in some types of land and common property in other land and resources
creditworthy:	Term used to characterize a borrower who is a good risk for a lender
custom:	Long established practice considered as unwritten law
deed registration:	Registration of title deeds
deep ecology:	a term coined by Norwegian philosopher Arne Naess to mean a fundamental reorientation of human values to remove the separation between humankind and nature
due process of law:	The regular and orderly course of the law through the courts
duty:	An act that is due by legal or moral obligation
emiment domain:	Inherent power of the state to take private property for a public purpose provided that any legal requirements for compensation are complied with
field:	A contiguous area of land under a common pattern of use or crop, which may be a parcel or part of a parcel
fixed boundaries:	Boundaries fixed by reference to points in a geodetic network
fixed rent tenancy:	A tenancy for which the rent is fixed
fixed rent:	A rent fixed in cash or a quantity of goods

formal tenure system:	A tenure system created by statute
fragmentation:	The state of a holding, consisting of several separate parcels
freehold:	Full private ownership, that is, free of any obligations to the state other than payment of taxes and observance of land use controls, imposed in the public interest
holding:	All the land held by a household or person in whatever tenure
immovable property:	Property in land and attachments (European Civil Law)
indigenous tenure system:	Tenure system of local origin
individual property:	Property held by a natural person
informal tenure system:	Unwritten, customary tenure system
inheritance:	The legal process by which land or other property passes from a deceased owner to his or her heirs
jural:	Pertaining to rights. The doctrine of rights
juridical:	Relating to, or acting in, the administration of justice
jurisprudence:	The science or philosophy of law
juristic person:	A body such as a corporation or association recognized by law as having rights and duties
land reform:	The attempt to change and thereby improve the distribution of land among land holders
land registration:	Recording in a register the ownership and other property rights in land. A broad, generic term
land survey:	Determination of boundaries and fixing the location of a parcel of land
land tenure system:	all the tenures provided for by a legal system, taken together
land tenure:	Right(s) in land
lease:	An agreement for temporary use by a lessee, who pays rent to the lessor (owner)

leasehold: Tenure for a specified period for payment of rent, conferred by the owner, whether state or private

locus standi: Place to stand. A right to be heard, a sufficient interest, or the legal capacity to challenge some decision

mandamus: A writ from the High Court ordering performance of a public duty

mortgage: A contract by which a borrower commits land as security for a loan

movable property: Property other than real property

nuisance: An unlawful interference with another's use, enjoyment of, or right over or in relation to, land, or damage resulting from such interference

open access resource: A resource to which access is open and uncontrolled

open access: use of a commons without controls

parcel: A contiguous area of land acquired as a unit, under one title

partition: Breaking up a parcel into smaller parcels, by division in inheritance or by sale of part of the parcel

personal property: Property other than real property (Anglo-American usage)

plot: A synonym for parcel; also used to indicate a piece of land within a parcel managed by someone other than the parcel owner

police power: Inherent governmental authority to regulate matters of safety, health, welfare, environment, morality and other matters pertaining to the protection of the public interest

possession: Having control of land or another resource

prescription period: The minimum time which land must be held to acquire it by prescription, usually in lieu of interest

prescription: Acquiring ownership of something by possession over a long period of time which is open and without permission of the owner, and during which the possessor acts as if he were an owner

private property: Property held by private persons, natural or legal

property: A set of rights and responsibilities concerning a thing, often stated as rights in a thing, to show they are rights against everyone

public property: Property held by any level of government

public trust: a historical doctrine that imposes a duty on public officials to supervise the private use of public resources so as to ensure the protection of the public's interest

real property: Property in land and attachments (Anglo-American usage)

repugnancy: Inconsistency of two or more laws or provisions of a law

resource tenure: Right(s) in land and other resources including water and forests

right: That to which a person has a just or legal claim to or an interest which is recognized and protected by a rule of law

riparian: Relating to the bank of a river or stream. A riparian owner may take and use water for ordinary purposes relating to tenement if the water is restored unaltered in character and substantially undiminished in value

security of tenure: Tenure held without risk of loss; alternatively, tenure held without risk, and for a long time; alternatively, tenure resembling full private ownership. The second is the preferred use of the term

security: Something the borrower promises to the lender if the loan is not repaid on time

sharecropper: A tenant paying as rent a percentage of the production of the land

sharecropping:	Farming land as a tenant under a share rent
sporadic registration:	Registration of a parcel separately from others in the area, voluntarily and general at the initiative and expense of the owner
state:	A politically organized community under a sovereign government. The criteria for statehood are a permanent population, defined territory, government and capacity to enter into relations with other states
sub-division:	Breaking up a parcel into smaller parcels, by division in inheritance or by sale of part of the parcel
succession:	The legal process by which land or other property passes from a deceased owner to his or her heirs
systematic registration:	Registration of all parcels in an area at the same time, usually compulsorily and therefore without charge to the owner
tenement:	Property held by tenure
tenure niche:	An area with a distinctive tenure arrangement, usually related to the particular use to which the land is put
tenure reform:	The attempt to alter and so improve the rules of tenure
tenure:	Right(s) in a landholder's resource
title deed:	The contract transferring ownership (title) to land
title registration:	a land registration which confers a guarantee of the title by the government
unimodal agrarian structure:	A distribution for land in which most land is owned by holders with average-sized holdings
usufruct:	Individual or household rights of use which exist under communal tenure systems

Notes

1. This glossary is reproduced with minor changes with permission from Bruce, J. 1994. *A Review of Land Tenure Terminology*. Madison, Wisconsin: Land Tenure Center.

References

Ackerman, B.A. 1977. *Private Property and the Constitution*. New Haven: Yale University Press.

Admassie, Y. 1992. *The Catchment Approach to Soil Conservation in Kenya*. Nairobi: Regional Soil Conservation Unit, Swedish International Development Authority.

Aliro, O.K. 1993. Natural soap washes away a deadly bug. *Panoscope*, April, pp. 5–6.

Alper, J. 1993. R&D alliances give biggest bang for buck. *Bio/Technology* 11.

Anderson, D., and R. Grove, eds. 1987. *Conservation in Africa: People, Policies and Practice*. Cambridge: Cambridge University Press.

Andrews, W.J. 1987. "Public Interest Perspective." In *Environmental Protection and the Canadian Constitution*, edited by D. Tingley. Edmonton: Environmental Law Centre.

Anthony, K.B., *et al.* 1979. *Agricultural Change in Tropical Africa*. Ithaca, New York: Cornell University Press.

ASAL Team. 1993. *Land Use and Land Tenure Systems in the Arid and Semi-Arid Lands of Kenya*. Composite Report to the World Bank's Resident Mission in Eastern Africa. Nairobi: The World Bank.

Ayensu, E.S. 1983. "Endangered Plants Used in Traditional Medicine." In *Traditional Medicine and Health Care Coverage*, edited by R.H. Bannermany *et al.* Geneva: World Health Organization.

Babcock, H.M. 1995. Has the US Supreme Court finally drained the swamp of takings jurisprudence?: The impact of *Lucas* v. *South Carolina Coastal Council* on wetlands and coastal barrier beaches. *Harvard Environmental Law Review* 19(1): 1–67.

Baker, G. 1984. *Water Resources and Water Management in South-Western Marsabit District*. IPAL Technical Report, B-4. Nairobi: United Nations Educational, Scientific and Cultural Organisation.

Bakshi, P.M. 1987. Environmental litigation. *Journal of the Indian Law Institute* 29: 260–261.

REFERENCES

Balandrin, M., *et al.* 1985. Natural plant chemicals: Sources of industrial and medicinal materials. *Science* 228(4704): 1154–1160.

Banuri, T., and J. Holmberg. 1992. *Governance for Sustainable Development: A Southern Perspective*. Islamabad and London: International Institute for Environment and Development.

Baraclough, S., and K. Ghimire. 1990. *The Social Dynamics of Deforestation in Developing Countries: Principal Issues and Research Priorities*. Discussion Paper No. 16. Geneva: United Nations Research Institute for Social Development.

Barrett, H., and D. Yach. 1986. The teaching of jurisprudence and legal theory in British universities and polytechnics. *Legal Studies* 5: 151–171.

Barrow, E.G.C. 1986. "The Value of Traditional Knowledge in Present Day Soil Conservation Practice: The Example of the Pokot and Turkana." In *Soil Conservation in Kenya: Proceedings of the Third National Workshop, Kabete*, edited by D.B. Thomas *et al.* Nairobi: University of Nairobi and the Swedish International Development Authority.

Barrow, E.G.C. 1992. *Tree Rights in Kenya: The Case of the Turkana*. Biopolicy 8. Nairobi: ACTS Press.

Barrows, R., and M. Roth. 1989. *Land Tenure and Investment in African Agriculture: Theory and Evidence*. Madison, Wisconsin: Land Tenure Center.

Barton, B. 1986. "Cooperative Management of Interprovincial Water Resources." In *Managing National Resources in a Federal State*, edited by J.O. Saunders. Toronto: Carswell.

Baxter, P.T.W., and R. Hogg, eds. 1987. *Property, Poverty and People: Changing Rights in Property and Problems of Pastoral Development*. Manchester: University of Manchester.

Beatley, T. 1994. *Ethical Land Use: Principles of Policy and Planning*. Baltimore: The Johns Hopkins University Press.

Becker, L.C. 1977. *Property Rights*. London: Routledge and Kegan Paul.

Bentham, J. 1967. *The Theory of Legislation*, translated by R. Hildreth. London: Trubner and Co.

Berkes, F., ed. 1989. *Common Property Resources: Ecology and Community-Based Sustainable Development*. London: Belhaven.

Berkes, F., and T. Farvar. 1989. "Introduction and Overview." In *Common Property Resources: Ecology and Community-Based Sustainable Development*, edited by F. Berkes. London: Belhaven.

Berlin, K. 1993. Just compensation doctrine and the workings of government: The threat from the Supreme Court and possible responses. *Harvard Environmental Law Review* 17: 97–150.

Bhalla, R.S. 1984. *The Institution of Property: Legally, Historically and Philosophically Regarded*. Lucknow: Eastern Book.

Bhalla, R.S. 1990. *Concepts of* Jurisprudence. Nairobi: Nairobi University Press.

Bienz-Tadmor, B. 1993. Biopharmaceuticals go to market: Patterns of worldwide development. *Bio/Technology* 11(2): 168–172.

Birgegård, L.-E. 1993. *Natural Resource Tenure: A Review of Issues and Experiences with Emphasis on Sub-Saharan Africa*. Uppsala: International Rural Development Centre, Swedish University of Agricultural Sciences.

Blumm, M.C. 1994. Public choice theory and the public lands: Why "multiple use" failed. *Harvard Environmental Law Review* 18: 405–432.

Boeninger, E. 1991. "Governance and Development: Issues and Constraints." In *Proceedings of the World Bank Annual Conference on Development Economics*. Washington, DC: The World Bank.

Bosselman, F., D. Callies and J. Bante. 1973. *The Takings Issue: An Analysis of the Constitutional Limits of Land Use Control*. Washington, DC: Council on Environmental Quality.

Brainard, J.M. 1981. Herders to farmers: The effects of settlement on the demography of the Turkana population of Kenya. PhD diss., State University of New York, Binghamton.

Brandl, E., and H. Bungert. 1992. Constitutional entrenchment of environmental protection: A comparative analysis of experiences abroad. *Harvard Environmental Law Review* 16: 1–99.

Brokensha, D., and E.H.N. Njeru. 1977. *Some Consequences of Land Adjudication in Mbere Division, Embu*. Institute of Development Studies Working Paper No. 320. Nairobi: University of Nairobi.

Bromley, D.W. 1989. Property relations and economic development: The other land reform. *World Development* 17(6): 867–877.

Bromley, D.W. 1991. *Environment and Economy: Property Rights and Public Policy*. Oxford: Blackwell.

Brown, L.H. 1971. The biology of pastoral development as a factor in conservation. *Biol. Conserv.* 3(2): 93–100.

Brown, P.G. 1994. *Restoring the Public Trust: A Fresh Vision for Progressive Government in America*. Boston: Beacon Press.

Brownlie, I. 1973. A survey of international customary rules of environmental protection. *Natural Resources Journal* 13: 179–189.

Brubaker, E. 1995. *Property Rights in the Defence of Nature*. London: Earthscan Publications.

Bruce, J.W. 1994. *A Review of Land Tenure Terminology*. Madison, Wisconsin: Land Tenure Center.

Bruce, J.W., and L. Fortmann. 1988. "Why Land Tenure and Tree Tenure Matter: Some Fuel for Thought." In *Whose Trees? Proprietary Dimensions of Forestry*, edited by L. Fortmann and J.W. Bruce. Boulder, Colorado: Westview Press.

Bruce, J.W., and M.S. Freudenberger. 1992. "Institutional Opportunities and Constraints in African Land Tenure: Shifting from a 'Replacement' to an 'Adaptation' Paradigm." Draft Concept Paper for the Land Tenure Center, Madison, Wisconsin.

Bruce, J.W., A. Hoben and D. Rahmato. 1994. *After the Derg: An Assessment of Rural Land Tenure Issues in Ethiopia*. Madison and Addis Ababa: Land Tenure Center and Institute of Development Research.

REFERENCES

Bruce, J. W., and S.E. Migot-Adholla, eds. 1994. *Searching for Land Tenure Security in Africa*. Dubuque, Iowa: Kendall/Hunt.

Burhenne-Guilmin, F., and W. Burhenne. 1991. "Competent Authorities and Levels of Decision-making in Wetland Protection." In *Legal Aspects of the Conservation of Wetlands* edited by J. Untermaier, pp. 43–56. IUCN Environmental Policy and Law Paper No. 25. Gland, Switzerland and Cambridge, UK: IUCN-World Conservation Union.

Burke, K. 1987. "Property Rights in 'Animals of Strangers': Notes on a Restocking Programme in Turkana, N.W. Kenya." In *Property, Poverty and People: Changing Rights in Property and Problems of Pastoral Development*, edited by P.T.W. Baxter and R. Hogg, pp. 129–136. Manchester: University of Manchester.

Caldwell, L.K. 1984. *International Environmental Policy: Emergence and Dimensions*. Durham, North Carolina: Duke University Press.

Caldwell, L.K., and K. Shrader-Frechette. 1993. *Policy for Land: Law and Ethics*. Boston: Rowman and Littlefield Publishers.

Campbell, A.H. 1942. A note on the word "jurisprudence". *Law Quarterly Review* 58: 334–339.

Campbell, D.J. 1993. "Land as Ours; Land as Mine: Economic, Political and Ecological Marginalization in Kajiado District." In *Being Maasai: Ethnicity and Identity in East Africa*, edited by T. Spear and R. Waller. London: James Curry.

Chalamwong, Y., and G. Feder. 1988. The impact of land ownership security: Theory and evidence from Thailand. *World Bank Economic Review* 5: 187–204.

Chambers, R., and M. Leach. 1987. Trees to meet contingencies: Savings and security for the rural poor. ODI Social Forestry Network Paper. London: Overseas Development Institute .

Chesman, D. 1984. "Constitutional Aspects of Water Law." In *Water Law and Policy Issues in Canada*, edited by H.I. Rueggeberg and A.R. Thompson. Vancouver: Westwater Research Centre, University of British Columbia.

Ciriacy-Wantrup, S.V., and R.C. Bishop. 1975. "Common property" as a concept in natural resources policy. *Natural Resources Journal* 15: 713–727.

Clark, R. 1991. *Water: The International Crisis*. London: Earthscan.

Clawson, M. 1982. "Private Forests." In *Current Issues in Natural Resource Policy*, edited by P.R. Portney and R.B. Haas. Washington, DC: Resources for the Future.

Cleaver, F., and D. Elson. 1995. *Women and Water Resources: Continued Marginalization and New Policies*. Gatekeeper Series No. 49. London: International Institute for Environment and Development.

Commander, S. 1986. Managing Indian forests: A case for the reform of property rights. *Social Forestry Network*, October.

Copestake, J.G. 1993a. "Kenya: Country Overview." In *Non-Governmental Organizations and the State in Africa: Rethinking Roles in Sustainable Agri-*

cultural Development, edited by K. Wellard and J.G. Copestake. London and New York: Routledge.

Copestake, J.G. 1993b. "Zimbabwe: Country Overview." In *Non-Governmental Organizations and the State in Africa: Rethinking Roles in Sustainable Agricultural Development*, edited by K. Wellard and J.G. Copestake. London and New York: Routledge.

Cotterrell, R. 1989. *The Politics of Jurisprudence: A Critical Introduction to Legal Philosophy*. London: Butterworths.

Coval, S., and J.C. Smith. 1986. The foundations of property and property law. *Cambridge Law Journal* 45: 457–475.

Critchley, W. 1991. "The National Soil and Water Conservation Project—Machakos District." In *Looking After Our Land: New Approaches to Soil and Water Conservation in Dryland Africa*, edited by O. Graham. Oxford: Oxford University Press.

Dais, R.W.M. 1979. *Jurisprudence*. 4th ed. London: Butterworths.

Darkoh, M.B. 1990. Kenya's environment and environmental management. *Journal of Eastern Africa Research and Development* 20: 21–25.

Davis, C., *et al.* 1993. *Biotechnology in Thailand: Scientific Capacity and Technological Change*. Biopolicy International 10. Nairobi: ACTS Press.

Davis, R.K. 1970. Some issues in the evolution, organization and operation of group ranches in Kenya. IDS Working Paper No. 93. Nairobi: Institute of Development Studies, University of Nairobi.

Denman, D.R. 1969. *Land Use and the Constitution of Property*. An Inaugural Lecture. Cambridge: Cambridge University Press.

Denny, P. 1993. "Eastern Africa." In *Wetlands of the World I: Inventory, Ecology and Management*, edited by D. F. Whigham, D. Dykyjová and S. Hejny. Dortrecht: Kluwer Academic Publishers.

Dias, A. 1994. Judicial activism in the development and enforcement of environmental law: Some comparative insights from the Indian experience. *Journal of Environmental Law* 6(2): 243–262.

DiMasi, J., *et al.* 1991. Cost of innovation in the pharmaceutical industry. *Journal of Health Economics* 10: 107–142.

Dorm-Adzobu, C., and O. Ampadu-Agyei. 1995. "The Malshegu Sacred Grove, Ghana." In *Towards Common Ground: Gender and Natural Resource Management in Africa*, edited by A. Sigot, L.A. Thrupp and J. Green. Nairobi and Washington, DC: ACTS Press and World Resources Institute.

Dorm-Adzobu, C., O. Ampadu-Agyei and P.G. Veit. 1991. *Community Institutions in Resource Management: Agroforestry by Mobisquads in Ghana*. Washington, DC and Nairobi: World Resources Institute and ACTS Press.

Duverger, M. 1977. *Élements de Droit public*, 8è éd. Paris: Presses Universitaires de France.

Ecosystems Ltd. 1985. Turkana District Resources Survey, 1982–1984. Report for the Republic of Kenya, Ministry of Energy and Regional Development, Turkana Rehabilitation Project. Nairobi: Ecosystems Ltd.

REFERENCES

Ekins, P. 1991. The sustainable consumer society: A contradiction in terms? *International Environmental Affairs* 3: 243–158.

Elias, T.O. 1956. *The Nature of African Customary Law*. Manchester: Manchester University Press.

Elisabetsky, E., and D.S. Nuñes. 1990. Ethnopharmacology and its role in Third World countries. *Ambio* 19(8): 419–421.

Ellefson, P.V. 1992. *Forest Resources Policy: Process, Participants and Programs*. New York: McGraw-Hill.

Elster, J. 1995. "The Impact of Constitutions on Economic Performance." In *Proceedings of the World Bank Annual Conference on Development Economics 1994*. Washington, DC: The World Bank.

Ely, J.W. 1992. *The Guardian of Every Other Right: A Constitutional History of Property Rights*. New York: Oxford University Press.

Emmenegger, S., and A. Tschentscher. 1994. Taking nature's rights seriously: The long way to bicentrism in environmental law. *The Georgetown International Environmental Law Review* 6: 545–592.

Emmett, A. 1992. Where East does not meet West. *Technology Review* 95(8): 50–56.

Engdahl, D.E. 1987. *Constitutional Federalism*. St. Paul, Minnesota: West Publishing Co.

Epstein, R.A. 1985. *Takings: Private Property and the Power of Eminent Domain*. Cambridge: Harvard University Press.

Eriksson, A., ed. 1992. *The Revival of Soil Conservation in Kenya: Carl Gösta Wenner's Personal Notes, 1974–1981*. Nairobi: Regional Soil Conservation Unit, Swedish International Development Authority.

Eshiwani, A. 1993. *The Decentralization Process in Kenya: The Place of Local Authorities*. ACTS Research Memorandum 2. Nairobi: African Centre for Technology Studies.

Falkenmark, M., and G. Lindh. 1993. "Water and Economic Development". In *Water in Crisis: A Guide to the World's Water Resources*, edited by P. Gleick. New York: Stockholm Environment Institute.

Fallers, L.A. 1969. *Law Without Precedent*. Chicago: University of Chicago Press.

Farnsworth, N., *et al*. 1985. Medicinal plants in therapy. *Bulletin of the World Health Organization* 63(6): 965–985.

Feder, G., and D. Feeny. 1991. Land tenure and property rights: Theory and implications for development policy. *World Bank Review* 5 (January): 135-153.

Fernandez, J. 1993. State constitutions, environmental rights provisions, and the doctrine of self-execution: A political question? *Harvard Environmental Law Review* 17: 333–387.

Field-Juma, J. Mugabe and J.B. Ojwang. 1995. Science, technology and environmental governance: A policy research agenda of the African Centre for Technology Studies. *ACTS Research Memorandum 11*. Nairobi: African Centre for Technology Studies.

Fortmann, L. 1988. "The Tree Tenure Factor in Agroforestry with Particular Reference to Africa." In *Whose trees? Proprietary Dimensions of Forestry*, edited by L. Fortmann and J.W. Bruce. Boulder, Colorado: Westview Press.

Fortmann, L., and J. Riddell. 1985. *Trees and Tenure: An Annotated Bibliography for Agroforesters and Others*. Nairobi and Madison, Wisconsin: International Council for Research in Agroforestry and the Land Tenure Center.

Fortmann, L., and D. Rocheleau. 1985. *Women and Agroforestry: Four Myths and Three Case Studies*. Nairobi: International Council for Research in Agroforestry.

Franke, R.W., and B.H. Chasin. 1980. *Seeds of Famine: Ecological Destruction and the Development Dilemma in the West Africa Sahel*. New Jersey: Rowman and Allanheld.

Frankin, D.P., and M.J. Baun, eds. 1995. *Political Culture and Constitutionalism: A Comparative Approach*. Armonk, New York: M.E. Sharpe.

Franson, R., and A.R. Lucas. 1978. *Environmental Law and Case Digest*. Vol. 1.

Freyfogle, E.T. 1993. Ownership and ecology. *Case Western Reserve Law Review* 43: 1269–1290.

Friedmann, W. 1973. *Dictionary of the History of Ideas*. New York: Scribners.

Fry, P.H., and J.T. McCabe. 1986. *A Comparison of Two Survey Methods on Pastoral Turkana Migration Patterns and the Implications for Development Planning*. London: Overseas Development Network.

Galaty, J. 1994. "Rangeland Tenure and Pastoralism in Africa." In *African Pastoralist Systems: An Integrated Approach*, edited by E. Fratkin, K.A. Galvin and E.A. Roth. Boulder, Colorado: Lynne Rienner Publishers.

Georgescu-Roegen, N. 1971. *The Entropy Law and the Economic Process*. Cambridge and London: Harvard University Press.

Gertzel, C.J., et al., eds. 1969. *Government and Politics in Kenya: A Nation Building Text*. Nairobi: East African Publishing House.

Ghai, Y.P., and J.P.W.B. McAuslan. 1970. *Public Law and Political Change in Kenya*. Nairobi: Oxford University Press.

Gibson, D. 1973. Constitutional jurisdiction over environmental management in Canada. *University of Toronto Law Journal* 23: 54.

Gillis, M., et al. 1983. *Economics of Development*. New York: W.W. Norton.

Glazewski, J. 1994. The environment and the interim constitution. *Consultus* (South Africa), April, pp. 22–27.

Gleick, P., ed. *Water in Crisis: A Guide to the World's Water Resources*. New York and Oxford: Stockholm Environment Institute.

Gluckman, M. 1955. *The Judicial Process among the Barotse of Northern Rhodesia*. Manchester: Manchester University Press.

Gluckman, M. 1965. *Ideas in Barotse Jurisprudence*. Manchester: Manchester University Press.

Good, C., and U.N. Kimani. 1980. Urban traditional medicine: A Nairobi case study. *The East African Medical Journal*, pp. 301–316.

REFERENCES

Goodland, R., *et al.*, eds. 1991. *Environmentally Sustainable Economic Development: Building on Brundtland*. Paris: UNESCO.

Goulet, D. 1990. "Development Ethics and Ecological Wisdom." In *Ethics of Environment and Development: Global Challenge, International Response*, edited by J. R. Engel and J. G. Engel. Tucson: University of Arizona Press.

Grandin, B.E. 1987. "East African Pastoral Land Tenure: Some Reflections from Maasailand." In *Land, Trees and Tenure*, edited by J.B. Raintree. pp. 201–210. Nairobi and Madison, Wisconsin: International Council for Research in Agroforestry and the Land Tenure Center.

Gregory, D.D., *et al.* 1972. *The Easement as a Conservation Technique*. IUCN Environmental Law Paper. Gland, Switzerland: IUCN-World Conservation Union.

Grootenhuis, J.G. 1991. "Disease Research for Integration of Livestock and Wildlife." In *Wildlife Research for Sustainable Development,* edited by J.G. Grootenhuis, S.G. Njuguna and P.W. Kat, pp. 97–102. Nairobi: Kenya Agricultural Research Institute, Kenya Wildlife Service and the National Museums of Kenya.

Guillien, R., and J. Vincent. 1978. *Lexique de Termes juridiques*, 4è éd. Paris: Dalloz.

Gulliver, P.H. 1963. *Social Control in an African Society*. London: Routledge and Kegan Paul.

Gupta, A. 1993. Losing the edge. *Down to Earth* 2(5), July 31.

Gutto, S. 1995. Environmental rights litigation, human rights and the role of non-governmental and peoples' organisations in Africa. *South African Journal of Environmental Law and Policy* 1: 1–14.

Hamilton, P.H. 1986. Destruction of Habitat in Tsavo National Park. Unpublished report. Nairobi: Wildlife Conservation and Management Department.

Hamnett, I. 1975. *Chieftainship and Legitimacy: An Anthropological Study of Executive Law in Lesotho*. London: Routledge and Kegan Paul.

Hansen, H.B., and M. Twaddle, eds. 1991. *Changing Uganda: The Dilemmas of Structural Adjustment and Revolutionary Change*. London and Kampala: James Currey and Fountain Press.

Hanssen, K. 1986. "Constitutional Aspects of Federal Spending Power." In *Constitutional Aspects of Water Management*, edited by D. Gibson. Winnipeg: The Agassiz Centre, University of Manitoba.

Hardin, G. 1968. The tragedy of the commons. *Science* 162: 1243–1248.

Harding, A.J. 1989. *Public Duties and Public Law*. Oxford: Clarendon Press.

Hauriou, A., and J. Gicquel. 1980. *Droit Constitutionnel et Institutions Politiques*, 7è éd. Paris: Editions Montchrestien.

Hertz, M.T. 1976. Interprovincial, the Constitution and the conflict of laws. *University of Toronto Law Journal* 26: 84–90.

Heyer, J., J. Maitha and W. Senga. 1976. *Agricultural Development in Kenya*. Nairobi: Oxford University Press.

Hirji, R., and L. Ortolano. 1991. EIA effectiveness and mechanisms of control: Case studies of water resources development in Kenya. *Water Resources Development* 7(3): 154–167.

Hobday, S.R., ed. *Coulson & Forbes on Waters and Land Drainage.* 6th. edition.

Hodgeson, G.M. 1993 *Economics and Evolution: Bringing Life Back into Economics.* Cambridge, UK: Polity Press.

Hogg, P.W. 1985. *Constitutional Law of Canada.* Toronto: Carswell.

Hogg, R.S. 1978. Development in Kenya: Drought, desertification and food scarcity. *African Affairs* 86(342): 47–58.

Hogg, R.S. 1986. Building Pastoral Institutions: A Strategy for Turkana District. Unpublished report to Oxfam, Nairobi.

Hollowell, P.G. 1973. "On the Operationalisation of Property." In *Property and Social Relations*, edited by P.G. Hollowell. London: Heinemann.

Homer-Dixon, T.F., *et al.* 1993. Environmental change and violent conflict. *Scientific American*, February, pp. 38–45.

Huffman, J.L., and G.C. Coggins. 1986. "The Federal Role in Natural Resources Management in the United States." In *Managing Natural Resources in a Federal State*, edited by J.O. Saunders. Toronto, Calgary and Vancouver: Carswell.

Hunt, A. 1988. The role and place of theory in legal education: Reflections on foundationalism. *Legal Studies* 9: 146–164.

Hunter, D. 1988. An ecological perspective on property: A call for judicial protection of the public's interest in environmentally critical resources. *Harvard Environmental Law Review* 12: 311–383.

Hyden, G. 1992. "Governance and the Study of Politics." In *Governance and Politics in Africa*, edited by G. Hyden and M. Bratton. Boulder, Colorado: Lynne Reinner.

Hyden, G., and M. Bratton, eds. 1992. *Governance and Politics in Africa.* Boulder, Colorado: Lynne Reinner.

IDRC. 1980. *Traditional Medicine in Zaïre: Present and Potential Contribution to Health Services.* Ottawa: International Development Research Centre.

IGADD. 1993. *Report on IGADD Subregional Case Study for the Intergovernmental Negotiating Committee on an International Convention to Combat Desertification in those Countries Seriously Affected by Drought and/or Desertification Particularly in Africa (draft).* Djibouti: Intergovernmental Authority on Drought and Development.

Ingold, T. 1980. *Hunters, Pastoralists and Ranchers: Reindeer Economics and Their Transformation.* Cambridge: Cambridge University Press.

Ingram, H., and C.R. Oggins. 1992. The public trust doctrine and community values in water. *Natural Resources Journal* 32(3): 514–537.

IUCN. 1990. *Biodiversity in Sub-Saharan Africa and its Islands: Conservation, Management and Sustainable Use.* Gland, Switzerland: IUCN-World Conservation Union.

REFERENCES

IUCN. 1995. *Forest Cover in Kenya: Policy and Practice*. Nairobi: IUCN-World Conservation Union.

IUCN/UNEP. 1986. *Review of the Protected Areas System in the Afrotropical Realm*. Gland, Switzerland: IUCN-World Conservation Union.

James, R.W. 1971. *Land Tenure and Policy in Tanzania*. Nairobi: East African Literature Bureau.

Jenkins, I. 1980. *Social Order and the Limits of Law*. Princeton: Princeton University Press.

Jensen, C.L. 1987. Effects of Fire and Grazing on Establishment of a Perennial Grass in Tsavo West National Park. Progress Report September 1986–July 1987. Unpublished report.

Johnson, L.E. 1991. *A Morally Deep World: An Essay on Moral Significance and Environmental Ethics*. Cambridge: Cambridge University Press.

Juma, C. 1989a. *Biological Diversity and Innovation: Conserving and Utilizing Genetic Resources in Kenya*. Nairobi: ACTS Press.

Juma, C. 1989b. *The Gene Hunters: Biotechnology and the Scramble for Seeds*. London and Princeton: Zed Books and Princeton University Press.

Juma, C. 1991. "Sustainable Development and Economic Policy." In *Gaining Ground: Institutional Innovations in Land-use Management in Kenya*, edited by A. Kiriro and C. Juma. Nairobi: ACTS Press.

Juma, C., J. Mugabe and P. Kameri-Mbote. 1995. *Coming to Life: Biotechnology in African Economic Recovery*. Nairobi and London: ACTS Press and Zed Books.

Kanyeihamba, G.W. 1975. *Constitutional Law and Government in Uganda*. Nairobi: East African Literature Bureau.

Kanyinga, K., A.S.Z. Kiondo and P. Tidemand. 1994. *The New Local Level Politics in East Africa: Studies on Uganda, Tanzania and Kenya*. Research Report No. 95. Uppsala: Nordiska Afrikainstitutet.

Karp, J.P. 1993. A private property duty of stewardship: Changing our land ethic. *Environmental Law* 23(3): 735.

KENGO. 1989. *Seeds and Genetic Resources in Kenya*. Nairobi: Kenya Energy and Environment Organizations.

Kenya, Republic of. 1965. *African Socialism and its Application to Planning in Kenya*. Sessional Paper No. 10 of 1965. Nairobi: Government Printer.

Kenya, Republic of. 1971. *National Report on the Human Environment*. Nairobi: Government Printer.

Kenya, Republic of. 1972. *Kenya's National Report to the United Nations Conference on the Human Environment*. Nairobi: Professional Printers and Stationers Ltd.

Kenya, Republic of. 1974. *Development Plan 1974–1978*. Nairobi: Government Printer.

Kenya, Republic of. 1976x. *Machakos District Annual Report*. Nairobi: Ministry of Agriculture.

Kenya, Republic of. 1976x. *Policy on Wildlife Management in Kenya*. Sessional Paper No. 3 of 1976. Nairobi: Government Printer.

Kenya, Republic of. 1979. *Development Plan 1979–1983*. Nairobi: Government Printer.

Kenya, Republic of. 1982. Tsavo Regional Land Use Study. Final Report for the Ministry of Tourism and Wildlife. Nairobi: Ecosystems Ltd.

Kenya, Republic of. 1983a. *Development Plan 1984–1988*. Nairobi: Government Printer.

Kenya, Republic of. 1983b. *Statistical Abstract 1983*. Nairobi: Central Bureau of Statistics.

Kenya, Republic of. 1984. *Machakos District Development Plan 1984–1988*. Nairobi: Ministry of Finance and Planning.

Kenya, Republic of. 1986. *Economic Management for Renewed Growth*. Sessional Paper No. 1 of 1986. Ministry of National Planning and Development. Nairobi: Government Printer.

Kenya, Republic of. 1987. *Constitution of Kenya*. Nairobi: Government Printer.

Kenya, Republic of. 1988. *Arid and Semi-Arid Lands (ASAL) Development Programme: Summary of Technical Reports on the Strategy, Policy and ASAL Development Programme 1988–1993*. Report No 0131-KE, November. Nairobi: Government Printer.

Kenya, Republic of. 1989a. *Development Plan 1989–1993*. Nairobi: Government Printer.

Kenya, Republic of. 1989b. *Machakos District Development Plan 1989–1993*. Nairobi: Ministry of National Planning and Development.

Kenya, Republic of. 1990a. *Machakos District Annual Report*. Nairobi: Ministry of Agriculture.

Kenya, Republic of. 1990b. Report on the Environmental Study of the Mau and Transmara Forests. Nairobi: Ministry of Environment and Natural Resources.

Kenya, Republic of. 1990c. *Statistical Abstract 1990*. Nairobi: Central Bureau of Statistics.

Kenya, Republic of. 1991a. *National Food Policy*. Sessional Paper No. 4. Nairobi: Government Printer.

Kenya, Republic of. 1991b. *Statistical Abstract 1991*. Nairobi: Central Bureau of Statistics.

Kenya, Republic of. 1992a. *Economic Survey 1992*. Nairobi: Central Bureau of Statistics.

Kenya, Republic of. 1992b. *National Water Master Plan* (draft). Nairobi: Ministry of Land Reclamation, Regional and Water Development.

Kenya, Republic of. 1993a. *Development Plan 1994–1996*. Nairobi: Government Printer.

Kenya, Republic of. 1993b. *Economic Survey 1993*. Nairobi: Central Bureau of Statistics.

Kenya, Republic of. 1994a. *Economic Survey 1994*. Nairobi: Central Bureau of Statistics.

REFERENCES

Kenya, Republic of. 1994b. *Kenya Population Census 1989*, Volume 1. Central Bureau of Statistics. Nairobi: Government Printer.

Kenya, Republic of. 1994d. *Recovery and Sustainable Development.* Sessional Paper No. 1 of 1994. Nairobi: Government Printer.

Kenya, Republic of. 1994e. *The Kenya National Environmental Action Plan.* Nairobi: Ministry of Environment and Natural Resources.

Kenya, Republic of. 1994f. *Kenya Forestry Master Plan.* Nairobi: Government Printer.

Kenyatta, J. 1938. *Facing Mount Kenya.* London: Secker and Warburg.

Kerruish, V. 1991. *Jurisprudence as Ideology.* London: Routledge.

Khasiani, S.A., ed. 1992. *Groundwork: African Women as Environmental Managers.* Nairobi: ACTS Press.

Kiamba, C.M. 1990. The introduction of private landed property in Kenya. *Development and Change* 20(1): 121–147.

Kiamba, C.M. 1994. *Land Use Conflicts and Resource Management in Kenya's Marginal Areas: The Case of Maasailand.* Mimeo.

Kiondo, A.S.Z. 1994. "The New Politics of Local Development in Tanzania." In *The New Local Level Politics in East Africa: Studies on Uganda, Tanzania and Kenya*, edited by K. Kanyinga, A.S.Z. Kiondo and P. Tidemand. Research Report No. 95. Uppsala: Nordiska Afrikainstitutet.

Kiriro, A., and C. Juma. 1991. *Gaining Ground: Institutional Innovations in Land-use Management in Kenya* , rev. ed. Nairobi: ACTS Press.

Kiss, A.C., ed. 1983. *Selected Multilateral Treaties in the Field of the Environment.* Nairobi: United Nations Environment Programme.

Kituyi, M. 1990. *Becoming Kenyans: Socio-economic Transformation of the Pastoral Maasai.* Nairobi: ACTS Press.

de Klemm, C. 1989. The conservation of biological diversity: State obligations and citizens' duties. *Environmental Policy and Law* 19(2): 50–57.

Kondratyev, K., *et al.* 1992. Priorities for global ecology now and in the next century. *Space Policy*, February, pp. 39–48.

KWS. 1990a. *A Policy Framework and Five-Year Investment Programme*, rev. ed. Nairobi: Kenya Wildlife Service.

KWS. 1990b. *A Policy Framework and Development Programme, 1991–96. Annex 4: National Park and Reserve Planning.* Nairobi: Kenya Wildlife Service.

KWS. 1990c. *A Policy Framework and Development Programme, 1991–96. Annex 6: Community Conservation and Wildlife Management Outside Parks and Reserves.* Nairobi: Kenya Wildlife Service.

KWS. 1991. *Development Policy and Activities 1991–96.* Nairobi: Kenya Wildlife Service.

Lamprey, H.F. 1983. Pastoralism yesterday and today: The overgrazing problem. In *Ecosystems of the World 13: Tropical Savannas*, edited by F. Bouliere, pp. 643–666. Amsterdam: Elsevier Scientific Publishing Co.

Lane, C. 1990. Barabaig natural resource management: Sustainable land use under threat of destruction. Discussion Paper 12. Geneva: United Nations Research Institute for Social Development.

Lane, C., and J. Swift. 1988. East African pastoralism: Common land, common problems. Dryland Programme Issues Paper No. 8. London: International Institute for Environment and Development.

Lawry, S.W. 1990. Tenure policy toward common property natural resources in sub–Saharan Africa. *Natural Resources Journal* 30(2): 404–422.

Lawson, F.H. 1958. *Introduction to the Law of Property*. London: Oxford University Press.

Lazarus, R.J. 1993. "Shifting Paradigms of Tort and Property in the Transformation of Natural Resources Law." In *Natural Resources Policy and Law: Trends and Directions*, edited by L. MacDonnell and S. Bates. Washington, DC: Island Press.

Leach, G., and R. Mearns. 1988. *Beyond The Woodfuel Crisis: People, Land and Trees in Africa*. London: Earthscan.

Lederman, W.R. 1975. Unity and diversity in Canadian federalism: Ideals and methods of moderation. *Canadian Bar Review* 53: 597–615.

Lee, A. 1775. *An Appeal to the Justice and Interests of the People of Great Britain, in the Present Dispute with America*, 4th ed. New York.

Lee, T.H. 1971. Strategies for transferring agricultural surplus under different agricultural situations in Taiwan. Paper presented at the Conference on Agriculture and Economic Development, Japan Economic Research Centre, 6–10 September.

Lele, U. 1989. Sources of growth in East African agriculture. *World Bank Economic Review* 1 (January): 119–144.

Lemma, A. 1991. "The Potentials and Challenges of Endod, the Ethiopian Soapberry Plant, for Control of Schistosomiasis." In *Science in Africa: Achievements and Prospects*, edited by AAAS. Washington, DC: American Association for the Advancement of Science.

Lewington, A. 1990. *Plants for People*. London: Natural History Museum.

Little, P.D., and D.W. Brokensha. 1987. "Local Institutions, Tenure and Resource Management in East Africa." In *Conservation in Africa*, edited by D. Anderson and R. Grove. Cambridge: Cambridge University Press.

Locke, J. 1946. *The Second Treaties of Civil Government and A Letter Concerning Toleration*, edited by J.W. Gough. Oxford: Basil Blackwell.

de Loe, R.C. 1991. The institutional pattern for water quality management in Ontario. *Canada Water Resources Journal* 16(1): 28–33.

Loudiyi, D., and A. Meares. 1993. *Women in Conservation: Tools for Analysis and a Framework for Action*. Washington, DC: IUCN-World Conservation Union.

Lucas, A.R. 1987. "Natural Resources and Environmental Management: A Jurisdictional Primer." In *Environmental Protection and the Canadian Constitution*, edited by D. Tingley. Edmonton: Environmental Law Centre.

Lundgren, L. 1993. *Twenty Years of Soil Conservation in Eastern Africa.* Nairobi: Regional Soil Conservation Unit, Swedish International Development Authority.

Lutz, R.E. 1976. The laws of environmental management: A comparative study. *American Journal of Comparative Law* 24: 447–520.

Lynch, O.J., and J.B. Alcorn. 1994. "Tenurial rights and Community-based Conservation." In *Natural Connections: Perspectives in Community-based Conservation,* edited by D. Western and R.M. Wright with S.C. Strum. Washington, DC: Island Press.

MacCormick, N. 1982. *Legal Rights and Social Democracy.* Oxford: Clarendon Press.

MacKenzie, K.C. 1961. Interprovincial rivers in Canada: A constitutional challenge. *University of British Columbia Law Review* 1: 499–509.

MacLean, R.A. 1986. Saskatchewan Water Corporation. *Canada Water Resources Journal* 11(3): 62–63.

Makau, B., J.B. Ojwang, and C. Juma. 1990. *Environmental Impact Assessment in Kenya: Indicative Capability, Potential and Legal Issues.* Nairobi: Norwegian Agency for Development Cooperation.

Marekia, E.N. 1991. "Managing Wildlife in Kenya." In *Gaining Ground: Institutional Innovation in Land-Use Management in Kenya,* edited by A. Kiriro and C. Juma, rev. ed. Nairobi: ACTS Press.

Mathias-Mundy, E., O. Muchena, G. McKiernan and P. Mundy. 1990. Indigenous Technical Knowledge of Private Tree Management. Report of the Centre for Indigenous Knowledge for Agriculture and Rural Development, Iowa State University, USA.

Mbiti, J.S. 1969. *African Religions and Philosophy.* London: Heinemann.

McAuslan, P. 1975. *Land, Law and Planning.* Weidenfeld and Nicolson.

McCabe, J.T. 1985. Livestock management among the Turkana: A social and ecological analysis of herding in an East African pastoral population. PhD dissertation, State University of New York, Binghamton.

McKenna, N. 1993. Third World plants may offer AIDS treatment. *Panos Features,* March 5.

Meier, G.M. 1984. *Leading Issues in Economic Development.* Oxford: Oxford University Press.

Meltz, R. 1994. Given-ness and gift: Property and the question of environmental ethics. *Environmental Law* 24(1): 1–31.

Meyers, L.R. 1981. *Organization and Administration of Integrated Rural Development in Semi-Arid Areas: The Machakos Integrated Development Programme.* A report for the Office of Rural Development and Development Administration. Washington, DC: United States Agency for International Development.

Migot-Adholla, S.E, *et al.* 1991. Indigenous land rights systems in sub-Saharan Africa: A constraint on productivity. *World Bank Economic Review* 5 (January): 155–175.

Migot-Adholla, S.E., F. Place and W. Oluoch-Kosura. 1994. "Security of Tenure and Land Productivity in Kenya." In *Searching for Land Tenure Security in Africa*, edited by J.W. Bruce and S.E. Migot-Adholla. Dubuque, Iowa: Kendall/Hunt.

Milne, D. 1986. *Tug of War: Ottawa and the Provinces under Trudeau and Mulroney*. Toronto: James Lorimer & Co.

Mugabe, J., et al. 1994. *Institutional Support for the Protection of Biodiversity in East Africa*. FAO/UNDP/GEF Field document no. 6. Dar es Salaam: Food and Agriculture Organization of the UN.

Mugabe, J. 1994. *Technological Capability for Environmental Management: The Case of Biodiversity Conservation in Kenya*. PhD Dissertation, University of Amsterdam.

Munn, R.E. 1977. *Environmental Impact Assessment*, 2nd ed. Toronto: John Wiley and Sons.

Murphree, M. 1994. "The Role of Institutions in Community-Based Conservation." In *Natural Connections: Perspectives in Community-based Conservation*, edited by D. Western and R.M. Wright with S.C. Strum. Washington, DC: Island Press.

Mutiso, G. 1991. "Managing Kenya's Arid and Semi-arid Areas." In *Gaining Ground, Institutional Innovations in Land-Use Management in Kenya*, edited by A. Kiriro and C. Juma, rev. ed. Nairobi: ACTS Press.

Myers, N. 1981. *The Sinking Ark: A New Look at the Problem of Disappearing Species*. New York: Pergamon Press.

Neumann, F.L. 1953. The concept of political freedom. *Columbia Law Review* 53: 901–925.

Niamir, M. 1990. *Community Forestry: Herders' Decision-making in Natural Resources Management in Arid and Semi-arid Africa*. Rome: Food and Agriculture Organization of the UN.

Norconsult Ltd. 1990. Report of a consultancy on an environmental study of Turkana District, Kenya. Nairobi: Norconsult.

Nyeki, D.M. 1992. *Wildlife Conservation and Tourism in Kenya*. Nairobi: Jacaranda Designs Ltd.

O'Connor, D. 1994. *Managing the Environment with Rapid Industrialization: Lessons from the East Asian Experience*. Paris: Organisation for Economic Cooperation and Development.

Oba, G. 1989. Impact of irrigated agriculture on floodplain ecology of the Turkwell River, North Western Kenya. Paper presented at the Conference on the People's Role in Wetland Management, Leiden, The Netherlands.

Oba, G. 1994. *The Role of Indigenous Range Management Knowledge for Desertification Control in Northern Kenya*. Linköping, Sweden: Environment, Policy and Society, Uppsala and Linköping Universities.

Ochieng, W.R. 1985. *A History of Kenya*. London: MacMillan Publishers.

Odegi-Awuondo, C. 1990. *Life in the Balance: Ecological Sociology of Turkana Nomads*. Nairobi: ACTS Press.

REFERENCES

Odero, P.W.J. 1975. Administration of water laws in Kenya. LLM diss., University of Nairobi.

Ogolla, B.D. 1988. "The Role of Environmental Law in Development." In *Contemporary Conceptions of Social Philosophy*, edited by E. Panou et al., pp. 118–129. Stuttgart: Franz Steiner Verlag Wiesbaden.

Ogolla, B.D. 1992. Environmental management policy and law. *Environmental Policy and Law* 22(3): 164–175.

Ogot, B.A., ed. 1976. *Kenya Before 1900*. Nairobi: East African Publishing House.

Ojwang, J.B. 1990a. "Constitutionalism: In Classical Terms and in African Nationhood." In *Constitutional Government and Human Rights in Africa*, edited by N.S. Rembe and E. Kalula. Maseru: Lesotho Law Journal.

Ojwang, J.B. 1990b. *Constitutional Development in Kenya: Institutional Adaptation and Social Change*. Nairobi: ACTS Press.

Ojwang, J.B. 1992. *Environmental Law and Political Change in Kenya*. Ecopolicy Series 1. Nairobi: ACTS Press.

Okidi, C.O. 1984. Management of natural resources and the environment for self-reliance. *Journal of Eastern African Research and Development* 14: 92–111.

Okidi, C.O. 1988. Reflections on teaching and research on environmental law in African universities. *Journal of Eastern African Research and Development* 18: 128–144.

Okidi, C.O. 1994. *Review of the Policy Framework and Legal and Institutional Arrangements for the Management of Environment and Natural Resources in Kenya*. Eldoret, Kenya: School of Environmental Studies, Moi University.

Okoth-Obbo, G.W. 1985. A conceptual analysis of environmental impact assessment as a legal mechanism for the protection and management of the environment: The Kenya case. LLM diss., University of Nairobi.

Okoth-Ogendo, H.W.O. 1974. Property Theory and Land-Use Analysis: An Essay in the Political Economy of Ideas. IDS Discussion Paper No. 209. Nairobi: Institute of Development Studies, University of Nairobi.

Okoth-Ogendo, H.W.O. 1976. "African Land Tenure Reform." In *Agricultural Development in Kenya: An Economic Assessment*, edited by J. Heyer et al. Nairobi: Oxford University Press.

Okoth-Ogendo, H.W.O. 1979a. "The Imposition of Property Law in Kenya." In *The Imposition of Law*, edited by S.B. Burman and B.E. Harrel-Bond. London: Academic Press.

Okoth-Ogendo, H.W.O. 1979b. Land Tenure and its Implications for the Development of Kenya's Semi-arid Areas. Nairobi: Institute of Development Studies, University of Nairobi.

Okoth-Ogendo, H.W.O. 1987. "Tenure of Trees or Tenure of Lands." In *Land, Trees and Tenure*, edited by J.B. Raintree. Nairobi and Madison, Wisconsin: International Council for Research in Agroforestry and the Land Tenure Center.

Okoth-Ogendo, H.W.O. 1988. "Issues in the Legal Organization of Irrigation in Africa." In *Reflections on Management of Drainage Basins in Africa*, edited

440

by C.O. Okidi. Occasional Paper No. 51. Nairobi: Institute of Development Studies, University of Nairobi.

Okoth-Ogendo, H.W.O. 1991. *Tenants of the Crown: Evolution of Agrarian Law and Institutions in Kenya.* Nairobi: ACTS Press.

Okoth-Ogendo, H.W.O., and D. Brokensha, eds. 1987. "Report of the Regional Working Group on Africa." In *Land, Trees and Tenure,* edited by J.B. Raintree, pp. 335–339. Nairobi and Madison, Wisconsin: International Council for Research in Agroforestry and the Land Tenure Center.

Okoth-Ogendo, H.W.O., W. Oluoch-Kosura and S. Wanjala. 1991. Kenya Land Policy. Mimeo.

Okoth-Owiro, A. 1988. "Land Tenure and Land Use Legislation Issues in Agroforestry Development." In *Soil Conservation in Kenya,* edited by D.B. Thomas *et al.,* pp. 267–274. Nairobi: Dept. of Agricultural Engineering, University of Nairobi and the Swedish International Development Authority.

Okoth-Owiro, A. 1989a. "Land Tenure and Land-Use Legislation Issues in Agroforestry." In *Agroforestry Development in Kenya,* edited by A.M. Kilewe *et al.* Nairobi.

Okoth-Owiro, A. 1989b. Legal framework for plant protection in Kenya. *Environmental Policy and Law* 19(2): 59–62.

Okoth-Owiro, A. 1990. Law and genetic resources in Kenya. Paper presented at the Environment 2000 Conference, 23–26, October, UNEP Headquarters, Nairobi.

Olindo, P.M., I. Douglas-Hamilton and P.H. Hamilton. 1988. Tsavo Elephant Count 1988. Nairobi: Wildlife Conservation and Management Department, Ministry of Tourism and Wildlife.

Omari, C.K. 1990. "Traditional African Land Ethics." In *Ethics of Environment and Development: Global Challenge, International Response,* edited by J.R. Engel and J. Gibb Engel. Tucson: The University of Arizona Press.

Ominde, S.H., and C. Juma, eds. 1991. *A Change in the Weather: African Perspectives on Climate Change.* Nairobi: ACTS Press.

Omoro, B. 1987a. *Marginal Soil, Marginal Farms.* London: Panos Publications.

Omoro, B. 1987b. *Why Kenyans Save their Soil.* London: Panos Publications.

Ondiege, P. 1992a. "Local Coping Strategies in Machakos District, Kenya." In *Development from Within: Survival in Rural Africa,* edited by D.R.F. Taylor and F. Mackenzie. London: Routledge.

Ondiege, P. 1992b. "Group Activities in Local-level Development: A Case Study of Machakos District of Kenya." In *Reviving Local Self-reliance: People's Responses to the Economic Crisis in Eastern and Southern Africa,* edited by W. Gooneratne and M. Mbilinyi. Nairobi: United Nations Centre for Regional Development.

Ondiege, P. 1994. Sustainable construction industry activities in Kenya. Paper presented at the National Environmental Action Plan Workshop, January, Naivasha, Kenya.

Ondiege, P., and J.M. Kiamba. 1994. Sub-Sahara Africa: A Survey of the Socio-political and Economic Situation, 1985–1994. Report prepared for the Japan External Trade Organization.

Ontario Law Reform Commission. 1989. *Report on the Law of Standing.* Toronto: Ministry of the Attorney General.

Orban, E. 1991. "Constitution and Regional Cleavages: A View From Quebec." In *After Meech Lake: Lessons for the Future,* edited by D.E. Smith *et al.* Saskatoon, Saskatchewan: Fifth House Publishers.

Oruka, H.O., ed. 1994. *Philosophy, Humanity and Ecology: Philosophy of Nature and Environmental Ethics.* Nairobi: ACTS Press and the African Academy of Sciences.

Ostrom, E. 1990. *Governing the Commons: The Evolution of Institutions for Collective Action.* Cambridge: Cambridge University Press.

Ottichilo, W.K., *et al.* 1991. *Weathering the Storm: Climate Change and Investment in Kenya.* Nairobi and Stockholm: ACTS Press and Stockholm Environment Institute.

Oweyegha-Afunaduula, F.C. 1982. "Vegetation Changes in Tsavo National Park (East), Kenya." MSc Thesis, University of Nairobi.

Parsons, K.H. 1971. Customary Land Tenure and the Development of African Agriculture. Land Tenure Centre Report No. 77. Madison: University of Wisconsin.

Paton, G.W., and D.P. Derham, eds. 1972. *A Textbook of Jurisprudence.* London: Oxford University Press.

Paul, E.F. 1987. *Property Rights and Eminent Domain.* New Brunswick: Transnational Books.

Paul, E.F., and H. Dickman, eds. 1989. *Liberty, Property, and Government: Constitutional Interpretation Before the New Deal.* New York: State University of New York Press.

Penelope, F. 1992. *Japanese Economic Development: Theory and Practice.* London: Routledge.

Picardi, A., and W. Siefert. 1976. A tragedy of the commons in the Sahel. *Technology Review* 78: 42–51.

Principle, P.P. 1989a. "The Economic Significance of Plants and their Constituents as Drugs." In *Economic and Medicinal Plant Research,* vol. 3, edited by H. Wagner, H. Hikimo and N.R. Farnsworth. London: Academic Press.

Principle, P.P. 1989b. *The Economic Value of Biological Diversity Among Medical Plants.* Paris. Organisation for Economic Cooperation and Development.

Principle, P.P. 1991. "Valuing the Biodiversity of Medicinal Plants." In *Conservation of Medicinal Plants, edited by* O. Akerele *et al.* Cambridge: Cambridge University Press.

Radin, M.J. 1988. The liberal conception of property: cross currents in the jurisprudence of takings. *Columbia Law Review* 88: 1667–1696.

Raintree, J., ed. 1987. *Land, Trees and Tenure.* Proceedings of the International Workshop on Tenure Issues in Agroforestry. Nairobi and Madison, Wisconsin:

International Council for Research in Agroforestry and the Land Tenure Center.

Regharan, C. 1990. Drug firms robbing Third World's medicinal plants. *Weekly Topic* April 24.

Reid, W.V. 1994. "Biodiversity Prospecting: Strategies for Sharing Benefits." In *Biodiplomacy: Genetic Resources and International Relations*, edited by V. Sánchez and C. Juma, pp. 241–268. Nairobi: ACTS Press.

Riddell, J.C. 1987. "Land Tenure and Agroforestry: A Regional Overview." In *Land, Trees and Tenure*, edited by J.B. Raintree, pp. 1–16. Nairobi: International Council for Research in Agroforestry and the Land Tenure Center.

Riddell, J.C., and C. Dickerman. 1986. *Country Profiles in Land Tenure: Africa 1986*. Madison, Wisconsin: Land Tenure Center.

Rocheleau, D. 1987. "Women, Trees and Tenure: Implications for Agroforestry Research and Development." In *Land, Trees and Tenure*, edited by J.B. Raintree. Nairobi and Madison, Wisconsin: International Council for Research in Agroforestry and the Land Tenure Center.

Rocheleau, D. 1993. *Land Use Change and the Dry Forest in Ukambani: A Case Study and Analysis of Alternative Options*. Nairobi: African Centre for Technology Studies.

Rocheleau, D., and D. Edmunds. 1995. Women, men and trees: Gender, power and property in forest and agrarian landscapes. Draft discussion paper prepared for the CG-PROP E-mail Conference, June–December, 1995.

Rolston III, H. 1988. *Environmental Ethics: Duties and Values in the Natural World*. Philadelphia: Temple University Press.

Rose, C. 1990. Property rights, regulatory regimes and the new takings jurisprudence: An evolutionary approach. *Tennessee Law Review* 57: 577–594.

Rose, C. 1994. *Property and Persuasion: Essays on the History, Theory and Rhetoric of Ownership*. Boulder, Colorado: Westview Press.

Roth, M., J. Unruh and R. Barrows. 1994. "Land Registration, Tenure Security, Credit Use, and Investment in the Shebelle Region of Somalia." In *Searching for Land Tenure Security in Africa*, edited by J.W. Bruce and S. Migot-Adholla. Dubuque, Iowa: Kendall/Hunt.

Rutten, M.M.E.M. 1992. *Selling Wealth to Buy Poverty: The Process of the Individualization of Land Ownership among the Maasai Pastoralists Kajiado District, Kenya, 1890–1990*. Nijmegen Studies in Development and Cultural Change. Saarbrucken and Fort Lauderdale: Verlag Breitenbach.

Sagoff, M. 1990. "Takings, Just Compensation, and the Environment." In *Upstream/ Downstream: Issues in Environmental Ethics*, edited by D. Scherer, pp. 158–178. Philadelphia: Temple University Press.

Salih, M.A.M. 1990. Pastoralism and the state in African arid lands: An overview. *Nomadic Peoples* 25–27: 7–8.

Salmond, J. 1966. *Salmond on Jurisprudence*, 12th ed., edited by P.J. Fitzgerald. London: Sweet and Maxwell.

Sánchez, V., and C. Juma, eds. 1994. *Biodiplomacy: Genetic Resources and International Relations*. Nairobi: ACTS Press.

Sandford, S. 1983. *Management of Pastoral Development in the Third World.* London: Overseas Development Institute and John Wiley and Sons.

Sarokin, D., and J. Schulkin. 1991. Environmentalism and the right-to-know: Expanding the practice of democracy. *Ecological Economics* 4: 175–189.

Sasson, A. 1992. *Biotechnology and Natural Products: Prospects for Commercial Application.* Nairobi: ACTS Press.

Saunders, J.O. 1988. *Interjurisdictional Issues in Canadian Water Management.* Calgary: Canadian Institute of Resources Law.

Sax, J.L. 1971. Takings, private property and public rights. *Yale Law Journal* 81: 149–186.

Sax, J.L. 1984. Takings and the police power. *Yale Law Journal* 74.

Sax, J.L. 1993. "Bringing an Ecological Perspective to Natural Resource Law: Fulfilling the Promise of the Public Trust." In *Natural Resources Policy and Law: Trends and Directions,* edited by L.T. MacDonnell and S.F. Bates. Washington, DC: Island Press.

Scherr, S.J. 1989. *The Legislative Context for Agroforestry Development in Kenya.* Fachbereich forstökonomie und forstpolitik. Zurich: Institut für Wald—Und Holzforschung. Arbitsberichte des fachbereichs Nr. 89/7.

Schramm, G., and T.J. Watford, eds. 1989. *Environmental Management and Economic Development.* Baltimore: The Johns Hopkins Press.

Schultz, D. 1993. Political theory and legal history: Conflicting depictions of property in the American political founding. *American Journal of Legal History* 37: 464–495.

Scoones, I. 1995. *Living with Uncertainty: New Directions in Pastoral Development in Africa.* London: Intermediate Technology Publications.

Scott, F. 1955. The constitutional background of taxation agreements. *McGill Law Journal* 13(1).

Seagle, W. 1965. *The History of Law.* New York: Tudor Publishing Co.

Sears, C. 1992. Jungle potion. *American Health,* October.

Seidman, R.B. 1986. *The State, Law and Development.* Cambridge: Harvard University Press.

Sheddick, V.G. 1954. *Land Tenure in Basutoland.* London: H.M. Stationery Office.

Shepherd, G. 1985. Social forestry in 1985: Lessons learnt and topics to be addressed. Social Forestry Network Paper 1a. London: Social Forestry Network, Overseas Development Institute.

Shepherd, G. 1986. Forest policies, forest politics. London: Social Forestry Network, Overseas Development Institute.

Shepherd, G. 1991. Communal Management of Forests in the Semi-arid and Sub-humid Regions of Africa. Report prepared for the FAO Forestry Department. London: Social Forestry Network, Overseas Development Institute.

Shipton, P. 1987. The Kenyan Land Tenure Reform: Misunderstandings in the Public Creation of Private Property. Discussion Paper No. 239. Cambridge: Harvard Institute for International Development.

Shivji, I.G. 1994. *A Legal Quagmire: Tanzania's Regulation of Land Tenure (Establishment of Villages) Act, 1992*. Pastoral Land Tenure Series 5. London: International Institute for Environment and Development.

Sigot, A., L.A. Thrupp and J. Green, eds. 1995. *Towards Common Ground: Gender and Natural Resource Management in Africa*. Nairobi and Washington, DC: ACTS Press and World Resources Institute.

Sinclair, A., and J. Fryxell. 1985. The Sahel of Africa: Ecology of a disaster. *Canadian Journal of Zoology* 63: 987–994.

Smiley, D.V. 1987 "The Two Themes of Canadian Federalism." In *The Canadian Political Tradition: Basic Readings*, edited by R.S. Blair and J.T. McLeod. Toronto and New York: Methuen.

Sorrenson, M.P.K 1967. *Land Reform in Kikuyu Country: A Study in Government Policy*. Nairobi: Oxford University Press.

Spalding, B.J. 1993. Biopharmaceutical firms up R&D spending 71%. *Bio/Technology* 11(2).

Spear, T., and R. Waller, eds. 1993. *Being Maasai: Ethnicity and Identity in East Africa*. London: James Currey.

Starke, J.G. 1978. "Human Rights and International Law." In *Human Rights*, edited by E. Kamenka and A.E.S. Tay, pp. 113–131. London: Edward Arnold.

Stein, L.A. 1979. "The Theoretical Bases of Locus Standi." In *Locus Standi*, edited by L.A. Stein. Sydney: The Law Book Co.

Stone, C. 1974. *Should Trees Have Standing? Toward Legal Rights for Natural Objects*. Los Altos, California: William Kaufmann.

Storas, F. 1987. "Intention, or Implication: The Effect of Turkana Social Organization on Ecological Balance." In *Property, Poverty and People: Changing Rights in Property and Problems of Pastoral Development*, edited by P.T.W. Baxter and R. Hogg, pp. 137–146. Manchester: University of Manchester.

Street, H. 1972. *The Law of Torts*, 5th ed. London: Butterworths.

Swift, J. 1977. Sahelian pastoralists: Underdevelopment, desertification and famine. *American Anthropologist*. 6: 457–478.

Swift, J. 1988. *Major Issues in Pastoral Development with Special Emphasis on Selected African Countries*. Rome: Food and Agriculture Organization of the UN.

Swift, J. 1995. "Dynamic Ecological Systems and the Administration of Pastoral Development." In *Living with Uncertainty: New Directions in Pastoral Development in Africa*, edited by I. Scoones. London: Intermediate Technology Publications.

Swynnerton, R.J.H. 1955. *A Plan to Rectify the Development of African Agriculture in Kenya*. Nairobi: Government Printer.

Task Force on Canadian Unity. 1987. "The Anatomy of Conflict." In *The Canadian Political Tradition: Basic Readings*, edited by R.S. Blair and J.T. McLeod. Toronto and New York: Methuen.

Tawney, R.H. 1922. *The Acquisitive Society*. London: G. Bell and Sons.

Teerink, J.R., and M. Nakashima. 1993. *Water Allocation, Rights and Pricing: Examples from Japan and the United States.* World Bank Technical Paper No. 198. Washington, DC: The World Bank.

Thomas-Slayter, B., C. Kabutha and R. Ford. 1991. *Traditional Village Institutions in Environmental Management: Erosion Control in Katheka, Kenya.* Washington, DC and Nairobi: World Resources Institute and ACTS Press.

Tiffen, M. 1992. *Environmental Change and Dryland Management in Machakos District, Kenya 1930–90: Farming and Income Systems.* ODI Working Paper No. 59. London: Overseas Development Institute.

Tiffen, M., M. Mortimore and F. Gichuki. 1994. *More People, Less Erosion: Environmental Recovery in Kenya.* London and Nairobi: John Wiley and ACTS Press.

Treitel, G.H. 1970. *The Law of Contract,* 3rd ed. London: Stevens and Sons.

Tribe, L.H. 1988. *American Constitutional Law,* 2nd ed. Mineola, New York: The Foundation Press.

Trudeau, P. 1980. "Transcript of the Opening Remarks to the First Ministers Conference on the Constitution." September 8–12. Ottawa: Document 800-14/083. Cited in *After Meech Lake: Lessons for the Future,* edited by D.E. Smith *et al.* Saskatoon, Saskatchewan: Fifth House Publishers.

Turner, B.L. II, G. Hyden and R. Kates, eds. 1993. *Population Growth and Agricultural Change in Africa.* Gainesville: University Press of Florida.

Uganda, Republic of. 1992. *The Draft Constitution of the Republic of Uganda.* Kampala: Uganda Constitutional Commission.

UNDP. 1994. Public Sector Management, Governance, and Sustainable Human Development. New York: United Nations Development Programme.

UNEP and KWFT. 1988. *People, Parks and Wildlife.* Nairobi: United Nations Environment Programme and Kenya Wildlife Fund Trustees.

UNEP. 1987. *Kenya: National State of the Environment Report.* Nairobi: United Nations Environment Programme.

UNEP. 1989. *New Directions in Environmental Legislation and Administration Particularly in Developing Countries.* Nairobi: United Nations Environment Programme.

UNEP. 1989. *Sustainable Water Development and Management: A Synthesis.* Nairobi: United Nations Environment Programme.

UNEP. 1991a. *Legal and Institutional Arrangements for Environmental Protection in Developing Countries.* Nairobi: United Nations Environment Programme.

UNEP. 1991b. *Register of International Treaties and Other Agreements in the Field of the Environment.* UNEP/GC.16/Inf.4. Nairobi: United Nations Environment Programme.

Unger, R.M. 1977. *Law in Modern Society: Toward a Criticism of Social Theory.* London: Collier Macmillan Publishers.

UNIDO. 1991. *Industry and Development: Global Report 1991/2.* Vienna: United Nations Industrial Development Organisation.

United Nations. 1993. *Report of the United Nations Conference on Environment and Development (Agenda 21)*. New York: United Nations.

USAID. 1995. *Forest Management in Kenya: An Overview of Natural Resource Management and Forestry Related to Forest Reserves*. Nairobi: United States Agency for International Development.

USAID. 1988. *Policies, Legislation, Institutions and Activities in Natural Resource Sectors in Kenya*. Nairobi: United States Agency for International Development.

Veblen, T. 1978. "The Natural Rights of Investment." In *Property: Mainstream and Critical Positions*, edited by C.B. Macpherson. Oxford: Basil Blackwell.

Verhelst, T.G. 1990. *No Life Without Roots: Culture and Development*. London: Zed Books.

Violetta, D.M., and L.G. Chestnut. 1986. *Valuing Risks: New Information on Willingness to Pay for Changes in Fatal Risks*. Washington, DC: United States Environmental Protection Agency.

Wachter, D. 1992. *Land Titling for Land Conservation in Developing Countries?* Environmental Department, Divisional Working Paper No. 1992-28. Washington, DC: The World Bank.

Waldock, H. 1980. The effectiveness of the system set up by the European Convention on Human Rights. *Human Rights Law Journal* 1: 1–12.

Walker, D.M. 1980. *The Oxford Companion to Law*. Oxford: Clarendon Press.

Walsh, V. 1993. Demand, public markets and innovation in biotechnology. *Science and Public Policy* 20(3): 138–156.

Walston, R. 1989. The public trust doctrine in the water rights context. *Natural Resources Journal* 29(2): 586.

Walters, M. 1991. Ecological unity and political fragmentation: The implications of the Brundtland Report for the Canadian constitutional order. *Alberta Law Review* 29(2): 420–446.

Wamalwa, B. 1991. "Indigenous Knowledge and Natural Resources." In *Gaining Ground: Institutional Innovations in Land-use Management in Kenya*, edited by A. Kiriro and C. Juma, rev. ed. Nairobi: ACTS Press.

Wanjala, S.C. 1990. *Land Law and Disputes in Kenya*. Nairobi: Oxford University Press.

Wanjigi, J.M. 1972. "Agriculture and Land Tenure in Kenya." In *East Africa: Its Peoples and Resources*, edited by W.T.W. Morgan, pp. 177–188. Nairobi: Oxford University Press.

WCED. 1987. *Our Common Future*. World Commission on Environment and Development. Oxford: Oxford University Press.

Weiss, E.B. 1989. *In Fairness to Future Generations: International Law, Common Patrimony, and Intergenerational Equity*. Tokyo and New York: United Nations University and Transnational Publishers.

Wellard, K., and J.G. Copestake, eds. 1993. *Non-Governmental Organizations and the State in Africa: Rethinking Roles in Sustainable Agricultural Development*. London and New York: Routledge.

Western, D. and R.M. Wright. 1994. "The Background to Community-Based Conservation." In *Natural Connections: Perspectives in Community-based Conservation*, edited by D. Western, R.M. Wright with S.C. Strum. Washington, DC: Island Press.

Western, D., R.M. Wright with S.C. Strum, eds. 1994. *Natural Connections: Perspectives in Community-based Conservation*. Washington, DC: Island Press.

Wheeler, G.J. 1896. *Confederation Law in Canada*. London: Eye and Spottingswoode.

WHO. 1976. *African Traditional Medicine*. Afro-Technical Report Series No. 1. Brazzaville: Regional Office for Africa, World Health Organization.

Whyte, A.G.D. 1994. "Post-graduate Research Education in Forestry: A New Zealand Approach and Philosophy." In *Proceedings of the First International Workshop on Capacity Building in Forestry Research in Africa*, edited by S.L. Kwaje and F.B. Mwaura. Kampala, Uganda.

Wieacker, F. 1990. Foundations of European legal culture. *American Journal of Comparative Law* 38: 1–29.

Wilkinson, G.K. 1985. *The Role of Legislation in Land Use Planning for Developing Countries*. FAO Legislative Study No. 31. Rome: Food and Agriculture Organization of the UN.

William, G.K. 1985. *The Role of Legislation in Land Use Planning for Developing Countries*. FAO Legislative Study No. 31. Rome: Food and Agriculture Organization of the UN.

Winstanley, T. 1995. Entrenching environmental protection in the new constitution. *South African Journal of Environmental Law and Policy* 1: 85–97.

Woodley, F.W. 1988. *Tsavo National Parks East and West. Brief Review of 40 Years April 1948–April 1988*. Nairobi: Wildlife Conservation and Management Department.

World Bank. 1988. *Kenya: Forestry Subsector Review*. Report No. 6651-KE; Eastern Africa Department. Washington, DC: The World Bank.

World Bank. 1989. *Sub-Saharan Africa: From Crisis to Sustained Growth*. Washington, DC: The World Bank.

World Bank. 1992a. *Governance and Development*. Washington, DC: The World Bank.

World Bank. 1992b. *Kenya: Protected Areas and Wildlife Service Project*. Staff Appraisal Report 9981-KE; Eastern Africa Department. Washington, DC: The World Bank.

World Bank. 1992c. *World Development Report 1992*. Oxford, UK: Oxford University Press.

World Bank. 1994. Governance and civil service reform: A regional program. *Findings*, Africa Region, No. 2, August. Africa Technical Department. Washington, DC: The World Bank.

World Resources Institute *et al.* 1994. *World Resources 1994–1995*. Oxford: Oxford University Press.

Yeager, R. 1987. *Africa's Conservation for Development: Botswana, Kenya, Tanzania and Zimbabwe.* Hanover, New Hampshire: African Caribbean Institute, Dartmouth College.

Yost, N.C. 1982. *The Governance of Environmental Affairs.* New York: The Aspen Institute for Humanistic Studies.

Contributors

Calestous Juma is Executive Secretary of the Secretariat for the Convention on Biological Diversity in Montreal, and former Executive Director of the African Centre for Technology Studies (ACTS) in Nairobi. He has a PhD from the University of Sussex. He is winner of the 1991 Pew Scholars Award in Conservation and the Environment and is a UN Global 500 laureate. He is co-editor of *Biodiplomacy: Genetic Resources and International Relations* (ACTS Press, 1994) and has published widely on property rights, biodiversity and institutional change.

J.B. Ojwang is Professor of Law at the University of Nairobi and an Advocate of the High Court of Kenya. He is member of the Kenya Law Reform Commission and Fellow of the Kenya National Academy of Sciences. He holds a PhD from the University of Cambridge and has written widely on constitutional issues. He is author of *Constitutional Development in Kenya: Institutional Adaptation and Social Change* (ACTS Press, 1990). He is co-author of the *International Encyclopaedia of Environmental Law* (Kenya Monograph) (Deventer: Kluwer, 1996).

Edmund G.C. Barrow is Regional Community Conservation Coordinator with the African Wildlife Foundation (AWF) and former Research Fellow at the International Centre for Research in Agroforestry (ICRAF) in Nairobi. He specializes in community-based natural resource management in arid and semi-arid areas.

R.S. Bhalla is former Associate Professor at the Faculty of Law at the University of Swaziland and holds a PhD from the University of Edinburgh. He has practised law in India and taught law in Nigerian, Australian and Kenyan universities. He has written extensively on constitutional law, legal theory and property theory. His publications include *The Institution of Property: Legally, Historically and Philosophically Regarded* (Eastern Book, 1984).

John W. Bruce is with the Land Tenure Center (LTC) at the University of Wisconsin-Madison, USA. He is former director of LTC, member of the Faculty of Law at the University of Khartoum, and Legal Advisor to the Ministry of Land Reform and Administration, Ethiopia. He is co-editor of *Searching for Land Tenure Security in Africa* (Kendall/Hunt, 1994).

Siri Eriksen is a Researcher at the African Centre for Technology Studies (ACTS). She is studying development geography at the University of Oslo and Middlesex University. She has previously written on water resource management, climate change and transportation policy.

451

Alison Field-Juma is Associate Director of the African Centre for Technology Studies (ACTS) and former Research Associate at the International Centre for Research in Agroforestry (ICRAF). She holds an MSc in natural resource policy from Cornell University and is a member of the IUCN Commission on Environmental Strategy and Planning. She is co-author of *Agroforestry in Dryland Africa* (ICRAF, 1988).

Hadley H. Jenner is Co-Country Representative of the Mennonite Central Committee (MCC) in Kenya. He has previously worked as a land use planner and is currently a member of the Kenya Pastoralist Forum. He holds a Masters degree in environmental planning from the University of Pennsylvania, USA. He has written on dispute settlement in pastoral areas.

Isaac Lenaola is a Nairobi-based advocate specializing in land matters in pastoral areas and Lecturer at the Kenya Utalii College. He studied law at the University of Nairobi and is an Advocate of the High Court of Kenya. He is Chairman of the Legal Sub-Committee of the Kenya Pastoralist Forum. His research interests include the constitutional aspects of customary land rights.

Njeri Marekia is Lecturer in the Faculty of Environmental Studies at Kenyatta University, Kenya, and Adjunct Lecturer at St. Lawrence University (USA). She holds degrees in environmental studies and law from York University (Canada) and the University of London, respectively. Her areas of research include environmental policy, wildlife conservation, gender relations and community development.

John Mugabe is Executive Director of the African Centre for Technology Studies (ACTS). He is former Director and founder of the ACTS Biopolicy Institute at Maastricht, The Netherlands. He holds a PhD from University of Amsterdam and is co-editor of *Coming to Life: Biotechnology in African Economic Recovery* (Zed Books and ACTS Press, 1995). His research interests include biodiversity conservation.

Albert O. Mumma is Senior Lecturer at the Faculty of Law, University of Nairobi, and an Advocate of the High Court of Kenya. He is formerly Assistant Editor of *Sweet and Maxwell Encyclopaedia of Environmental Law* in London. He holds a PhD in law from the University of Cambridge and specializes in freshwater resource management. He is the author of *Environmental Law* (McGraw Hill, 1995).

Albert Mwangi was Director of the Contract Research Bureau at the African Centre for Technology Studies (ACTS). He holds a PhD from Michigan State University in resource economics and taught in the Department of Forestry at Moi University, Kenya. His research interests include natural resource management policies and resource valuation.

Bondi D. Ogolla is Legal Officer at the United Nations Environment Programme (UNEP), Nairobi. He holds a PhD in law from the University of Bordeaux in France. He has taught environmental law at the University of Nairobi. He is a member of the Kenya National Academy of Sciences and the IUCN Commission on Environmental Law. His research interests include environmental law and land tenure issues. He is co-author of the *International Encyclopaedia of Environmental Law* (Kenya Monograph) (Deventer: Kluwer, 1996).

Arthur Okoth-Owiro is Senior Lecturer in the Faculty of Law at the University of Nairobi. He holds a Masters degree in law from the University of Nairobi and has taught and written on environmental law, legal theory, criminal law, land tenure, medicinal plants and indigenous knowledge.

Phoebe N. Okowa-Bennun is Lecturer at Bristol University, UK, and an Advocate of the High Court of Kenya. She received her DPhil in law from the University of Oxford. Her main areas of research include public international law, environmental law and dispute settlement.

Peter O. Ondiege is Director of the Housing and Building Research Institute and Senior Lecturer at the University of Nairobi. He holds a PhD in economics from Tsukuba University, Japan. He has researched widely on land use, urban development policy and rural development and has conducted research and consultancy for various national and international organizations.

Kenneth K. Orie teaches law at the School of Environmental Studies, Moi University, Kenya. He is a Barrister and Solicitor of the Supreme Court of Nigeria and obtained his Doctor of Laws degree from McGill University, Canada. He has practised law in Nigeria and Canada and specializes in environmental law with particular emphasis on water rights.

Evans Ouko is a Researcher in the Environmental Governance Programme at the African Centre for Technology Studies. He holds a BSc in forestry from Moi University, Kenya, where he is completing his MPhil in environmental studies.

Cleophas O. Torori is Director of the Environmental Governance Programme at the African Centre for Technology Studies (ACTS). He previously taught Political Science at Moi University, Kenya, and is co-author of *Adaptive Economy: Economic Crisis and Technological Change* (ACTS Press, 1993). He specializes in environmental governance and community-based resource conservation.

Timothy Wichert is a Mennonite Central Committee (MCC) volunteer seconded to the United Nations Quaker Office (QUNO) in Geneva. He has practised law in Canada and worked on human rights and refugee issues. He has previously worked with the African Centre for Technology Studies (ACTS) on secondment from MCC. His areas of interest include conflict resolution in pastoral areas.

Index

District Commissioner 63
District Development
  Committee 216, 219
District Focus for Rural
  Development Strategy
  14
district environment com-
  mittees (DECs) 354
dominium eminens 5, 107
drainage basins: the Tana,
  Athi, Ewaso Nyiro, Rift
  Valley and lake Basin
  146
drugs 282; plant 282–285

easements 165, 373
East Africa Protectorate
  238
East African Wildlife So-
  ciety (ENWLS) 217,
  218, 219, 220, 221
Eastern Europe 56
eastern Africa 233
ecology 11, 16; principles
  of 1, 3, 10, 11;
  stewardship 2; ignorance
  3; awareness 133, 325,
  326
economic efficiency
  paradigm 95
economic growth 10
Ecosystem Ltd 266
EEC-funded ASAL devel-
  opment programme 137
Egypt 282
ekwar 267, 268, 269, 270,
  271, 272, 276
Elgeyo-Marakwet District
  138
Elli Lilly 282
Emperor Justinian 166
English Registered Land
  Act 152
enkiguana 252
environment impact as-
  sessment 49, 56, 355
environment ix, ii; envi-
  ronmental conservation
  x, 44, 130; regimes of
  50; conservation ethics
  1, 95, 225, 317, 319,
  320, 335; degradation

41, 44, 51, 93, 117, 181;
  economics 10; health 53,
  54
epaka or *amire* 266, 267,
  270
ere 267
Eriksson 137
Establishment of Villages
  Act 24
Ethiopia 21, 23
ethnomedicine 297–298
European Missionary 347
European settlement 19
ex situ conservation 296
exclusive ownership 22;
  control 105; concept of
  exclusive use 23
Executive authority 301
extra-ordinary (Secondary)
  purposes 155, 158

Factories Act 45, 46
fanya juu terracing 137
Feder and Feeny 124
federal spending power 344
federalism 338, 352; co-
  ordination and coopera-
  tive 338, 351, 356, or-
  ganic 339
Fertilizers and Animal
  Food Stuffs Act 45
Feyfogle 365
Fisheries Act 295
Food and Agricultural Or-
  ganization (FAO) of the
  UN 134
Food and Agricultural Or-
  ganization of the UN
  232
Food, Drugs and Chemical
  Substances Act 45
Foreign Jurisdiction Act
  (1890) 238
Foreign Statutes list 415t
foreign exchange 88
Forests Act 45, 105, 113,
  132, 163, 181, 184, 193,
  273, 290, 294, 301, 354
forests as energy source 91;
  industrial raw material
  91; value of 175–176;
  Forest Department 179,
  273; management of
  179; state ownership of

182–184; in the USA
  186; privatization of
  185; of New Zealand's
  commercial forests 186;
  leaseholds of 186–188;
  Forest Extension Ser-
  vices Division 193; Ru-
  ral Afforestation and
  Extension Division 193
freehold subject to conditions: 246

Galaty 235, 250
gender issues 168, 186,
  190, 365
German Mucheim-Kearlich
  Case 346
Gillis *et al.* 122
Glaxo (UK) 281
Global Biodiversity Strategy 39
global commons 50
Goodland *et al.* 39
Gossypium (male contra-
  ceptive) 282
governance ix, 3, 9, 11, 13,
  56, 367; defining con-
  cept of 12; systems 11,
  21, 36, 93, 171; tradi-
  tional systems of 161,
  271, 275
Government Lands Act
  104, 242, 245, 246
government 12, 51; of
  Kenya 241
Grass Fires Act 45, 191
gratis 10
Great Britain 154, 165, 185
Green Revolution tech-
  nologies 121
Ground Water Division 159
Group 245; concept of 245
Gura valley in Nyeri Dis-
  trict 125

Hamnett 313
harambee 32
Harding 96, 239, 240, 383
Haridas Chhagan Lal v.
  *Kericho Urban District
  Council* 65
Harvard University's Dana
  Farber Cancer Institute
  284

180, 203, 209, 211, 239, 254
land use 85, 95, 96, 103, 114; policies 234
landed oligarcy 239
landlessness 182
Law ix, 4, 9; contract 44, 48, 73, 312, 315; torts 44, 45, 48, 73, 312, 315; Roman 152, 166; constitutional 50; copyright 296; agrarian 20; international 41, 42, 46, 47, 65; public 43, 44, 45, 47, 50, 327; criminal 44, 50; African customary 204, 205, 243, 244, 247, 271, 292, 322, 337, 372, 409; administrative 44, 50; common 44, 68, 102, 143, 150, 153, 159, 166, 207, 286, 288, 291, 315, 319, 364, 372; private 44–47; property 46, 292, 315; of nuisance 45, 75, 156; tax relief 47; facilitative 48; municipal 65, 78; River 152; domestic 50; environmental 39, 50, 366, 367; rule of 65
Le Dain 340, 341
legal theory 39
legal-structural authoritarianism 238
legislature 349; bicameral 349, 356; unicameral 349, 356
legitimacy of the public realm 13
Lele 126
Lesotho 282, 313
Local Government Ordinance of 1960 65
Local government 77; Act of 109, 113, 289, 354, 370
locus standi 46, 287, 328, 346, 380, 382, 383
Lord Viscount Simon 340
Lucas v. *South Carolina Coastal Council* 75
Luo 97

Maasai and the Samburu 98

MacCormick 54
Machakos District 118, 135; County Council of 131
Machakos Integrated Development Programme 137
Madagascar 282
Magistrates' Court Act 63
Magistrates' Jurisdiction (Amendment) Act (1981) 128
majimbo 349, 351
Malaria Prevention Act 163
Mali 272
Maritine Zones Act 295
Marx's dogma 10
Mau and Transmara forests 179
mbari 98
Mbere Division 131
mechanistic economic models 10
medicinal plants 279
Mediterranean Countries 185
Meir 120
Merchant Shipping Act 45
Merck 281
Mexico 122
Meyers 136
Migot-Adholla 125
Ministry 24; of Agriculture and Livestock, 24, 134
Ministry of Environment and Natural Resources 55, 150, 193
Ministry of Land Reclamation, Regional and Water Development 150
Ministry of Lands and Settlement 150
Ministry of Water Development 160
Mobisquads (in Ghana) 14
mobu ke oa sechaba 313
Mozambique 21, 23, 282
multi-party system 351
Mumpree 32, 36
muramati 98
musyi 136
Mwathe 215
mwethya self-help groups 136, 139

Nairobi area 46, 408t, 411t
Nairobi's Uhuru Park 370
Nandi and Kipsigis 98
Narok County Council 113
Narok District 100
National Audubon Society v. *Superior Court* 327, 371
National Contaminated Sites Remediation Program 345
National Environmental Action Plan 353
National Environmental Policy Act (1970) of the US 53
National Environmental Secretariat of Kenya 55, 219, 354, 357
National Institutes of Health 284
National Lands Commission 25
National Museums of Kenya 219
National Parks Ordinance (1945) 203
National Soil Conservation Programme 135
National Water Conservation and Pipeline Corporation 150
national concern doctrine 341
nationalizing trees 265
Native Land Tenure Rules of 1956 244
Native Land's Trust Ordinance (1938) 104
Native Lands Trust Board 104
Native Trust Land Areas 99
native lands 19, 180, 203
natural resource ix, x, 3; management of ix, x, 3, 12, 17, 29, 43, 52, 64, 85, 272, 276, 296, 351, 354; traditional management of 236, 265, 275, 318
neoclassical economists 10
Netherlands 216
Newmann 316
ng'undu 125